TIBER

BRUCE WARE ALLEN

TIBER

Eternal River of Rome

ForeEdge

ForeEdge

An imprint of University Press of New England

www.upne.com

© 2019 ForeEdge

All rights reserved

Manufactured in the United States of America

Designed by Mindy Basinger Hill

Typeset in Garamond Premier Pro

For permission to reproduce any of the material in this book,
contact Permissions, University Press of New England,
One Court Street, Suite 250, Lebanon NH 03766; or visit www.upne.com

Library of Congress Cataloging-in-Publication Data

Names: Allen, Bruce Ware, author.

Title: Tiber: eternal river of Rome / Bruce Ware Allen.

Description: Lebanon, NH: ForeEdge, an imprint of University Press
of New England, 2019. | Includes bibliographical references and index.

Identifiers: LCCN 2018022308 (print) | LCCN 2018031668 (ebook) |
ISBN 9781512603347 (epub, pdf, & mobi) | ISBN 9781512600377 (cloth: alk. paper)

Subjects: LCSH: Tiber River (Italy)—History. | Rome (Italy)—History.

Classification: LCC DG975.T5 (ebook) | LCC DG975.T5 A45 2019 (print) |
DDC 945.6/32—dc23

LC record available at https://lccn.loc.gov/2018022308

5   4   3   2   1

CONTENTS

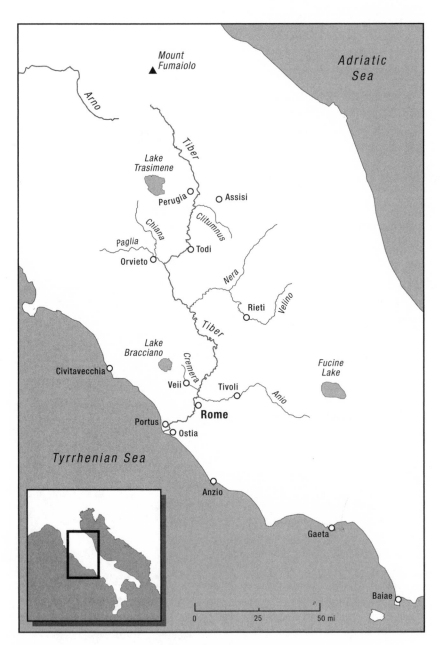

THE TIBER AND SOME TRIBUTARIES

INTRODUCTION

I've trod the Forum and I have scaled the Capitol.
I've seen the Tiber hurrying along, as swift and dirty as history.
Henry James to his brother William, 1869

James wrote at a time when Rome was still vitally connected to the Tiber,[1] when small boats, lighters and barges, still floated olives and wine and grain downriver from Tuscany and Umbria to the curved baroque white marble of the Ripetta wharf; or more exotic goods were pulled upriver with aid of oxen and against the current, from river mouth at Ostia to the wharves and quays of Rome's city center at the Porto Leonino and to the Ripa Grande near Porta Portese. Once arrived, crewmen and stevedores lounged as agents sought out buyers, and only then off-loaded the cargo and watched the goods disappear into the business of the city, just as their predecessors had done for over two thousand years.

In less commercially active stretches along the river, mud and river grass and clay and bulrushes, and occasional sand, sloped down to the water. On hot days, children and other idlers could wander down and cool their feet in the running water and watch the scenery, just as their predecessors had done for centuries. Painters could still find for their canvases good views of aging palaces and ancient ruins against the river, symbols of change and decay.

The year following James's visit, everything had changed. In December of 1870, the river rose and flooded the city, as the river had done for millennia. Every time, Rome had grieved and endured, sometimes talked about ways of eliminating this problem, and inevitably sighed and shrugged and moved on. This time, however, things were different. Modernity had come to Italy. The various states had been unified under one government, the king of Savoy, Victor Emmanuel, chosen as head of state, and Rome, the new capital, was not going to be subject to the whims of a temperamental river. For the first time in three millennia, in the ongoing struggle with this part of nature, *something would be done.*

It was something of a new attitude. Early Romans had been deferential to the Tiber, treating it chiefly with affection and always with respect. No surprise there. Rivers, places of lurking divinity, are an extension of weather. Like weather, they are both generous and dangerous—very godlike qualities—and the earliest inhabitants treated the river with the same deference one does any capricious deity. Rites were performed, offerings made, insults avoided, and, when the river silted up or overflowed, forgiveness was readily granted. The ancient historian Pliny is reserved in his criticism, and tries to find an upside to the Tiber's excesses of AD 105: "No river is more circumscribed and shut in on either side; yet of itself it offers no resistance, though it is subject to frequent sudden floods, the inundations being now here greater than in the city itself. But in truth it is looked upon rather as a prophet of warning, its rise being always construed rather as a call to religion than as a threat of disaster."[2]

The attitude was not entirely wrongheaded. The river was, first of all, a source of life. It provided fish to eat, water to drink and grow crops with, a medium for transporting trade goods.

Water was also a barrier against hostile neighbors, just as it was to be for Venice and the Netherlands. For a traveler wandering the city today, the swamps and streams and high slippery banks surrounding the seven hills are difficult to imagine. To get to the Romans' high ground, the enemies—Etruscans, Gauls, Sabines—had to pass over the river or through a mephitic swamp known only to locals. Sabine warriors, retaliating for the abduction of their women, made do with the help of Tarpeia, a local girl who showed them how to negotiate the narrow and slippery approaches to the city. She was killed for her troubles—the Sabines had no love of traitors—but the attack failed regardless. Janus, god of gates and doors, a friend of rivers and Rome, sent up a geyser of boiling water to ward the Sabines off.

Later visitors besides James, beguiled by years of schooling in Latin, Roman history, and art, found that the reality did not live up to the dream. The Englishman Richard Lassels in 1670 or so "wondered to finde it such a small river, which poets with their hyperbolical inke had made swell into a river of the first rate."[3]

He wasn't alone. A disappointed David Garrick wrote in 1763: "It is strange that so much good poetry should be thrown away upon such a pitiful River; it is no more comparable to our Thames, than our modern Poets are to their Virgils and Horaces";[4] Tobias Smollett in 1765 called it "foul, deep, and rapid";[5] the fictional Mrs. Ramsbottom (1825) wrote, "The Tiber is not a nice river, it looks yellow."[6] William Hazlitt (1826)—"The golden Tiber is

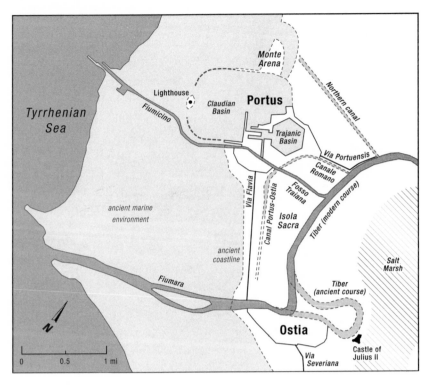

OSTIA AND PORTUS

a muddy stream."[7] Nathaniel Hawthorne (1858)—"The Tiber has always the hue of a mud-puddle; but now, after a heavy rain which has washed the clay into it, it looks like pease-soup."[8]

(At the same time, Hazlitt went on to say that "St. Peter's is not equal to St. Paul's [in London]," which suggests some considerable bias, or discomfort on his trip. Presumably he liked the food . . .)

Robert Burn (the English classical scholar, not Burns the Scottish poet) in 1871 dismissed the river as "too large to be harmless, too small to be useful."[9] He was thinking of London's tidal estuary, which at that time was a working seaport on a scale that even at its busiest the Tiber could not have matched. Nevertheless, earlier ages would have found the comment perplexing. Biondo Flavio described the river in 1572 as "great, navigable, and most useful . . . crowned by a thousand victories."[10] By no means was it too small to be useful, and for centuries, of all the roads that lead to Rome, the Tiber was the most important. At the height of the empire, a column of barges weighted

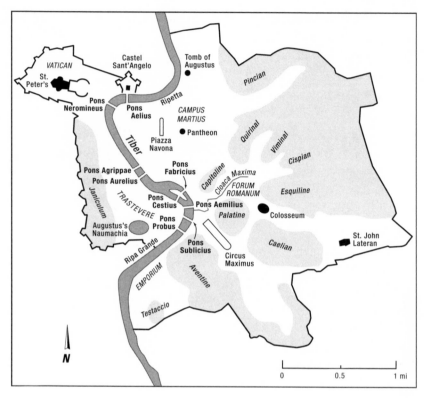

ROME

down with grain and wine stretched the full eighteen miles from the wharves at Rome to the river's mouth at Portus and Ostia, where cargo ships from across the Mediterranean and beyond brought the food that fed a million people, and the spices from India and silks from China that diverted those who could afford them. Traffic was heavy enough that the emperors toyed with the idea of carving a straight parallel causeway to Ostia to help ease some of the congestion.

They might have done so, too, except for religious scruple—water, claimed the naysayers, is powerful and, like cats, roams where it wants, and—also like cats—can make trouble for anyone who tries to get in its way. When the emperor Nero fell ill in AD 45 and was near death, his more pious subjects attributed the calamity to his having bathed in the source of the Aqua Marcia; even the emperor cannot profane sacred water, springwater still less, and least of all water that exits the ground at a bracing forty-six degrees Fahrenheit.[11]

The Tiber's fee for all its benefits was periodic flooding, a tribute in lives and landmarks tactfully not mentioned by the Roman poets. Historians recorded the worst of the damage, but never reproached the river god responsible. Rome's greatness is tied to the river, and Latin writers preferred to dwell on his kinder moods, and to note and praise the river god and his connection to their success. *Pater Tiber*, Father Tiber, the most common of images. *Dominus, regius, sceptifer*, Lord, regal, scepter bearing. He was a powerful patron looking out for his underlings, a leader whose occasional outbursts must be weathered and accepted as the price for the good that he brings. It was, after all, Tiberinus, "the very god of the place," who welcomed Aeneas when that hero slept by the riverside.[12] It was the river that refused to drown Romulus and Remus, ensuring that they survived long enough to found an empire. It was while engaged in religious observations at the riverside that Romulus was finally transported to a better place. (Or so the story goes. Others claim that he was killed and dismembered by accompanying senators, who carried the pieces away under their cloaks.)

The Tiber became the earliest symbol of Rome, at least as powerful as the she-wolf that suckled Romulus and Remus. Other nations have lifted from it. The fledgling capital of America for years had a tributary of the Potomac called Tiber Creek (which was in fact a small, slow, and decidedly dirty stream that ran through Rock Creek Park and has long since been paved over by Connecticut Avenue, its presence unsuspected even to longtime residents, the answer to a trivia question). The river Tiber snakes through the city on its way to the sea; it separates the bulk of civil Rome from the Vatican. Protestants embracing the Catholic faith are said to be crossing the Tiber.

The river's symbolism was powerful enough that Mussolini redrew provincial borders so that the source at Monte Fumaiolo was no longer in Tuscany, but in his native province of Romagna. In a beech grove high in the mountains, he erected a marble column, topped by an eagle, to honor the twin springs that mark its origins: "Qui nasce il fiume sacro ai destini di Roma" (Here is born the river sacred to the destiny of Rome). The column is still there. The border has since been ceded back to Tuscany.[13]

Of what practical use is the river these days? These days, not much.

River traffic is now reduced to the odd sculler, perhaps a police boat, a tour boat carrying passengers up and down the length of the city, its docent pointing out those few sites in view of the water—the bridges, the squat cylinder of Castel Sant'Angelo, the odd palazzo now safe behind the protective embankments. Summertime brings the occasional traveling market of cheap goods, but the area is still more a backwater than a destination, and despite the cobbled bicycle path running from Ponte Milvio in the north to the distant reaches of EUR, Mussolini's district of the future, the river is rarely a logical path between two points. A pair of barge restaurants are tied to the banks, with a view of little except the dirty water, dirty travertine walls, and a clean sky. The heavy scooter, car, and truck traffic on the Lungotevere, the road running parallel to the river, makes peering over the wall more trouble than it is worth. The odd suicide still finds final oblivion in the water.

For all that, access to the banks is possible, if awkward, and can repay those who make the effort with relative quiet and some good views of the bridges. Plane trees overhang long sections of the riverbank and announce the changes of the seasons. The riverside is a stony oasis in a vibrating city, a resource in search of a purpose.

And it has a history, both swift and dirty.

TIBER

GODS, KINGS, AND MEN

In which gods speak to men, Trojans found a empire, citizens expel a king

and import alien gods, healthy people harvest salt, sick people get well,

Cicero goes to law, and Cleopatra settles by the riverside.

Father Tiber

Rivers are constantly alive, sometimes resting, sometimes running, alternately cheerful, morose, angry, bored, dozy. In a good mood, gentle and playful, refreshing and invigorating. Sit next to a river for any length of time, and you can easily imagine it chattering and chuckling, mostly to itself, just this side of incomprehension. In a bad mood, water can be murderous. Rivers are stronger than any single man and more relentless; they fight back.

How can an observant person not be impressed? For early man, a running river was a constant reminder that, for good or for ill, in sickness and in health, the gods were living beside you, like the pre-creation universe, without shape or form, but palpable, as visible as the sun or moon but within reach and touchable, their power instantly apparent. Genesis declares that the Spirit of God moved upon the face of the waters; gentiles have noticed something similar.

Back in the golden days when men lived in peace under divine law, Rome's river spirit went by the name Albula. Virgil writes about him: "Then kings arose, and fierce Thybris with giant bulk, from whose name we of Italy have since called our river Tiber; her true name ancient Albula has lost."[1]

Note the spelling—you will also find "Tybris" and "Tibris," and scholarly explanations for all of them. The historian Livy claims the name comes from

Tiberinus Silvius, a later king of Alba Longa, who fell into the river Albula and drowned, and was thereafter considered the godhead as well as the new namesake.[2] The philologist Varro acknowledged Livy's story but suggests that the king in question was ruler of Veii.[3] Or possibly the king got his name from the river, which in turn was named for its godhead Tiberinus, one of the three thousand sons of Oceanus and Tithys, all of them river deities.

There are more stories equally uncertain—take your pick. By the time of the Roman Empire, Albula has become Tiber Pater—Father Tiber—respected by and familiar to all Romans. Virgil gives the god a speaking part in the *Aeneid*, in which he favors our hero with a prophetic dream, giving him a glimpse of everything that his descendants in this part of the world will accomplish.

He takes on human form, as gods sometimes do when they need to talk to mortals directly. Virgil describes him:

> Tiberinus, the old river god himself,
> Lifted his head amid the poplar leaves
> Draped in a fine, grey-linen mantle,
> His hair crowned with shady reeds[4]

The poet Ovid called upon the god at one time on a point of scholarship, and to hear Ovid tell it, the god arose from the water in the form of a somewhat befuddled old man happy to talk about the old days, before Rome was founded, when, "if I recall correctly" (*si memini*), he went by the name of Albula.[5] Ovid was never the most respectful of poets, and stressing an immortal's age as if he were human was a bit of cheek. (Ovid himself was banished from Rome to the provincial reaches of the Black Sea for unspecified crimes against morality; possibly this kind of verse was a factor.)

Roman sculptors give the river god a human figure, dripping long hair and beard. The earliest, now in the Louvre, was discovered in 1512, acquired by the church, stolen by France in 1797, and would have been returned to Rome in 1815 had not the pope bequeathed it to the restored Bourbon monarch Louis XVIII in recognition of his Christian faith. A later copy can be seen in Rome on the Capitoline as one half of a flanking pair, the other half being Nile. He is reclining—it is hard to imagine a river god doing anything else—with one elbow resting on the wolf that suckled Romulus and Remus, and next to her are the twins themselves. He is also holding a cornucopia, a horn of plenty, suitable for a god whose element is required for growing food.

There is more to that story. The original horn belonged to the Greek river god Achelous. In that dry country, he could expect a good deal of respect. It was his misfortune to fall in love with the nymph Deianira. So had Hercules. Achelous counted on his watery ability to change shape to win her over. It was not enough, as she herself explains:

> Acheloüs, who in triple form appeared
> To sue my father Oeneus for my hand,
> Now as a bull, now as a sinuous snake
> With glittering coils, and now in bulk a man
> with front of ox, while from his shaggy beard
> Runnels of fountain-water spouted forth.[6]

The matter came to blows, as was so often the case with Hercules. Achelous entered the ring in the form of a bull, and in the ensuing struggle, Hercules tore off one of the horns. Achelous then morphed into a snake. Hercules just laughed. He was famous for having killed two vipers when he was still in his cradle. The river god gave in. Even years later he didn't like to talk about the encounter ("It is a mournful task you have required, for who can wish to tell his own disgrace?").[7]

Who indeed? As to how Father Tiber wound up with the cornucopia, that's another story, now lost along with many other things dropped into the river.

Aeneas to Romulus and Remus

> from the ship Aeneas sees a grove
> And through its midst a pleasant river running,
> The Tiber, yellow sand, and whirling eddy
> Down to the sea. Around, above and over,
> Fly the bright-colored birds, the water-haunters,
> charming the air with song. The order given,
> The Trojans turn their course to land; they enter
> The channel and the shade.
> *Aeneid*

So Virgil describes the arrival of Aeneas and his fellow Trojan refugees to their final destination.[8]

As we have seen, the newcomers had a cordial relationship with the river god, who favored these men over the indigenous Italians. Father Tiber goes so far as to bring the river's flow to a standstill just long enough for the Trojans to row their boats upstream, as far as Pallantium (future Rome), then occupied by Greek wanderers under a King Evander of Pallene (Arcadia).

Good fortune, in that although Greek, these Greeks had left their own native lands some sixty years before the Trojan war and were without any anti-Trojan prejudice. Indeed, Evander and Aeneas could cite a common ancestor.

War would follow. The divine quarrels that had sparked the war back in Troy were not entirely burned out (Juno in particular was not done with punishing Trojans wherever she might find them, least of all Aeneas, the son of her rival Venus). But with help from Evander, Aeneas and his Trojans were able to defeat Turnus and other unwelcoming aborigines and set the foundations of Rome's future greatness.

The gods, we are told, assured Aeneas, expelled from Troy, that he and his followers would settle Alba Longa and that their descendants would astonish the world, as indeed they did. Virgil's epic, never finished to the author's satisfaction (on his deathbed Virgil asked friends to burn it, a directive they ignored), stops in medias res, with Aeneas fighting his enemy Turnus to the death. The story was well enough known that the unwritten parts were, and are, superfluous. Aeneas ends his days quietly, full of years, in Lavinium, the city he founded, upstream from Pallantium, leaving descendants to build on what he had begun.

Everything up to now has been a prequel, for Rome, unusual among nations, has not one, but two foundation myths. Some years pass in Lavinium, ruled by Aeneas's posterity, until there appears the bad seed in the person of the wicked and ambitious Amulius. Desirous of the throne held by his uncle Numitor, he killed Numitor's sons and forced Numitor aside. The king's daughter, Rhea Silva, he compelled to become a Vestal Virgin. She, however, had coincidentally been raped by the god Mars and given birth to the twins Romulus and Remus.

Amulius was in an awkward position, and given every other example of abandoning infants, his solution seemed predestined to fail. One can, however, see a kind of brutal logic to the order. If the mother was lying and the father was some anonymous rake, then the boys would likely die, like all unwanted and exposed infants. If, however, the two were in fact half divine and, worse, favored by the gods, then their safe passage was, if not assured, at least not Amulius's problem.

Floating inconvenient but chosen infants on rivers to die, only to have them survive and go on to great things, is a familiar enough trope. Consider Moses of the Bible, Karna of the Mahabharata, Sargon of Akkad. Given Rome's proximity to the Tiber, the surprise would have been a foundation myth that did not involve a water baby or two.[9] In this story, if Mars was indeed the father, he appears to have had nothing further to do with the boys, leaving their fate to Tiberinus, who guided the basket to the bank where the she-wolf heard them crying and suckled them. While so engaged, they were found by Faustulus the shepherd, who gathered the twins and raised them with his wife Laurentia.

The boys grew up, somehow learned the truth of their background, and either from a sense of familial piety or sheer love of adventure, one day headed back upstream to Alba Longa, overthrew Amulius, and reinstated their grandfather Numitor as king.

We can only assume that the Alba Longa they liberated did not live up to the Alba Longa of their imagination. They had proved their gumption to anyone who might have doubted it, as well as their favor with the gods. Presumably they were heirs apparent to the throne of the now aging Numitor. Despite all this, the city apparently did not sit right with them. The next we hear of them, the twins had decamped and headed downstream and stopped at the bend in the river near Tiber Island. (What had happened to Pallantium the ancient sources leave unaddressed.)

Where to drop stakes? On the right bank there was the Janiculum Hill, relatively high and surrounded by fertile ground, defensible, close to Tiber Island. On the left were several hills surrounded by low swampy ground subject to flooding, difficult to cultivate. They chose to settle the left bank—Romulus the Palatine Hill, Remus the Aventine.

Which gets us to the second cliché in the twins foundation myth, that of siblings murdering sibling over property, or just out of pique. It's an ancient trope—Cain killed Abel, Seth killed Osiris, Eteocles and Polynices kill each other, and Romulus killed Remus. It didn't have to happen that way. Having arrived at the site of what would become Rome, they disagreed over whether to center on the Palatine Hill or the Aventine. Unable to agree or to settle both, they turned to auguries. Birds in this case. Remus saw six, Romulus saw twelve. Divinely approved or not, the decision did not go down well with Remus. Again, details on what happened next are sketchy. One story goes that Remus insulted Romulus by jumping over the as yet not too tall city wall. The insult led Romulus's friend Celer to strike Remus, leading in turn to an all-out riot between the brothers and their respective partisans. Remus got the worst of it.

Or possibly not. Alternative stories from various ancient writers have all manner of extraneous and contradictory details, chiefly meant to whitewash fratricide.[10] For those uncomfortable with morally repugnant outcomes, we can conclude this episode by including the version of Egnatius, who wrote that Remus was never killed but in fact lived on to a ripe old age, longer even than Romulus. Egnatius appears to be alone in this take on the story.[11]

To cement the gods' favor involved a second step.

Valerius Maximus would have us believe it was the Tiber itself that sealed Rome's greatness, but that it had been a near thing. He writes that while Servius Tullius was king, a cow of exceptional size and beauty was born on a Sabine farm. Experts on oracles declared that this was a gift of the gods, and that whosoever sacrificed the animal at the temple of Diana on the Aventine, his people would rule the world. The cow's owner immediately drove the animal to Rome, anxious to get the matter over with. The priest had his own agenda. He addressed the man with the full authority of a man of the cloth:

"Stranger, what can you be thinking of? Surely you do not mean to sacrifice to Diana without first performing the act of purification. You must bathe yourself, before the ceremony, in a living stream. Down there in the valley the Tiber flows."[12]

The rebuked Sabine took the advice and wandered off. In his absence, the priest, a good Roman, carried out the sacrifice himself.[13] "The end results of this act were most agreeable to the king, and to the state."[14] Less so, no doubt, to the Sabines, whose reaction is not recorded.

The details are unimportant. One way or another, Rome found its place on the map, a small city of wattle and daub on a hilltop surrounded by swampland and in need of women (Romulus and his men famously stole these from Sabines farther upriver), a more imposing military presence, and a more functional infrastructure. Among other things, they needed a quick way to cross the river.

Age of Kings

Bridges are a form of cheating nature and, like flying, to be undertaken only with the greatest caution. They are by their nature an affront to the gods. The Greek poet Hesiod warned his readers that before crossing any river, one must at the very least pray and wash hands.[15]

Early Romans knew this. They understood the power of rivers, and their usefulness in keeping out enemies. Running water is not only an effective physical barrier, but a supernatural one as well; ghosts and spirits cannot cross a running stream. More-tangible threats, like soldiers, might stumble their way from one side to another, if the river is low and in a good mood, but the wise man shows respect in advance, the more so if he intends to make a habit of crossing. Swimming, or wading, or boating across the water was seen as a liberty, punishable by occasional drowning; building a permanent fixture across (and in) the water was even more of one.

Which explains in part why the Romans took as long as they did to build a bridge. Still, by the age of kings, the city was growing, and taboo or no, a bridge was the sort of thing that could turn the river from a simple barrier to a means of expediting both trade and territorial expansion. Building it, or even just convincing the Romans that it should be built, required a man of some strong will. That would be Ancus Marcius (c. 677–617 BC), fourth king of Rome.

Ancus, maternal grandson of Rome's second king, the pious pacifist Numa Pompilius, came to the throne by popular election after the sudden death of Tullius Hostilius. Tullius had died soon after performing a hurried sacrifice to Jupiter, a job he completely botched. He and the horse he was riding were killed by a lightning strike, their bodies turned to ashes.

Ancus Marcius naturally made placating the gods his first order of business, and published all the rites and obligations of Rome across the city to ensure none were ever left undone, or done badly. Prudence required nothing less.

Rome's Latin enemies took their measure of the man. They observed his initial acts and assumed that pacifism ran in his blood, that this reflected the sum of the man, that he was weak, unwarlike, and liable to fold at the first sign of danger. They were mistaken. As Livy puts it, "He had in him something of Numa and something of Romulus as well."[16] Forced to wage war, he proved more than equal to the challenge. Realizing that wars are not won on defense, Ancus took the battle to Rome's enemies. Previous kings had done the same, multiple times. In a foreshadowing of later Roman policy, those of the enemy who survived were brought back to Rome and installed on one of the seven hills—Sabines on the Capitoline, Albans on the Caelian—and allowed to live as Romans. Ancus followed this precedent. The first set of defeated Latins were brought back to Rome, given citizenship, and settled on the Aventine, more or less peacefully (though Livy pointedly adds that crime increased as citizenship was expanded). A few more years were needed before Ancus and his army could defeat, and co-opt, the Latins utterly.

In times of peace, a prudent ruler prepares for war. Ancus had ditches dug around the city perimeter. He then looked across the river and considered threats from that direction. The Tiber served as a first-rate line of defense, one reason Rome was built where it was. The right bank, however, was home of the Janiculum Hill, potentially a stronghold for Rome's enemies. Rather than trust to the river alone for Rome's safety, Ancus Marcius had the city boundaries extended across the water, to encompass that hill.

The new stronghold brought a new problem. The heights, now Rome's first line of defense on the right bank, would, presumably, sooner or later be attacked. Rome would then need quick access to those hilltops. Stress on "quick." Rome had boats; but boats are slow and limited in the number of men they can carry at one time. They can be worse than useless if an army needs to retreat, or if reinforcements need to reach the front line. Something better was needed. In 642 BC Ancus announced that he would build a bridge.

It says something for the king's standing that this bold announcement was accepted without any great objection. Necessity was part of the reason. Rome was attracting the attention of violent neighbors and needed all the advantages it could muster. Clearly too, Ancus Marcius was a man who had won back the favor of the gods, which tends to calm the more fretful of any population. To allay any residual doubts among the citizens, Ancus Marcius made certain to follow certain religious guidelines that would make the project less obnoxious to the gods. The official put in charge of construction was given priestly status, the pontifex—bridge builder—who made certain that no mistakes either small or large infected the building of the bridge.

The Pons Sublicius, Sublician bridge, was made of wood (*sublicius,* wooden piling, the base on which it was built) and only of wood.[17] Iron fasteners were considered an unnatural component and not to be used. The bridge would also stand alone, a matter of necessity if Rome was to survive, and as such acceptable to the gods (who presumably wanted Rome to survive). The Sublicius, whether from taboo or necessity, would be the only Roman bridge across the Tiber for the next three hundred years.

Beyond the sheer practical use of the bridge, the Sublician was also a political statement. The Roman enterprise was not only no longer bounded by the Tiber, but so long as the bridge stood, that enterprise enjoyed tacit approval from the river gods.

Such approval came at some cost. For all the good that the river brings to Rome, the Tiber also has a tendency to flood, at times catastrophically. To the extent that this was a measure of the gods' displeasure rather than some random act of nature, the Romans made an effort to placate Father Tiber against whatever offense they might have caused. Each year in mid-May, the sacred college of pontiffs oversaw the procession of the Argei, in which the priests, the Vestal Virgins, and the praetors (magistrates) marched through the city to twenty-seven stations, gathering straw men that had absorbed the local evil spirits over the previous twelve months. The rite culminated with the Vestals' standing in the middle of the bridge and tossing the effigies into the river.[18] The city was cleansed for another year.

(Modern commentators refer to these figures as dolls or puppets, but the Greek and Roman writers are not so specific. Plutarch and Dionysius of Halicarnassus both use the word εἴδωλα, idols, representations; Ovid, Varro, and Macrobius refer to *simulacra*; Festus, to *effigies*.[19] It is, granted, easier to imagine a dignified, white-gowned vestal tossing a modest-size doll into the river, rather than have her hefting a full-scale dummy over the side, but is it accurate? Surely if one hopes to displace the sins of an entire city, or to buy a year's worth of indulgence from the gods, a prudent resident would want the largest possible gift. Food for thought, in any event.)

Of Ancus Marcius, there were a few more wars, all victorious, footnotes to his greater achievements of expanding Rome and taking the boundaries across the river and down to the river mouth, where he founded Ostia, the port of Rome, essentially Rome's first colony. He is also credited with establishing the first saltworks.

If the Sublicius was indeed the first bridge to cross the Tiber, we may suppose that the second was the unnamed structure built farther upstream, at a strategic point along the Anio tributary, by Sabines, a tribe less favored by the gods than were the Romans. Their bridge too was wooden, and we would not have heard of it at all except for its role in one of the early wars between the two tribes.

The battle in question, the first record of fighting on the Tiber in fact, came under the rule of Ancus Marcius's successor, Lucius Tarquinius Priscus (616–579 BC), fifth of the seven Roman kings.[20]

Priscus, also known as Tarquin the Elder, wandered into Rome from Etruria, much as Dick Whittington wandered into London, accompanied not by a cat but by his wife Tanaquil. They were Corinthian Greeks who had been in Tarquinia (Tuscany), where their Greek origin limited his opportunities, and so they went to Rome, where kings were elected, not born, and ability was prized. As the pair rolled along the countryside on a horse-drawn wagon, an eagle swooped down from the sky, stole Priscus's cap, then returned it. An unusual event at any time, and Tanaquil assured him that this was not just an unpleasant happenstance, but a sign of favor from the gods. Ancus Marcius was still king, and he, and the rest of Rome, seemed to have agreed. Ancus Marcius designated Tarquinius Priscus as guardian to his sons the princes.

Years passed, and Tarquin was fastidious in his labors. He was also cunning and knew how politics work. When the king died, Tarquin sent the boys, now nearly men, off on a hunting expedition, while he stayed behind and launched what amounted to a political campaign. It was unheard of at the time, but Tarquin was ambitious. Rather than wait to be called to service, he made speeches praising the now deceased Ancus Marcius as his friend, mentor, and inspiration. Who better than he, Tarquinius Priscus, a Roman by choice rather than by birth, to take up the reins laid down by such a man? The elders agreed. Tarquin was elected. The princes sink into obscurity.

Among Tarquin's early acts was to increase the size of the senate by a hundred members (creating a hundred grateful clients) and declaring war on neighboring Latins (creating a windfall for the Roman treasury). He called for public games, and began construction of a defensive wall. The latter was clearly needed—Sabine troops from upriver managed to cross the unfinished works and draw blood in the streets of Rome itself before being pushed back. Like his mentor, Tarquin was keen to take the fight to the enemy, but on his own terms. He concentrated on building up a large force of cavalry, and once this was arranged to his satisfaction, delivered the fight to the enemy.

It is the first record of fighting on the Tiber, and involves a bridge, presumably wooden, at a strategic point along the Anio tributary, on a spot more useful to the Sabines than to the Romans. Tarquin saw the practical and psychological significance of the structure, and ordered his cavalry upriver, where they gathered a pile of dried wood, set it on fire, and pushed the works onto the water. Soon the ad hoc raft was entangled on the bridge and had set it ablaze. Other Romans had already begun fighting the Sabines, who, seeing their escape route in peril, were wrong-footed. Some retreated in hopes of crossing the bridge while they still could—in vain hope, as it turned out. Others were forced back to the water's edge and slaughtered.

The remains of the bridge and equipment and the bodies of the dead Samnites floated down the river into the Tiber and past the city of Rome, mute evidence for its citizens that Tarquin had won.[21] The Sabines surrendered themselves and their territory to Rome. Latins soon followed suit. War was over. Tarquin could now turn his attention to transforming Rome into the city it deserved to be. A temple to Jupiter headed the list, and is mentioned by the ancient writers. Other than its foundation stones, the temple is long gone, but one project he began, river related and cheating nature in a different way than bridges, continues to function to this day.

It was Cloaca Maxima, the Greatest Sewer.

Cloaca Maxima

Athens had its Parthenon, Rome had its drains. The Romans were practical men.

The cloaca began life as little more than a ditch. In nature this first sewer was the spring-fed Forum Brook. We have to imagine a primitive, marble-free Rome, more grass than stone, surrounded by wetlands and streams, and a lot closer to sea level than it is now. The current elevation of the Roman Forum is fourteen MASL (meters above sea level).[22] The original pathway from the Forum Romanum to the Velabrum, a small stream leading to the Tiber, was just under six MASL.[23] At flood tide, water reached nine MASL[24]—clearly an untenable situation for anyone who wanted to live in the area year round.

Untenable, but it took some considerable willpower to correct matters. Not surprisingly, the willpower came from the top. Tarquinius Priscus, fifth of Rome's seven kings, set the project in motion. It was wrong, he felt, that his people should have to put up with the inconvenience of living next to a swamp. Rome was a growing city, a city beginning to turn from wood to stone. He and his successors had begun to erect stone temples to Jupiter and Diana, visible from a distance to anyone approaching upriver or downriver.

Rome was not, however, Athens, certainly not Alexandria, not yet a world power. Temples were an undeniable good, but how impressed was a cosmopolitan foreigner—an Egyptian, say, or a Persian—going to be by a few wattle-and-daub houses surrounded by a waterlogged marsh prone to flooding? Rome could do better. One more flood during Tarquin's reign proved the last straw—the water pooling around the hills had to go.

Initially the idea was to raise the low area higher above the flood lines. (Recent core samples have turned up bluish clay laid down in early days.)

Priscus ordered large parts of what is today the Roman Forum filled with an estimated twenty thousand cubic meters of fill, raising the swampy basin by several meters and creating dry land on either side of the watery channel, something you could walk on.[25]

The result was utilitarian, but not visually stunning. The cloaca ditch now ran about one hundred meters from the river to the Forum Romanum, open air with occasional walkways across it. The new course followed the stream's original bent, twisting and curving according to whims of nature, nature being indifferent to Euclid's observation that the shortest distance between two points is a straight line. Why did the Romans not employ linear geometry and lay a straight line through the Forum? Professor Gregory Aldrete suggests that maintaining the cloaca's winding nature was a mark of respect for, or perhaps fear of, whatever gods were peculiar to that particular tributary.[26]

The project was, like medieval cathedrals, destined to become a multi-generational affair, from Tarquinius Priscus (615–576 BC) to Servius Tullius (576–531 BC) and finally Tarquinius Superbus (532–509 BC), last of the kings of Rome.

Over time, the kings became more ambitious. To answer the problem of runoff, Tarquinius Superbus ordered the ditch to be lined with large slabs of cappellaccio tuff (a volcanic rock) measuring some 1.25 meters square by 0.3 meters thick.[27]

The stone upgrade was not initially a popular idea. It was one thing to shove a little dirt around and coax an existing stream along its way, quite another to ham-fistedly force the issue with a stone-lined canal. In no way could the proposed canal be mistaken for a natural waterway. This was clearly the work of men determined to bend nature to their own ends.

The gods, said the pious, do not care to be manipulated. Water was, after all, a living force, with moods and whims and enough power to destroy mere mortals. Anything that prevented river water from doing whatever river water wanted to do was risky. This went double for water that was allied to the Tiber itself, a river that had done Rome a lot of good but that periodically lost its temper.

On a more mundane level, the man in the Roman street may not have been very confident about holding off marauding enemies. The marsh was an equalizer. Draining the wetland and burying the streams around the settled hills was in effect stripping Rome of one part of its natural defenses. Rome was still a young enterprise, empire and superpower status a long way off. Hostile armies still marched on the city, and its defense system mattered.

Feelings ran so high that men forced to work on the project started running away or committing suicide. There is no record of what the injury rate on the project was, but the engineers had required massive blocks of stone. The ancients had experience with large stone, of course, but shifting such things in a waterlogged swamp was dangerous in novel ways.

New technology or not, approved or not, Tarquinius Superbus was not a man to be denied. The order went out that the project would proceed. Shirkers would be crucified. Work resumed.[28] The marshes were drained. The Forum was paved over, and a pleasant, stone-lined brook, a creation of unknown suffering and presumably death, ran through it, for all of which the people did not thank Tarquinius. On top of this outrage, he permitted a political ally to get away with the rape of an honorable Roman matron. That was too much. Shortly thereafter, Superbus was run out of the city, whose citizens decided that seven had been enough, and they were through with kings.

He will return to our story in the next chapter, but for now we can consider the greatness of his achievement.

And it was great. In later years, Pliny wrote admiringly of the construction's durability, the fact that it could withstand heavy carts passing over without its cracking.[29] Falling buildings (shoddy construction was not uncommon in Rome—building codes were lax and tenant litigation rare) did not move it, earthquakes did not shift it. The cloaca and its tributaries withstood the haphazard urban renewal made necessary by the Gauls' sack of Rome in 386 BC, with the result that, as Livy writes, "the old sewers, which originally were carried under public ground, now run everywhere under private houses, . . . the conformation of the City resembles one casually built upon by settlers rather than one regularly planned out."[30]

Pliny and Livy weren't alone in their interest in such public works. Dionysius of Halicarnassus (c. 60 BC–after 7 BC), a sensible man, lists a trio of Rome's achievements: roads, aqueducts, and sewers.[31] Strabo (63 BC–AD 23) commended the early Romans for their foresight in both bringing freshwater into town and flushing sewage away.[32] Cassiodorus (c. 485–c. 585) goes a bit far, referring to the "rivers enclosed, so to speak, in hollow hills, and flowing through the huge plastered tunnels; you may see men sailing the swift waters in boats prepared—with great care, lest they suffer a seafarer's shipwreck in the headlong torrent."[33] An alarming prospect. Perhaps he was joking.

It still had the power to impress two millennia later. Goethe, whose expectations of Rome came from his study of Piranesi's prints, found most of what he saw disappointing, excepting only the Cloaca Maxima, the reality of which was "even more colossal than Piranesi had led me to expect."[34] As late as 1869, Henry James declared after taking a brief tour of the place by torchlight: "It gave me the deepest and grimmest impression of antiquity I have ever received."[35]

What had begun as little more than a drainage canal, a more efficient way of channeling excess water from the Forum to the river, began to grow off shoots into the spreading city. And the huge drain got a companion. Roman archaeologist Rodolfo Lanciani wrote in 1889,

> In canoeing along the left bank of the Tiber, I had long noticed the mouth of another cloaca, a trifle larger than the Maxima, and separated from it by an interval of some three hundred feet. I had heard it called the cloaca of the Circus Maximus, but I was ignorant on whose authority and by what reason such a name had been applied. Six years ago, at the bottom of the valley which separated the Palatine from the Coelian, between the Arch of Constantine and the church of S. Gregorio al Monte Celio, a cloaca even larger and higher than the Maxima was discovered, three quarters of a mile from its opening into the Tiber, at the depth of forty feet. The enormous size of its blocks, the beauty and perfection of its masonry, and the wonderful preservation make it compare most advantageously with its rival, the Maxima, to which it is altogether superior as regards length and extent of district drained.[36]

The secondary drain was inevitable. Over time, the Cloaca Maxima had come to take on a new function, not simply a storm drain but an active sewer, daily ridding the city, by one estimate, of some one hundred thousand pounds of waste.[37] This raises the question of how human waste was dealt with in old Rome. In truth, raw sewage had its uses. The fullers collected urine to bleach cloth, a need so firmly established that the emperor Vespasian put a tax on the liquid, famously noting to his disapproving son Titus that the money collected this way had no smell. Columella wrote that human solid waste made excellent fertilizer, and given its widespread use in other times and places, we have to take him at his word.[38] Nasty stuff, of course, but nothing more than that. Disease? Disease was just an unhappy fact of life. Something to do with the air. . . .

Accordingly, night-soil collectors scrounged the city; some of their takings might have gone to agriculture, though a good deal of it was dumped near the cemetery at the Esquiline Hill. Even so, we have to assume Rome produced more than could be put to use, and so—off to the river it went.

If the river was offended by the liberties taken by the kings and subsequent rulers, it got periodic revenge, backfilling the sewers and regurgitating ripe effluent into the city, which was a strong disincentive to connecting one's house to the main sewer lines. The drain did on occasion stop up, as drains will, and there was credit to be had for anyone who set things back to rights. Marcus Agrippa in 33 BC, having cleared some stoppage (or having paid for others to do so), made a point of standing erect as his boat sailed away up the tunnel to prove that all was right between man and sewer.[39]

As to the relationship between man and the divine, the Romans acknowledged the vital role their imposition had on the water spirits. Under the rulership of Sabine king Titus Tatius, contemporary of Romulus and Remus while the twins were still on their respective hills, a statue of a woman was found in the proto-cloaca. Titus called the statue Cloacina for lack of any identifier, and had a little festival scheduled for her. In due course, and in an effort to boost the brand, so to speak, he set the goddess up with Venus herself, as Venus the Purifier, Venus the source of life itself.

The goddesses were accorded a small, circular shrine in the Forum Romanum, just in front of the Basilica Aemilia, outfitted with a stone manhole cover leading to the waterworks below. The shrine is long gone, its place marked by a circular outline on the ground, easily overlooked by casual visitors. Coins of the late republic show two female figures in dignified clothing standing on a dais, one holding up what appears to be a branch. The figures represent both Venus and Cloacina, just to be on the safe side. Love and sewage wore a dual mantle that could have given rise to cheap jokes, but for which, among the Romans, let us assume there was nothing but healthy respect (not least of all when the drain backed up).

Which is more than Cloacina got from the English. At least one Briton used his knowledge of the classics to come up with this water-closet doggerel:

> O Cloacina, Goddess of this place,
> Look on thy suppliants with a smiling face.
> Soft, yet cohesive let their offerings flow,
> Not rashly swift nor insolently slow.[40]

Some claim it was written by Lord Byron. The lines do not appear in any edition of his collected works, but—some claim—they are written in the lower stall at his ancestral house at Hampstead Abbey.

John Gay (1685–1732) features the goddess in his *Trivia: Walks in the City of London,* where she appears to have wandered off from the Eternal City and, now something of a down-and-outer in London, fallen in love with a mortal:

> Then Cloacina (Goddess of the Tide
> Whose sable Streams beneath the City glide)
> Indulg'd the modish Flame; the Town she rov'd,
> A mortal Scavenger she saw, she lov'd[41]

And he her, it seems. The offspring of this mixed marriage (more of a one-night stand, as Gay has it) is in due course given various bits by his mother's fellow gods and suitably prepared for the trade of bootblack.

> His treble Voice resounds along the Mews
> And Whitehall echoes—"Clean your Honour's Shoes"[42]

Having set the boy up in business, the mother dives into Fleet Street Ditch, we may hope as a first leg of a journey down the Thames to the sea and back to Rome where she was appreciated.

Certainly London in Gay's time had serious problems with sewage. Rome, more respectful of the spirits that inhabit the waters, had a better experience, and the Cloaca Maxima functions as a storm drain to this day. Given the abysmal state of London waste treatment at that time, so bad in the steaming summer of 1858 that they had to close down Parliament, a little more respect might have been in order. London didn't even begin work on *its* sewers until the 1860s.

What does remain from the cloaca's public face is the five-foot, nine-inch sewer cover, the so-called Bocca della Verità. This disc of Phrygian marble (high-quality stuff then and now), carved with a face, is now upright in the portico outside Santa Maria in Cosmedin. The cover is similar in size to the opening at the Round Temple in the nearby Forum Boarium, slightly concave on its face, its eyes and mouth pierced clean through. Possibly the image is a rendering of Oceanus, king of all water, lobster claws sprouting from his head. It likely dates to the reign of Hadrian.[43] Legend, presumably medieval, holds that any bearer of false witness who puts his hand in the god's mouth will have it bitten off.

An eighteenth-century English grand tourist was told that in older times the clearly guilty party was made to put his hand within to clear himself. Conscientious priests, hidden behind the stone and ready with hot iron, were ready to burn the offender's fingers, thus assuring the spectators of the fellow's guilt. "When this account was given us, a good Catholick present, observ'd upon the occasion, 'I Preti di quei Tempi erano Bricconi, comme sono alcuni dei nostri'"—The priests of those times were tricksters, and some of ours are no better.[44]

We have a written record that the cloaca was cleaned again in 1742 (presumably not the only time since Marcus Agrippa in 33 BC), and it seems to have worked fine ever after.[45] Improvements have continued down to the modern day. After the backwash of water into the Forum during the flood of 1901, the Cloaca Maxima was connected to the city's main sewer lines.[46]

Three Heroes of the Republic

We now return to Tarquinius Superbus and his travails.

The year was 598 BC. Tarquin, the seventh and last king of Rome, was expelled when he attempted to shield a relative who had raped the respected wife of a patrician. The senate established a republic, to be ruled by patricians and elected consuls, instead of a king.

Tarquinius Superbus did not take well to forced retirement. For two years, he licked his wounds and nursed his grudges, an exile at the court of Lars Porsena, a fellow Etruscan and king of Clusium. Tarquinius repeatedly warned Porsena that the very idea of republicanism was dangerous to men like themselves, and should be quashed as quickly as possible. In the end, Lars Porsena agreed to gather his considerable forces and head south. He had delayed two years, which proved to be a mistake. Had he acted sooner, he might have exploited man's natural discomfort with change.

For however objectionable Tarquinius had been, not all Roman citizens, in particular the masses of the less well off, were convinced that this new arrangement was in their interest. To convince them otherwise, the senate arranged to tax the rich more, the poor less, and to end price gouging on salt. Taken together, and allowed two years to become familiar, these measure seem to have done the trick, so that by the time the Etruscans were on the march, the citizens, by now accustomed to the new order, were antipathetic to the very word king.

Put to the test, however, the Roman spirit failed. Despite holding the high ground of the Janiculum Hill, the Roman soldiers were soon streaming away from Lars Porsena's forces toward the one bridge that connected this outpost with the city of Rome.

Not all citizens were that useless. Trying to hold back the tide of panicked men was Horatius Cocles, a one-eyed veteran of other wars, grabbing as many soldiers as possible and shouting that if the bridge were lost, Rome itself would be lost.

Only two men, the patrician-born Spurius Lartius and Titus Herminius, chose to stand with him. Together the trio baffled the first onslaught, while calling on their fellow Romans to tear up the bridge behind them. As the demolition wound down, Lartius and Herminius retreated at Horatius's urging. Let Livy continue the story:

> Once more Horatius stood alone; with defiance in his eyes he confronted the Etruscan chivalry, challenging one after another to single combat, and mocking them all as tyrants' slaves who, careless of their own liberty, were coming to destroy the liberty of others. For a while they hung back, each waiting for his neighbour to make the first move, until shame at the unequal battle drove them to action, and with a fierce cry they hurled their spears at the solitary figure which barred their way. Horatio caught the missiles on his shield and, resolute as ever, straddled the bridged and held his ground. The Etruscans moved forward, and would have thrust him aside by the sheer weight of numbers, but their advance was suddenly checked by the crash of the falling bridge and the simultaneous shout of triumph from the Roman soldiers who had done their work in time.[47]

Horatius now called out to the spirit of the river: "Tiberinus, holy father, I pray thee to receive into thy propitious stream these arms and this thy warrior."[48] And so he jumped and swam back to the safety of his fellows.

The story has been the stuff of Romantic painting, of opera, and Victorian poetry:

> O Tiber! Father Tiber!
> To whom the Romans pray,
> A Roman's life, a Roman's arms
> Take thou in charge this day.

That would be Macauley, from his *Lays of Ancient Rome*, a classic of its time.

Horatius had done well, but the war between Etruscans and Romans continued. Porsena had a navy, which he called out to block the coast and disrupt corn imports. Despite the loss of the bridge, he was able to cross the river elsewhere and savage Roman farms, steal their cattle, besiege the city. At this dramatic point in the narrative, C. Mucius, a noble youth, stepped up and declared to his fellow Romans:

"I wish to cross the river and to enter, if I can, the enemy's lines. My object is neither plunder nor reprisals, but with the help of God, something more important than either."[49]

What Mucius had in mind was assassination. He set out with the city's blessing, swam the river, and somehow managed to get within striking range of his target. Too quick for anyone to stop him, he closed with his victim, pulled a dagger from under his cloak, pushed himself forward, and landed a single killing thrust. Etruscans immediately seized him, and only then did he learn that he had got the wrong man.

Mucius was brought before Porsena, who demanded details of Rome's situation. Mucius refused. Porsena ordered a fire built around him until he spoke. Mucius told him not to bother, and to underscore the point, stuck his right hand in the kindling dish and let the fire roast his flesh. The body, he declared, is nothing to those intent on glory. Porsena, impressed, declared that Mucius could leave now unmolested. Mucius thanked him, then added that there were hundreds more Romans just like him, only one of whom had to be luckier than himself.

Porsena immediately sued for peace.

The story did not end there. Part of the deal was that Porsena take Roman hostages, male and female, among them the virgin Cloelia. She, dissatisfied with the situation, jumped on a horse and led some of the other female hostages to the riverside to swim home. Delicate diplomacy was called for if all were to save face. Porsena regretted the loss only because it was outside protocol. He was, he said, willing to release her, but only after she returned voluntarily. Were she not to return, the treaty would be voided, the war would resume.

She returned. Porsena, once again impressed by Roman gumption—greater, he said, than that of Horatius or Mucius—declared that she could take half of the remaining hostages. She chose young men rather than the women. This seemed odd, even wrongheaded, and when asked why she made this choice, she said that they would make the best soldiers in the war she saw as unfinished.[50] Porsena realized that these were not the kind of people whom he, or Tarquin, or anyone else, really, could hope to dominate. This time he proposed new peace terms, terms that made the two powers allies.

Horatius and Mucius, now called Scaevola ("Lefty") for having burned his right hand, were given tracts of land across the Tiber, Horatius's defined by whatever acreage he could plow in a day. Cloelia earned an equestrian statue at the head of the Sacred Way. Horatius also got a bronze statue, non-equestrian; his was in the Forum. Neither survives.

Those are the stories, in any event, and they are good ones for building a national spirit. Certainly they have proved rich fodder for artists and poets ever since, even into modern times. That later Romans fell far short of these people is not too surprising, given human nature.

The stories serve a secondary function as well, beyond that of giving young Roman boys and girls models for heroic behavior; they also remind the audience that the river was, ultimately, their natural ally against all enemies. It is always heartening to have the gods on your side.

Valesius, Ogulnius, and Asclepius

The stories of the river's healing powers are many and old. One of the earliest concerns Valesius the Sabine, who invoked the gods' help on behalf of his sick children. A voice answered, instructing him to sail down the river to the shrine of Dis Pater and Proserpina at Tarentum and boil some river water. Tarentum is the modern Taranto, over five hundred kilometers away in Southern Italy. A daunting prospect, but he set out regardless, eventually stopping for the night at Campus Martius. Chatting with the locals, he learned that this place too was called Tarentum. Better yet, he learned that if he dug at a certain spot he would find an abandoned altar to Dis and Proserpina. It was a short matter then to heat the water, head home, cure the children, and initiate the rites for the Ludi Tarentini, aka Saeculares. The games became an annual event, marked each time by digging up the altar beforehand and reburying it afterward.[51]

The annual games were an extreme expression of gratitude. Most people confined themselves to tossing votive offerings, small clay replicas of affected body parts, into the water, whether in hope for cures expected, thanks for cures attained, or dismay for cures misplaced. Scores of these objects—arms, hands, eyes, ears, breasts, legs, knees, feet—have been found near and around

Tiber Island. Shops leading from the Campus Martius to the Pons Fabricius sold the things in quantity; the remains of one of these shops was discovered in 1885, which trove included life-size torsos, open for inspection, perhaps as an aid for the unwell but undecided. Collect enough of the votives and you can build a creditable mannequin.

Valesius's games were good, but were not a cure-all. By 293 BC, the city needed stronger medicine. The reason was plague.

Rome was lousy with it. So were the outlying areas of Latium. Pleas to Apollo went unanswered, and so the city elders turned to the Sibylline books.[52] The Sibylline books were a Roman institution that went back to Tarquinius Superbus, with a story of their own.

One day, an old woman unknown to Rome approached the king and offered to sell him nine books, sight unseen, for an outrageous price. He refused. She took three of the nine and put them in a nearby brazier to burn. She then offered the remaining six for the same price. Again, he refused, but more uncertain. Three more went to the fire. One last chance, the remaining three for the same price. He gave her what she asked.

The woman turned out to be the Cumaean Sybil, priestess of the Apollonian oracle near Naples, one of various Sybils dotted around the ancient Mediterranean, and the books she offered turned out to be prophecies specific to Rome's future, with advice on how to deal with future catastrophes. Once clearly identified, the books were taken into safekeeping in the Temple of Jupiter, and were to be consulted only when a genuine emergency, such as the plague, arose.

In this instance, the books' answer was straightforward enough: Asclepius—none other than the god of medicine—must be taken from Epidaurus to Rome.[53] An embassy was arranged, led by Quintius Ogulnius Gallus, and made its way to Greece to see what could be arranged.

Their request did not go over well. The temple priests were not unsympathetic, but observed that the Sibylline books had put both parties into an awkward situation. It was quite impossible that the god statue should leave, and highly irregular that anyone should ask to take it. Perhaps they had misinterpreted the books? Oracles can be tricky.

The Romans insisted otherwise, and the argument went on into the night, without conclusion, and so was deferred until the next day. Ogulnius was permitted to spend the night in the temple, in case he might dream. As indeed he did. The statue itself spoke to him. Ogulnius, it seemed, should consider the snake that entwined the caduceus. He, Asclepius, promised that he would morph himself into such a snake, albeit larger and more powerful, and accompany Ogulnius to Rome.

By morning, all interested parties gathered at the temple, and Ogulnius told his story. As if on cue, the temple began to tremble. From the base of the statue there emerged a gold-skinned snake of heroic size. The creature circled the temple three times and then made its way to the main ship, slithering aboard and settling himself in with his head facing the stern. Good enough for the priests. They got to keep the temple; the Romans, the snake.

As Ogulnius and crew rowed up the Tiber, the surviving Romans lined the banks, doing their best to make the god feel welcome. Altars dotted the riverside, incense rising from each one. The snake roused itself, considered the choices on offer, then, near Campus Martius, slipped overboard and made straight for Tiber Island. The plague abated, the people rejoiced. His temple was built in 289 BC, and the island was clad in stone, giving it the form of a ship, to honor the expedition. You can still see remains of the caduceus carved into the side.

God or no god, priests and doctors were limited by the state of knowledge at the time. They did what they could, first avoiding harm, starting off the consultation with religious rites, following with some preliminary diagnosis—sacred oils, dog licking, snake licking—and if these failed, the administration of drugs. As at Epidaurus, the drugs were not curative, but intended to induce in the patient a dream-filled sleep. With luck, the godhead would appear and either grant good health on the spot or prescribe a course of treatment. This was better than nothing, and the placebo effect can only have been for the good. As of 195 BC (the date of his temple), the god Faunus aided the dream portion of the diagnosis.[54] Those who were not given a sign were reduced to asking passers for anecdotal advice and old wives' cures. The number of amateur and quack treatments was probably no greater than they are today.

Cure rates were presumably low, and the island inevitably served also as a hospice or, worse, as a dumping ground for inconveniently longtime dying. Useless slaves ended up this way often enough that the emperor Claudius, to discourage the practice, guaranteed freedom to any slave who should recover. The sources give no word on how well this worked out.

There were regardless some remarkable cures that the temple proprietors could boast of, and they did. A large Greek-language inscription relates the anecdote of a blind man, Gaius (blindness was a common ailment in the ancient world), who was instructed in his dream to walk from right to left, then to place five fingers on the podium, then to touch his eyes. His vision returned. Cure. The procedure does not appear in any of the ancient medical texts, though various other alarming prescriptives (the bile of certain fish, for example, for eye irritation) come highly recommended well into the Renaissance, and with some scientific basis.

There were skeptics, of course. Cicero sneered at votive offering as so much foolishness.[55] Horace notes and disdains the mother who pledges that her feverish son will "stand naked in the Tiber" (*nudus in Tiberi stabit*). The results, the poet notes, will be that "the idiot mother will kill her son, sticking him in the mud, renewing his fever."[56] Then as now, parenting skills of others were a source of criticism.

Salt

Salt was indispensable, the reason for Rome's first colony at Ostia at the mouth of the Tiber, where sandbars created a barrier between the wider Mediterranean and the Italian mainland, lagoons of brackish water, a place where flats could be laid out and shallow water allowed to be steamed off by the sun, leaving salt crystals behind. Livy claims that Ancus Marcius established the first saltworks (*salinae Ostienses*) there.[57] Some suggest that the Pons Sublicius was built at least in part to expedite the transport of salt from downriver across to the city proper.

Salt is crucial; it allowed fishermen to preserve the daily catch. Mountain people used it to preserve excess game. It was useful in making cheese. It provides iodine, a vital nutrient, and brings out flavor in otherwise insipid food.

For all these reasons, salt can be extremely lucrative. So much so that in the first year of the Roman republic, the senate, eager to get support from the lower classes who still had to be convinced that throwing off the king was in their interest, appropriated the privately owned salt pans and established a government monopoly, providing the stuff to the people at cost.[58]

Rutilius (fl. fifth century AD) describes the arrangement:

> It is on this score that value is set upon the salt marsh,
>   where the sea-water, running down through channels in the land, makes entry,
>   and a little trench floods the many-parted ponds.

But after the Dog-star has advanced his blazing fires,
when grass turns pale, when all the land is athirst,
then the sea is shut out by the barrier-sluices,
so that the parched ground may solidify the imprisoned waters.[59]

The dog-star being Sirius, prominent in the hot months, the time best suited for evaporation. Natural heat is best; also cheap.[60]

The science is straightforward enough. Salt in water breaks down into sodium and chloride ions, which are then surrounded by water molecules. When water evaporates, it cannot take the ions along for the ride, which leaves them free to recombine into salt and precipitate to the bottom of the pans. Salt gatherers can at that point rake the crystals into moist piles, scoop them out, and move on to the next step. The less water there is to break down the salt, the more salt solids precipitate to the bottom of the pans.

From the earliest days, the main road heading inland from Rome has been called the Via Salaria, the Salt Road—note that it starts from Rome, where salt ships would have brought the product upstream from the river's mouth. An entire district was called the Salinae, translated as either "saltworks" or "salt flats," where presumably the stuff was packaged and sold. The area retained that name well into the fifteenth century, long after its salt connection was gone.[61] Saltworks were a significant source of revenue for anyone who controlled them (the church in Middle Ages, which leased them out).

Taking from nature is taking from the gods, and a suitable acknowledgment is always in order. In Rome, a duty of the Vestal Virgins was to prepare *mola salsa*, sacred meals, the leftover grains and salt of which were solemnly tossed from the Pons Sublicius. Salt has, in its way, as strong a magic as water; tossing salt over the left shoulder is an attack on whatever devils might be perching there.

There is a widely held myth that Roman soldiers were paid in salt or that salt was used as currency or that the word "salary" comes from *sal*, salt. This bit of folk etymology goes back at least as far as Pliny, but nothing supports it.[62] Soldiers like salt as much as anyone, but they prefer precious metals. At the height of Rome's financial crisis in the third century AD, they were the only government employees who could demand, and get, their pay in gold. You can buy a lot of salt with gold.

Alien Gods

There is a spot where the rapid Almo flows into the Tiber
and the lesser stream loses its name in the greater.
There does the hoary priest in his purple vestments
lave the lady goddess and her sacred utensils in the waters of the Almo.[63]

The words are Ovid's, the lady goddess described being the Acus Matris
Deum, Cybele's Needle, a black meteorite that embodied Cybele, the Almo
being a small tributary not too far from Rome where the priests periodically
washed the stone down. They had their reasons, which dated back to the Punic Wars, when things were not going well for Rome. Winter had come, and
although combat was suspended for the season, Roman soldiers in camp were
suffering a fatal and contagious disease that the army commander thought
would surely be their end. A remedy needed to be found, and in fact was
found.

In the year 204, stones fell in quantity from the sky. The senate agreed that
this justified opening the books, where they read that whenever a foreign
enemy will have entered Italy, he could only be driven away and vanquished
if the Idaean Mother were transferred from Pessinus to Rome. By happy coincidence, Roman ambassadors had recently returned from the Oracle at
Delphi on an unrelated matter of gift giving and had heard a pronouncement
suggesting that a strong victory and much treasure were in Rome's future.
People hear what they want to hear, and armed with the two predictions,
Rome sent a delegation on five quinqueremes east, stopping again at Delphi
just to confirm that their interpretation was correct. It was, and added to
the prediction were instructions to approach King Attalus of Pergamum (in
modern Turkey) with their request. The king not only smiled on the request,
but accompanied them to Pessinus to expedite the transfer. The committee
carried the goddess stone out of the city, placed her aboard a reliable ship,
and sailed back to Rome, where the ship became stuck on a sandbank at the
river's mouth. A troubling omen, or some kind of Greek trick. Teams of men
pulled on ropes to break the ship free but, despite their best efforts, failed.

Of course the stone could simply have been offloaded and carried over-
land, but that would ruin the point of the story, which has a happier, if somewhat clichéd, ending. Once the men had exhausted themselves and all but
given up, one Claudia Quinta, a matron whom gossips accused of impurity

(Ovid writes that she dressed provocatively, changed her hairstyle frequently, and talked back to men), came forward and shouted to the goddess that if she, Claudia, were indeed virtuous, the goddess should allow her to shift the boat.[64] Nothing else was working, so Claudia was permitted to try. Eschewing the rope, she took off her sash (*infula*) and twined it on the prow of the ship and began to pull.[65] As with Arthur and Excalibur, the ship moved with minimal effort, but would only do so when the right person pulled.

It was no surprise that Cybele was the protector of women and children and a bringer of luck in general. The stone, having made its point, was carried to the temples until a proper home could be built, and every year eunuch priests carried the stone from its temple home on the Palatine to the pure spring-fed waters of the Almo, where it and the implements for her worship would be ritually bathed.[66]

The stone itself had an after history—Augustus dedicated a temple to it and to Cybele. The mad emperor Elagabalus removed the stone to a private chapel in the imperial palace, where it stayed, uninteresting to centuries of looters and treasure hunters, until it was rediscovered by the antiquarian Monsignor Francesco Bianchini in 1730. He describes "a stone nearly three feet high, conical in shape, of a deep brown color looking very much like a piece of lava and ending in a sharp point."[67] Scholar though he was, Bianchini failed to make the connection, and the stone has long since disappeared.

Claudia, as a vestal, was not the only religious patron to baffle nature in dealing with the Tiber. Livy mentions the followers of Dionysus, semisecret cultists less reserved in their worship than followers of Cybele. He writes: "The women, in the habit of Bacchantes, with their hair disheveled, and carrying blazing torches, ran down to the Tiber; where, dipping their torches in the water, they drew them up again with the flame unextinguished, being composed of native sulphur and charcoal."[68]

The general tolerance of Romans for strange and alien religions did have its hiccups.

Isis, another import, this time from Egypt, initially caught on in Rome as an object of veneration for slaves, women, lower classes, and immigrants. She, like Cybele, was the goddess of good fortune, a protector of the weak, especially women and infants. She looked out for sailors, too, which perhaps facilitated her leap from Alexandria to Rome. She was the goddess of regeneration and ensured the harvest; she was a healing goddess, and the mother of rivers and all those mythical creatures who watch over them. She, even more than her consort Osiris, who watched over the dead, was as close to a universal god as one was apt to find.

The senate frowned on the cult. Rome had enough gods already to propitiate without having to deal with a celestial turf war. The ambivalent view of Egypt might have had a hand in this as well. It was one thing to admire the old culture and power of that kingdom, quite another to let that culture infiltrate that of Rome itself. Then there were all those stories one heard, grim stories having to do with human sacrifice, with people thrown into the Nile for obscure cultish reasons.

Augustus considered the sect a scandal and passed measures to restrict its spread. Cleopatra, after all, had declared herself a reincarnation of the goddess, and then had seduced both Julius Caesar and Mark Antony from honorable Roman marriages (in the case of Antony, from Augustus's sister Octavia). A cult army dedicated to that kind of woman was the last thing Rome needed. Augustus stepped up official denunciation of the religion and tried to bring back the old republican virtues of chastity and moderation.

In the end, nothing he could do could prevent either vice or Isis, in Rome or even in his own household. Isis had become fashionable to such an extent that his own granddaughter was said to be a devotee. This having been added to her other crimes—chiefly sexual dissipation—she found herself exiled to a small island and forgotten.

The low point for the cult came under Tiberius. The historian Josephus tells the pitiful story of Paulina and Mundus.[69]

Paulina was a good Roman married to the equally good Saturninus, both of them devotees of Isis. Mundus, a rich Roman, fell in love with Paulina and thought that money would get him a night of paradise. Of course he was wrong. He then fell in with Ida, a priest of the temple, who suggested that if someone—say, Ida—could convince the loving couple that Anubis himself had fallen for Paulina, she and her husband might be more open to outrage. And so it turned out. Mundus paid Ida a good sum and got free rein of the temple for three consecutive nights of passion. Paulina seemed none the worse for wear, and Saturninus was pleased to share his wife with a god.

Like so many rich and powerful men, Mundus could not keep the joke to himself. He revealed himself to Paulina, presumably presuming that she would keep the matter to herself. She didn't. She told her husband, who told Tiberius, who came down hard. He had Ida and the priests crucified, the temple destroyed, and the statue of the god thrown in the Tiber.

And Mundus? Mundus got off with exile.

The faith proved stronger than the scandal; indeed, the scandal seems to have provoked an opposing reaction. Tiberius's successor Caligula, perhaps from innate perverseness, not only approved of the cult, but actively encouraged it. Whole temples, not just private chapels, were built. Holidays were entered into the civil calendar, most significantly March 5, when a statue of the goddess was placed on a boat and taken for a river cruise, on the good ship *Navigium Isidis*, as though back on the Nile. The celebration allowed Caligula to dress up as a woman, which he seemed to enjoy. Apuleius (AD 125–170) has a long description of their doings in his novel, *The Golden Ass*.

Nero was generally tolerant of the cult, though one theory holds that after the great fire of AD 64, he blamed the fire on Isis worshipers, not Christians.[70] No matter. He would be gone in another four years, and out of the wreckage of AD 69—the Year of Four Emperors, all but one killed within months of taking the crown—the cult found a new patron in Vespasian.

Vespasian had reason to favor Egypt. He had many allies there, dating from his time as a senior official in North Africa. And as he was founding his own imperial dynasty, the Flavians, and in effect regenerating the Roman Empire, who better as a benefactress than the goddess of the Nile? Vespasian had lived in and fought in areas—the Middle East, among others—where water was a lot less abundant than in central Italy. He was never a man to neglect the true value of things. Best to have the goddess smiling on Rome than not. Isis, it seemed, had come to stay.

Even so, the goddess still had her detractors. Juvenal writes of a female devotee putting herself in some New Year's discomfort to ward off the worst of the coming year's trials:

> In winter she will go down to the river of a morning, break the ice, and plunge three times into the Tiber, dipping her trembling head in its whirling waters, and crawling out thence naked and shivering, she will creep with bleeding knees right across the field of Tarquin the Proud.[71]

Male adherents seem to have gotten a pass on this particular rite.

Neither Isis nor the old river gods, however venerable, could survive Christianity. Their festivals fell out of favor, their holidays were co-opted. The river lost its divinity. Rome's traditional priesthoods were abolished by AD 400.

Cui Bono? Roscius and the *Poena Cullei*

One summer night in the year 81 BC, Sextus Roscius, a prosperous farmer from Armeria, some distance north of Rome, was visiting Rome and, after dinner with a friend, happened to be walking home through the city's dark, dirty streets. The Social War of 91–88 BC, a war that had torn Italy apart, was now over, the victorious Sulla ran the city with an iron hand, and various lieutenants and honest citizens could be grateful that the fighting was over. Sextus could be confident that he was no man's enemy, least of all Sulla's, and although rich, he seems not to have been as well guarded as he should have been. Rome was not Armeria, and in an alley near the baths, he was assaulted, a dagger thrust in his gut, his body thrown in the Tiber. It was the sort of thing that could happen to anyone visiting the big city, and might have passed without record or memory outside his immediate family, if not for the aftermath.

Roscius's body was recognized by a fellow Armerian and relative T. Roscius Magnus, who happened to be in Rome, and who sent word back to T. Roscius Capito of the man's death. Capito informed Chrysogonus, one of Sulla's lieutenants who was responsible for the disposition of properties forfeited by proscription—essentially judicial theft for the benefit of Sulla and his friends. Roscius had owned thirteen separate farms, most facing the Tiber and as such particularly attractive.

By rights the estate should have gone to the man's son, also named Sextus Roscius. The problem was not insuperable. It would require only a moment with pen and ink to add the dead man's name to the (officially closed) proscription list, squeezed in at the very bottom, and thus put the Roscius estate in forfeiture. An auction was quickly arranged, and real estate and chattels worth six million sesterces fell under the hammer to an unknown buyer for two thousand.

It didn't seem right to the locals, and as the dead man was well regarded in town and his politics were at best middle of the road, some Armerians banded together to protest the events to Sulla. Roscius should never have been on the proscription list, and his property should not have been sold. Unfortunately, one of their number was T. Roscius Magnus, the man who tipped off Chrysogonus in the first place. The delegates met not with Sulla, but with his trusted agent Chrysogonus, who listened attentively and assured the men that Roscius senior would be stricken from the list and his property restored to his son. They left, satisfied that things would soon be put right.

Things were not put right. Chrysogonus, the unknown buyer, knew that he could not keep the deceit hidden indefinitely. What would render the question of ownership moot was the sudden and prudently arranged disappearance of the younger Roscius. A few attempts were made and, surprisingly, failed. Roscius took the hint and left town and headed to Rome, where he might disappear among the rest of the penniless rabble and survive on handouts, or maybe, just maybe, find a way of getting justice.

Justice would be difficult. His story might be convincing, but making accusations against a man as powerful as Chrysogonus, a man favored by the decidedly unsentimental Sulla, would be professionally unwise. In any event, Roscius was soon found in Rome, and rather than just have him killed outright, Chrysogonus went a step further. He hired the finest prosecutor then in practice and had a charge of parricide laid against the young Roscius. For the defense, Roscius managed to hire a young and ambitious man with a gift for oratory. The defense of Sextus Roscius was the first case for Cicero.

In war, the best defense is a good offense, and Cicero was very good on offense. Having dismissed the charge of parricide as nonsense that only a fool would believe, he went after two men of Armeria. One now owned a small section of the grand estate that Chrysogonus had bought for a pittance; the other got a plum job as overseer of the rest—obviously rewards for perjury. Having dealt with the small fry, Cicero now went for the big fish. He gestured up to the rich houses on the Palatine Hill, pointing to the home of Chrysogonus, a former slave, a Greek former slave at that, rich through base means, golden haired, perfumed, unspeakably arrogant, certainly not much of a Roman, the very antithesis of sturdy yeomen like Sextus Roscius, senior and junior. At the end of the day, Cicero asked the crucial question—Who benefited? *Cui bono?*

The crowd loved nothing more than a good speech, and the tyro Cicero had certainly delivered, his words the more thrilling since Sulla was not known as a forgiving man; and although Cicero had stressed that none of this repellent behavior was any reflection on the great dictator, who must not have known of any of it, this was playing close to the line. Perhaps Sulla was amused by the lawyer's impudence. Perhaps he felt that the likes of Chrysogonus had gone too far. In any event, Cicero now became a prized and well-paid advocate, well on his way to greatness. Chrysogonus disappears from the record, we can assume to enjoy his ill-gotten gains, as does Roscius, who can be grateful that he was unlikely to be chased down and killed. At least we can be sure that he was not punished for parricide.

Which would be welcome news, since the punishment for parricide, or matricide, was the *poena cullei*, punishment by the bag.

The sack (*culleus*) in question was the same sort of leather arrangement used to transport wine in bulk, essentially the skin of an entire cow. The punishment is first mentioned by Livy as the fate of one Publicius Malleolus, a man guilty of matricide. The year was 101 BC; the recipe was to tie the guilty party in a large leather bag and throw him into the sea.[72] This was later expanded to include the river. (The river was the final resting place for dead gladiators; or rather, those gladiators who had failed to fight the good fight, who showed cowardice. Such men were as bad as cowards in war, *noxii*, a stain on the city, and so forfeited the right of proper burial.) Cicero, as part of his defense of Roscius, goes into some detail on the punishment:

> [Our ancestors] stipulated that parricides should be sewn up in a sack while still alive and thrown into a river. What remarkable wisdom they showed, gentlemen! Do they not seem to have cut the parricide off and separated him from the whole realm of nature, depriving him at a stroke of sky, sun, water and earth—and thus ensuring that he who had killed the man who gave him life should himself be denied the elements from which, it is said, all life derives? They did not want his body to be exposed to wild animals, in case the animals should turn more savage after coming into contact with such a monstrosity. Nor did they want to throw him naked into a river, for fear that his body, carried down to the sea, might pollute that very element by which all other defilements are thought to be purified. In short, there is nothing so cheap, or so commonly available that they allowed parricides to share in it. For what is so free as air to the living, earth to the dead, the sea to those tossed by the waves, or the land to those cast to the shores? Yet these men live, while they can, without being able to draw breath from the open air; they die without earth touching their bones; they are tossed by the waves without ever being cleansed; and in the end they are cast ashore without being granted, even on the rocks, a resting-place in death.[73]

The punishment takes on more elaborate details in later years. Seneca mentions the addition of snakes.[74] Juvenal adds a monkey.[75] By the fourth century, the Greek grammarian Dositheus ups the number by including snakes, a monkey, a cockerel, and a dog.[76] Cold, wet, noisy, painful, confusing, and unpleasant for the condemned and his companions, but a clean end of an evil for the high-minded, a gruesome entertainment for the bloody minded. The emperor Augustus seems to have found the punishment distasteful and even in cases of manifest guilt attempted to lead the guilty away from full confession ("You surely did not kill your father . . . ?"), without which the punishment was not to be used.[77] His grandson Claudius, by contrast, is said to have condemned more men to the sack than to crucifixion.[78] Perhaps he thought it more merciful.

The most notable matricide of antiquity was Nero, who had his mother Agrippina placed in a collapsible boat in AD 58 in hopes she would drown. She didn't. She made it to shore, where Nero had underlings finish the job with swords.

That he was not charged comes as no surprise, given human nature. What is dispiriting is that his adviser, the stoic philosopher Seneca, went so far as to write a letter to the senate explaining that she had been planning a coup and that all should be grateful that Nero had come out of the situation alive. Of all present, not one objected. The closest anyone came was Thrasea, who, rather than go on record, walked out in silence, "as he could not say what he would, and would not say what he could."[79] (Private sentiment was less restrained. Cassius Dio writes that by night someone hung a leather bag over one of Nero's statues; further explanation was superfluous.) [80]

The punishment was outlawed in the ninth century, to be replaced by immolation. It was later taken up in central Europe, the last case occurring in Germany, only to be outlawed in the eighteenth century.

Cicero and the Woman

Habes hortos ad Tiberim. ("You have gardens on the Tiber.")
Cicero, Pro Caelio

The subject of the charge being Clodia Metellus (94 BC–?), daughter of Appius Claudius Pulcher and as such of as ancient a family as Rome could provide. Rich, too. First-year Latin students will know her as the Lesbia of Catullus's easy-to-parse poetry. *Odi et amo*—I love and I loathe.

She had a taste for young men, did Clodia, and so did they for her. Catullus, one of her more naive and sentimental lovers, immortalized her as Lesbia, first with happy, even euphoric love poems, later, disillusioned, with savage invective. She broke his heart, and when he turned, he turned hard indeed, and the private poetry began to make the rounds. The name Lesbia was a cover, but tissue thin in gossip-loving Rome. He described his former paramour as a high-born trollop—*quadrantaris*, two-bit (whore)—who trolled the taverns and alleys for rough trade, and favored the grinning Spaniard who kept his teeth white by brushing with his own urine—those who mattered knew whom he was talking about, even if we do not.

It might have ended there, a curious footnote to history, had she not taken as her new lover the unsentimental Caelius Rufus. In this case he, it seems, dumped her.

Clodia was not to be mocked, and lacking Catullus's talent for poetry, went to law. She had formulated a list of outrageous crimes, from peculation to attempted murder, not only of herself, but of an Egyptian ambassador. This too might have passed into history's memory hole had not Caelius hired as defense counsel his good friend Marcus Tullius Cicero.

Accordingly, second-year Latin students meet Clodia again in the defense speech, *Pro Caelio*, a remarkable work of subtle and not so subtle invective by the greatest speaker of his age. He had his own reasons to dislike the family. Just two years earlier, Clodia's brother Publius Clodius Pulcher, as tribune, had a law drafted that saw Cicero temporarily banished, then took advantage of the orator's absence to destroy his various real estate holdings. Offered the chance to take down this man's sister while helping out a friend, Cicero did not need much persuasion.

Drawing on a full arsenal of rhetorical weaponry, Cicero was able to fillet the reputation of this powerful member of the old aristocracy, all the time keeping just on the right side of libel.

Those gardens on the Tiber mentioned—"You have deliberately chosen that particular site because that is the very place where all the young men go to swim"[81]—that was just for starters. He goes on, first praising the woman's considerable ancestry, then regretting that it should be associated with such a squalid affair as this trial, involving a woman whom so many men have considered not an enemy but rather a cherished *amica*—here the audience laughs; *amicus* meaning friend or client, in the feminine form, *amica*, friend or mistress. Indeed, he would impugn her the more except for the fact that he, Cicero, had such personal differences with her husband.

Did I say husband? Sorry, I meant *brother*. I always make that mistake.

All of which would have gotten another laugh from the gossip-loving audience that had heard stories of Clodia's sharing her bed with Pulcher.

The speech is worth reading in its entirety; suffice it to say that the case was dismissed, and she fades a bit from history, while Cicero goes on to greater glory in court and in politics, making friends and enemies in both. A decade later, writing about luxury real estate opportunities with his friend Atticus, Cicero professes to admire the infamous riverside gardens very much, though he believes that she is unlikely to wish to sell. Perhaps Atticus could arrange a private purchase? It appears he could not.[82]

Not that it mattered much. Roman politics soon heated up again, honorable men assassinated Julius Caesar, and factions arose. In the initial confusion, Cicero sided with Octavian and wrote philippics against Mark Antony. When, briefly, Octavian and Antony reconciled and formed a triumvirate with Lepidus, all three agreed to let each proscribe old enemies. Octavian argued to spare Cicero, but successful politicians tend to be cold-blooded in cutting off underlings they no longer find necessary. Soldiers found the orator at his villa at Formiae; he offered his throat to the soldier sent to kill him. Mark Antony had ordered the hands that had written the philippics cut off, and the head to be nailed to the Rostra.

Before the head was put on public display, however, Clodia's niece—Mark Antony's second wife, Fulvia—took the opportunity to have it brought to her so that she could, with a golden hairpin, repeatedly stab the orator's tongue. Much good it did her. Soon after, Mark Antony dropped her and married Augustus's sister Octavia (eventually dumping her to marry Cleopatra).

Such at least has been the standard story for decades. More recent scholars have a more benign view of Clodia, and some argue that "Lesbia" might be someone else entirely.[83] Scholarship never ends.

Caesar and Cleopatra

The man in the street has largely forgotten Clodia; nobody has ever forgotten Cleopatra.

Short refresher—49 BC, Cleopatra, age twenty, and her brother Ptolemy XIII, age twelve, co-regents of Egypt and last of a line dating back to a lieutenant of Alexander the Great, were at war, largely thanks both to Ptolemy's advisers and weakness of character. Cleopatra had proved too officious for Ptolemy's minders, and she had been forced into exile. By chance, Rome was also in contention, with Julius Caesar fighting against his onetime co-ruler Pompey, and defeating him at the battle of Pharsalus in 48 BC. Pompey had now arrived in Egypt, with hopes of sanctuary and rebuilding his army. Caesar was no doubt not far behind, forcing Ptolemy to consider where his best interests lay. Ptolemy, or rather his advisers, placed his bets on Caesar, and so when Pompey appeared, Ptolemy had him assassinated. Good news for Caesar, if not quite as Ptolemy might have hoped. The Egyptian had rid Caesar of a meddlesome competitor, but a competitor who still had supporters back in Rome. Ptolemy's action allowed Caesar to lay blame for the crime on a dishonorable foreigner, and justify Roman interference with Egypt. Enter Cleopatra, famously smuggling herself into Caesar's quarters by means of a rolled carpet. Sparks flew, and soon he conflated his own personal war with that of Egypt. Within a year, Ptolemy XIII was drowned in the Nile (rivers are dangerous), Cleopatra was again regent (another brother, Ptolemy XIV, was co-regent), Alexandria had been largely torched (including much of its great library), and effective control of the country had gone to Rome. Cleopatra was also carrying Caesar's child. With their child Caesarion delivered, Cleopatra headed to Rome to join her victorious lover.

What a disappointment it must have been! Cleopatra had grown up in Alexandria, first city of the Mediterranean, all gleaming white boulevards and seaside views, marked by a great lighthouse, the Serapion, the tomb of Alexander, the magnificent library. From this to a hilly city of narrow streets and brick-and-wood buildings was a lesson in how appearance does not necessarily reflect power, much less potential.

Cleopatra spent her time at one of Caesar's riverside villas, the Horti Caesarum, just south of the city wall. Was Caesar embarrassed by his native river? However pleasing the Tiber might be, it is no patch on the Nile, and the city of Rome, even with its recent additions of Pompey's Forum, of Caesar's Forum, of the Temple of Jupiter looming over the city on the Capitoline Hill, could only look pathetic when considered against the white stone of seaside Alexandria.

Not only was Cleopatra's new situation a comedown after a lifetime as a princess and queen on the Nile; it was also something of an insult. Julius tried to make sweeten the pill, to flatter her vanity. He ordered a gilded statue in her image placed in the city's temple of Venus Genetrix, which can only have raised a few eyebrows, or prompted a few filthy jokes, given that not only Rome in general, but Caesar himself in particular was famously descended from Venus. Regardless, the gesture changed nothing. The statue could remain, but Roman law forbade a foreign head of state (like Cleopatra) from spending the night within the *pomerium*, the sacred boundaries that encircled Rome proper.[84]

Visitors, fascinated by the strange stories out of Egypt, crossed the river to see the young woman had so beguiled the soldier Caesar, most notable among them being Cicero. He didn't much like her (*Reginam odi*, "I loathe the queen"), and complained in a letter that, having crossed the river just to see her, he had not received a gift he had been promised.[85] A proper gossip would have continued with this vein, adding salacious details, but no, Cicero goes on to other less interesting topics, disappointing both rumormongers and historians.

Cicero was not alone in his antipathy, and even as a mistress, Cleopatra did Caesar no real good: "For she had come to the city with her husband and settled in Caesar's own house, so that he too derived an ill reputation."[86] She was in town when the dictator was killed at the Curia of Pompey (the plan to throw his body in the Tiber failed), but left soon after, there being nothing for her in Rome. Civil war distracted Rome for some years, in the course of which Mark Antony, in need of military support, came calling in Alexandria, and fell for the queen even harder than Caesar had, going so far to divorce his wife (Octavian's sister) in absentia. After some years of Antony and Cleopatra's complex relationship (incidentally producing three children), war came to them. Mark Antony lost the battle of Actium to Octavian and died a suicide, ending any hopes she had for power in Rome. Unable to seduce Octavian and unwilling to be the main attraction in his inevitable triumphal parade (which would likely end in a ritual strangulation), she committed suicide, possibly by snakebite, forcing Octavian, now Augustus, to substitute a living queen with wax effigy, complete with wax asp. Just as well, really; even the Romans found the execution of a woman harder to swallow than the execution of a man. There was no such sympathy for Caesarion, her son, Julius Caesar's son, who had hoped to escape to India and safety but never got there. Augustus, his quasi half-brother, ordered him killed on the way, then claimed all of Egypt for Rome. The surviving children of Antony and Cleopatra graced Octavian's triumph (gold shackles), but were afterward raised in Octavia's household with Antony's other children.

As to the villa on the Tiber—Caesar had bequeathed it to the people of Rome.

Tributary—Cremera

"Slight and short of water," according to the Renaissance scholar Biondo Flavio.[1]

Which did not stop the Etruscans from dedicating a temple to it. Well they might—Cremera's water fed the city of Veii, crown jewel of the Etruscan League. Veii, "not inferior to Rome itself in buildings and possessed of a large and fruitful territory, partly mountainous and partly in the plain. The air was pure and healthy, the country being free from the vicinity of marshes, which produce a heavy atmosphere, and without any river which might render the morning air too rigid. Nevertheless there was an abundance of water, not artificially conducted, but rising from natural springs, good to drink."[2]

Veii was something of a sore point with early Romans. The first kings of Rome had been Etruscan, and although the last had been kicked out in 509 BC, there was always the chance that they could return. Veii, some twenty kilometers northwest of Rome, comfortably rich, well armed, was too close for comfort. The Veiians had begun to make occasional raids, not enough to call for outright war, but not enough to qualify as peace either.

Eventually, the Romans had had enough. In 479 BC the head of the Fabia family, *gens Fabia*, as patrician as a family of Romans could be, declared his clan was willing to take full responsibility for countering the Veiian trouble-makers, leaving the rest of Rome free to get on with their lives. The offer was accepted. All Rome cheered as the Fabii and their friends and clients headed across the Tiber and up the Cremera. Arrived outside Veii, the small army established camp and remained there for the next two years, an active reminder to the Etruscans that Rome would not tolerate any nonsense.

And indeed, raids against Rome grew fewer. Some fights large and small broke out, the Fabii generally besting the Etruscans. Over time, however, the Fabii began to have problems of logistics. Rome was not regular with food. To carry on, the Fabii began to raid the local farms, essentially becoming what they had come to fight.

It was now the Veiians' turn to be furious. They determined on deception. For some months, they countered raids on their farms with ineffective defenders who fled at the first show of Roman force, leading the Romans to think the Etruscans had gone soft. New raids followed, each a little farther from the river and the main camp. One day, the Romans saw a herd of cattle on the far side of the plain, and only a small number of men tending them. Easy prey, and various Fabii headed out in no particular order and rushed the herd, which, predictably, scattered. The Fabii kept up the haphazard chase, diluting their own strength.

At which point the Veiians rose up in force. The Romans found themselves surrounded by a circular shield wall of men. Etruscan javelins targeted the Romans' shrinking core. With some difficulty, the Fabii managed to form a flying wedge, break out of the circle, and gather on higher ground, but it was too little, too late. More Etruscans appeared and began the slow slaughter of the entire family, some 306 men.

Nearly, but not all. Quintus Fabius Vibulanus, scarcely more than a boy, managed to survive, either at the battle or, underage for battle, at Rome. Which was just as well. The family needed a root to grow on; the Fabii would have much to offer Rome in coming centuries.

Veii would survive as Etruscan for another eighty years, then fall, like Troy, to a ten-year siege, after which it became Roman Veii, a pleasant mountain retreat, eventually abandoned and allowed to fall into ruin. The remains are scarcely more than some tufa foundations, near impossible to build a mental picture of what was once a great and rich fortress city.

RIVER OF EMPIRE

In which Romans stage mock naval battles, arrange for free food,

build canals and tombs, commit suicide, build an extra hill, mess about

in boats, move obelisks, and endure emperors' behaving disgracefully.

Naumachia

In 46 BC Julius Caesar returned to Rome to celebrate his triumph over the
Gauls. He bankrolled forty days of public celebration, including a mock sea
battle. To set the stage, he had men dig out a basin in the area of the Campus Martius. Once satisfied, he had the river fill it in. Ships followed, oared
vessels of two to four banks, to reprise in small a battle between Tyrians and
Egyptians for the benefit of those Romans who had missed the real thing. It
could as well have been a real battle. Arguably it *was* a real battle, absent the
geopolitical element. Four thousand oarsmen, one thousand marines, all of
them prisoners of war or condemned prisoners; for them, as for all combat
troops, once the fighting started, it was personal. Those who survived that
day, we may assume, could look forward to freedom. Knowing that this was
not a mock event, they were more apt to fight like they meant it.

But who cared about the combatants? For the Roman mob, it was also the
spectacle of a lifetime, whatever the outcome. They lined up in their thousands, camping outdoors for better position, jostling, shoving on the streets
to the point that many were crushed to death before the event even began.

There is no record of the show itself, but some things can be inferred. The
standard naval tactics of the Roman navy would be replicated, a straightforward matter of ramming the enemy ship, swarming aboard, then engaging

the enemy sailors sword to sword. These were not the one-on-one gladiatorial contests where individual crowd favorites could be singled out and cheered on. This was large-scale combat—anonymous, murderous, loud, smelly, bloody, inglorious. It would be difficult not to get caught up in the excitement, assuming one has a taste for such things.

The spectacle was a one-off, the basin eventually filled in, either to placate the river god or to prevent the area from becoming a fetid and malarial swamp.[1] Or possibly in response to an outbreak of plague.[2]

It was memorable, in any event. Caesar had a talent for what was memorable.

No surprise then that his successor Augustus, once settled in power, decided to stage a repeat. He carved out his inlet on the right bank below the Pons Aemilius. To avoid the possibility of creating a swamp, he built an aqueduct to draw water some thirty kilometers away, water so bad that it was useless for anything other than lake fill. For the show, he ordered thirty boats with rams, other boats, three thousand men (all names now lost). The theme was the battle of Salamis, Persians versus Athenians. The spectacle was significant enough to be included on his *Res Gestae*, the official record of achievements, copied and posted on bronze placards all over the empire from Spain to the Levant, far beyond the reach of those who actually saw the battle. The official description of the basin was exact—eighteen hundred by twelve hundred Roman feet (530 by 350 meters).[3] Pliny writes of an island in the middle.[4]

The new venue was permanent, the shows infrequent and only on extraordinary occasions. It isn't easy to get thousands of men willing to kill each other for sport. The lake itself was picturesque enough to attract those in need of a discreet place for a tryst, heartfelt or purely commercial.[5] The erotic poet Ovid, never much a one for blood sport, thought the show absurd, but found the crowds a good place to find women, presumably dragged unwillingly to the show and open to other diversions: "In that crowd, who *didn't* find someone to love?"[6]

Who indeed? Still, the play was the thing, and the most spectacular was to be played out during the reign of Claudius, not on some man-made pond, but on the Fucine Lake.

The lake was a shallow basin without outlet and potentially rich farmland. All emperors since Julius Caesar had considered draining it, but had not. Entrepreneurs asked Claudius if they could try. He agreed, and they spent the next eleven years digging a channel through solid rock to reach the lake. When they were nearly done, Claudius decided to mark the occasion with the greatest mock sea battle ever seen, to be followed by a gushing draining of the lake into the Liri River.

For days before the event, workmen built a wooden wall around the lake and stands for the spectators. Fifty ships, divided into opposite sides, took part, one line imitating Sicilians, the other, Rhodians.[7] Nineteen thousand men would take part in one capacity or another.[8] Nor were the ships scaled-down stage vessels. With the whole of Fucine Lake to work with, Claudius had brought in full-scale triremes and quadriremes, fully equipped and ready to show the punters what a real naval battle looked like. There were also praetorian cohorts, on rafts, manning catapults and ballistae to ensure that none of the nineteen thousand crew members tried to make a run for it.

On the day of the show, people rushed to fill all available seats; luckless latecomers contented themselves on the shore, on nearby hills, on the crests of nearby mountains. This was not the sort of thing one wanted to miss. Claudius appeared, along with his wife Agrippina in a chlamys of golden thread.

The commanders of each flotilla approached the imperial dais, raised their arms. It is now (and only now) that we hear the phrase "Hail Caesar, we who are about to die salute thee."[9]

This was stirring stuff, but Claudius was either excited, or playful, or bored. His offhand, less quoted, reply to this was "or not" (*aut non*).[10] A mistake. Some jailhouse lawyer among the combatants interpreted the words as a blanket pardon and said so. His fellows took up the point and refused to fight.

This stumped Claudius. The crowds were ready, and the actors were in effect going on strike. It took a combination of threat and cajoling to get them back on board and the show back on schedule. "The signal was sounded on a horn by a silver triton, which was raised from the middle of the lake by a mechanical device."[11] The oars rose and dipped as ships on both sides engaged in a little preliminary feinting and parrying, until finally getting down to the murderous business at hand.

Did Claudius get his money's worth? Tacitus suggests he did: "The battle, though one of criminals, was contested with the spirit and courage of freemen, and after much blood had flowed, the combatants were exempted from destruction."[12]

Less satisfying was the aftermath. Unfortunately, the engineers who planned to break the final barrier between lake and gravity had miscalculated, and the expected torrent was more of a trickle. Years passed before Claudius got credit for seeing through "an engineering marvel scarcely describable."[13]

Claudius's show could not easily be topped, but that did not stop his successor Nero, arguably the most theatrically inclined of emperors, from trying.

In AD 57, he ordered the building of an amphitheater on the Campus Martius. The various accounts are confused and confusing. It was made of wood.[14] (Seating, perhaps, but what of the space to hold water?) It was covered with a blue awning with stars.[15] It was filled with seawater.[16] (For what possible reason, and how?) It was stocked with fish and other sea creatures.[17] (What could they add to the show?) Many questions, few answers. He had faux Persians and Athenians reprise the battle of Salamis (like Augustus), after which the basin was drained and the surviving combatants finished the contest on dry, that is to say muddy, land. The amphitheater burned in the great fire of Rome (64 AD), but not before one more animal hunt, one more sea battle, one more gladiatorial combat, and one more public banquet.[18] (In a few centuries, it would silt up to a pond, the Cavone, property of the nuns of San Cosimato.)

The last of the great mock sea battles was under Titus as part of the dedication of the Colosseum in AD 80.[19] Two, in fact—the Colosseum had seating for about fifty thousand, this in a city of over a million souls, and Titus wanted to please everyone. He ordered the old Augustan pond across the river again fitted out, and three thousand men reenacted Athenians attacking Syracusans on the small island that represented their city.

The poet Martial was present and gave us his impressions. He is a little thin on the details—what exactly was the "trained bevy of Nereids" doing along the shore?—but assures us that the spectacle was better even than the show Claudius had put on:

> Let not the Fucine lake and the mere of dreadful Nero be told of: of this seafight alone let the ages know![20]

(Two years after its initial completion, the Colosseum received an upgrade. Its *palestra* was drained one last time and a warren of small chambers for animals and gladiators and condemned prisoners built where water had once been. The area was covered over with wooden planks, which in turn were covered with sand to soak up blood. Engineers built mechanical lifts to raise the performers and the condemned up into the sunlight. Presumably these improvements spelled the last of the sea battles, though with the drainage system and the aqueduct's extension still intact, a thorough rinse job both above and below should still have been possible, not to say highly desirable in the hottest months.)

And the Colosseum? The Colosseum was a poor venue for water sports, especially given the other options. True, it could be filled with aqueduct water and drained into Rome's main drain. The arena, however, was seventy-nine by forty-seven meters, a wading pool compared to Augustus's lake (never mind the Fucine Lake). The water portion of the entertainment could pass as a novelty, even a comedy act, but soon gave way to the more familiar killing of gladiators, exotic animals, criminals, and Christians. The drains served only to wash away the refuse that comes from that sort of entertainment, eventually winding up back in the Tiber. Indeed, Titus's brother and successor Domitian, not having been associated with the Colosseum to the extent his father and brother were, went so far as to create his own water park near the Tiber, which he surrounded with seats and in which he "gave sea-fights almost with regular fleets."[21]

Suetonius adds the odd comment that he watched these contests in pouring rain, *inter maximas imbres*.[22] Vespasian and Titus were generally thought to be of a sunny disposition; Domitian was something of a depressive.

Rain or shine, the shows continued to be popular. Sidonius Apollonaris refers to Rome's naval spectacles as late as AD 467, nearly four hundred years after the Colosseum was built, which suggests a healthy appetite for the medium, to say nothing of the money required to put them on. By that time, however, their days were numbered.[23]

Villas

On the banks of the Tiber and overlooking it there are perhaps
more villas than on all the other rivers of the entire world.

Pliny wrote that in the early days of the empire. In the early days of the republic such land was awarded to outstanding heroes for services to the people. Cash eventually replaced virtue as the price of a river view, and wealthy Romans built villas upstream to escape the city's brutal summer heat.

Cicero, Horace, Pliny, Propertius, Catullus, and others all either had rural land or wrote wistfully of how fine it would be to get some, and, as with any prized limited good, how unfair it was that the undeserving should have any. Pliny the Younger wrote of the odious Regulus, who "is retired to his gardens across the Tiber, where he has covered a vast extent of ground with huge porticoes, and crowded all the shore with his statues." "Across the Tiber" meant Trastevere, known even then as not the nicest part of town; but Regulus was, to Pliny, a cheap, nasty man who liked to show off at the least possible expense.[24]

Pliny could go on at some length concerning his own Tuscan villa (one of several), where although it "abounds with great plenty of water, there are no marshes; for as the ground is sloping, whatever water it receives without absorbing, runs off into the Tiber."[25] It has yet to be identified.

One villa that has been identified, upriver some nine miles north of Rome, belonged to Livia, wife of Augustus. The story goes that she was visiting the site when an eagle dropped a white chicken holding a sprig of laurel in its beak into her lap. This sort of thing grabs one's attention. For lack of any specific guidance, she planted the laurel nearby, and over time it took root and prospered mightily, and all Caesarian crowns for official occasions thereafter were taken from the tree that it became.[26]

The white chicken prospered as well, even giving its name to the villa (Ad Gallinas Albas) and multiplied—in itself unusual, since white chickens tend to sterility. In time the bird's familial line waned, the last of the line dying with the last of the Julio-Claudian emperors, that is to say, with Nero.[27] The villa was uncovered in 1863 (along with the life-size portrait statue of Augustus, the so-called *Prima Porta Augustus*, now in the Vatican museum) and has been restored, still pleasing for visitors. In the basement, filled in with and therefore protected by dirt, archaeologists found a mural, continuous on all four walls, no windows, lit only by sky light and depicting an idealized low-walled garden full of laurel (of course), roses, daisies, fir, oak, oleander, myrtle, pine trees, apple, and pomegranate, and spotted with an alarming number of birds, flying, walking, pecking at fruit, grooming themselves, feeding their young, singing. As a sign that life is complicated, the artist included one bird in a cage, which, along with the wall, is the only sign that man has had anything to do with this place.

Augustus and His Tomb

You can tell a lot about people from the way they dispose of their dead. Burial at sea is an expedient dating from the days before refrigeration. Burial at river is an expedient for sub rosa deaths, generally murder, by which the guilty parties are looking for quick disposal with a minimum of effort. It is usually done by night. Under these circumstances, a river can hardly be called a burial ground, much less a tomb.

Riversides are another matter. Old Jewish chronicles speak of tombs on the side of the Aventine, but archaeologists have had no luck finding them. Recently, archaeologists have found a Jewish cemetery across the river in Trastevere, dating from the mid-fourteenth to the mid-sixteenth century when the area was still outside the city and as such suitable for suspect aliens. And after 1645, Pope Urban VIII built new city walls, and the Jewish cemetery was moved to—the Aventine Hill. The chroniclers were ahead of their time.

Urban VIII's other notable graveyard story involves the tomb of Flavius Agricola, whose marble casket was found intact under the nave of Saint Peter's. It features the subject reclining and holding a small bowl on top of the box on which was carved a lengthy verse advising the reader to "mix the wine, bind the garland round your brow, drink far from here. And do not withhold the pleasures of love with beautiful women."[28] Urban was so appalled that he ordered the inscription broken up and thrown in the Tiber. The statue itself, happily, can be seen at the Indianapolis Museum of Art.

Two other tombs, both imperial Roman, grace the riverside and are impossible to miss. The first was the tomb of Augustus.

He thought ahead, did Augustus, and began work on his tomb shortly after he defeated Mark Antony at the battle of Actium (31 BC). He was thirty-one at the time.

He had good reasons for the project. If he was to take control of Rome, he had to stake his credibility with the senate and people of Rome, to which end, propaganda was the order of the day. And so—his tomb, an acknowledgment of mortality.

For starters, consider its location. It was outside the *pomerium*, discreet, but not out of reach for the average Roman citizen. Moreover, it was not a stand-alone destination. Casual strollers would see his Ara Pacis, the Altar of Peace, the monument commemorating his putting an end to years of strife. The more scientifically inclined might contemplate his oversize sundial (an

Egyptian obelisk and markings for shadows). All of these were placed in a park overlooking the less commercial reaches of the Tiber, all very tranquil, all meant to affirm the impression of himself as the bringer and guarantor of peace—a bold contention, given that he had been a major force in promoting the recent civil war in the first place.

The tomb aped the Mausoleum at Halicarnassus, one of the seven wonders of the world, built for the Persian king Mausolus. The man in the Roman street could either be appalled at the impudence, or proud that a fellow Roman was thinking on such a large scale. The geographer Strabo saw it in 7 BC and described it as

> a great mound near the river on a lofty foundation of white marble, thickly covered with ever-green trees to the very summit. Now on top is a bronze image of Augustus Caesar; beneath the mound are the tombs of himself and his kinsmen and intimates; behind the mound is a large sacred precinct with wonderful promenades; and in the centre of the Campus is the wall (this too of white marble) round his crematorium; the wall is surrounded by a circular iron fence and the space within the wall is planted with black poplars.[29]

It was drum shaped, of brick sheathed with travertine, eighty-seven meters in diameter and forty-two in height (Halicarnassus was forty-five meters high), with cypress trees planted on the top. Inside the building were funerary urns made of gold (all of them later stolen). A pair of obelisks, since removed, flanked the entrance.

Over time, as family members died off, its various niches held the ashes of all five Julio-Claudian emperors, the good, the bad, and the dangerous to know, along with a good number of their family members—not including, by Augustus's firm insistence, his granddaughter Julia, shame of the family (we are told) on account of her alleged licentious behavior. He had no way of knowing what exactly was coming in Caligula or Nero.

The structure would be taken by the Colonna family in the Middle Ages and converted into a small fortress. They held it until 1167, when they lost it to the Commune of Rome and the Count of Tusculum. With no more respect than its previous tenants had shown, the new tenants plundered the tomb for parts and let what was left fall to ruin.

By the Renaissance, the area was not fashionable. When Pius V (1504–1572) launched his crusade against Roman vice in 1566, he expelled prostitutes to the Ortaccio district on the banks of the river near the Mausoleum of Augustus[30]—an interesting juxtaposition for the old pagan who was, if anything, even more opposed to vice than the pope himself. One wonders if the irony crossed Pius's mind.

Further insults followed. By the 1700s it was said to be a bullfighting arena, and later a circus pit. Augustus's tomb served as a music hall in the early twentieth century, until Mussolini ordered it stripped down to what remained of its ancient form. The roof is long gone, the outer circle now below ground level, giving the impression of a building upright in a pit. The tomb is far from the imposing presence it once was. *Sic transit*, but it was an inspiration for older Romans. The tomb meant for the ages is an abused relic and unappreciated by those to whom it was handed down. It was not always so. Martial (c. AD 38–104) features it in one of his more double-edged poems:

> Pour me a double measure, of Falernian, Callistus,
> and you Alcimus, melt over it summer snows,
> let my sleek hair be soaked with excess of perfume,
> my brow be wearied beneath the sewn-on rose.
> The Mausoleum tells us to live, that one nearby,
> it teaches us that the gods themselves can die.[31]

Nero was the last of the Julio-Claudians, and was succeeded by three interim emperors, who in turn were succeeded by the three Flavians, who had their own family mausoleum. The last internee in Augustus's tomb was the decent but very non-Julio-Claudian emperor Nerva.

Nerva was succeeded by Trajan, who was in turn succeeded by Hadrian, who also built a tomb, very like Augustus's but, as we shall see, with a far greater impact on the city's history.

A Million Mouths to Feed

For the living it all comes down to bread.

Also wine and olive oil, but mostly bread. Or rather, grain with which to make bread. But essentially—bread.

Rome had changed since 509 BC. By the late Republican era, large landowners had displaced the self-supporting yeoman farmers, and preferred high-return cash crops and vineyards to grain. The city of Rome is famously the first metropolis to break the million mouth mark, all of whom needed to be fed. There was little choice but to import grain from overseas. Sardinia,

Sicily, North Africa, and most of all, Egypt, where the Nile made possible the production of grain on a scale impossible in the Tiber valley.

How did it work?

The process begins with money. Maritime trade had a long history in the Mediterranean well before the Romans got their feet wet. Greeks and Levantines, when not making war, had been shifting trade goods for centuries and had worked out systems of managing the risk of a highly risky business.

Rome itself had no shortage of money looking for investments in Rome (Aulus Gellius, writing in the second century AD, notes sadly that commercial real estate would be an excellent investment if only buildings didn't burn down so often).[32] The senatorial class required a million sesterces to join. The snag was that senators by law were prevented from engaging in trade. More specifically, as of 218 BC, senators were forbidden to own ships (*maritamam navem*) for commercial gain; or rather, they were allowed, but only up to a capacity of three hundred amphorae, enough for personal use (senators were rich by definition and had their own households to feed).[33]

Of course as senators set the law, workarounds were found. To be fair, this was, after all, a question of whether the city as a whole survived or died, and what kind of arrangements capital and entrepreneurs could come to.

Plutarch explains how Cato the Elder (234–149 BC) did it: "He required his borrowers to form a large company, and when there were fifty partners and as many ships for his security, he took one share in the company himself, and was represented by Quintio, a freedman of his, who accompanied his clients in all their ventures. In this way his entire security was not imperiled, but only a small part of it, and his profits were large."[34]

Of ways to make money on loans, this was, says Plutarch, "the most disreputable of all."[35]

Why so? Most loans had an interest cap at 12 percent.[36] A handsome return, but people are greedy. Maritime loans played to that greed, and given that food was a matter of life and death, Roman lawmakers were willing to be flexible. If a lender took the entire risk of a given voyage on himself—cost of goods, ship insurance, *traecticia pecunia*—he could charge whatever the market would bear.[37]

On the other hand, if a ship sank, the loan was forgiven.

The system seems to have worked for them, and for several hundred years. (Of course, Plutarch's outrage may have been at the notion of a man of Cato's rank having anything to do directly with business at all; Romans were snobbish about the origins of their wealth, and commerce was so far down the list that, technically, the senatorial class was barred from participating—a technicality overlooked in the doing, as we have seen.)

If the patrician class could not deal in trade, who then? *Negotiatores*, *mercatores*, and *naviculari*—go-betweens, merchants, and sailors, generally freedmen and foreigners, the sort of men from whom anything could be expected. If in fact they fronted for senators, well, what can one say? Profits like that were just too much to be ignored.

We have any number of monuments attesting to the wealthiest merchants' achievements. Better than that, however, we have Trimalchio, the ex-slave featured in Petronius's *Satyricon* who gives us an idea of what a successful entrepreneur could hope for. Riding on the back of a small inheritance, he informs us,

> I built five ships, loaded up with wine—it was worth its weight in gold just
> then—and sent them off to Rome. You might have supposed I'd ordered it so!
> if you'll believe me, every one of the ships foundered, and that's a fact. In one
> day Neptune swallowed me up thirty millions. Do you imagine I gave in? Not
> I, by my faith! the loss only whetted my appetite, as if it were a mere nothing.
> I built more ships, bigger and better found and luckier, till every one allowed
> I was a well-plucked one. Nothing venture, nothing win, you know; and a big
> ship's a big venture. I loaded up again with wine, bacon, beans, perfumery and
> slaves. Fortunata was a real good wife to me that time; she sold all her jewelry
> and all her clothes, and laid a hundred gold pieces in my hand; and it proved
> the leaven of my little property. A thing's soon done, when the gods will it.
> One voyage I cleared a round ten millions. . . . So your humble servant, who
> was a toad once upon a time, is a king now.[38]

Adjusting for satiric intent, and considering what we know about later plutocrats, the portrait does not strain credulity. On harder evidence, we have the tomb of Flavius Zeuxis, merchant of Hieropolis, whose epitaph boasts of his seventy-two trips round Cape Malea to Italy.[39]

Numerous scholars have worked out the figures, minimum amounts of grain brought in every year, the yield being 237,000 metric tons of wheat per annum—more, counting in loss and spoilage—18,000 tons of olive oil, and wine, creating a minimum of 1,692 shiploads per year.[40] Bear in mind that the sailing season lasted from April to September, so, an average seventeen ships per day in season.

So, with financing in place, ships in place, the process begins. Agents in, say, Alexandria, make the best deal they can from farmers and arrange for transport to the grain fleet. If anyone should worry about fraud, there were safeguards.

A discarded receipt in Egypt of AD 211 describes a master of eight boats and terms of sold wheat, swearing that it is unadulterated, with no admixture of earth or barley, untrodden and sifted. The form was originally in triplicate.[41] We also read of samples of grain, sealed in leather pouches or small pots, confirming the uniform quality of what was promised with what was delivered.[42] A physical example survives attached to a small jar of red clay, some 14.5 centimeters high, 17 centimeters in diameter, along with a tag that reads: "This is a sample of the cargo for which he has taken consignment from the harvest in the 28th year of Augustus's reign. . . . We have loaded the cargo from the 2nd of Hathyr to the 4th of the same month, and we have affixed [on this jar] both our respective seals, that of Ammonius which features a figure of Ammon, and that of Hermias, which features a figure of Harpocrates Year 29 of Augustus."[43]

Details to notice—the ship took two days to load, and the men who guaranteed the cargo used seals of Egyptian gods. The text is in Greek. We are, again, talking international trade.

The ships were privately held, though the emperor could requisition them in time of war. For normal trips, the ships also carried soldiers, *frumentarii*, to make sure that the army's interests were kept paramount. When Saint Paul traveled to Rome in AD 60, he came as a civilian passenger on a grain ship, along with 276 fellow passengers. Their crossing was unusually rough, and he mentions the centurions who stopped the crew from jumping ship once the weather turned bad; simply to keep the boat afloat, the passengers jettisoned the chief cargo of grain—more work for lawyers.[44]

The ships sailed in convoys. The voyage from Alexandria to Ostia and later Portus at the mouth of the Tiber generally took three weeks, and the ships were not small. Lucian of Samosatos (AD 120–?) describes a *naus*, a grain ship from the Alexandria fleet that had blown off course, and it caused so much excitement on the docks that the author considered the five-mile trek from Athens to Piraeus well worth his time just to see it: "180 feet long, the man said, and something over a quarter of that in width; and from deck to keel, the maximum depth, through the hold, 44 feet."[45] Lionel Casson estimates her cargo capacity at anywhere between twelve hundred to thirteen hundred tons burden.[46] (Lucian claims that the ship would carry enough grain to feed Attica for a year, but Lucian likes to exaggerate.)

In comparison, the *Sea Witch*, a state-of-the-art extreme clipper ship dating from 1846, was 179 feet long and 33 feet abeam, with a cargo capacity of just over four hundred tons burden. Granted, clipper ships were designed primarily for speed, but the comparison is nonetheless striking. Even to the jaded Italians, the arrival of the grain ships was something of an event. Seneca (c. 4 BC–AD 65) describes the scene: "Suddenly there came into our view today the Alexandrian ships,—I mean those which are usually sent ahead to announce the coming of the fleet; they are called mail-boats. The Campanians are glad to see them; all the rabble of Puteoli stand on the docks, and can recognize the 'Alexandrian' boats, no matter how great the crowd of vessels, by the very trim of their sails."[47]

Puteoli is nice, but it isn't Rome. It's not even close to Rome. The mouth of the Tiber, however, has no natural harbor and is given to sandbars, the runoff from the river itself. Large ships carrying grain to Rome waited offshore while flat-bottomed lighters came out to offload cargo and bring it to land. This was not efficient, not for the numbers of people waiting upriver to be fed. That most of their corn was alien should have been concerning.

It took the famine year of 40–41 for the then emperor Claudius to take the hint. His officials informed him that there was grain enough for perhaps one week, and after that—nothing. The problem presumably was saved by a late arrival of food, but the off-loading must have been agonizingly slow. The close call was enough to goad Claudius into action on making Rome a proper port. He ordered a protected area built, two large moles, breakwaters, to reach out into the ocean and provide safe harbor for the grain fleet. A century later Trajan expanded this enterprise by building the sexagonal harbor of Portus. You can see the outlines of it if you fly into Fiumicino airport.

Busy? Juvenal says so. "Look at our ports, our seas, crowded with big ships! The men at sea now outnumber those on shore. Whithersoever hope of gain shall call, thither fleets will come."[48] Again, adjusting for Juvenal's being a satirist, there must have been some truth, or the joke would not have worked.

A ship's arrival was as complicated then as now. The harbormaster assigned an incoming ship an empty berth, officials and merchants came aboard to break the seal on the sample container, confirm the goods in the hold were consistent with the goods in the container, and tally the amounts. All required signatures were given and received, after which guild members stepped in, their tasks specific and not to be infringed upon by outsiders: *saccarii*, stevedores who hefted sacks of grain, not to be confused with *phalagarii* who carried amphorae filled with wine or oil, or *saburrarii*, who arranged sand used for ballast. General dockworkers, *geruli*, were not to overstep the prerogatives of *horrearii*, warehouse workers, which warehouses were guarded by *custodiarii*, who may have kept a sharp eye on *mensores frumentarii*, who kept track of goods leaving the river and entering the warehouse (and vice versa). None of these men would have jobs at all without the *fabri navales* who built the ships in the first place. Each one of them was vital if goods were to get to carts and then to warehouses (*horrea*) or directly to *navis codicaria* on the Tiber that would take them upriver to the city for storage and distribution.

A short mast in front, to take advantage of what offshore wind there might be, and, when the winds failed, to secure tow ropes for the oxen (or perhaps men, as Volga boatmen) for passage upriver (Procopius describes towpaths).[49] All involved—stevedores, measurers, small-boat and barge men—were members of their specialized guilds that had a vested interest in keeping all transactions more or less honest, if not necessarily cheap.

A brief letter from a crew member at Ostia to his brother in Alexandria provides a personal view: "I reached land [Portus or Ostia] on the 6th day of the month of Epeiph [June 3], and we finished unloading on the 18th of the same month [July 12]. I went up to Rome on the 25th of the same month [July 19], and the place received us as the god willed. We are daily expecting our discharge, so that up to today nobody in the grain fleet has been able to leave."[50] The letter is dated August 2, at some time in the second or third century. What on earth was the holdup? Bureaucracy of some kind, we can assume. Or a disinclination to sail outside of a convoy.

The Vatican museum has a third-century wall painting from Ostia showing us the loading of the good ship *Isis Giminiana*. At the stern is Farnakes, shipmaster, who idles as a pair of stevedores tote sacks of grain up from the dock while a man named Arascantus keeps a sharp eye on his progress and that of a third man who dumps grain into a *modius*, a barrel of known volume. A third man with a tally stick watches their progress, as does a man seated at the bow next to another speech balloon, on which is written the caption "*feci*"—I'm done! A very cosmopolitan affair—*Isis Giminiana* suggests an Egyptian flag for the ship; Farnakes takes his name from the first-century BC kings of Pontus (modern Turkey).

The number of craft heading up and down the Tiber at peak shift would have been considerable, and there were inevitably accidents. In AD 62 we read of one hundred vessels heading up the Tiber catching fire and burning (this on top of two hundred in harbor sunk by a passing storm).[51] There are no details, but presumably one blazing ship was abandoned, floated downriver, struck and ignited a second ship and set off a chain reaction down the line. Where the fire broke out and how many ships were upriver of it (and whether they escaped) we are not told.

Having crossed the Mediterranean and been off-loaded, some grain remained in warehouses at Ostia and Portus for later distribution, the rest taken upriver to Rome. Procopius gives us a written record of the oxen yoked by the side of the river that dragged the barges against the current (adding that the straight stretches could exploit sail power).[52] The trade was enough to support 258 members, if the guild inscription is to be believed; and like cabbies outside railway stations, there were generally some ready and waiting for business. The journey took three days and nights, with all traffic stopping after sundown. Maneuvering oxen and boats around tight corners by lamplight would have been more than even the most grasping entrepreneur would have wanted to tackle. We will assume that buffalo and oxen were used; there is, however, a bas-relief in Arles that shows a boat carrying barrels being towed by two men. If, as seems likely, the water is the Rhône, they were pulling against the strongest river in France.

Once arrived at the wharves at Rome, the cargo would fall under the purview of a new set of stevedores and officials. The area between the river and the foot of the Aventine Hill held the major grain warehouses, the *horrea,* from where the goods could be distributed over the leaner winter months. The grain was precious stuff, and the *horrea* were built like blockhouses not simply to keep out heat and water and rodents, but also to prevent theft. And to guard against flooding, of course. They were notably massive, their floors not open dirt but raised and paved with stone, their walls thick, their windows high.[53]

Keeping them in order was a job sufficiently responsible that Seneca, comforting a friend facing a recent professional setback, reminds him that it could be worse, that in times of shortage (like that after Caligula died), he at least does not have to be the one tasked with ensuring that "corn from oversea poured into the granaries, unhurt either by the dishonesty or the neglect of those who transport it, in seeing that it does not become heated and spoiled by collecting moisture and tallies in weight and measure."[54]

Annona, or the Dole

The poet Juvenal was referring to the *annona* in his tenth satire:

> Long ago, when they lost their votes, and the bribes; the mob
> That used to grant power, high office, the legions, everything,
> Curtails its desires, and reveals its anxiety for two things only,
> Bread and circuses.[55]

There are misconceptions about the bread part of bread and circuses, and this as good a place as any to clear them up.

For starters, the dole was not universal. A specific group of adult male citizens were eligible. They could sell the perquisite or pass it on to their children, and for some the dole was a mark of distinction. You will see it on grave markers, where the deceased may have had nothing else noteworthy in his life—but at least he wasn't a no-account noncitizen unworthy of receiving free food. The amount of grain (and it was grain; you had to find your own baker) was not enough to feed a family, or really, the recipient.

And, of course, the dole began modestly and with the best of intentions. Livy refers to the famine year of 440 BC when "many of the poorer people, their last hope gone, covered their heads and drowned themselves in the Tiber to escape the anguish of prolonging their miserable lives."[56]

Desperate measures were called for. The narrative continues with the arrival of one Spurius Maelius, a rich plebeian who bought up all available wheat and distributed it at cost. His social betters thought he was pandering and aiming at dictatorship, and so had him murdered.[57] The grain was distributed, and the laws written to prevent it from ever happening again.

The idea was revived under Gaius Gracchus (154–121 BC), younger of the Gracchi brothers. Part of Rome's tax revenue came in the form of grain, which corrupt officials sold on the open market, skimming a bit off the top. Gracchus changed all that. He cut out the middleman and sold directly to the people at a fraction of market value.

The idea did not go over well with traditionalists, who pointed to Spurius Maelius. Lucius Calpurnius Piso (called Frugi for his care for money) argued against the law but, once it passed, could be found in line waiting for his share. Confronted with this paradox, he said, "I should not wish, Gracchus, for you to distribute my property to every man in Rome, but if you insist on doing so, I would like to get my share."[58] Sallust (86–35 BC), among others, argued that free grain discouraged labor, and that qualifying farmworkers migrated to the city to live a life of ease, if not plenty.[59] Eventually, Gracchus and his followers were crushed, their bodies, at least three thousand, thrown into the Tiber.

The precedent, however, had been set. In 59 BC Julius Caesar threatened to make grain free.[60] In 58 BC, Publius Clodius Pulcher (93–52 BC), with his Lex Clodia Frumentaria, actually did so, specifically for the poor. The cost was staggering, a fifth of the state revenues, but once the scheme was rolling, it was hard to stop.[61] Caesar himself, on taking power, was only able to cut the rolls from 320,000 to 150,000.[62]

Augustus, assuming the throne after Caesar's assassination (and fifteen years of civil war), continued the practice, juggling the figures somewhat in an attempt to keep it practicable. For the have-nots, the dole made the emperor's new world order more palatable. For the haves, government's underwriting the cost of moving grain jump-started the cross-ocean transport, allowing for greater traffic, a significant factor in the rise of the Roman economy under the emperors. Everyone, it seemed gained.

No later emperor dared repeal the subsidies. Indeed, Trajan added wine; Septimius Severus added olive oil; Aurelian added pork, and also took over the bother of baking bread. By the third century AD, the *annona* was open to all Roman citizens. When the empire's capital moved to Constantinople, responsibility for the dole went to the senate, and a little later, to the church. Both did their best in the face of little money and invading barbarians. When Justinian took Italy back in AD 550, he promised to keep up the *annona* as well as maintenance for the Tiber and the ports. Whether he was able to do so may be doubted.

In the end, there was no free lunch.

Eighth Hill of Rome

In 1739, French traveler Charles de Brosses described one of Rome's more unusual antiquities:

> This is a hill entirely composed of broken pots. Legouz and I passed an hour
> in digging into this mountain of broken crockery. What a smashing of pottery
> there must have been in Rome—in a town five or six times as populous as
> Paris now. I believe this hill to be formed entirely of new pottery: the potters

have their manufactories in this quarter of the town, on the banks of the Tiber, on account of the nearness of the water required in their work; and I think that this mount consists of the broken refuse of all the manufactories.[63]

The man-made hill in question is Monte Testaccio, loosely, Mount Crockery, from Latin *testacium*, ceramic, or baked clay, and is not the refuse of all manufactures, but only of amphorae that held olive oil, mostly from Spain. It's an impressive creation, centuries in the making (first century BC to sometime in the third century AD), each shard requiring some individual to retrieve the empty pot, break it apart (sharp edges, many small cuts), bring the pieces to the dump, heft them up the incline and add them to the ever-rising pile. And add them not in any haphazard way, it should be noted. Archaeologists have found method to the sherd stacking, a crude but stable architecture of layered terra-cotta. This is not a hill given to landslide.

Recycling seems not to have been a concern. It's an impressive pile, and unique, which raises the question of why. Why were these terra-cotta containers of olive oil disposable? Why not returned to point of origin? Presumably because the process of sorting and storing and waiting for a ship to carry them was cost prohibitive. Then there was the possibility of fraud—each handle was stamped with its point of origin, and as such the sort of thing a good olive grower would not want holding someone else's oil.

They were also useless for building. Olive oil residue—and these amphorae were limited to the olive oil trade—reacts badly with lime, preventing the jugs from being mixed with cement. The clay is also notably resistant to grinding.

The Welsh priest and chronicler Adam of Usk, at Rome in 1404, refers to the hillock only as *montis omnis terre*, so-called because it was, as he put it, made up of leftovers from all around the world. He informs us that on Shrove Sunday (anytime from early February 1 to March 7), "at the cost of the Jews, four carts covered with scarlet cloth, in which are eight live boars, being placed on the top of the mountain of all the earth . . . are yoked with eight wild bulls; and, [the carts] being shaken open by the swift descent down hill and the beasts set free, the whole becomes the prey of the people. And then every man pell-mell rushes at the beasts with his weapon; and, if it so happen that any one brings not home to his wife some part of the spoil, he is accounted a poor spirit and a craven who shall not have her company till the feast of Saint Pancras [May 12]." There could be a secondary incentive for taking part: "And often in the scuffle they cut down or wound in particular the courtiers [*curte-sanis*] whom they hate for wrongs done to wives and daughters."[64]

In Renaissance times, Testaccio served as Golgotha in passion plays. In 1849, it served as a gun emplacement for Garibaldi when holding back the French. It also serves more secular and peaceful ends. Long ago, men tunneled inward at the base to create wine cellars—the temperature being uniformly cool and steady. The tradition is that a Roman out on a day's hunt had stashed his lunch in a small crevice he noticed in the hill, his lunch including a bottle of wine. When he returned he found the drink admirably cool. He in turn told some wine sellers, who began to make their own commercial-size caves in the side of the mountain. Tavern keepers followed, and even householders. So, at least, goes the story. Certainly the cellars are still there.

The sides and summit are now largely overgrown with grass, shrubs, and evergreen trees, the tawny shards forming an intermittent hardscape in this haphazard garden. Before the new century it was freely available for unambitious hikers and picnickers, a small piece of artificial countryside in the middle of the city. Today, entry is by appointment only, through officially guided tours, and not very many of those. It is worth the trip, if you can arrange one.

Stones

"So many merchant ships arrive here, conveying every kind of goods from every people every hour and every day, so that the city is like a factory common to the whole earth. It is possible to see so many cargoes from India and even from Arabia Felix, if you wish, that one imagines that for the future the trees are left bare for the people there and that they must come here to beg for their own produce if they need anything."[65]

Aristides was a Greek visitor to Rome around the year AD 155, declaiming to the imperial court the sort of thing successful people like to hear. He was not exaggerating. Life in second-century Rome was as good as it was to get, at least for those in a position to get the finer things in life. Those things included ebony, ivory, jewelry, artwork, slaves, exotic animals, fine unguents and all the excess that makes life pleasant. The so-called Muziris papyrus mentions a cargo of spikenard, ivory, and cloth from India worth seven million sesterces.[66] Specialists in all these goods had offices and warehouses at the river ports of Ostia and Portus. The city itself had three distinct off-loading spots: the Ripa Grande, the Ripetta, and the Ripa Graeca.

The market for stone was large enough to warrant its own quay, the Marmorata. The name is Renaissance, the trade ancient. Augustus famously claimed to have found Rome a city of brick and left it one of marble. Rome was, in fact, heading that way regardless. Marcus Lepidus (120–77 BC) kicked off the vogue for decorative stone when he imported a block of yellow marble from Numidia and used it as a doorsill. "Vilissimo usu," a most sordid use, in Pliny's opinion.[67]

Pliny was clearly in the minority. The novelty (and conspicuous expense) of colored stone was soon the fashion. Lucullus was known as an epicure (or glutton) so consumed by consumption and excess as to become a byword. Lucullan feasts trace back to him. Four years after the doorsill, L. Lucullus decorated parts of his house with pink, white, gray, and black marble from Anatolia, soon to be known as Lucullan marble.

Contemptible as Lepidus and Lucullus were, even worse was Mamurra, a military engineer who became obscenely rich in the Gallic Wars under Julius Caesar. He went so far as to clad his entire house with marble veneer—a first in Rome—and to top that off, had columns from Luna (white marble) or Carystos (green/white). Vulgar and disgraceful, to be sure, but what could one expect of someone like that? This was, after all, the man the poet Catullus repeatedly calls Mentula (prick), a man notorious for gambling and debauchery, a man able to plunder Gaul only because he was Julius Caesar's boy toy (*pathicus*).[68] Oh, and he was a bad poet, besides.[69] (Catullus later apologized for the insult, and was next seen dining with the great dictator, all, apparently, forgiven.)

Stones flowed to the Tiber from quarries in Anatolia, Spain, Gaul, North Africa, and beyond, some of them a good distance from the sea and difficult to access, evidence of just how nouveau riche and frivolous Rome had become. Spanish broccatello, lapis lazuli from Afghanistan by way of Syria; from France, black marble. North Africa, yellow marble *giallo antico*, more alabaster, and onyx; flawless snow-white Parian marble from Greece, finest for sculpture, as well as marbles of red and greens, Pentelic marble the color of butter. The trade was so brisk that special ships had to be built just to carry such cargo—*navis lapidariae*, stone boats, for stone columns of exotic marble and granite, a nice change from all that pure white limestone closer to home. Exotic stone had become so widespread that the normally encyclopedic Pliny drops the subject, noting, "It is not important to mention the colours and species of marbles when they are so well known, nor is it easy to list them when they are so numerous."[70] And then there was Egypt.

The Nile delta and upriver was, is, chockablock with colored mineral—alabasters of red, yellow, and brown; granites of green, pink, gray, and black; black and green basalt; purple porphyry, reminiscent of the regal purple that trimmed senatorial robes, and perfect for the oversize tubs and basins that graced imperial public baths.

Rome's medieval and Renaissance descendants found it easier to just tear down and recycle rather than to import anything new. The variety of decoration found in later churches and palazzi across Italy is testimony to the seemingly insatiable appetite of old Rome for novelty and the ability to feed that appetite. Determining with ever more precise exactitude where some of the various greens and purples and yellows and reds came from is an ongoing work. A wall on the Capitoline Museum in Rome gives samples of the most common. Alternatively, visit the Sistine Chapel and look down on the floor rather than up at the ceiling.

Once the Romans got a taste for exotic stone, nothing would do but to go large. Greek statues (painted to make them look more realistic) were taken as a given. Egypt, home of pyramids and sphinxes, posed a different problem.

How to Shift an Obelisk

Ancient Egypt periodically becomes fashionable. Europe went through a phase after Napoleon's brief misadventures in archaeology; Europe and America's fascination was sparked when Howard Carter unearthed Tutankhamen's tomb. Imperial Rome was likewise beguiled. That Romans felt inferior to and aped Greek culture is a cliché; we tend to forget that they were also entranced by the sheer antiquity of Egypt and the scale of its achievements.

With Augustus's victory over Antony and Cleopatra came Egypt's subservience to Rome. As it was a military victory, there had to be a triumph. Normally the defeated enemy would be part of the spectacle, but since Cleopatra was dead by asp and useless for any victory parade, something else would have to do. The event did include hippos and rhinos and other exotic things—but these were ephemeral, soon forgotten. Augustus needed something more substantial, but also suitable and possible.

It proved a tricky question. Pyramids were immovable, the mammoth sculptures of Thebes as well. Tearing out walls for the hieroglyphics would seem more like vandalism, and where could he put them? There were some middle-size statues, but these were bulky and might not fit in with a Roman aesthetic. In the end, that left obelisks. From the Greek *obeliskos*, ὀβελίσκος, or small skewer. Of pink granite quarried near Aswan, extremely hard, difficult to work, to the point that even today it is unclear how exactly it was done.

Originally dedicated to the sun, they were simple in shape but impressive; clearly Egyptian, but suitable for many settings. Long and thin, they could fit nicely in boats.

If one, why not two? The so-called Solare (21.79 meters) and Flaminio (24 meters), one for the center at Circus Maximus, the other as a sundial on the Campus Martius (now at the Piazza di Montecitorio and the Piazza del Popolo respectively).

The problem was how to get them to Rome. The solution was custom-built boats—superships, really, specific for the job and which "attracted much attention from sightseers. That which carried the first of two obelisks was solemnly laid up by Augustus of Revered Memory in a permanent dock at Pozzuoli to celebrate the remarkable achievement; but later it was destroyed by fire."[71]

It was as nothing to the boar used by Caligula, "the most amazing thing that had ever been seen at sea," a tourist attraction at Ostia until Claudius had it moved to the end of the jetty at Portus, filled with concrete, and sunk to become the foundation for his lighthouse.[72] (Sinking the ship also served as a small act of *damnatio memoriae* against Caligula, something that Claudius worked out with the senate that had colluded in the earlier emperor's assassination.)

The Lateran obelisk, at 32.18 meters, put an end to this competition. Ammianus Marcellinus credits Constantius II with the moving, and refers to a purpose-built ship "of a burden hitherto unexampled, requiring three hundred rowers to propel it."[73] The Tiber itself "seemed as it were frightened, lest its own winding waters should hardly be equal to conveying a present from the almost unknown Nile to the walls which itself cherished."[74] Ammianus claims that Augustus had left this one alone because "it was consecrated as a special gift to the Sun God" and as such was not to be profaned.[75] Probably wise. Once raised in Rome, the stone was topped with "a brazen sphere, made brighter with plates of gold"—which was immediately struck by lightning and destroyed.[76]

Four more obelisks came from Egypt, smaller in size and weight. The supply, however, was limited, and Romans soon realized that the things were not all that difficult to make, and so began to farm out the work to locals. These were kept to more manageable sizes, under seventeen meters.

The ship that Augustus used was a tourist attraction for years. Caligula's ship—the one Claudius sunk for a lighthouse—may have been the inspiration for Giovanni Battista Alberti when he wrote one of his Aesop-like fables in 1437:

"A ship, having brought a large obelisk to Rome, heard the story of Aeneas's ships that had set sail from port and become sea goddesses, and hoping to do the same, withdrew to the open seas only to be lost in the deep."[77]

That's all he wrote. One line, no moral. Alberti was a busy man.

Canals

Show is all well and good, but the empire ran on money, which meant trade, which meant roads, and along with roads, at least in theory, canals.

Canals are one area where Rome's predecessors set the standard. The Fertile Crescent was crisscrossed with them for centuries, but what really caught the Romans' engineering attention was the canal that connected the Nile to the Red Sea.

The so-called Necho canal, the Canal of the Pharaohs, was ordered by the Pharaoh Psammetic I and ran for 140 kilometers, its breadth enough that two triremes could pass each other coming and going. Herodotus claims that 120,000 men died in the making of it (Herodotus can be loose with figures, but no doubt it was not an accident-free job). Work was suspended when an oracle said that the canal would benefit barbarians more than it would Egypt, and indeed, a hundred years later, the Persian king Darius I invaded and finished the job. The canal served the country well—the journey in either direction took four days, expediting traffic between east and west. Shifting sand had made it unusable by the time Julius Caesar arrived, but even in its useless state, it stood as testimony of what was possible. If the Egyptians and Persians could do it, so could the Romans.

Caesar's exact plan was to "divert the Tiber just below the city into a deep channel, which would bend round towards Circeii and come out into the sea at Terracina, so that there would be a safe and easy passage for merchantmen to Rome. Then too he proposed to drain the marshes by Pometia and Setia and to create a plain which could be cultivated."[78]

The schemes died in committee, but Caesar had a backup plan. In July of 45 BC, Cicero wrote to his friend Atticus with all the latest news from Rome: "Capito happened to speak of the proposed expansion of the city: the Tiber, starting from the Milvian Bridge [upstream of the city], is to be re-channeled alongside the Vatican hills, and the Campus Martius opened up to development. The Vatican fields in turn will become a sort of Campus Martius. . . . 'This law will be passed,' Capito said; 'Caesar wants it.' "[79]

Caesar wanted a good many things, but he wasn't to get them. Brutus, Cassius, and Mark Antony made sure of that. The dream, however, did not die. Indeed, it grew. Claudius, as part of his enterprise to build a proper port at the mouth of the Tiber, introduced a pair of flood canals from a bend in the lower Tiber out to the sea, thus increasing the outflow in times of flood and providing a means for river boats to take goods from the newly built harbor of Portus. The wider the drain, the less backup near Rome.

An inscription commemorated the achievement:

"The emperor Claudius, . . . while building a port for Rome, freed the city from the danger of floods by constructing canals that led from the Tiber into the sea."[80]

The canal may have helped commerce, but it did not stop floods.

Nero, as great as Caesar in his own mind and never one for modest measures, had even bigger dreams. He conceived his own waterway from Ostia down to Lake Avernus near Naples and ending at Baiae—Baiae being the Ibiza of its day, a playground for the patrician class, or at least the very wealthy, who may or may not have been patrician. The canal would also service commercial traffic. Nero's canal would be smooth inland sailing, 240 kilometers all told in length, and wide enough to allow the passage of two quinqueremes, five-bank galleys, abreast.

To make this dream come true, Nero hired "Severus and Celer, whose genius and ambition led them to attempt things impossible by their nature and thus to waste the treasure of the prince."[81] The labor force he calculated would require the prison population of the entire empire.

As to why the Romans should bother, the answer has to do with weather. Northerly winds predominate on the west coast of Italy, which is fine for sailing from Rome to North Africa and the eastern Mediterranean, less fine for bringing the cargo ships north. A sheltered canal from the easily reached bay of Naples made a good deal of theoretical sense.

It remains one of the great might have beens. The Great Fire of Rome (64 AD) required the workforce be reassigned to clearing rubble from the city, loading it into barges, and dumping it downriver near the more marshy areas around Ostia. Nero's imagination now focused on a new project, that of enclosing the city of Rome as far as Ostia (in defense of what it is difficult to say) and digging a straight canal from port to city and in so doing eliminate time-consuming twists and angles and saving a good deal of time.[82]

Neither project flourished. By the time his slave army could get back to canal work in earnest, Nero, a victim of politics and finance, had committed suicide. His successors had other priorities. Tacitus, writing forty years later, notes that the scars of the initial work, "traces of his disappointed hope," could still be seen on the hills near Lake Avernus.[83]

As to the Necho canal, Julius Caesar's inspiration—some forty years after Nero's death, the emperors Trajan and Hadrian got it back up and running, boosting Roman trade with India and China. Nero's plan of a canal connecting Naples and Rome was a nice idea, but for an empire at the height of its power, easy trade with the east took precedence. (The canal was closed in AD 770 by the Abbasid caliph Abu Jafar because enemies were using it for military reasons. But that's another story.)

Boats

Of making many boats there is no end. In Roman texts, we read of the *caudicaria, lenuncularus, scapha, navigium, slatta, acutaria, lembus, naves onerariae, carina, peotas, bombarda, lusoria, felluca, barca, tartanes, traiectus* (Italian *traghetto*), *galea, lintra,* and more besides, lists suitable for the professional or the collector of trivia, or of words, or of trivial words. None so trivial that someone didn't take a keen interest in the distinction.

Chiefly we read of *scaphae* and *lintres, lenunculi* and *caudicariae.*

Scaphae, lintres, and lenunculi were rowboats, the latter requiring more than one oarsman. The boatmen had five separate guilds at the port of Ostia, which says something about their importance. The two most notable were *lenuncularii tabularii auxiliarii,* those who manned towboats, and *lenuncularii traiectus Luculli,* those who manned ferries. Juvenal refers to a point-nosed Numidian reed boat (*canna . . . prora . . . acuta*), which carried fish sauce.[84]

There were craft even more specialized than that. Archaeologists digging in the area near the river mouth uncovered a small Roman fishing boat (officially known as Fiumicino 5) with a fish-holding tank with narrow holes to allow seawater to pass through during long journeys. This life-extending measure allowed for exotic fish to be brought upriver alive and fresh, and more expensive than the same fish that was dead and salted.

River traffic above Rome required lighter craft with shallower drafts. Martial refers to these, comparing them to quality sleep-inducing carriages untouched by "the cry of the boatswain or the noise of hawsers, although the Milvian bridge is near, and the ships are seen gliding swiftly along the sacred Tiber."[85] For ships, read *carina*, which can also mean "keel." Propertius writes of the *lintres* that plied the Tiber so swiftly and contrasts them with the barges (*rates*) that are hauled upriver so slowly.[86]

Trimalchio, our nouveau riche entrepreneur of Petronius's *Satyricon*, goes on at some length to describe the marvelous things money and his fleet of ships bought him, but fails to mention any pure pleasure craft. Such things did exist for the superrich and the rulers of empires, and Petronius could have had a field day with the topic. The stoic philosopher Seneca moots this sort of excess when discussing generosity to a possible foe: "I would not send triremes or bronze-beaked ships, but I would send pleasure boats and cabin cruisers" (*lusorias et cubiculatas*).[87] A missed opportunity—then again, we are missing large parts of the *Satyricon*.

That having been said, it was as difficult for satire to keep up with reality in Roman times as it is today. Caligula's barge, which was outfitted with mosaic floors, hot and cold running water, fountains, rotating statues, vines, and fruit trees—it had been described in Suetonius, and its location at the bottom of Lake Nemi was known as early as the Renaissance (fishermen trolled for artifacts, while more serious scholars were stymied by lack of adequate diving equipment)—was treated with skepticism until Mussolini's engineers were able to drain the lake enough to reveal the thing. It had been deliberately sunk after Caligula's assassination, its more valuable fittings removed, but clearly would have been difficult even for someone like Petronius to top.

An 1856 guidebook refers to the *batelli a vapore* that carried passengers from the Mediterranean upriver, and inland produce—wine, lumber, coal—downriver.[88] These days, the Tiber hosts a tourist boat or two, the odd sculler, or sculling team, and the river police on guard against criminal mischief or misadventure. The rich boating life that predated the embankments is gone.

Boats make for a good spectacle. Naval vessels, with their added frisson of blood and danger and, we hope, victory, make for even better spectacle. The army had its triumphal parades, the navy (technically, the navy was part of the army, but let us leave that distinction aside) had water. Once the Roman military began to enjoy victory across the sea, there arose the question of how best to show off victory to the people back home. Traditionally, triumphs were a matter of the general leading troops and treasure through the wider streets of Rome. What was the Tiber if not a watery boulevard? As such, the river inevitably drew a crowd. Aemilius Paullus, who had defeated Perseus in 167 BC, was able to bring the enemy's flagship upriver as a war prize. The same year, Anicius Gallus and Gnaius Octavius arrived in their own fleet.[89]

Plutarch describes Cato the Younger arriving home from his successful governorship in Cyprus in 56 BC:

> The Romans did not fail to hear of his arrival with his ships, and all the
> magistrates and priests, the whole senate, and a large part of the people
> went to the river to meet him, so that both banks of the stream were hidden
> from view, and his voyage up to the city had all the show and splendour of
> a triumph. Yet some thought it ungracious and stubborn that, although
> the consuls and praetors were at hand, he neither landed to greet them, nor
> checked his course, but on a royal galley of six banks of oars swept past the
> bank where they stood, and did not stop until he had brought his fleet to
> anchor in the dock-yard.[90]

Gnaius Calpurnius Piso, in returning to Rome from Syria in AD 20 to face charges of sedition and having killed Germanicus, heir to the throne, deliberately took the last leg of his journey by boat, down the Nera and Tiber, alighting near the Mausoleum of Augustus.[91]

Caligula used a bireme to bring his mother's and brother's ashes from Ponza, a solemn occasion for all who witnessed it. The allusion to the river Styx would not have been lost on them. Which gets us to our next subject.

Suicide

Suicide by Tiber was something of a comic device in hard-hearted writers. Horace spends a good deal of his third satire with Damasippus, an amiable wastrel who, having squandered his fortune on art and real estate, is steered away from the Fabrician bridge ("a Fabricio ... ponte reverti") by the oracle Stertinius, who wins him over to Stoic philosophy; Damasippus, with the fervor of the convert, now must buttonhole Horace and bore him to tears with this newfound insight.

Juvenal has a slightly different conversation with one of his friends; the fellow Postumus hasn't lost his fortune, but he is considering getting married. Juvenal argues against such a rash act, and suggests that there are quicker and easier ways to end his life: "Can you submit to a she-tyrant when there is so much rope to be had, so many dizzy heights of windows standing open, and when the Aemilian bridge offers itself to hand?"[92]

For Christians, suicide is potentially a mortal sin. For the Romans, suicide was a matter of individual conscience. What mattered was the means, whether the act demonstrate one's *dignitas*, or lack of it. Your reputation was at stake, and one must choose wisely. Death by river was for traitors and the worst sort of criminals, their bodies left for the gods to deal with. At the very least, drowning was in decidedly poor taste. Self murder by water was accordingly a degraded choice, proof of despair, which ran counter to the hardy discipline a proper Roman was expected to embody.

Upright Romans favored falling on one's sword, in emulation of dying in battle; or, for the more philosophically inclined, the methodical and stoic vein letting: both of them honorable deaths, demonstrative of courage and steadiness of nerve. Petronius, Nero's onetime arbiter of taste and part-time satirical writer, out of favor and having learned he must die, turned his final hours into an occasion worthy of a light-minded Socrates. Friends were invited to his last supper, during which he settled in his bath where he alternately ate, drank, conversed, opened his veins, then bound them for a time, to repeat the process and let the party last that much longer. A macabre event, but as a final rebuke to the emperor, it had a magnificent, if an unnerving, flavor.

Three years later came Nero's turn. Aware that the senate and Praetorian Guard had in mind a fate worse than death, he announced to his rapidly shrinking retinue that he would take his own life. He chose a knife—very theatrical—but found he wasn't up to the job. He tried to find a good blade man to do the work for him, but the gladiator he had in mind was himself being killed in the Forum. Poison would do the trick, but unfortunately his personal stash, ill-advisedly stored in a small gold box, had been stolen. In despair, Nero ran to the river, intending to throw himself in: "*quasi praecipitaturus se in Tiberim.*"[93]

He managed to restrain himself, and slunk back home from where, under cover of darkness, he and a small band of loyal followers headed out to a country estate, hoping for a reprieve. Instead he got word that the senate had confirmed his sentence, "in the usual manner," which involved being struck by heavy rods (not subjected to *poena cullei*, oddly enough). He now wept, stalled, asked his few companions to set an example by doing themselves in.

They demurred. He tested the points of two daggers; both proved disturbingly sharp.

Dawn broke, and the senate's horsemen could be seen in the distance. At this last minute, he did manage to drive one blade across his own throat, but ineptly, and needed the help of a slave to finish the job. Even so, he was still alive when the senate's representative entered the room. But—at least he hadn't jumped into the Tiber!

From Nero's death in AD 69 there followed the Year of the Four Emperors, four men in contention for the prize, and one winner, Flavius Vespasian. That genial emperor, builder of the Temple of Peace as well as the Colosseum and much else besides, was notoriously, proudly, frugal, and able to take a joke. He died after a decade of stable rule, and despite his cheap ways, his funeral procession was sumptuous. As per custom, a mime wore his face mask, the better to play the part of the deceased for the crowds that lined the streets. At one point, he called out to the procurators leading the parade and asked just how much the affair was expected to cost. Ten million sesterces, they said. In true Flavian horror, the mime shouted: "Give me a hundred thousand and just fling me into the Tiber."[94]

Suicide didn't stop with the ancients. Casanova had to discourage a friend thwarted in love from considering to end it all in the river (happily, the couple were eventually reunited). Napoleon's arrival in the city and his subsequent conscription of young men cast a pall over the average citizen. Irish traveler John Chetwode Eustace reports that Roman mothers, "when deprived of their sons, have been known to pine away or throw themselves into the Tiber in despair."[95]

It still goes on. The newspapers report a few every year, the bodies generally extracted near the Fabricius bridge, under which the current is particularly strong and the chance of timely rescue slight.

Lurid Tales of Nero

Of all Roman emperors, none has more connections to the river than Nero, nor quite as many outlandish stories. A twelfth-century (and not altogether trustworthy) German epic poem *Die Kaiserchronik* has the emperor expressing a desire to give birth to a child.[96] His physicians, none too clever men, gave him a potion that effected half of his desire. His belly swelled, and he was in due course delivered of—a frog. Or perhaps a toad.

Frog or toad, the important part of the story was that the sight of this unexpected spawn caused the bystanders to shout *"lata rana"* (frog-born), which somehow became the name of Nero's palace, later adopted by the papal palace, the Lateran palace. (Modern scholars prefer the theory that the area was once owned by the Plautii Laterani family.) The Getty Museum has an anonymous illuminated manuscript of the event, and the frog (or toad) later on escaping into the Tiber.[97] The frog (or toad) was later captured, killed, and burned.

This lunatic fable appears to be a throwback to older traditions. The ancient record describes one of Nero's many stage performances, specifically, his work as Canace Parturiens (Canace in childbirth) in Euripides's play (now lost) *Aiolos*. The finer points of his performance were over the heads of his soldiers. When asked, "What is the emperor doing?" one answered, "He is in labor."[98] The frog aspect is presumably a medieval calumny based in part on the belief that frogs could live comfortably inside other animals for long periods of time.[99]

To further muddy the waters, there's Plutarch, who relates that the dying Nero morphed not into a god but into a viper (in commemoration of his killing his mother, vipers being, according to the ancients, the death of their mothers when born).[100] Whatever divine spirits had control over this process took some pity on the would-be singer and changed him instead into a vocal creature, frequenter of marshes and lakes.[101] To wit, a frog.

A mad tale, misheard, repeated, embroidered, retold with advantages, and likely owing its final ingredient to the near contemporary account of Nero's wedding at the AD 64 party of Tigellinus. Nero was famous, not to say notorious, for the number and scope of his celebrations, but this one, even Tacitus, writing thirty years after the event, said was the one to remember.

The setting was Rome's Stagnum Agrippae, an artificial pool at the Campus Martius, built by Agrippa, son-in-law to Augustus, great-grandfather of Nero himself. This lake was fed by a purpose-built aqueduct, and drained into the Tiber, some eight hundred meters away, by the Euripus canal. Nero's impresario Tigellinus (prefect of the Praetorian Guard) had arranged everything. Exotic birds and beasts were on display, and sea creatures lurked in the pool (how they survived freshwater is not explained). Nero and his guests lounged on a raft supported by empty wine casks and covered with purple cloth, attended to by dancing girls and prostitutes of both sexes. Catamites arranged by age and sexual skills (*scientiam libidinum*) gently rowed gold and ivory boats that pulled the raft around the lake.[102]

Crowds gawked at this magnificent excess from the shore, comforted with the knowledge that their own immediate pleasures were not neglected. Around the lake, Tigellinus had erected brothels, one side stocked with women of high rank, the other, open-air prostitutes. There were food stations, and stages on which, whether voluntarily or under imperial pressure, nonprofessionals of all sorts were seen to be dancing or singing or both to the best of their abilities. Modesty had no place at this party. Society low to high was on offer, and abuses against decency the norm. Once-respectable wives and daughters disported with slaves and gladiators while their husbands and fathers looked on, or found other distractions. With darkness came lamps, and general good time (or brawling and fighting, if we are to believe Dio. Arguably both.)[103] A few days later, to cap the entire event, Nero, outfitted in the finest bridal finery, mimed marriage to a man named Pythagoras.

Some months later, Rome burned.

Nero was away when the fire broke out, down the coast at Antium (Anzio), not fiddling, but preparing for a singing contest, in which he himself would be taking part. His subject—the fall of Troy. It would be some hours before he learned of what was happening in Rome, and the initial reports did nothing to break his concentration. It was only the third update, delivered after he had won the competition, that moved him to order his galley prepared for the trip back to the capital.

As his flotilla came up the Tiber, he could see the rising smoke visible first, staining the sky, then smell the remnants of the scorched city. From here on in, his actions become creditable, even admirable. He had temporary shelters built on the Campus Martius, opened his own gardens and other public buildings for the newly destitute, and, local storehouses having gone up in flame, had grain brought up from Ostia and distributed at cut-rate prices. Once the ashes had cooled, he began the task of rebuilding.

Logic and foresight prevailed, for a wonder. Surveyors were soon busy describing new streets, wider than the cramped alleys and mews of the old city, with colonnades to shelter pedestrians (this latter embellishment was at Nero's personal expense). The emperor also ordered that all boats bringing grain up the Tiber be filled on the returning trip with rubble unsuitable for recycling, ultimately to be used as landfill for marshy areas.

He had a bridge built across the Tiber, the Pons Neronianis, connecting the westernmost Campus Martius to the Campus Vaticanus, improving access to Caligula's circus and some of his own family land, a common good.

Of course, given the vast swaths of the city destroyed and his own efforts at restoration, it stood to reason that he should have some tangible recognition in return. We can imagine him in the ruins of his house on the Palatine Hill gazing down on the leveled center of Rome and getting the inspiration that there, on the edge of the Forum, was just the spot for a formal garden and urban villa. He set his prime architects, Severus and Celer, to work on making a complex worthy of an emperor: the Domus Aurea, Golden House, where he would famously claim he could finally live as a human being.

He would be dead in four years.

Trajan and His Port

The emperor Trajan (AD 53–117) was fortunate. His immediate predecessors, chiefly Domitian (AD 51–96), had restored and refurbished Rome's crucial infrastructure by the time he took over in AD 98, leaving him nearly twenty years to concentrate on more personally flattering projects. He was also flush with a pile of Dacian gold, prize money from two wars that ended decisively in AD 106. Money changes everything, and with this windfall, he was able to build a stone memorial to his victory over Dacia (Trajan's column), a new commercial center (Trajan's Forum), the baths of Trajan, the aqueduct of Trajan, as well as less obvious but no less vital work in shoring up the banks of the Tiber.

And he was able to add considerable value to Claudius's harbor.

The seawall and moles were functional, but still subject to occasional problems. The storm of AD 62 showed that even with the moles, the sea could still do considerable damage to ships. Trajan had a place of greater safety in mind, a place where ships in quantity could dock and unload with greater efficiency. He, or his architects, had a greater sense of style than Claudius had had. His contribution involved digging into the coastline and fashioning an inner harbor in the shape of a hexagon, each side some thirty-five meters in length, resulting in a basin covering about 33.25 hectares (82 acres) at a depth of five meters. It was unique in shape for a harbor, possibly the work of Apollodorus of Damascus, who designed Trajan's Forum in Rome. The enclosure was less threatened by ocean storms and still had plenty of room for plenty of ships to service the bulging population in Rome.

Four of the six sides were dedicated to warehousing, one to a *navalia* (shipyard), one to the entry to Claudius's harbor. Recent study suggests a total warehouse space of ninety-two thousand square meters, which would put it on the level of, say, all the floor space of London's Harrods department store, or half that of Macy's flagship store in New York.[104]

There was more to Portus than just warehouses and docks. There was a small amphitheater dating from the third century AD, along with baths, both no doubt welcome for the laborers, and what are believed to be housing for the small army of workers who serviced the ships and their cargoes. Also hostels for out-of-towners. Saint Jerome recommended one owned by Pammachius, a onetime Roman senator (later a saint) who gave it all up to become a monk and set up a small hospice for strangers.[105]

With the arrival of Portus, Ostia became something of second-tier port, even something of a commuter town (though more of a high-end suburb, from the evidence), the place where deals were struck and fortunes were made. This is the beginning of Edward Gibbon's happy time, when "if a man were called to fix the period in the history of the world, during which the condition of the human race was most happy and prosperous, he would, without hesitation, name that which elapsed from the death of Domitian to the accession of Commodus."[106]

Of course it couldn't last.

Hadrian and His Tomb

"At the entrance of the Roman city there is a certain fortification built with wondrous craft and of wondrous strength; before its gateway there is built a very precious bridge across the Tiber, which can be crossed by those coming to and departing from Rome, and there is no other route except across it. No crossing, however, can be made unless with the permission of those guarding the fortification."[107]

So wrote Liutprand, bishop of Cremona, in the late tenth century. Today it is called Castel Sant'Angelo, but it began life as Hadrian's tomb. Repurposing is a constant in Rome. Hadrian's tomb has had more than its share.

It gets a single line in the *Historia Augustae*: "He built a bridge and a tomb on the Tiber with his own name."[108]

The bridge was redundant, since Nero had built one (now gone) just a few yards downstream. Cassius Dio's claim that Augustus's tomb was full seems, given the size of the place and the size of a funerary urn, at least open to question.[109] At best it can only have been an excuse for Hadrian to exercise his passion for building things, preferably things on a grand scale. (He did, admittedly, build on the small scale as well—tombs for his horses and dogs, for example.)

And the building is grand, without question. Of monuments visible from the river, it is (after the better bridges) without question the most striking man-made structure, the one building that painters and photographers hoping to incorporate the river in their work invariably turn to. In form, it is a sort-of twin to the Mausoleum of Augustus. Its footprint is a shade smaller, but if you're traveling upriver, it's the first of the two you'll see; the Mausoleum of Augustus by contrast is easily missed altogether. The tomb is a three-part creation, a square base of eighty-four meters per side, ten in height, on which rests a squat drum of sixty-eight meters in diameter, twenty-one meters high. The tomb was originally topped with statues of men and horses, which proved useful in 537 when Romans needed heavy objects to throw on invading Goths. A fragment of Cassius Dio describes a bronze statue of the emperor, a chariot, and four horses, so large that "the bulkiest man could walk through the eye of each horse."[110] It would be nice to think that such a statue graced the tomb, and some early medieval fragments suggest one did, but Dio was not specific, and would-be corroboration is flawed.

The building itself housed the ashes and urns of Hadrian; Antoninus Pius and his wife, Faustina; Lucius Verus; Marcus Aurelius and his son, Commodus; Septimius Severus and his wife, Julia Domna, and sons Geta and Caracalla. Commodus was as cruel and vicious as Caligula but without the charm; his mistress Marcia attempted to kill him with poison, and when that was too slow, had him strangled by his wrestling coach Narcissus. She and he narrowly escaped punishment chiefly because the senate, if anything, feared and loathed Commodus even more than she had, going so far as to vote against his entombment and for his being tossed into the Tiber. It was only thanks to the greater piety of his successor Pertinax (amiable, only mildly debauched, and deposed in under three months) that Caracalla was placed inside the tomb, discreetly, after dark.

Hadrian, or his architect, or whoever planned the thing, was shrewd about the setting. The area in Roman times was pleasant—the empress Domitia (c. AD 53–55 to c. 126–130) had public gardens, the Horti Domitia Longina, laid out just across Nero's bridge, which may have been a factor in deciding where to place the tomb. It was a fine place to walk about, so long as Rome was at its peak and utterly secure from external enemies.

My soul, my pleasant soul and witty,
The ghest and consort of my body,
Into what place now all alone
Naked and sad wilt thou be gone?
No mirth, no wit, as heretofore,
Nor Jests wilt thou afford me more.
Henry Vaughan, 1652

Animula vagula blandula
Hospes comesque corporis
Quae nunc abibis? In Loca
Pallidula rigida nudula
nec ut soles dabis Iocos.

Hadrian himself died at Baiae, up the coast from Naples, having failed to see the finished project, and it was up to his successor and adopted son Antoninus Pius to exhume his body, cremate the remains, and place them in the tomb. They might have rested there indefinitely, if it were not for the sheer bulk and position of the structure. The building would survive the worst that nature and man could throw at it, and over the centuries have an afterlife as a prison, a fortress, and much else besides, all involving reworking to accommodate its owners' shifting needs, as we shall see.

Although the idle pedestrian could easily reach the tomb by the (now long gone) Pons Neronianus just a short walk downstream, the builder in Hadrian could not rest until he had his own bridge, the Pons Aelius (Aelius being Hadrian's family name). Just as the tomb is now better known as the Castel Sant'Angelo, the bridge is now better known as Ponte Sant'Angelo, without question the most striking of all the Tiber's bridges.

The bridge's earliest representation is on an ancient medallion, which, if anything at all similar to reality, suggests that the Ponte Sant'Angelo has always been the most striking of Rome's bridges. The medallion depicts the approaches, which extended a short way out from either bank, then rise steeply some forty degrees, nearly doubling the bridge in height (if we take the medallion seriously), or fifteen degrees (if we do not).[III] The central span rested on three arches. Gracing the high walkway were four pillars (eight, assuming they are paired), topped with human statues at least life size. The statues are long gone now, presumably burned for lime in the years after Rome's first fall, and the Bernini figures that have replaced them, however impressive, seem trifling in comparison—again, if we take the medallion seriously.

The Pons Aelius was suitable for the periodic funeral processions and any other traffic that needed to get to the other side and straight into the tomb. For the tomb's future occupants, there would be a mournful procession of prefects in black robes, choristers chanting dirges, trumpeters blowing horns, mimes in masks of beeswax representing the dead, and near relatives and friends carrying the urn itself. Bringing up the rear would be the great man's clients, and slaves set free under the great man's will.

After Severus was buried there, history goes silent until Procopius, who visited Rome in the sixth century and from whom we will hear more in due course.

Later Mad Emperors

If the river could cleanse the city of filth, could it not also cleanse the individual of sin? Apparently so. Tertullian, a church father of the third century, writing on the beneficial effects of baptism, notes with disapproval that "among the ancients" a ritual wash could erase the stain even of murder.[112] Pagans and Christians had different views on the spiritually cleansing powers of river water.

Elagabalus, one of the more lunatic later emperors, was assassinated (not without good reason) and proved too large to be stuffed down a sewer and so was simply tossed into the river, earning the nickname Tiberinus (possibly a witty reference to Tiberinus Silvius, mentioned earlier as the king of Alba Longa who gave his name to the river when he accidentally fell in and drowned).[113]

Stories of Roman emperors, stories already wild enough in their own times, became wilder still the farther away history moved from the events under discussion. The *Kaiserchronik*, last seen slandering Nero, tells the story of Gallienus (AD 218–268, whom the author seems to conflate with the physician Galen), in which that emperor catches out a would-be assassin attempting to slip poison into his wine. He forces the man to drink the goblet himself, and watches as the man's eyes bug out in prelude to death. Gallienus, unnerved, heads upriver with a bronze casket filled with poison, which he dumps into the Tiber in hopes of its wiping out his ungrateful subjects. End of story. No word on whether this harmed more people than fish.[114]

Tributary—Anio

Delicatissimus Amnium, "most gentle Anio," in Pliny's words.[1] Gentle, but bear in mind that it is sourced in the Abruzzi, tough country, and that *amnis* can also mean fast flowing, a torrent. He goes on to describe what the gentlest river could do when fully aroused:

> [The river] has almost entirely rooted up and carried away the woods which shaded its borders. It has overthrown whole mountains, and, in endeavoring to find a passage through the mass of ruins that obstructed its way, has forced down houses, and risen and spread over the desolation it has occasioned. The inhabitants of the hill countries, who are situated above the reach of this inundation, have been the melancholy spectators of its dreadful effects, having seen costly furniture, instruments of husbandry, ploughs, and oxen with their drivers, whole herds of cattle, together with the trunks of trees, and beams of the neighboring villas, floating about in different parts.[2]

The Anio joins the Tiber at Antemnae (*ante amnem posita*, "in front of the river," is the alleged derivation), capital of the Sabines and accordingly the source of the Sabine women snaffled by Romulus and his followers. It was also the place where, in 390 BC, Gauls under the chieftain Brennus marched in the Tiber valley and to the Etruscan city of Clusium. Rome sent three members of the gens Fabii (the family having rebuilt its stock) to negotiate a peace. They instead started an argument, a fight, resulting in the death of a Gaulish chieftain. Brennus demanded the heads of the Fabii; Rome instead appointed the three to lead three armies.

It was a bold gesture, but not a wise move. The Romans had not quite mastered the techniques that would later procure them an empire. Faced with a crush of murderous Gauls under a skilled general, the Roman commanders ordered a retreat, not to Rome, which in those days was unwalled and open, but to Veii, now Roman and easy to defend. The Gauls entered Rome, took what they liked, destroyed a good deal, and spent the next seven months besieging the remaining locals on the Capitoline Hill. On July 18, the defenders capitulated. They agreed to pay the Gauls a thousand pounds of gold for their departure.[3]

The 18th of July was forever after considered bad luck.

There was a satisfying aftermath, at least for the Romans. While the ransom was being weighed out, scattered Romans under the command of Marcus Furius Camillus appeared. He declared the terms null and void and ordered the Gauls to leave. They naturally refused, and fighting broke out, leading to the Gauls making a strategic retreat northward. Camillus followed and, eight kilometers away, engaged in a final battle, annihiliating the invaders. The city of Rome would be free of foreign invaders for the next eight centuries. (There would be a few domestic invasions, but that's another matter.)

Anio water was prized for drinking. Quintus Marcius Rex, praetor in 144 BC and as such manager of a new aqueduct project, wanted to tap the water flow close to the headwaters at le Serene, some ninety kilometers up the Anio valley at Arsoli-Agosta. Money was no object—four years earlier, Roman troops had defeated Corinth in battle, slain its men, sold its women and children into slavery, and stolen its treasure. Bureaucracy, however, in the form of the Sibylline books interfered—the water must not be taken from the area Marcius had in mind, but must be come from the river itself. The Sibylline books were, however, open to interpretation, and after a few days of debate in the senate, Marcius got his way.[4] He trooped his engineers and laborers to the source and provided the best water for Rome, distinguished for its excellence above all others, a gift of heaven to the state through mountains and over aqueducts.[5]

The water was so good that by law it was banned for any purpose other than drinking. Gardeners and cleaners must settle for lesser, though still readily available, water. But who does not want the best when it can be had? Fullers, the men who cleaned and bleached cloth by treading and pounding it in vats of ammonia-saturated urine, wanted to rinse the end product before handing it back to their customers, and in Marcia water (as it was called), if possible. The aqueduct was tapped illegally, much as gas and electric lines are in some places today. Frontinus, Rome's water minister, bemoaned the practice and its results: "We have found even Marcia water, so delightful in its purity and coldness, used for baths, fulling mills, and for things so disgusting I cannot bring myself to write about them."[6]

CHRISTIAN TIBER

In which Christendom comes to Rome, barbarians storm the gates, a tourist

gawks at dubious attractions, a bureaucrat deals with a dangerous mob,

a wartime necessity spawns a Roman industry, mysterious creatures wash up

on the riverbank, and two women effectively rule Rome for forty years.

Crisis of the Third Century

The third century was not kind to Rome. Various reasons can be cited, not least of all, money. The government took in less than it spent. Nothing new in that; governments by nature spend beyond their means. Rome, however, was new to the situation and uncertain how to deal with it. At some point a committee, unfamiliar with Gresham's Law that bad money pushes out good, must have come up with the novel expedient of currency debasement.

One can see how it happened. The denarius, the standard coin of Roman commerce, depended on a steady supply of silver. As expenses rose (soldiers' pay, largely) there came a time when silver mines came up a bit short, too short to coin the same quantity of denarii as last year. What to do? Well, lead looks and weighs more or less the same as silver. Why not toss a bar or two of that into the melting pot? A few lead grains here or there per individual coin—who's to notice? No one, really. The books are balanced, life goes on. A year passes, the mines are up to speed, but the emperor has had an expensive war and the treasury is a little short. Perhaps some more lead would straighten out that problem, just this once. Another few grains should cover the shortfall. And again, there seemed no harm in it—if there were, of course, one would stop. But as there was no harm—another year, another few bars. Simplicity itself, and such a boon to the government's account books. It's all quite brilliant, really. Though one does notice that the feel of the coins has gotten a little odd of late. Not quite like the specie of old. Come to think of it, you don't find too many of those old coins anymore. And, oddly, prices seem to have gone up in recent years. Greedy merchants overcharging, no doubt; they really should be punished. In the meantime, there is a quick solution.

From the reign of Domitian (AD 96) to AD 268, when emperors' reigns could be measured in months and few died a natural death, the silver content in Roman currency plunged from 96 percent pure down to 5 percent. People noticed. Soldiers (barbarian mercenaries, most of them) in particular noticed, insisted on, and got, payment in gold. Good for them, but they couldn't solve the underlying problem.

The loss of money and the crisis in confidence were bad enough; the fracturing of the empire into separate entities (Gallic empire, Palmyrene empire) and the surprise appearance of Germanic tribes pouring over the Alps and down the boot of Italy toward Rome prompted outright panic in the capital. A near-run battle in 271 was followed by a huge public works project, the so-called Aurelian Walls, doubling the size of the city. The walls were, and are, impressive, but the message they sent was that Rome could no longer count on its reputation and its frontiers to keep the population safe. The most surprising, and most immediately dangerous, threat came in the form of a woman.

Zenobia

"Now all shame is exhausted, for in the weakened state of the commonwealth things came to such a pass that, while Gallienus conducted himself in the most evil fashion, even women ruled most excellently."[1]

The "now" referred to was the declining third century, and the specific shame was the capture in the battle of Edessa (AD 260) of the Emperor Valerian by Persian forces under Shapur I, marking the first time ever that a Roman emperor had been taken prisoner, and a sign that maybe the Roman Empire wasn't quite the powerhouse it had once been. Gallienus was Valerian's successor, a man not so much evil as very much distracted by Goths marauding in the north. Of the excellently ruling women, the specific woman was Zenobia, queen of Palmyra.

Palmyra was a small piece within the Roman province of Syria; it stretched from the upper reaches of the Euphrates River to the Lebanon mountains, and at the time of Valerian's defeat was run by Odaenathus, a local man, an ally of Rome, a *consularis*, more a governor than an independent ruler, but also a good general and, in 261, the man who pushed back against Shapur and defeated him.

Besting the man who had captured Valerian could give any man a swell head. More battles followed, generally a relief for Valerian's successor Gallienus, who had his own hands full with Goths up north. Odaenathus arrogated titles (king of kings) to himself; he was perhaps not quite entitled, but so long as his activities were a benefit to Rome, who was to argue? His luck ran out in 267. That year, he was assassinated (no evidence by whom), leaving behind his young wife Zenobia and their son, his heir, who was all of eight years old. The story was about to become interesting.

Zenobia (240?–274?) was another native Syrian, but collaterally related to the Ptolemies of Egypt; for the sake of her image, she claimed descent from Cleopatra, a name that, even in 275, still carried some weight. Some Arab historians argue she was Arab, some Jewish historians claimed that she was Jewish. The Roman histories say only that "her face was dark and of a swarthy hue, her eyes were black and powerful beyond the usual wont, her spirit divinely great, and her beauty incredible. So white were her teeth that many thought that she had pearls in place of teeth. Her voice was clear and like that of a man."[2]

She took up the role of regent, and to dispel any thoughts that Palmyra was ripe for being conquored, she continued her husband's battles, chiefly against the Sassanids, expanding her influence, building her reputation. In Rome, by contrast, the emperor Gallienus was assassinated and replaced by the ineffective Aureolus, who proved inadequate to dealing with the increasing troubles on Rome's northern border. His failures were widely noticed.

Success fuels ambition, and Zenobia had both. She also had, she thought, a more legitimate claim to Egypt than the Roman bureaucrats then in charge, and so turned her considerable army onto that land. The fighting might have been less one-sided had the Roman prefect not been busy elsewhere dealing with pirates, piracy having enjoyed a recent comeback in the Mediterranean after centuries of Roman peace. The Roman commander on land, anticipating defeat by the Palmyrene forces, committed suicide. Zenobia was now queen of Egypt.

Clearly the woman had a talent for war and, we may assume, an appetite for it as well. Having secured the Roman food source, she turned north, to Anatolia (modern Turkey), and soon controlled the east half of that territory. By 271, her influence extended over twelve hundred miles of the coastal Mediterranean, from Antalya to the border of modern Libya, hundreds of miles inland, and on both sides of the upper Red Sea.

Rome was, granted, not in the robust shape it had once been. Empires on the edge of decline are, however, most anxious about appearances, and apt to take arms against any suggestion of a slight. A quick succession of poor emperors ended with Aurelian, an up-from-the-ranks soldier. He was also a good general, and although he might have tolerated Zenobia's control of trade to the east, any foreign control of Egypt, Rome's breadbasket, was unacceptable. She cut off Rome's grain supply; he ordered the army to march.

The matter was settled in 272 at the battle of Immae, near Antioch. Aurelian, having dealt with rebellious Germans and rebellious Dacians, now marched into Syria, pushing the opposing armies back to Emesa (Homs). He laid siege. Zenobia and her son escaped and headed for Persia, but they were caught before she could reach the Euphrates. Her sudden empire fell under Roman control. Aurelian had effectively put an end (temporarily) to a near century of Roman fever.

The question becomes, why? Why did she bother pushing the boundaries in the first place, and against Rome itself? Aurelian asked her this very question. The alleged reply was, "You, I know, are an emperor indeed, for you win victories, but Gallienus and Aureolus and the others I never regarded as emperors. Believing Victoria to be a woman like me, I desired to become a partner in the royal power, should the supply of lands permit."[3] A nice balance of flattery and flat-footed realism; any ruler jealous of his land should take note. She went on the march because she could, and kept on marching until she could not.

Of course Aurelian couldn't just let her go. Rome was by now an old enterprise. There were procedures and traditions that must be followed. His first obligation was to serve her up as the centerpiece of his upcoming triumphal parade.

Some senators grumbled that her taking a spot usually reserved for male leaders was a poor reflection on Rome in general and Aurelian in particular. Aurelian's response to his critics: "Those very persons who find fault with me now would accord me praise in abundance, did they but know what manner of woman she is, how wise in counsels, how steadfast in plans, how firm toward the soldiers, how generous when necessity calls, and how stern when discipline demands. I might even say that it was her doing that Odaenathus defeated the Persians and, after putting Sapor to flight, advanced all the way to Ctesiphon."[4]

Certainly she made a stunning spectacle for the Roman citizenry, who were always up for the unusual. She was forced to walk the parade route, stopping frequently under the weight of oversize jewels and the golden fetters, shackles, and chains that bound her legs, arms, and neck, so burdensome that she needed a slave to help her bear the weight. Humiliating, but also more than a little awe inspiring. One likes to think that the crowd was on her side.

And after that? She seems to have been spared the ritual strangulation generally accorded defeated generals and kings. (There was precedent for mercy; Claudius spared the British ruler Caratacus when he was brought to Rome.) Some say she died soon after, of illness or suicide. A happier narrative has it that Aurelian, mindful of her earlier service to Rome, provided her with a villa at Tibur, overlooking the Anio.[5] True, it was a step down from being queen of Egypt, but she had had a good run, and there are plenty of worse places to live out one's twilight years than in an Italian riverside villa.

Constantine and the Milvian Bridge

Like Waterloo, the actual fighting was nowhere near its name place. But after two thousand years, complaint is futile, and so, the battle of the Milvian Bridge it is.

The battle was a consequence of an empire grown too large for any one man to govern. The emperor Diocletian had recognized this in AD 298 and determined to split it in two, with each region having an Augustus as its head and a Caesar as his second in command. The plan assumed too much of human nature. By 312, after some contentious bids for the four slots, the last men standing were Maxentius in Rome and his brother-in-law Flavius Valerius Constantinus in Gaul, both of whom thought the empire would do better with one man only in charge. To force the issue, Constantine gathered his army and marched into Italy, heading steadily southward, gathering strength as he went, down the Via Flaminia, which covers hills and mountains until in its latter stages it enters the narrow valley containing the meandering Tiber. Constantine stopped at Prima Porta, a small town some twelve kilometers north of the city. Rome, he knew, would be locked up and ready for a siege.

A good general takes care to know the territory and prefers to choose the field of battle. The Tiber valley floodplain is flat, wide, and good for cavalry, of which Constantine had a fair number. His army, however, was smaller than that of Maxentius. His best hope was that Maxentius would exit the city and he, Constantine, could maneuver him into a weaker position.

In Rome, Maxentius had his own concerns. For weeks, survivors of failed battles farther north had been retreating to Rome and telling stories of Constantine's success. Maxentius had to make a choice—to defend himself within Rome and its considerable walls, or to come out and fight. The people of Rome were said to be restless, unhappy with his rule, and even called out support for Constantine in the mob anonymity of the circus games (games presumably paid for by Maxentius). These were not the sort of people who would put up with a drawn-out siege. To maintain power, Maxentius thought it best to go out and destroy the enemy quickly, once and for all. And, like any prudent commander, he took advice where he could get it. He went to the Sibylline books, the standby and fallback source for Rome in times of crisis. Specifically, he wanted to know which way the battle would go.

The answer was clear: anyone who should try to harm the Romans would die a miserable death.[6] The ambiguity came in who could be called a Roman. Maxentius was actually in Rome, which was a point in his favor. Certainly the bookish prophecy did not *preclude* Maxentius from victory, which was also a plus. And he had the Praetorian Guard, undefeated crack troops, behind him. The prospects looked good.

Constantine did not have access to the books, but he did have visions. The accounts differ in detail, but only a little. The chroniclers write that Constantine slept and dreamed, or remained awake and daydreamed. He had a vision of a Latin cross, or perhaps the Chi-Rho sign. With the vision came the prediction, In hoc signo vinces, "In this sign shalt thou conquer." Or he looked up at the sun, saw the cross inscribed with the same message in Greek, "Εν Τούτῳ Νίκα." He either got the message immediately, or lacked the wit to understand its meaning.[7] A dream that night spelled the matter out for him: remove the pagan symbols from your standards and replace them with Christian totems.

At dawn on October 28, Maxentius opened the gates to the city and headed north on the Via Flaminia as far as the Milvian bridge, which he crossed and then destroyed. He had no need of it. A ways downriver he had ordered a prefabricated two-part pontoon bridge thrown over the Tiber, fastened at the center with an iron pin. Let Constantine approach the destroyed Milvian bridge and be dismayed. If worse should come to worst, Maxentius could head to the pontoon bridge, cross, and destroy it all but instantly. Initially, his men were to fight at Saxa Rubra, a small village near Prima Porta and, as a place of final approach to Rome, full of its own history. The plan must have looked better on paper.

The morning sun rose, and both sides lined up at their respective positions, Maxentius with his back to the river. Constantine made the first move, sending in his heavy Gallic cavalry and breaking Maxentius's line of horse. Taking immediate advantage of this success, Constantine ordered the infantry to follow up. There is little more detail about the battle. Praetorians, the emperor's personal guard, in what would be their last battle, fought bravely, if ineffectively. According to the generally sympathetic Zosimus, Maxentius's troops, both Roman and foreign, were less than enthusiastic, thinking him a hard master. Nevertheless, they did fight, and die, trampled by cavalry or killed by infantry. Maxentius and his best men were pushed back to the pontoon bridge. The bridge collapsed under the strain of too many people, sweeping all those on it into the river.

Maxentius himself, weighted down with armor, was among the drowned. His body was later recovered, the head severed and mounted on a pike by Constantine's men as a trophy. Later it was taken to North Africa to show skeptics that the political order had changed. Constantine somehow managed to cross the river and the next day made a triumphal entry into Rome.

The poets, sensitive to the moment, had a field day, singling out the river itself for its part in Constantine's victory:

Sacred Tiber, once adviser of your guest Aeneas, next savior of the exposed Romulus, you allowed neither the false Romulus to live for long nor the City's murderer to swim away. You who nourished Rome by conveying provisions, you who protected her by encircling the walls, rightly wished to partake of Constantine's victory, to have him drive the enemy to you, and you slay him. You are not always rapid and turbulent but moderate if the occasion demands it. You were calm when you carried Cocles in armor, the maiden Cloelia entrusted herself to your stillness; but now violent and turbid you sucked in the enemy of the State and, lest your service go unnoticed, you revealed it by disgorging his corpse.[8]

It was, take note, still acceptable to include completely pagan references while praising the emperor who would soon bring Christianity into the Roman fold.

Having conquered, Constantine restored the empire as the charge of a single ruler, to be headquartered in Constantinople. Anyone with an ounce of ambition in Rome followed him there. Rome's pagan temples began to turn into churches. Change had come quickly. Decay would follow at leisure.

A Million More Mouths

The fourth century may have been a time of decline, but it was an easeful decline. The crisis of the third century was history, those who suffered it long dead. The emperor had left Rome, and many with him, but life went on, temples and buildings still stood, trade still functioned, the rich still lived in fine houses, the masses still enjoyed the odd circus and daily bread. The bread may have been sourced abroad, but that is not to say it was not Roman.

There were some unanticipated long-term consequences to taking foreign taxes in the form of food. Most significantly, the Romans undermined their own agricultural sector. The government underwrote the basic delivery of government-sponsored grain, which for the *naviculari* meant that the cost of shipping any goods beyond the contracted grain was essentially zero. Accordingly, it was a simple matter for a North African farmer (whose marginal costs were low) to dump excess olive oil, say, into the olive-producing regions of Italy, undercutting the local Italian producers. Not surprisingly, wealthy Romans owned much of the land in North Africa. So long as they profited from the system, they were bound to support it.

That is to say, so long as the mechanism of foreign-sourced food operated properly, which was not always the case. Harvests were uncertain, even in Egypt; Mediterranean winds could be uncooperative; storms at sea could sink ships—none of which mattered to the unforgiving Roman mob. Tertullus, urban prefect of Rome in AD 359–361, was in charge of grain distribution and public entertainment—bread and circuses, if you like—and was held personally responsible for the bad weather that held up the fleet. A contemporary reports that the mob was getting ugly: "They anticipated famine, the worst of all ills; and this was utterly unreasonable, since it was no fault of his that food was not brought at the proper time in the ships, which unusually rough weather at sea and adverse gales of wind drove to the nearest harbours, and by the greatness of the danger kept them from entering the Porta of Augustus."[9]

A quick wit, a talent for oratory, and mutable weather probably saved his life. Hounded by the unreasoning crowd, Tertullus climbed onto the Rostra, his two young sons at his side, and with tears in his eyes declared: "Behold your fellow citizens, who with you (but may the gods of heaven avert the omen!) will endure the same fate, unless a happier fortune shine upon us. If therefore you think that by the destruction of these no heavy calamity can befall you, here they are in your power."[10] He followed this up with a quick trip to Ostia, where he sacrificed to the temple of brothers Castor and Pollux. It seemed to work. Gale-force winds gradually died down, the sea became smooth, and the grain ships offshore were able to enter the harbor; their cargo soon crammed the granaries.

It was a close call, and by no means the first ("he had often been disquieted by uprisings"), and credit, notice, went to the pagan gods.[11] Not all stories ended quite so happily. Quintus Aurelius Symmachus (c. 345–402), a good pagan in a Rome heading to Christianity, inherited Tertullus's old job, and the reader can wonder why he agreed to take it. The mob, as usual, was proving fickle, and we learn that in 375 "they set fire to Symmachus' beautiful house in the Transtiberine district, spurred on by the fact that a common fellow among the plebeians had alleged, without any informant or witness, that the prefect had said that he would rather use his own wine for quenching lime-kilns than sell it at the price which the people hoped for."[12]

It is a wonder that anyone was willing to enter public service at all, and no wonder that Symmachus the younger should have worried that the emperor was not taking the delivery of grain to Rome as seriously as he ought.[13] In 384, the fleet was running late, and the people were accordingly restless. Although the emperor was responsible for financing the dole, it was the prefect and the senate, men close at hand, who took the blame when things went wrong. Happily, Symmachus could write to his friend the Frankish general Ricomer, "I see with pleasure what grain arrives day by day, and what supplies from Macedonia have been brought into the warehouses of Rome. For, as you remember, because of delays in Africa, famine was almost at our doorstep when our most clement emperor, born for the salvation of all, prevented it, through mobilizing levies from this other area."[14]

Flattering the men who controlled the grain was part of his job, and the clement emperor no longer lived in Rome but hundreds of miles east in Constantinople, where odds were even if he remembered from day to day or year to year that Rome must be fed, it wasn't the emperor who would face the consequences of shortfall. We are fortunate to have this letter, but who knows how many other thank-you notes Symmachus had to send out to ensure someone would keep the emperor reminded.

Symmachus at Law

One vital element to the river trade were divers—*urinatores* in Latin, possibly based on the phenomenon of immersion diuresis, in which divers feel the urge to urinate. They formed part of the *corpus piscatorum et urinatorum*, the guild of fishermen and divers. The reason for the combination is not hard to see. Drop hooks or traps or dip nets are useless for fishermen with an interest in certain types of bottom-dwelling creatures (octopus, sponge, murex), and so they had little choice but to go down under in person. And those already accustomed to the requirements of diving could put the skill to other uses—collecting cargo that had fallen off boats in the harbor, say, or inspecting ship hulls. Given the traffic in Portus and on the Tiber, collisions and sinkings would have been fairly common. *Urinatores* would also be ideally suited to fitting the caissons used to hold bridge foundations during construction, pouring underwater concrete and smoothing it with rakes. They could inspect and clean boat hulls without the bother of a drydock. Some tasks were beyond them. Caligula once took his fleet to sea and found his personal quinquereme, all four hundred rowers worth, was slower than the rest. It was a *urinator*, kept on board in case of need, who found the offending (and undescribed) sea creature attached to the rudder.[15] Some fish! Caligula was predictably annoyed, but the inspector had no choice but to say he could not do much about it.

Urinatores could also serve as expert witnesses under law, as occurred when the aforementioned Symmachus was named prefect of Rome and inherited a two-year-old legal squabble from his predecessor.

The facts of the case were as follows: two men, Cyriades and Auxentius, had been contracted to build a basilica (possibly Saint Paul outside the Walls) and reconstruct the Pons Probi near the Aventine Hill. Time passed, work proceeded, but before completion, the bridge collapsed. Both men (senators, as it happened) blamed each other, with charges and countercharges of embezzlement on one side and shoddy workmanship on the other. Prior investigations had led nowhere, Auxentius had disappeared, Symmachus called in experts, the investigation continued:

> Craftsmen estimated the cost or repair at twenty gold coins, at the outside. But the collapse of this part [of the bridge], which was as yet separated from the rest of the structure, did not seem to have damaged in any way the more distant sites. Cyriades, of the distinguished order of senators, assured us that it would not be a difficult building operation to repair it. A second site was examined, and a block of stonework was discovered with gaps in it. Cyriades, *comes* and civil engineer, giving us the advice of his specialist knowledge, told us that the stones had been set in this way so the material could be run in later and the parts separated by gaps would thus be bound together. His successor in the work ought to have taken great care to do this, but he was said, instead of doing it, to have contrived that open places should be filled with bales of hay and esparto [a grass fiber] so as to bring the originator of the works into discredit. He supported this by quoting from the record of work done, and the skilled diver did not deny that was what had been done, but he said that it was in accordance with normal building practice, and not with a view to dishonoring Cyriades, of the distinguished order of senators, that this kind of measure had been adopted.[16]

How to square all the conflicting testimony? Torture. The unfortunate witness confessed to perjury, but claimed that it was because Cyriades had threatened him. Since, however, his new testimony came out under torture, he could not be believed. And then—

Unfortunately, the record breaks off here. Symmachus might have been tired of the whole affair. By this point it had dragged on for five years, and he was a busy man.

Julian the Apostate

One of the odder stories from the twelfth century *Kaiserchronik* concerns Julian the Apostate (330–363) in his pre-emperor days and the pious widow who accused him of stealing money entrusted to his care.

Julian was the last of the pagan emperors, hopeful of returning Rome to the ancient gods whose abandonment was arguably the cause of the empire's clear instability. For that reason alone the Christian writers had no choice but to blackguard the man and his works. Theft from a poor widow is the kind of offense that will evoke sympathy in any audience that is not heartless or disciplined enough to wait for the facts.

In this case, Julian denied the accusation, and the court believed him, in consequence of which the poor widow was forced to labor as a washerwoman on the banks of the Tiber. One day while rubbing cloth against the rocks, she found a statue of the god Mercury left over from pagan days. Nothing remarkable in that, but this particular statue housed an evil spirit, which told her to carry him to the next church service and bring up the question of her lost money again. She did so, demanding that Julian place his hand in this pagan statue's mouth and then swear again that he did nothing wrong. Despite the pagan origins of the statue, the pope approved, Julian did as he was told, whereupon the statue bit him and refused to let go until Julian retracted the story and returned the money. Which he did.[17]

And then the story gets strange.

With that unpleasantness behind them, the pagan devil and Julian become friendly. The statue tells him that he, Julian, will soon succeed Constantine, so long as he is willing to forswear Christianity, rebuild the temples, and start persecuting the faithful, starting with two men called John and Paul. Julian takes the statue up on the offer, and a long narrative of persecution follows.

One gets the impression that the author became a little desperate at this point and needed a way to wind up the story. His solution, weak by modern standards, is to introduce a ghostly horseman who kills Julian and conveys his body to Constantinople, where it will remain until the day of judgment.

Alaric the Goth

Theodosius the Great (347–395) was the last emperor to rule over both eastern and western empires, working from his base in Milan.

In 395 the poet Claudian could praise Theodosius with some inspiring panegyrics about how he pushed the enemy back across the Alps, but it was largely bluster. Theodosius died young, leaving his son Honorius to take the western throne, his other son Arcadius the eastern. Honorius was eight years old, too young by any measure. Fortunately his father had appointed a competent and loyal soldier, Stilicho, as his guardian.

Stilicho was a Vandal, but a Christian Vandal, married to Theodosius's niece and sworn to serve Rome; he was also a skilled general. In 397, Gildo, *magister utriusque militiae per Africam* and son of King Nubel of Mauretania, sensing a power vacuum, halted grain shipments to Rome. Stilicho was forced to put aside another war and gather two fleets, one to get stopgap grain from Gaul and Spain, another to get troops to North Africa and take care of Gildo.

After the fact, Claudian wrote a lengthy encomium to Stilicho's brilliant action, asking rhetorically, "Has it ever happened before that Tiber's wave has carried grain from the fertile north over the ploughing of whose fields the Lingones [a Celtic tribe] have toiled?"[18] Apparently not. The poem mentions the bread riots that had occurred in the past when grain failed to make it on time. As to the grain officials from Africa, once Gildo was defeated, they were marched through Rome as part of Stilicho's triumph and either killed or freed, depending on the whim of a whimsical mob. Their exact fate is unknown for certain, but not hard to guess.

Back in Italy, when Alaric the Goth crossed the Alps and surrounded Milan in 402, it was Stilicho who broke the siege and sent Alaric running. It was a feat for which Stilicho received a triumphal parade in Rome—the last, as it happened.

The young emperor Honorius, unnerved by the siege, fled to Ravenna, surrounded by marshland, as a place of greater safety than Milan or Rome, where he could indulge in his taste for raising chickens. He did rouse himself long enough to enter Rome in 404, taking the precaution, as Claudian notes, of praising the river and using its waters to make a libation ("when in greeting to Father Tiber thou hast poured a libation of his waters thou art welcomed by Rome's arches and all the magnificent buildings which line the roads of that noble city's suburbs").[19] His obligations met, Honorius hurried back to Ravenna and his sycophants, his palace, and his poultry. The details of imperial administration he would leave to others. He was, unfortunately, not always best served by his advisers, which in less interesting times might have been tolerable, but now, with a still powerful Alaric at his borders, was disastrous. Worse, Honorius failed to recognize just how critical his guardian was to the empire.

Within the court circle surrounding Honorius, Stilicho was hated for his success and had become the target of political intrigue too byzantine to describe. He was executed in 408, leaving Honorius without a competent general and Alaric with a stronger hand. Alaric offered terms. Honorious said no, and Alaric moved on Rome in 408, a prospect so alarming to the inhabitants that the pope even sanctioned pagan rituals, just in case. The sticking point was that he insisted the rituals be done in private, whereas the pagan priests said the rituals could work only if done in public. (It is worth pointing out that just a few years earlier, Stilicho was said to have burned the Sibylline books, which in retrospect may have been a mistake.)

In the absence of help from Honorius, or advice from the books, the senate elected to negotiate on their own. Gold and silver and slaves and silk and hides and pepper did the trick, and by year's end Alaric was gone, marching north to attend to the unfinished business of his prior demands on Honorius. Rome, at least for the moment, was safe.

Rome might have continued to be safe if Honorius had been even a little more realistic. He was not, and in 410 Alaric, uninterested in Ravenna, marched on Rome one final time.

As sieges go, this one did not last long. The game was over when a lone starving inhabitant opened the gates and allowed the Goths in. That there was much left to steal seems surprising, and it may be that the three-day free-for-all was more a matter of burning and smashing and rape than theft. The most striking physical evidence of their presence comes in the Forum's Basilica Aemilia, where, it is said, the coins that fell from the merchants' tables—apparently it was business as usual, despite the siege—were superheated and, as the basilica burned, fused to the stone floor. They're still there, faintly green from exposure, even if the walls and ceiling are gone.

To Alaric's credit (and these things are always relative), he, as another good Christian, took nothing from the basilicas of Saint Peter and Saint Paul. Satisfied for the moment, he and his men marched south, and en route he died of fever. According to legend, his men diverted the course of the Busento River just long enough to bury him and a massive treasure (*cum multas opes*), then returned the river to its normal path.[20] No one has claimed to have found it yet.

Honorius's attitude to the entire affair is summed up in the probably apocryphal anecdote that when news came that Rome had perished, his first reaction was surprise, since, as he said, "It is only an hour ago that he was feeding out of my hand." It took a moment for the chamberlain to explain that the Rome in question was his capital city. Honorius was relieved. "I thought, my good man (ἑταῖρε), that my chicken Rome had died."[21]

Hadrian's Tomb Undone

Alaric must take the blame for being in charge when Hadrian's tomb was ransacked, its urns smashed, its treasures taken. It had served its purpose as a mausoleum for just under 275 years. Still, the structure was intact, useful for anyone who needed a secure building at a strategic location. The record goes silent for a time; when the chronicles pick up again, they stop referring to Hadrian but instead call the structure the House of Theodoric (Domus Theodorici), or Theodoric's prison—Theodoric (454–526) being ruler of Italy as well as king of the Ostrogoths.[22]

Christian itineraries, early guidebooks for pilgrims, refer to certain oddities of the tomb, including a triple range of columns, fine sculpture on the roof, gilded peacocks, a bronze bull, and Belvedere pines—the source of all these is supposedly Leo I, the pope who faced Alaric, but the first written record is secondhand, by Pietro Manlio writing in 1160.[23] (A pair of gilded peacocks, thought to have survived Rome's numerous sackings, are now in the Vatican Museum.)

There will be more to say about the building in due course.

Barbarians at the Gates

Rome reeled, Rome recovered, after a fashion. Alaric's arson had been chiefly restricted to the central Forum area, and there were still enough people living in Rome to justify calling it a city. Battered but not entirely broken, the locals soldiered on, presumably uncovering the valuables they had hidden from the Goths.

Politics also went on. Honorius died (423), to be replaced by Valentinian III, who also had to negotiate peace rather than ensure it by force of arms. His opponent was Gaiseric, king of the Vandals, master of Carthage.

Carthage had been famously destroyed in the second century BC by the Romans egged on by Cato the Elder, who had ended each senate speech with the catch phrase "Carthage must be destroyed," an idea that through repetition eventually brought results. Carthage was destroyed, its people enslaved, its soil tilled with salt (actually, the salt story is a later poetic embellishment), then reprieved a few years later when the Romans realized that the location was ideal for trade with North Africa. Carthage was rebuilt, became rich, and in 439 was taken by the Vandals.

One of the more energetic of the barbarian tribes, the Vandals came from eastern Europe, crossed Gaul, then Spain, then in 428, under their leader Gaiseric (ca. 400–477), they crossed from Spain to North Africa, the western parts of which they found congenial and settled into. In 439, they took Carthage. Carthage had recovered brilliantly in the centuries after the Punic Wars, in good part on the basis of its agriculture, the fruits of which were largely shipped off to Rome.

Taking Carthage gave the Vandals its considerable merchant fleet, along with its navy, which proved useful in raiding the coastal towns of Sicily and Southern Italy. These raids were a tragedy for those locals, but for anyone living in Rome, they were less a worry than the fact that Gaiseric had made it clear that Carthage was not going to pay taxes.

That is to say, the dole, the staple of Rome for five hundred years, was now at an end.

It is sad to imagine knots of people waiting on the quays, staring out to sea, not fully believing that the annual arrival of the grain ships, as regular as migrating birds, would not be happening that year. How was it possible? They had heard rumors of troubles overseas, but their own day-to-day lives had not changed; their houses were as solid as ever, their routines unchanged, flowers bloomed, birds sang, slaves toiled, the aqueduct still brought clean water. The ships being tardy they could understand, but to be cut off entirely? How could God, or the gods, allow such a thing?

Politics and diplomacy were called for, and unlike Alaric and Honorius, Gaiseric and Valentinian were able to come to mutually satisfactory terms. General peace was guaranteed (i.e., fewer Vandal raids), trade reopened, but if Rome wanted grain, it would come at a cost. To cement this treaty, Valentinian pledged his daughter Eudocia in marriage to Gaiseric's son Huneric when the two came of age. All well and good, and whether through oversight or necessity, the fact was that Huneric was next in line to inherit the Roman Empire once Valentinian died.

Valentinian did die, in 455, assassinated by Petronius Maximus, who claimed the throne for himself. It was a bold move but ill advised, given Gaiseric's past history of blood and violence. This was a man who had not only taken over Carthage, but acquired its considerable navy and merchant fleet as well. In short order, this fleet carried his army of Vandals up the coast of Italy to the Tiber, ready to avenge the murder of his son's prospective father-in-law. As it turned out, there was little enough for him to do—the Roman mob had already stoned Maximus to death, preserving honor all around. By simply showing up to support the Romans, Gaiseric had proved a good and honorable ally, and the locals hoped he would have a safe voyage home.

Gaiseric has a different take on the matter. Having come this far, he saw no reason to waste the trip. He was a Vandal, Vandals sack cities, and just because the man who was the reason he had come was now dead did nothing to change those facts. Pope Leo I came out to discuss the matter and managed to strike a bargain. Gaiseric agreed that he would neither kill nor enslave the people of Rome. The goods of Rome, however—those Gaiseric would be taking with him, along with the royal widow and her two daughters.[24]

For the next two weeks, Gaiseric's men methodically went through the city and gathered everything of value not nailed down (and in some cases, like the bronze roof of the temple of Jupiter—gilded, not the solid gold they had hoped for—much that was nailed down), loaded it into carts and into the boats waiting in the river, then sailed down to Ostia and back to Carthage. The chroniclers mention the copper cooking pots in the imperial kitchens of the Palatine. Those same people who had sat by the seaside a few years earlier waiting in vain for the grain ships now watched as the very ships that once had been their sustenance were now piled high with the wealth of centuries. What was to become of them? Easeful urbanites now had to envy the country mice cousins who had managed to maintain the ancient Roman virtues of working the land.

There is evidence that this gloomy view was not the whole story, or even close to it. The dole may have gone, but markets continued to function, the ships to sail, tourists and pilgrims to visit. Some Roman rich had fled from Carthage when the Vandals first showed up, but those who remained there found that the new overlords were content to live a life of some luxury in their conquered real estate. Carthage boomed in the wake of Gaiseric's expedition, and to the extent that trade declined at all, it did so slowly.

Sidonius Apollinaris

There are dangers in the Tiber that are invisible to the naked eye. Four general groups of troubling microzoa inhabit the waters: enteric viruses, bacteria, parasitic protozoa, and parasitic worms.[25] Rotovirus, parvovirus, and enterovirus, salmonella and parasitic protozoae, hookworms, threadworms, whipworms, roundworms, flatworms, typhoid, and dysentery—the sub-list is endless.

And then there is malaria.

Malaria's path into Italy seems to have been from North Africa by way of Sardinia. The arrival date is contested. Possibly as early as the fourth century BC, possibly as late as the first. Possibly the less virulent strains of *Plasmodium malaria* and *Plasmodium vivax* mutated into something worse. These infestations were regularly endured, occasionally fatal, never welcome. Initially the same swamps that skirted the hills of early Rome were the breeding ground for the disease-bearing mosquitoes. Their number declined somewhat as those swamps were drained, but there were other habitats for the insect, and the disease was still a serious concern well into the empire. Sidonius Apollinaris, a saint, scholar, son-in-law of the emperor Avitus, caught the fever in 467 and described the symptoms to his friend Herenius: "Fever and thirst ravaged the very marrow of my being; in vain I promised to their avidity draughts from pleasant fountain or hidden well, yes, and from every stream present or to come, water of Velino clear as glass, of Clitunno ice-cold, cerulean of Teverone, sulphureous of Nera, pellucid of Farfa, muddy of Tiber; I was mad to drink, but prudence stayed the craving."[26]

Who, one wonders, gave him this odd advice? Not drinking while suffering malaria is a ticket to renal failure. He survived. Other of the many pilgrims to Rome through the seventh and eighth century did not. The first Saint Augustine of Kent, first Archbishop of Canterbury, was bitten in 587 in Rome and finally died in 604; Alcuin, abbot of Tours, caught the fever in 798 and suffered for the remaining six years of his life. The list of pilgrims high and low who paid this price for their piety is unknowable, but no doubt considerable.

Malaria's life cycle is depressingly simple. A female anopheles mosquito seeking nutrient-rich mammalian blood injects her victim with a bacterium that seeks out and settles on the liver, breeds enormously, then sends its posterity into the bloodstream in search of red blood cells. Capillaries are soon clogged with dead blood cells, the spleen and kidneys are stressed, the patient loses weight and begins to suffer chills and fever, stomach cramps, nausea, vomiting, headache, and eventually, possibly, death.

Ancient gods did nothing to stop this annual scourge, nor it seems did Christian faith fare much better. Sixth-century Rome dedicated a church to the Madonna della Febbre, Our Lady of the Fever, but even so, the disease lingered on well into the early twentieth century. It was Mussolini who brought the disease to an end. His engineers laid down the pipes and fired up the water pumps that would drain the Pontine marshes and set the stage for the growth of Rome in the later twentieth century. A more praiseworthy legacy than making the trains run on time.

Belisarius's Mills

In 535, the eastern emperor Justinian decided that a split Roman Empire was less desirable than a single empire under himself. Accordingly, he dispatched Belisarius, arguably the finest general of his age, to recover territory taken by the upstart Ostrogoths. A string of victories from North Africa to Sicily to Naples to Rome soon followed, which, in 537, led the Ostrogoth king Vitiges to set out to even the score. More scuffles followed, until we find Belisarius trapped inside Rome preparing for what would become a yearlong siege. Among Vitiges's first acts was to cut off all fourteen aqueducts, including those feeding the gristmills on the Janiculum Hill.

This was dramatic, but not critical. Cisterns, wells, and the river could provide drinking water, and the warehouses were adequately stocked with grain. The mills, however, were a concern; for whatever reason, the Roman cattle and slaves that provided the bulk of grain grinding were not up to the job.

Belisarius came up with the solution. If stationary mills could take advantage of falling aqueduct water, there was no reason why floating mills could not do the same with flowing Tiber water. Soon, just below the Pons Aurelius (site of the later Ponte Sisto),

> he fastened ropes from the two banks of the river and stretched them as tight as he could, and then attached to them two boats side by side and two feet apart, where the flow of the water comes down from the arch of the bridge with the greatest force, and placing two mills on either boat, he hung between them the mechanism by which mills are customarily turned. And below these he fastened other boats, each attached to the one behind in order, and he set the water-wheels between them in the same manner for a great distance. So by the force of the flowing water, all the wheels, one after the other, were made to revolve independently, and thus they worked the mills with which they were connected and ground sufficient flour for the city.[27]

Vitiges countered by floating some Roman dead to foul the works, then floating logs to destroy the mills. Belisarius was neither intimidated nor flummoxed. He countered this with iron chains that shielded the mills from river flotsam, and the Goths were stymied. The Goths eventually left; the mills remained.

Belisarius would return twice to the Tiber and to Rome, each time facing the even more formidable Ostrogothic king Totila. Belisarius's aide and historian of the war Procopius outlines at some length the series of clashes over both river and city, with one side prevailing, then the other, besieged Romans reduced to eating nettles and rats (fish, oddly, are not mentioned, even though the river abounds in them). The stories are told at length in *The Gothic Wars*, and make for exciting reading.

Belisarius, like Stilicho, was not a political general and had been too successful too far away for too long. In the end he was replaced, and Justinian had him blinded and cast out, and he settled, if that's the word, at Rome's Pincian gate. There he sat, calling out to passersby, "Date obolum Belisario"—spare an obol for Belisarius—obols being the smallest coin then in circulation. The dramatic figure in his despair has inspired painters and poets from Matteo Renzi to Wordsworth, and stands as a sharp reminder of shabby treatment accorded war veterans by ungrateful masters.

Happily, the obol story and the blinding are largely doubted by modern scholars. Score one for the soldier.

And if Belisarius, and Vitiges, and Totila all drifted into memory, the legacy of the mills carried on for centuries. The Romans know a good thing when they see it. One of the mills is mentioned in a document from the year 1005 listing privileges granted to the church of Saints Cosmos and Damien.[28] Others feature in pictures from Renaissance woodcuts to nineteenth-century landscape paintings.

The basic plan involved two houseboats flanking a waterwheel and anchored to the shore by chain and pylon. The larger houseboat was closer to the bank and contained the gears and shafts and millstone. Both structures could reach three stories high, room enough for raw grain, finished flour, and the men who worked the operation, at least one servitor and assistants, and two *caricatori* who toted the sacks of raw material and end product.

The individual mills had names, chiefly taken from nearby landmarks or saints. The setup was not cheap—the cost of building, maintaining, and operating even one of machines was considerable, never mind the rent and never mind the guild's civic obligation (duly noted in the guild charter of 1496, but possibly in place earlier) to keep the riverbed clean.[29] Grain itself was regulated, generally belonging to the church and the rich families that owned inland estates in Umbria and Tuscany. Volume would have been considerable, and the millers kept busy. By 1800 there were about twenty mills on the river, serving a population of perhaps 150,000.[30]

They did so at their risk. Despite their size and the chains that bound them, these structures were on the river on sufferance. Bad floods could, and did, force the mills loose and smash them against bridges downstream, a considerable capital loss, and worse. Crescenzo Del Monte (1868–1935), a poet of Jewish Romanesco dialect, wrote of the 1846 flood and its effect on the mills:

. . . La mola? Fu una notte di teróre!
La fiumana 'a strappò in men d'un minuto
e bùuum . . . ! ì a sbàtte a ponte! àah! chi gelore!

E tre òmmeni che c'ereno serati
chi terore a sentilli: aiùuto . . . ! aiùuto . . . !
fintanto che non fureno salvati[31]

The mill? There was a horrible night
The floodwater cut it loose in under a minute
And bang! It ripped it from the bridge! Ah, what a scare!

And three men who were locked inside the thing—
What a horror to hear them: "Heeelp . . . ! Heeelp . . . !"
Until they were saved.

The following year there was a bureaucratic shake-up in the Presidenza dell'Annona. One of the new regulations forbade pack animals to shift raw or processed grain in favor of handcarts—fine for land-bound mills, less so for those on the river.

In 1871, the water mills were banned.

Procopius the Tourist

The Romans love their city above all the men we know, and are eager to protect all their ancestral legacy and preserve it, so that nothing of the ancient glory of Rome may be obliterated. Even though they lived long under barbarian sway, they preserved the buildings of the city and most of its adornments, those which could withstand so long a lapse of time and such neglect through the sheer excellence of their workmanship. Furthermore, all the memorials of the race that were still left are preserved even to this day.[32]

This day being AD 553, a century after the sacking by Gaiseric. Procopius was visiting from Constantinople as an aide to Belisarius himself. Their immediate task had been to recover Rome from barbarians and restore it to its rightful master, the Byzantine emperor Justinian. The city had been greatly worked over by invading outsiders, as we have seen, but even if the gold and bronze were largely missing, and the marble statuary perhaps not quite as plentiful as at the time of high empire, when it was said there were as many statues as living men, the city did still have a considerable heritage to draw on, both for the pilgrims—a staple of Rome's economy since the early days of Christendom—and for those whose curiosity was more secular. There were historical sites of interest—the cabin of Romulus and Remus, various museums and temples. Procopius, a native of Constantinople writing in the sixth century, who came to Rome on government business—actually, with Belisarius to win the city back for the empire, now headquartered in Constantinople—found the time to visit the various landmarks in town.

Some of the sites Procopius visited are the same that divert travelers today, including "the tomb of Hadrian, a wonder and remarkable work, built of large blocks of Parian marble, superposed and closely fitted together without cement or clamps to bind them."[33] We can imagine that he was being gulled by a local tourist guide. The marble was in fact clad to a superstructure of bricks and mortar. A minor point, and he goes on to the Parian marble statues of men and horse that cover the summit, useful as missiles when enemies come too close and proper weapons are not on hand, as Procopius elsewhere describes in discussing the attack in 537 by Vitiges and his Ostrogoths, in which both bronze and marble statues played their part in driving them off. In 1624, workmen pulled the so-called Barberini Faun, a life-size marble statue of a rather too relaxed faun, from the moat around the structure. The thing was badly damaged, having lost part of a leg, an arm, and head, which suggested to some art historians corroboration for Procopius's story. The faun in question appears to have been a one-off. It is now to be seen in the Glyptothek in Munich. (Also mentioned but now missing are the bronze statues at the Forum of Peace, including works by Phidias and Lysippus, "all the finest things of Greece [that have made] adornments of Rome."[34]

The most notable sight he mentions was an early boat, the very boat, in fact, that carried Aeneas from Troy to Rome over a thousand years before, and kept on display ever after in a purpose-built hangar where the curious, patriotic, and reverent could see it.

"The ship," Procopius writes, "is one of a single bank of oars and very long, being one hundred and twenty feet in length and twenty-five feet wide, and its height is all that it can be without becoming impossible to row. But there is nowhere in the boat any piecing together of timbers at all, nor are the timbers fastened together by any device of iron, but all the timbers are of one piece, a thing strange and unheard of and truly only, as far as we know, of the one boat. For the keel, which is a single piece, extends from the extreme stern to the bow, gradually sinking to the middle of the ship in a remarkable way and then rising against thence properly and in due order until it stands upright and rigid."[35]

He continues at some length on the construction of the vessel, showing a greater interest in its details than a more casual observer might take.

There is no (surviving) earlier record of the vessel, and a skeptic might think the artifact was cobbled together in later years to gull the rubes, but Procopius assures us that it is the real thing. He does just add, however, "none of these timbers has either rotted or given the least indication of being unsound, but the ship, intact throughout, just as if newly constructed by the hand of the builder, whoever he was, has preserved its strength in a marvelous way."[36] Occam's razor suggest that we dismiss the provenance and the antiquity of the boat, though it should be noted that modern museums shelter wooden boats of comparable age (if not provenance), with little pushback from visitors, or scholars.

Dragons

Where would they come from, one wonders. Dragons are generally associated with the sea, or craggier sorts of mountains, and yet they turn up in Tiber literature, if only during the river's more intemperate moments. Norman Douglas sees such creatures in the mountain streams of Southern Italy when "from placid waterways they are transformed into living monsters, Ægirs or dragons, that roll themselves seaward, out of their dark caverns, in tawny coils of destruction."[37] Not a bad description of a seriously angry river.

Gregory of Tours (538–594), writing about the flood of 589, tells us that it swept away pagan temples and monuments, proof to some Christians that their god was wiping out the old ways. Harsh proof, given that it also swept away private dwellings and inundated the city's warehouses, warehouses full of grain overseen by the church, a few thousand *modi* of of which were lost or spoiled in an instant, with nothing coming before spring.[38]

Gregory adds that the flood also carried down a dragon "as large as a tree trunk."[39] A considerable beast, then, a creature that the river and the city were well rid of, dragons being, after all, creatures of evil. Or, alternatively, the snake of Asclepius, abandoning (or being forced out of) the city it had served so well in pagan times.

Besides the usual devastation and illness mentioned elsewhere, and the dragon large as a tree trunk, there were an "innumerable multitude of serpents . . . that also rode the channel of the Tiber river, down into the sea."[40]

And then?

"The beasts choked on salty sea waves, then shortly afterwards washed up on the beach, and rendered the area putrid with their stink."[41]

Paul the Deacon (c. 720–799) repeats the story, neglecting the death by saltwater element, but adding the detail that water was so high it flowed over the very walls of the city itself (*super muros urbis influerent*).[42]

It is difficult to say which is the harder story to swallow.

This was not the first or the last dragon to be reported, either. Saint Crescentinus, a Christian convert in Rome fleeing persecution under Diocletian, traveled upriver to "Thifernum Tiberinum Città di Castello," where he killed a local dragon, which gave weight to his evangelizing. He was eventually beheaded. Pope Sylvester I, credited with baptizing Constantine the Great, is also said to have slain a dragon, in some traditions a Palatine-dwelling dragon, in others, a Tiberine-swimming dragon. In the year 1458, the people of Todi were troubled by a Tiber-side beast until the bishop of Todi, Bartolomeo Alaleoni, sent a squadron of soldiers to snag the beast.[43] He chained the creature for seven days for the benefit of the curious, then killed it outright.

Todi also suffered from the Regulus, either a cock with a serpent's tail or a winged dragon, depending on whom you ask. Whatever he looked like, his glance was fatal, or perhaps it was his breath. This one was killed by Saint George, or a clever and brave merchant, who emulated Perseus and confronted the beast with nothing more than a sword and a mirror.

Better attested to are the events of 1475–1476; twenty-eight days of rain flooded the Tiber, raising waters to such a degree that the pope was forced to the highest reaches of the Castel Sant'Angelo, and many who could, left town. It was a deluge beyond any in living memory. A Milanese envoy reports to his masters that those who did leave town missed the sight of a dragon. Fellow Milanese Giovanni Marchus elaborates, singling out four live serpents in particular, green like the others, and in size that of an arm, "groseza de la mittate duno bracho, verdi cum le ale." This according to a Milanese reporting in Roman dialect to a Venetian, which raises a question or two. *Verdi cum le ale*—if we read *cum* as *come*, then "green like the other [snakes]"? Green is unusual for Italian snakes. Or possibly the snakes had wings, *con ali*? Wings are suitable trappings for a dragon, and definitely worth writing home about. On the other hand, Marchus also admits that he did not actually see the creatures himself, but he has it on the authority of over a thousand who had. More scholarly folk recalled the 590 apparition and worried about the pestilence to follow.[44]

Dragon or no dragon, the floods were real enough, and worse than dragons was to follow. Bubonic plague, in the case of the 589 flood, hovering around Mediterranean ports for the previous five years, now began to spread across Rome and environs, taking Pope Pelagius himself. Coincidence, perhaps, the flood and the plague coming together, but for those seeking patterns and hoping to tease out divine temper, a very meaningful coincidence.[45] The scientifically minded Luis Gomez, writing in 1532 about the 1531 flood, put such phenomenon down to the snakes that, having been taken from their habitat, drowned at sea, washed back on shore, then putrefied; and between their corpses and the unsettled mud, pestilence follows.[46] Pelagius's successor as pope, Gregory the Great, would see the city through the worst of it and the final return of God's favor to Rome.

Dragons turn up occasionally in later literature. In November 1661, a hunter shot a dragon from the sky near Rome, described as young, about the size of a dog, and green, the remains of which are now lost.[47] Also lost are the remains of the dragon found in 1674 by Cornelius Meyer in the marshes near Rome (*nelle paludi fuori di Roma*).[48] Meyer was a Dutch engineer who came to Rome in that same year with a brief to improve navigation on the Tiber (he wrote *L'arte di restituire à Roma la tralasciata navigatione del suo Tevere*). Something of a polymath, he spent a good deal of time in unrelated areas, and in 1696 published *Nuovi ritrovamenti divisi in due parti* (New findings divided into two parts) for Rome's highly regarded Accademia Fisico-Matematica. Part one (there was no part two) features an etching of the winged dragon mentioned above, against a background of the river Tiber and possibly the Ponte Milvio. After thumbing through some striking pictures of eyeglasses and monocles, other chapters on raising sunken cannon, on breaking glass by sound waves, on Archimedes in his bath, and so forth, the reader will find another sketch purporting to be the now dead dragon and its mostly skeletal remains mounted for display. Exciting stuff, though the display has long since been lost.

Alas for romantics, biologists at Fayetteville State University of North Carolina argue that the skeleton is something of a bony hodgepodge—head of dog, ribs of fish, spine of beaver, limbs of bear—in short, not a dragon at all.[49] They have no specific answer for the wings, tail, beak, and horn, or who might have cobbled the thing together, or why.

Since then, reports of dragons are all but nonexistent.

Gregory the Great

Pope Gregory the Great arrived in Rome in 590—a bad time for the city. A flood had ruined the grain stores and left behind poisonous serpents, and his predecessor had died of plague. Clearly God was angry. (To be fair, a pagan might argue that the snakes were Asclepius abandoning the city for its lack of respect, and the plague to follow was proof that he had withdrawn his protection.) On the feast of Saint Mark, Gregory called on the citizens of Rome to join him in a penitential procession. He gave a long and impassioned speech to the crowd, then ordered a portrait of the Virgin (said to have been painted by Saint Luke himself) brought forth and carried through the city streets at the head of the parade. The faithful, all silent and shuffling, prayerful and hopeful, trailed behind the portrait and the pope, waiting to see what, if anything, would happen.

Their prayers were answered when the procession, and more important, the portrait, reached the Pons Aelius. A celestial voice rang out:

> Regina coeli laetare
> Quia quem meruisti portare
> Resurrexit sicut dixit
> Alleluia

> Rejoice o queen of heaven
> for one who is worthy to carry
> has risen as it was spoken
> Alleluia!

Gregory took up the cue: Ora pro nobis Deum—Pray for us to God—Alleluia! The crowd repeated the words. An angel then appeared in the sky, first brandishing a sword, then sheathing it. Eighty people in the procession had stumbled, fallen, and died, victims of the plague, but that was the end of it.[50] Rome was now free of the illness, and the picture was placed in the Aracoeli church, where it still remains. The bridge itself took on the name Ponte Sant'Angelo, by which it is still known.

The episode was a good start for Gregory, and he went on to be one of three popes dubbed Great, as well as earning a sainthood.

Saracens

Rome's population declined, but only a bit. All the factors that had nurtured Romulus and his followers—the river, the countryside, the climate—were there. Additionally there was a wealth of abandoned but perfectly functional buildings, as well as building material. Most important, there were still the churches of Saint Peter and Saint Paul and, for the hierarchically minded, the seat of the pontifex.

The rise of Christianity proved a declining Rome's saving grace, so to speak. As the final stop for both Saints Peter and Paul, the city had an attraction for pilgrims, regardless of its lost grandeur. There were plenty of churches, but none so sacred as Saint Peter's. Accordingly, it required a suitable decoration. Seventh- and eighth-century popes seemed to be in competition to see who could add the most silver and gold. The *Liber pontificales*, an early biography of Dark Age popes, goes into some detail:

> Honorius I (625–638) added silver to Peter's *confessio* (the area beneath the
> high altar and above his tomb, accessible from the back of the altar).[51]
> Sergius I (687–701) placed a silver ciborium at the back of the apse.[52]
> Gregory III (731–741) added six columns clad in silver.[53]
> Paul I (757–767) donated a silver gilt statue of the Mother of God of 150
> pounds.[54]

Hadrian I (772–795) went further. He installed a ciborium over the altar, weighing in at 134 pounds of silver, two silver doors and steps paved with 150 pounds of silver, and a number of silver vessels (*delphines*) at 180 pounds (among other such silver). Where there had been silver images of Jesus, the

Virgin Mary, Saints Peter and Paul and Andrew, Hadrian now installed new figures of pure gold at 200 pounds.[55]

Hadrian's successor Leo III (750–816), having crowned Charlemagne here in the year 800, went further still. He added statues of Jesus with Peter and Paul on either side, all with gem-studded crowns. The steps to the *confessiones* he paved with 453 pounds and six ounces of "excessively yellow gold," and he commissioned yet another apostolic statue of gold (19 pounds, 3 ounces), also studded with gemstones. To keep the common worshippers at a respectful distance, he installed a balustrade in front of the entire operation, itself made of silver.[56]

The lists go on, totaling up (assuming the source material is neither fanciful nor exaggerated) to a combined treasure in the two churches of three tons of gold and thirty of silver.[57] Even a fraction of that would mark a stunning amount of glitter. One would have liked to have seen it. Untold numbers of Christian pilgrims went to a great deal of effort to do just that.

Word of these marvels (and their location outside the city walls) was not, unfortunately, confined to respectful pilgrims. By the early ninth century, Muslim raiders had spread across Northern Africa to western Sicily. Palermo had fallen to Islam in 831 (all Sicily would follow by 901). Bari, just above the heel of the Italian boot, was raided and then taken in 841, and would become a Muslim emirate in 847. Southern Italy, old Magna Graecia, had come to a modus vivendi, often businesslike and at times even cordial, that their northern counterparts had not. Some southern Christians hired Muslim soldiers to fight intra-Christian wars (a practice that would play a role in the collapse of the Byzantine empire some centuries later). Muslim raiders working independently continued to expand their target range into central Italy. In 846 they reached the mouth of the Tiber.

Their intentions appear to have been strictly criminal, the kind of smash-and-grab action that pre-dates Islam, an example of the *ghazw*, the lightning raid against ill-defended targets and swift withdrawal with whatever the raiders could carry. Ships substituted for horse or camel, but the process was the same—find a target, moving or stationary, where the pickings were good and easy to pluck. Happily for the raiders, Rome's easiest and richest candidates for plunder were the old Saint Peter's Basilica and Saint Paul's, each thick with religious paraphernalia, each outside the protection of the walls.

Rome had been warned. Adelvertus, Count of Tuscany and Protector of Corsica, sent word on August 10, 846, that a large armada of Saracens was on its way to Rome. The figures he gives are eleven thousand men and five hundred horse on seventy-three ships (the numbers are probably inflated).[58] Men of power in the city gathered to consider their options. In the end they did little more than pass on Adelvertus's warning to the people of Rome and their outlying allies. They had probably received warnings like this before, and wait-and-see appears to have been the standard reaction.

The invaders—Hagarenes, *gens Aggarenorum*, sons of Hagar, or Saracens, *Saraceni*, sons of Sarah (both terms turn up)—landed near Ostia on Monday, August 23. Ostia itself should have been a tough nut to crack, between its high Roman walls (Emperor Aurelian) and moats and catapult towers (Pope Gregory IV, 827–844). Defensive works need manning, however, and the men of Ostia deserted the town rather than stay and fight. The invaders quickly sacked the place, then crossed the river to Portus. Portus having been emptied, they rested up for the main event.

By now Rome knew the raiders could not be wished away. City officials cobbled together a makeshift resistance, drafting foreigners—merchants, pilgrims, and students, but no soldiers—to head downriver and drive off the enemy. This improbable force made camp for the night not far from the invaders and was attacked the following morning. Christians fought back, and surprisingly, the invaders fell back, at least for the moment. Rome now sent real soldiers to join the their alien fodder; they stayed just long enough to see just how large the Saracen force really was, and rushed back to the safety of Rome, leaving the foreigners to deal with the matter as best they could.

Not well, once the Saracens now got down to business. The invaders routed the ad hoc combatants (whose appetite for a fight cannot have been great at this point) and made their way to Saint Peter's and Saint Paul's. The Romans countered by placing soldiers between the invaders and the Campus Neronis, presumably the Circus of Nero, outside the walls and between Saint Peter's and the Tiber. Prudence and self-preservation trumped honor.

At this point, the chroniclers begin to wander in their respective narratives. Did the two forces clash? Possibly. Even probably. Did the Saracens manage to loot Saint Peter's? Some say yes, others say nothing. One says that they left off looting Saint Peter's to loot Saint Paul's, but were stopped by a Campanian army. One account mentions slaughter of civilians, men and women.

All seem to agree that the raiding party did not reboard the boats (which were presumably busy carrying off booty to the home port) but remained in Italy, in part because the Mediterranean is not a body of water one wishes to cross in fall and winter months, in part because there were other targets of opportunity. They did not leave the country until April 847, having rendez-voused with their fleet at Gaeta.[59]

The whole affair was too much for Pope Sergius II, who died on January 27 of 847. His successor, Leo IV (847–855), spent the next four years in putting up a huge wall, imposing if not beautiful, and for the first time crossing the river and incorporating Castel Sant'Angelo. The idea had been floating about for at least fifty years.[60] Three kilometers of stone and brick some forty feet high, nineteen feet thick, strung along forty-one towers, open at three gates. Additionally, he had a chain placed across the mouth of the Tiber. The job's completion was celebrated with the pope leading an army of bareheaded and barefoot clerics dressed in sackcloth around the perimeter, casting holy water and beseeching celestial blessings for their city.

In 849, a fresh gathering of ships arrived at the mouth of the Tiber, this time a friendly coalition from Naples, Amalfi, and Gaeta, led by Cesario il Valoroso, Caesar the Brave, admiral of the Duchy of Naples. The Saracens, he said, were coming back for more. Would the pope like to bless the Neapolitan fleet before this happened? He would, and did.[61]

The benediction seems to have worked. The initial engagements were fierce but inconclusive; midway through the fighting, however, the skies went dark and the waves kicked up. Cesario had his ships return to the relative safety of the port. Muslim ships were forced to battle the waves, and proved largely unequal to the task. The vessels scattered, and many sank; a few survived long enough for the weather to grow calm, whereupon Cesario's men fell on them with a vengeance. For days afterward, flotsam and jetsam washed up on the shores, considerable pickings for the locals. The surviving Arabs were taken upriver and set to work on Leo's wall. The less fortunate were hanged near Portus, a grisly warning to anyone who would come back for more. To defend the river mouth, "a colony of Corsicans with their wives and children was planted in the station of Porto at the mouth of the Tiber; the falling city was restored for their use, the fields and vineyards were divided among the new settlers: their first efforts were assisted by a gift of horses and cattle; and the hardy exiles, who breathed revenge against the Saracens, swore to live and die under the standard of St. Peter."[62]

Pope Gregory IV (824–844) made a point of building strong walls, dig-ging moats, and equipping towers with catapults. Sycophants called this refurbished Ostia Gregoriopolis, a name that only more or less stuck over time.

The Muslim invasions did not end in 844, or even 846. Raids tended to focus on Southern Italy, but Latium was not immune from attack. Pope John X won a significant fight against them at Mount Circeo south of Rome, but on his own could do little more. Saracens had a stronghold south of there on the Garigliano River. In spite of John's initial victories, Muslim incursions continued, past Rome, to the upriver towns of Tivoli, Narni, Nepi, Orte.

The hope was conquest, and for a brief period it seemed possible. John X was forced to pay tribute. A Muslim emirate seemed all but inevitable. The tide turned, however, in 915 when John managed to build an alliance of Italian nobles with the express purpose of ridding Italy of the infidels. Pope John led men into battle at Garigliano, eliminating the greater part of "God's hated people."[63]

Muslims who had gotten a tenuous foothold on the Italian mainland were targeted, most notably in the little mountain town near Tivoli in the Aniene (Anio) valley where a group were cut off and surrounded. They were allowed to surrender and remain if they forswore Islam for Christianity. They agreed, and it is said their descendants are still there, gathered in a tiny mountain village called, suitably enough—Saracinesco.

This God-given victory rang loud enough in Roman history that seven hundred years later, Raphael was hired to commemorate the event on the walls of the Vatican's papal chambers.

Laban/Balan

Two hundred years on, a garbled version of these histories formed the basis of various French chansons de geste, largely involving Charlemagne and his circle of knights, the Twelve Peers, and most notably Roland and Oliver.[64] The story lines have a good deal of overlap, the earliest example being *La Destruction de Rome*, a prelude to more of the same, which features the Moorish antagonist Fierabras, and at times his sister Floripas, imposing children of Spanish sultan Balan (aka Laban).

The fifteen hundred alexandrine verses of the *Destruction* begin with Balan/Laban having lost ships to Christians, and deciding to sail to Italy with son Fierabras and daughter Floripas along with her fiancé, the warrior Lucifer, to sack Rome. There is some fighting near the mouth of the river, and in due course the Saracens reach the city.

The ships came up the Tiber, that fed the city's moat.
The platforms on their mast heads were raised, and as they rose
The Moors aboard were able, god curse their crafty souls,
To grapple hand to hand with defenders high and low.[65]

Traitors open the gates, holy sites are desecrated and relics stolen, and Charlemagne, arriving too late, calls on his colleagues the noble Roland and Oliver and Guy de Bourgogne to get the goods back. The two heroes enter Spain, and after much backing and forthing, they defeat and execute an unrepentant Balan while his children cast off Islam and embrace Christianity. Floripas falls in love with and marries Guy, who, together with Fierabras, rules Spain. All, with the exception of Balan, live happily ever after.

There are variations on the basic story. A French interpretation, *La chevalerie d'Ogier de Danemarche* (c. 1200) focuses on Oliver's stand-in, Ogier the Dane, one of whose exploits was to battle infidels on the banks of the Tiber (Toivre) and even on Tiber Island. In 1484 the English printer Caxton published *The Romaunce of the Sowdone of Babylone and of Ferumbras his Sone who conquered Rome*, in which Saracens conquer Rome, and two barrels of balm used on the body of the dead Christ are stolen by the infidels. Caxton's Oliver is shown drinking the stuff before tossing the remainder into the Tiber.

Further installments, assuming they ever existed, are now lost.

Formosus

Sad to say, the rise of Christendom did not see a corresponding decline in river violence. Even the papal tiara itself was no protection from outrage. In 892, Pope Formosus, a son of Ostia, took the papal throne after Stephen V. Stephen had made promises to Guy III of Spoleto. Specifically, in return for providing Rome protection against temporal threats, Guy would be named Holy Roman emperor, and his son Lambert his successor. Formosus agreed, but when Guy died, Formosus reached out to invite (the incidentally illegitimate) Arnulf of Carinthia to Rome to take the crown instead. An incensed Lambert declared war. Armies marched, cities fell, alliances were made, oaths abjured, principals were imprisoned, were released, died. In 897, Lambert finally made his comeback, seized Rome, and had friendly clerics put Formosus on trial in the Basilica of Saint John Lateran for perjury and violation of canon law.

The fix was in. The lawyer for the defense did not even bother to argue on his client's behalf. The verdict: guilty as charged, damned for eternity. All his canonical acts were nullified. The former pope was stripped of his papal robes, the three fingers of his right hand used to deliver benedictions were cut off. A cooperative mob then dragged him through the streets and into the Tiber. Formosus bore the mistreatment and humiliation well, as well he might—by the time his case reached trial and his appearance made in court, he had been dead for eight months.

The mutilated body washed up downriver and was found by the future Pope Theodore II. Faithful supporters of Formosus claimed that the body effected miracles—though not enough, it seems, to warrant sainthood or even beatification.

Lambert's cronies did not prosper. Soon after the trial, an earthquake brought down part of the basilica of Saint John Lateran. The Roman mob took this as a sign of God's displeasure and marched on the men responsible for the sham trial. Stephen VI (or VII), Formosus's puppet successor and point man in the so-called Cadaver Synod, was himself pulled from the papal chair and imprisoned in the Castel Sant'Angelo. A few months later, he was strangled.

His successor, Romanus, lasted only four months, to be replaced by Theodore II, who lasted only twenty days, to be replaced by Pope John IX (a native of Tivoli, bringing back the Tiber connection), who lasted two years, in which time he was able to bring some closure to these unfortunate events. Ordained by Formosus, he had that man's body exhumed from its pauper's grave and given proper burial. Liutprand writes that when the body was brought back to the church for burial, the stone images bowed in respect.[66]

Pornocracy

Pornocracy—literally, rule by whores—is an ungenerous label for the period between 904 and 964 when Rome was under the general control of the Theophylact family, most notably, the lady Marozia.

Marozia, born in 890, the daughter of Theodore Theophylact, Count of Tusculum, and Theodora, *senatrix* and *serenissima vestaratrix*, was on and off able to call the Castel Sant'Angelo home for the better part of four decades. That, and a family villa on the Aventine Hill overlooking the Tiber. She was arguably the most powerful woman of the tenth century, until it all went bad. Hers was a complicated family.

Her father was a shadowy figure, low key and competent, seemingly respectable. Her mother, at the very least her husband's equal in influence, was the subject of malign gossip. Their entrance on the stage begins with the accession of a cousin, Sergius III, to the papacy in 904, a feat accomplished with the help of Theodore, who had pull with the Holy Roman emperor. For this help, Theodore was named *sacri palatii vestararius*, essentially keeper of the papal treasure, in power second only to the pope.

Marozia was fifteen when the family moved to Rome. Good looking and intelligent, she was soon the focus of Sergius's attention, so much so (according to the hostile Liutprand) that she bore him a son, John.

It should have been a scandal, but shame is a rare commodity among the powerful. The *Liber pontificalis* is up front about the matter, referring to "John, by his father Pope Sergius."[67] Whether the relationship continued after the fact is unclear, but the family remained in power, passing on the appointment of sinecures to the benefit of their many family members and friends.

The unwed Marozia was still beguiling and available for new alliances. In 909, she partnered ("not as a wife, according to the evil custom of the time") with Alberic I, Duke of Spoleto, a wealthy man with a private army, and as such useful to the family.[68]

Theodora had been busy as well. Her husband had been less interesting to her than a young and good-looking priest from Ravenna. It wasn't terribly difficult to promote the priest, and after Sergius died, get him elected Pope John X, so that she, a shameless whore (*scortum impudens*), might have her lover close by.[69]

So far, so squalid, if true. John, in any event, proved to be an able pope, good for the city. In alliance with Alberic, he donned armor and rode south to the Muslim colonies that had begun to sprout up in recent decades and quashed them for good. All Rome rejoiced.

Alberic had further cause to celebrate—Marozia bore him a second son, Alberic II.

Years passed, Theodore died, as did Theodora, as did Alberic, leaving Pope John free of the Theophylact family and its influence. He placed his brother Peter in Theodore's old position and made an alliance with Hugh of Arles, king of Italy.

Marozia, a young widow and orphan with young children, could easily have settled down to a quiet life on her Aventine villa overlooking the Tiber.

She did not. A Roman since childhood (as John, Peter, and Hugh were not), she had maintained good relations with leading Roman clans, clans that did not like recent changes, least of all the appointment of the officious Peter. Dislike turned to open hostility, though as Rome's champion, Marozia lacked the means of imposing her will on the pope. This changed in 928 when she married Guy, Marquis of Tuscany, another man of wealth and power (and coincidentally Hugh's half brother). Together they brought a handful of soldiers to Rome, assassins really, and surprised both the pope and his brother at the Lateran palace. They killed the pope's brother and led the pope himself back to the Castel Sant'Angelo in chains. And then?

A contemporary chronicler, Flodoard of Reims, put the matter succinctly: "Pope John was deprived of his primacy by Marozia, a very powerful woman, and he was murdered while he was a captive. Some maintain that he was strangled."[70]

Liutprand, writing long after the fact, adds the detail of a cushion, "which they placed over his mouth by which they most wickedly suffocated him."[71]

Marozia now moved into the Castel Sant'Angelo, a sign of strength or weakness, depending on one's point of view. Her immediate problem was filling the now vacant papal throne. Even in those days of quick maturation, her sons were still a bit young, and so she arranged for tame, doddery stand-ins until her eldest came of age. His time came in 931. Guy was dead, as was the pope, and Marozia made certain that her son was settled in as John XI. The act raised eyebrows. On the accession of the supposed papal bastard to the throne, Benedict of Monte Soratte writes, "The power of Rome has been subjected by a woman's hand as we read in the Prophet, 'women dominate Jerusalem.' "[72]

Marozia did not stop there.

To consolidate her own position, she got in touch with her former enemy Hugh. It did neither of them any good to be unfriendly. Let bygones be bygones. Let them be married, and by her son the pope, who could designate the happy couple as emperor and empress of the west. He was already married? A shame. (Fortunately, the inconvenient wife died at a most opportune moment.) She was his half brother's widow, and therefore off limits under canon law? Not at all—his half brother, Hugh assured her, was in fact a bastard.

The wedding was a small affair, officiated by her son the pope, not in the cathedral of Rome, but rather with a small gathering of trusted friends and relatives in the comfort and safety of the Castel Sant'Angelo. The deal was sealed, the world their oyster.

Nothing is ever that easy. Marozia had reckoned without her second son, Alberic, legitimate in this case, and feeling understandably nervous about his place in this now very tangled family. Hugh didn't seem to like him very much, and it was common knowledge that the happy groom had blinded his own half brother Lambert of Tuscany. At the wedding banquet, Alberic was dutifully pouring water on the hands of his stepfather when, whether by accident or by intent, he spilled some. Hugo slapped him, which prompted the young man to leave the castle and go to the people of Rome, his people, to discuss the matter with them. He was his father's son, it should be remembered, a man who led armies to rid Italy of Saracen colonies. Liutprand gives Alberic a stirring speech: "The dignity of the Roman city is led to such depths of stupidity that it now obeys the command of a prostitute. For what is more lurid and what is more debased than the city of Rome should perish by the impurity of one woman, and the one-time slaves of the Romans, the Burgundians, I mean, should rule the Romans? If he hits my face, that is, the face of his stepson, and, what is more, when he is a recently arrived guest, what do you think he will do to you as soon as he has settled in?"[73]

He was persuasive, possibly helped by the fact that Hugh's arrival in Rome had coincided with what appeared to be a huge dragon, *draco immanissimus*, flying over the city of Rome for several hours before disappearing into the clouds, a bad omen in anyone's book.[74] The Roman mob, already irritated at the prospect of a foreign ruler and sympathetic to the native son Alberic, rose up and fell on the Castel Sant'Angelo, breaking into the private quarters, capturing both mother and pope, while Hugh managed to slither down the outer walls by a rope and flee. At a stroke, Alberic became ruler of Rome. Over the years Hugh made various attempts to retake the city; all failed. For the next twenty years, Alberic kept a heavy thumb on his brother, and when this pontiff finally died (in 936), Alberic appointed the next five popes, all obedient servants. Hugh gave up his Roman dreams, retired to Provence, and lived out his days in peace. Marozia? The record is silent. We may assume the worst.

Death comes to all men. When Alberic himself sensed his time was passing, he called the powers of Rome to his bedside and forced them to swear to have his bastard son Octavian made pope when the seat again opened. They so swore, and in due course, the teenaged Octavian became Pope John XII.

He was brave enough to lead armies, but not skilled enough to control the clans of Rome. Outside Rome, his chief opponent was Otto III, the Holy Roman emperor, whom he could never beat (and whose client Liutprand of Cremona is our main source for the Theophylact family history). It was, however, John's taste for women that did him in. In 964 he was caught in flagrante with a married woman, whose husband strangled him and tossed him out a window. Or possibly he suffered a heart attack while in the act.

And the tangled history of medieval Rome pressed on to further intrigues and outrages. The Theophylact decendants would take the name of Crescentii, and for a brief time gave their name to Hadrian's tomb (Castellum Crescentii) before the family exits history in the eleventh century.

Marozia herself, possible lover of one pope, mother of a second, grandmother of a third, all but ruler of Rome, is sometimes credited as being the source for the legend of Pope Joan.

But that is another story.

INTERLUDE

———

Tributary—Nera

Il Tevere non sarebbe il Tevere
Si la Nera non gli desse da bevere

The Tiber would not be the Tiber
If the Nera did not offer him drink.

Alternatively,

Tevere non cresce
Se la Nera non mesce

The Tiber doesn't rise
If the Nera doesn't pour

What sort of water, exactly? White and sulfurous, if Ennius and Virgil are to be believed.[1] The grammarian Servius (AD 363–438) wrote that *nar* was Sabine for sulfur, of which he claimed the river stank.[2] Not so these days.

Nera, or the Nar. The fifteenth-century geographer Biondo Flavio claims that the name originates from the twin springs that make up its source and which (he writes) resemble the nostrils (Latin *nares*) of some large animal.[3] Certainly the river is as wild as some large animals, its first ten miles of life full of gorges engorged with white water.

Water brings out the litigiousness in people, usually over parties upstream hogging from those downstream. In the case of the Nera, the complaints were reversed.

The problems date back two millennia and were over there being too much water. Consider the Nera's chief tributary, the Velino River, the chief source of water for the Rieti plateau.

In early Roman times, the plateau was all but cut off from the rest of Italy, a world of its own. Velino water created ponds and lakes and marshland, but did not drain. Agriculture was difficult, mosquitoes thrived, malaria was widespread.

Enter, in 290 BC, Marius Curius Dentatus, tribune of the plebs, three-time consul and holder of other high offices, including that of general. Pliny claims he got his surname ("Toothy") because he was born with a full set of teeth. He is credited with ending the fifty-year war with the Samnites, as well as expelling King Pyrrhus of Epirus from Italy. Dentatus was so high-minded that when Samnite envoys ventured to bribe him, he answered that he preferred ruling over the possessors of gold rather than possessing gold himself. (They found him roasting a turnip over an open fire, which should have been a clue.)

Then as now, the military was a repository of good engineers, and Dentatus, his enemies vanquished, began looking for suitable peacetime work. The waters of Rieti seemed a good candidate. With or without the approval of the gods or local deities, much less the senate, he ordered a channel cut by which the excess water of Lake Velino cascaded over what would become the Cascata delle Marmore, the largest man-made waterfall in Europe, down into the Nera River some 165 meters below.[4]

The results were spectacular. Several hundred acres of land rose above the receding water; mosquitoes died, malaria disappeared, and the newly exposed soil, the product of centuries of decayed organic matter, was so fertile that, people said, grass cut back on one day would grow back to the same height by the next.[5] Virgil called the area the *Rosea rura Velini*, "rosy country of Velino."[6] Varro referred to it as *Rose campestri*.[7] Pliny noted its abundance of grain and livestock and called it the udder of Italy.[8] A lake remained, but smaller, and healthier.

There was, of course, a downside, downstream, at the small town of Terni, home to the Interamnates, the "people between rivers," who were now overwhelmed by the water that once troubled the Reatians. They brought their complaints to Rome. Finding no satisfaction, they eventually took matters into their own hands and attempted to plug the gap, which upset the people of the plateau. The matter went to law, as Cicero reports to his brother: "The Reatians asked me to come to their area in order that I might argue their cause among the consul and the ten legates, against the Interamnates concerning the Lake Velino which Marcus Curius created."[9] Unfortunately, the record is silent on how this played out, or even if it played out at all.

Nature eventually did what the law would not. The locals failed to maintain the area, the cut was clogged, and much of the plateau reverted to its early swampy nature. There exist various references from the tenth to thirteenth century of flooding and to the existence of navigable lakes on the plateau.[10] With the Renaissance, several attempts were made to balance the competing interests; two new cuts were made, neither of them overly successful.

The cuts were not entire failures, however, and by 1775 were even something of a tourist attraction. Smollett had qualified praise: "The great part of its effect is lost, for want of a proper point of view, from which it might be contemplated. The cascade would appear much more astonishing, were it not in some measure eclipsed by the superior height of the neighboring mountains."[11] Smollett was ever the spoilsport, though in fairness he had shown up twelve years too early. It was not until 1787 that Pius VI got Andrea Vici to carve the area below the falls into a fashion that resolved the matter to everyone's satisfaction.[12] Byron saw the finished product and thought it superior to all other European waterfalls, with the possible exception of Schaffhausen, of which "I cannot speak, not yet having seen it."[13]

The falls are a part-time proposition these days. Mussolini redirected excess lake water so as to power electric turbines; the lake, long, narrow, and relatively wind-free, is the training ground for Italy's national sculling team. For the tourists, sluices divert water over the falls for only two hours a day, longer on holidays. The effect is quite dramatic. Smollett would have approved.

DARKNESS AND LIGHT

In which Martin Luther bristles at a statue of a woman,

a populist champion rises and falls, questionable prophecies are made,

a tomb becomes fortress, Pontius Pilate becomes a saint, yet more mysterious

creatures wash up on the riverbanks, a scholar lays down the law,

and a pope takes a pleasure cruise down the river.

Pope Joan

Martin Luther, after one of his trips to Rome gathering up more anticlerical material, wrote: "In a public square there is a stone monument to that female pope, and who gave birth to a child on that spot. I have seen this stone myself and I wonder that the pope allows it to stand."[1]

Pope Joan—or possibly Agnes, or possibly Gilberta—is said to have been pope from 853 to 855, or perhaps later. Or perhaps never. The first written mention of a female pope is found in 1250 as part the *Chronica universalis Metensis*, Chronicle of Metz, by Jean de Mailly. It's a short account, with no name provided, and the author places this Jane Doe in the year 1099. De Mailly ends the story with the pope giving birth while out riding. An outraged crowd then binds her feet and has a horse drag her for half a league while they stone her to death. They bury her where she died and erect the epitaph "Petre, Pater Patrum, Papisse Prodito Partum" (O Peter, father of fathers, betray the childbearing of the woman pope).[2]

Even by medieval standards the story is bizarre, and he gives no source, which inevitably raises the question, where had de Mailly heard about it?

Impossible to say. But consider that epitaph—it's a little strained, but it is also extremely alliterative, and as such calls to mind the tongue twister by the Roman poet Ennius, *O Tite tute Tati tibi tanta tyranne tulisti!* (You tyrant, Titus Tatius; such things you made happen!). Possibly de Mailly was delivering the punchline of a learned joke, a joke that the earnest author perhaps did not understand was a joke and took at face value. Or perhaps he made up the joke himself, along with the rest of the story.

The 1099 date is late enough that it could be checked and disproved even at the time of de Mailly's writing. (The official records say that Urban II and Paschal II were popes that year.) A genuine fraudster would presumably choose a pope from an earlier age, when the records become scantier. The ninth century, then, is where Martin of Troppau (aka Martinus Polonus), the author of the *Chronicon pontificum et imperatum*, writing in 1265, slips the prelate John Anglicus, born in Mainz, into the papal lists, John being a precocious girl schooled in the liberal arts and disguised as a man, who was unanimously elected to the papal seat and served for two and half years, until going into labor while on a procession between Saint John Lateran and Saint Peter's. Martin's acount is relatively bland. Nothing about a savage death, much less a statue or an enigmatic inscription. The place of death is noted, and said to be avoided, and John does not appear on official rolls because of her sex and the dubious nature of the whole affair (*ad hoc deformitatem*).[3] Later versions with various embellishments stem from these accounts. Despite her deep learning and ability, John succumbed to feminine weakness (*fragilitate feminea devicta*) and was impregnated by a onetime *dyacono secretario*.[4] The street was ever after call Vicus Papisse, while John took on nun's clothing and lived out her life in penitence. No aspect of the narrative has any evidence.

And yet the story was too good to disappear. Bartolomeo Platina, librarian for the Vatican Library (also the author of a cookbook), felt obligated to wedge "John VIII" into his *Lives of the Popes* (1479)—not, he assures his readers, because he believes it, but to avoid charges of obstinacy, and for the sake of completeness ("I had better mistake with the rest of the world"). Then there was also the off chance that the stories just might be true.[5]

True or not true, the stories were rich fodder for the more militant of the anticlericals, and not just Martin Luther. Jan Hus, mocking the Catholic Church, cited her (he used the name Agnes) at the Council of Constance (1414–1415), and none of the Catholic priests objected.

Then there was the question of the statue. Adam of Usk refers in 1404 to a stone carving of the lady pope and her son near Saint Clemente. Pope Innocent I had to ride past the pair to reach Saint John Lateran, but turned aside "out of abhorrence of Pope Agnes."[6] Presumably this is the same statue Martin Luther objected to.

There is nothing that matches the description in the area anymore; there are, however, noted various stories of various popes, Pius V (1566–1572), or Sixtus VI, or Clement VII, ordering it removed and thrown into the Tiber, and we may assume that one of them actually did so.[7] Elias Hasenmüller, a Jesuit turned Lutheran, can only claim, circa 1595, to have seen the place and pedestal on which the statue of Agnes/Joan used to stand—not nearly as compelling a story as Luther's.[8]

Rounding out the Tiber angle, an anonymous secondary hand amends the Martinus Polonus text and claims that Joan/John and the baby themselves survived the birth and the outraged mob, she to be shunted off to a nunnery and penance, the baby eventually to become bishop of Ostia.[9] There are many stories surrounding Pope Joan, endlessly fascinating to enthusiasts.[10]

Finally, that inscription—long gone, but there is reason to believe that de Mailly might have gotten it at least half right. Perhaps not all the words were spelled out. It might possibly it have been, as later writers suggest, "Pater Patrum PPP." Pater Patrum would be recognized in imperial Rome as a title of rank, specifically, that of a high priest of Mithras, something to be proud of, something to put on one's tombstone. And PPP? The three letters turn up on any number of ancient monuments, shorthand for *propria pecunia posuit*, "put up at his own expense." It was a good story while it lasted.

Copper Bottom

The Book of Luke informs us that early on in his reign, Caesar Augustus decreed that all the world should be taxed. Accordingly, shiploads of widows' mites from Judaea and bronze sestertii from Gaul and beyond were shipped off to Rome for the glory of the empire. And then? One tradition held that all this bronze was melted down, rolled into sheets, and used to line the bed of the Tiber.

The story originates in Persia and Iraq, both great centers of medieval Islamic learning. The Persian cartographer Ibn Khordadbeh (c. AD 820–912) describes a canal covered with copper plates, which suggests something not quite so large as a river. An aqueduct, perhaps. (Della Vida moots the Cloaca

Maxima, considered Rome's proud achievement.)[11] There is a snag— Khordadbeh calls the city Roum, capital of the empire. By his time, the empire had split, each half with its own political center; "Roum" can mean either Rome or Constantinople. Khordadbeh further describes the city as "washed by the sea on the Levant, the place was called the Canal of Constantinople."[12] So far as we know, Khordadbeh never actually visited either city.

One of his coevals, the Iraqi historian and geographer Harun ibn Yahya of Basra, did visit Constantinople, as a prisoner of war. He was able to wander the city and gives a lengthy description of the place, but has nothing to say about the copper canal. In 866, however, he traveled to the Italian Rome, the first Arab writer to do so. There, he reports, "the bed of the river is paved with copper; its two banks are also of copper and they have built copper bridges across it."[13] Encouraging, but not something found in any Western accounts.

Histories, when unexamined, can take root and grow, often mangled and improved in the retelling. Heading west, we find that of Abu Abd Allah Muhammad al-Idrisi al-Qurtubi al-Hasani al-Sabti (or simply Al-Idrisi, 1100–1165). This man, a Muslim born in Ceuta, was for eighteen years the court cartographer for the Arabo-phile Norman king Roger II of Sicily. Al-Idrisi compiled a considerable body of geographic knowledge from traveling merchants and pilgrims. He also made maps, most notably a disc, two meters in diameter, of solid silver. Concerning the Italian Rome, he repeats Ibn Khordadbeh's talk of a canal covered with copper plate some forty-six cubits long. He adds, however, that there is "a river the bottom of which is paved in copper plate, so that no ship can drop anchor." He also claims that the paving accounts for the modern calendar, "as [the Romans] say, 'from the day of the copper.'"[14]

The story is repeated in an Arabic translation of *Seven Books of History against the Pagans* by Christian writer Paulus Orosius (375–418). The translation includes a number of dubious insertions, including a claim that "in the fourth year of his reign, [Augustus] imposed upon the inhabitants of the world through the provinces a tribute in bronze, which ought to be supplied at any price, so that its price went up above the price of gold. Having collected a vast amount of it, thick planks and plugs were struck out of it, and he paved with them the river of Rome and its banks for a length of forty miles and an impressive width."[15]

From Muslim scholars and fantasists, we turn to Hebrew scholars. Spanish astronomer, historian, and philosopher Abraham ibn Daud (1110–1180) essentially repeats the story of Augustus taxing the world for copper to line the river with.[16] Moving on to Joseph ben Gorion's (tenth century?) *Sefer Yosippon*, we read that the Romans got the Tiber "to flow into other channels, and made a bottom to the river from one gate (of Rome) to the other, from its entrance to its exit, a distance of eighteen miles, all of which covered with brass, from the gate of Rome where it flows into the sea until the gate where it takes its source, a distance of eighteen miles, for three-fourths of the people were on one side of the river and one-fourth on the other side. The river flowed in the midst of the city, and the inhabitants of Rome paved its bed."[17] Rome, according to the author, feared ships from the emperor of Babylon.

The *abate* Bonino in 1660 cites an (alas!) unnamed and undated Hebrew scholar who claims that it was not only Augustus but other emperors as well who gathered the metal from abroad and so paved the riverbed. The task, it is said, was beyond mortal man and therefore could only have been the "work of demons"—"*che fu opra de' Demoni.*"[18]

As to the European Christian tradition: Pseudo-Isidore, author of a Christian history in ninth-century France, makes no mention of demons, but does repeat the story of Augustus's taking bronze as tribute and melting it, "making plates out of it, and flattened firmly the valley of the Tiber, twenty miles up the river and twenty miles down"[19] Spanish Christians living under Muslim rule repeat the story. Juan Ruiz, archpriest of Hita, in his 1335 *Libro de buen amor* credits the poet Virgil with meddling with the Tiber:

> The bed and channel he transformed where Tiber's waters flow
> Into a solid sheet of copper with an amber glow
> (E'en so lust's necromancy turns a maiden chaste as snow
> Into a brazen huzzy whom the lewd and unchaste know)[20]

By the fifteenth century, the story was wearing a little thin. Spanish traveler Pero Tafur (c. 1410–c. 1484) doesn't rule the truth of it out entirely, but does show a hint of skepticism: "Through the middle of the city runs a river, which the Romans brought there with great labour and set in their midst, and this is the Tiber. They made a new bed for the river, *so it is said*, of lead [*dizenque de plomo*], and channels at one and the other end of the city for its entrances and exits, both for watering horses and for other services convenient to the people, and anyone entering it at any other spot would be drowned."[21]

Which sounds like a confusion between a river and an aqueduct.

The story's last gasp appears to have been in the seventeenth century, when the Algerian scholar Al-Maqqeri (1578–1632), citing earlier authorities, writes: "Some, as Ibn Hayyan, Ar-razi, Al-hijalri, say that [Cordoba] was built by Octavius, the second Caesar of Rome, who conquered the whole earth, and he lined with copper [*sufr*] the bed of the Tiber; the same emperor from whom the Roman Aera, which began thirty-eight years before the Messiah, is computed."[22]

And with that, the story is quietly forgotten, a fantasy on the same lines as the copper city in *One Thousand and One Nights*, of interest chiefly to scholars of folklore, philology, and misguided history.

And yet—in 1590 diggers in Ostia found a "long canal or conduit of lead, with a certain gold medal of Honorius and Arcadius," the sons of Theodosius who failed so miserably in protecting Rome from Alaric in 410.[23] Sloppy archaeology—they do not record where it began or ended.

(Bronze seems to fascinate people. Harun Ibn Yahya of Basra, a visitor to Rome [c. 880–890], noted that the city was surrounded by gardens and olive groves.[24] He also described a bronze metal bird atop Saint Peter's, which, when the wind was right, whistled. More than a novelty item, the whistle in olive season attracted flocks of thrush, each bird carrying three olives, one by mouth, two by claw, which they dropped and which the clerical staff then gathered. The berries provided enough oil to light the church lamps for the coming year.[25] Wonders abound in Ibn Yahya's world.)

Prophecy of Malachy

Saint Malachy of Armagh (1094–1148), ordained in 1119, was a zealous promoter of the faith in an Ireland that had enjoyed a period of some religious laxity. A caretaker of the poor and needy, a scholar and proselytizer, a planter of apple trees, he was a man generally agreed to merit sainthood. He is most famous, however, for the *Prophetia Sancti Malachiae Archiepiscopi, de summis pontificibus.*

In 1139, Malachy was called from his native Ireland to Rome on church business. During his stay, he had visions, concerning which he wrote down 112 lines of Latin so explosive that they were deposited in the Vatican's secret archives and condemned to gather dust for the next 448 years.

The forgotten work is first mentioned in a letter dated June 1587 addressed to Cardinal Giovanni Girolamo Albani (1509–1591), one of several letters from a sycophant with a bent toward the supernatural and a desire that Albani become the pope. The author found encouraging signs for this ambition, referring to not one, but two works of prophecy, "not modern, but ancient; the first by Malachy, which concerns over 200 popes and mentions *De Rore Coeli*, which miraculously applies to us."[26]

Miraculously, and too clever by half. The logic is as follows: *de rore coeli*, "from the dew of the skies"; dew is a phenomenon of the dawn, dawn in both Latin and Italian being *alba*; Albani is the name of our would-be pope. QED.

Too clever, but in keeping with the sort of wordplay that could be construed from the rest of the Malachy document, which enters a second phase in 1595. In that year, a Benedictine cleric named Arnold de Wyon published *Lignum vitae*—The tree of life—his history of the Benedictine order. The audience would normally be narrow and scholarly, the work itself largely forgotten, except for his inclusion, on pages 307–311, of what purports to be Malachy's document. The document itself contained 112 short lines of Latin that would, if interpreted correctly, provide a capsule description of each of the 112 (not, it should be noted, "more than 200") popes since Pope Celestine II (1143) to his present day and into the future. The initial parts of the list involve the same sort of wordplay that connected Albani to the morning dew—references to names, place of origin, family crest, that sort of thing.

The project began credibly enough. Celestine II (1143–1144, just in time for Malachy's visit) aligns with *ex castro Tiberis*, from a castle on the Tiber; Celestine was born in Città di Castello, on the banks of the Tiber.[27] Similarly, Benedict XII, onetime abbot of Fontfroide, Cold Spring, slots in nicely as Frigigus Abbas. Pius III, a member of the Piccolomini family, is indeed *de parvo homine*, from a small man (Italian *piccolo uomo*).

Fitting fact to prophecy retrospectively makes for easy enough joinery, but once the list goes into the then unknown future, interpretation becomes somewhat like reading meaning in the prophecies of Nostradamus (who some claim is the true author of the *Vitae*, but who used Wyon as a front to ensure the work's credibility). More to the point, was there any point to it all?

Albani (who would die anyway in 1591) never got the tiara, and the lines *de rore coeli* corresponds with Urban VII (1521–1590), elected in September of 1590, a man chiefly noted for good works, banning the use of tobacco in any form, and for dying (malaria again) after a record thirteen days on the throne. Wyon, uninterested in the now-dead cardinal but for some reason obliged to keep his list credible, writes that Urban had been archbishop of Rossano in Calabria, where some of Italy's finest manna was collected.[28] Manna being, according the *British Pharmacopoeia* (1867) "a concrete saccharine exudation from the stem of the Fraxinus Ornu [manna ash]: and Fraxinus rotundifolia DC, which trees are cultivated for the purpose of yielding it chiefly in Calabria and Sicily."[29] In Wyon's day, and even to Victorian times, it was considered useful as a laxative and tonic, favored for children and pregnant women. Given the intended audience, however, the author presumably hoped that the Book of Numbers would come to mind—11.9 describes manna dropping "when the dew fell. . . in the night."

The papal throne was again open, and politicking had begun again. Pierre le Lorrain de Vallemont, a seventeenth-century French Jesuit, posits a theory that Wyon hoped to boost the chances of his friend Cardinal Girolamo Simoncelli (1522–1605), and to do so came up with the line *ab antiquitate urbis*, from the ancient town.[30] Simoncelli was a native of Orvieto, the Latin for which is Urbs Vetus. Old Town. The conclave might be forgiven for missing the link between Albani and morning dew, but the meanest intelligence could hardly fail to take the hint this time.

It's an ingenious theory, and may even be true. By the very nature of politicking, there is no known record of who promised what to whom in exchange for votes; and given the savvy nature of the Renaissance cardinals, it is difficult to believe that many would be persuaded by something as ephemeral and unremunerative as an ancient piece of paper of uncertain provenance and questionable interpretation. In the event, the tiara went to Gregory XIV. When Wyon finally published his book four years later, perhaps disappointed that his man failed to win, he didn't even bother to come up with a reason why Gregory should have been elected. (Why he bothered to include the list in the end product is another mystery—or not, if one rejects the theory that it was all about politics.)

Malachy's original document appears to have disappeared, and the church itself dismissed the list as arrant nonsense years ago. Still, official contempt has not prevented some men of ambition from taking it into consideration when planning their careers. Malachy's predictions were allegedly on Cardinal Spellman's mind just before the conclave of 1958. The upcoming pope, the text insisted, would be *pastor et nauta*, "shepherd and mariner." Not a common combination, but if those were the requirements, they could be met fairly easily. Cardinal Spellman was, they say, to be seen sailing up and down the Tiber on a rented boat filled with (presumably rented) sheep.[31] The effort was in vain; the conclave chose Angelo Roncalli (John XXIII), born to a family of sharecroppers (perhaps caring for sheep?), and later patriarch of Venice, the city that annually renews its vows to the sea with a golden ring.[32]

The last pope, according to the list, is to be known as Petrus, Peter, Pietro and will oversee the destruction of Rome itself. By Wyon's reckoning, Pope Benedict XVI (*Gloria olivae*—Glory of the Olives, referring perhaps to his role as a conciliator and peacemaker) was either the last pope, or the next to last, depending on how the final paragraph is read. As of this writing, we have pope Francis, not Peter. On the other hand, Francis took his name from Francis of Assisi, whose full name was Francis di Pietro di Bernardone.

Nero—Nuts and Dams

In 1099, an evil spirit was troubling the area near the gates of today's Piazza del Popolo. Locals prayed for help, and soon the Madonna appeared to Pope Paschal II in a dream. The problem, she said, was that the body of the emperor Nero was buried in a tomb nearby, underneath a walnut tree that had grown out of the wicked man's heart. The spirit would remain so long as the plant was alive, and walnut can live a long time. She suggested taking an ax to the tree and a hammer to the tomb. The following day, Paschal led a procession of cardinals and civilians to the site and set to this unlikely work. The chips began to fly, the tree was felled in short order, and the tomb was revealed. Inside, Nero's bones were still present. The pope gathered these and threw them into the river, following up this act with a general exorcism of the grave site. The project completed, all present applauded. Peace had been restored.

In later days, the church of Saint Mary was built, final triumph of Christendom over paganism.[33] Would that all earthly problems could be solved so easily.

It is not the only instance of anti-pagan arboricide on record. Lombards in the city of Benevento, far down the coast, were known for out-and-out tree worship. Their custom was to gather around a certain walnut tree, place an animal skin on its branches, then turn and walk away in an ever widening circle. At a given moment, all turned and rushed the tree, striking the skin.

Barbatus, a local Christian, found the practice hateful and in the year 663 took an ax to a tree, bringing down the trunk, then tore up the root and piled dirt on the remains.[34]

A bold gesture, given the nature of the locals, but instead of treating him as he had the tree, all turned Christian and elected him bishop of Benevento. One version has it that taking down the offending tree was a test, that Constans II was outside the city ready to attack, but that once the tree had come down, he left, proof enough for the Lombards that Barbatus's god was stronger than theirs.

Gentler spirits were found back at the Tiber, upriver. Saint Francis of Assisi, preacher to birds and flowers and sheep and wolves, could see the Tiber from his hometown. There is a tradition that he came to the water's edge near Pantenello and preached the good word to the fish. More to the point, they stopped to listen.

Another riverside cleric was Saint Benedict, who began his religious life as recluse in a cliffside cave near Subiaco. For three years, food was lowered to him by basket, after which time he emerged and founded the monastery and order, both of which still stand. It's rugged country, high, narrow valleys and steep mountainsides, but visually striking, a good place to exercise the soul. The monastery hosts a fresco of Benedict sitting by one of Nero's three ancient dams with a fishing pole in his hand, which stands to reason. Benedict forbade the eating of meat from four-footed animals; chicken and fish were acceptable.

The dams. Dams are not thick on the Tiber, nor were they then, in part because of religious scruple. By the time Nero became emperor, respect for the river seems to have waned considerably. While it was acceptable for a pagan Roman to swim in the full flush of the Tiber, it was quite another to take a dip in the upriver springs. Nero's doing so was a scandal at the time, and the cause, it was said, of his serious (if only temporary) illness. More egregious than his swimming was his constructing a series of three dams in the gorge near his riverside villa in Subiaco, creating three lakes and a magnificent view.[35] The pious were shocked, concerned that this was an insult to the river spirits. It came as no surprise to the good pagans that he should come to a bad end four years later.

Insulting to Father Tiber the dams may have been, but the gods seem to have gotten over it. Trajan tapped into the resulting lake as a source for the Aqua Novus.

Unlike much of the rest of Roman building, the dams proved remarkably durable. They survived intact and fully functional well into the 1300s and would have survived longer still had not a pair of monks, concerned that an autumn overflow was flooding their fields, tried to lower the water level a bit by adding a spillway. This was no easy task, nor one to be undertaken lightly, but they were men of God, and the whole thing looked simple enough.

You can just see them trundling along the rim of the stonework, hammers and chisels in hand, water on one side, air on the other, taking care to maintain their balance as they discuss which is the best spot to correct the ancient builders' mistakes, and then kneeling down, arranging their tools, and setting about unloosening the first stone. Brimming with the confidence of the amateur, but unschooled in the intricacies of dam construction, and unaware just how interdependent each block was to the next and to the whole, or just how much potential energy there is in thousands upon thousands of gallons of standing water, they played on.

Eventually they managed to pull out the first block. The water began to flow, slowly at first, and no doubt to their satisfaction. Then a little faster, probably to their unease. Then increasing pressure began to unseat another block or two, almost certainly to their alarm. Then more blocks, in rapid succession.

There followed total, sudden, utter collapse. A contemporary gives the following account:

> That spreading flood destroyed not only the opposing buildings near at hand, but also bridges, despite their strong piles, at that time were struck and cast down; indeed, the water even tore up the foundation of the Pantanellus bridge. The same force tore the exceptional mill house at Mandra down to its very foundation. Then the lake fell through the Varcus fields of the Subiaco plain with a horrid crash, and its coursing seized the peasants busy in the fields, as this sudden disaster did not afford to these oppressed wretches either higher places of greater safety, [or] time to avoid the increasingly violent currents: And so as the water widely occupied the field, men and beasts and cattle without distinction perished miserably. By that horrendous flooding of the Anio valley it spread across tracts of many miles, destroying villages, crops, orchards, and herds.[36]

You can still find the dams' remains on the valley floor, much picked over by later scavengers who were not going to let perfectly good building stone go to waste. Whether the two monks survived the catastrophe, the chronicle does not say.[37]

Dante at Ostia

By the year 1000, the old port at the mouth of the Tiber had degenerated into a poolside settlement with no ocean connection and only a ditch to connect it to the river. It was not a place one went to without a very good reason.

Even so, as early as 1100, when it was not much more than a commune, with a population of perhaps three hundred people (down from perhaps eighty thousand at Rome's height), Ostia qualified as a bishopric.[38] The region by then had little enough to offer, other than fish, salt, and the lumber that still could be had in the surrounding area, two bargeloads of which the pope expected every year. Malaria had returned.

It was to this Ostia that Dante (1265–1321) and his guide Virgil emerged from their tour of Hell. He described Ostia and the river's end as a place of mixed quality, "Dove l'acqua di Tevere s'insala" (where the Tiber water grows salty)—bad, but not quite so bad as the regions they had just escaped. From here the dead lined up to board the vessels that would carry them across the Mediterranean into the Atlantic and ultimately to the base of Mount Purgatory.[39] The question arises, why Ostia? The downsides of the area in Dante's time were evident enough—all pine barrens, reeds, grass, poverty, malaria. One can see how the Florentine (and anyone else, for that matter) would consider the place less than paradisiacal.

There is another way of looking at it. Ostia is a place of transition and shifting qualities, its brackish lagoons half fresh, half salt, not quite river, not yet sea, its ancient buildings half standing, half ruin; by the shore even its flat horizon half earth, half sky. The entire area is a reflection of purgatory, a halfway mark for the half saved.

Amid all the melancholy of the area, whom should Dante meet but his old friend Casella, the man who put his words to music, a singer of songs, not a bit put out by the dismal nature of the place, but rather pleased, given the lesser option, and very pleased indeed at the prospect of his eventual journey to heaven itself. One can see his point.

About 130 years later, Ostia was seen as a kind of memento mori, a warning to any upbeat Renaissance men not to get too cocky. Biondo Flavio (1392–1463) could describe "something that should make every person of good sense wary of trusting too much in human capacities—that lavish expense and considerable effort on the part of emperors (very powerful emperors, too) were not enough to keep the structures of the city of Ostia, the city and port of Anzio, or the harbor of Rome intact for as much as a thousand years; but as in the days of old, Ostia still remains without a harbor after 500 years."[40] The less sentimental Renaissance humanist and antiquarian Poggio Bracciolini (1380–1459) visited the ruins with his patron Cosimo de' Medici in search of antiquities, of which there were many. Acting fast was advised—"As Cosimo and I arrived to see the port, we found no plaques, since the temple was being demolished by the lime burners."[41] All the place lacked was its Ozymandias.

Cola di Rienzo

In 1303, French pope Clement V, wearied of the difficulties of life in Rome, packed up the necessities of the church administration and moved his base of operations to Avignon, France, where he and his entourage were less likely to be killed, and where the papacy would remain for the next seventy-two years.

The effect on Rome was the same as the removal of any large employer from any major city. Rome, like Washington, was a town that produced nothing but depended on the work and goods of people living far away. The church, recipient of tithes from across Christendom, had been the chief moneymaker for the city. Once it had gone, the money and the talent soon followed, and the people left behind watched as their city went into steep decline.

Law and order broke down, social services became spotty, businesses struggled, and power went to the most ruthless: in the case of Rome, families like the Colonna, Caetani, Orsini. Rome had yet to build the Renaissance palaces familiar even now; the men of power instead repurposed the sturdiest of Roman ruins, including the Colosseum (Frangipane); the tomb of Augustus (Colonna); the Theater of Marcellus (Orsini); the Castel Sant'Angelo (Crescenzi); and oddly, the Arch of Constantine (Frangipane again), into inelegant fortresses from which they controlled, more or less, the roaming bands of young toughs who terrorized the city.

There was government—senators and such, but without much in the way of enforcement power, largely ineffective against, for example, the malefactors who set Saint John Lateran on fire in 1308.

Into this squalor came Cola di Rienzo (1313–1354), son of a tavern keeper and water carrier. An unusually bright boy whose brightness was combined with grit and enthusiasm and a strong sense of outrage, he was fortunate in getting an education in the classics, most particularly the writers connected to his hometown, men like Livy, Cicero, and Seneca. From them he learned that in the past, the rich had been cowed, the people championed, and he believed that Rome, with help that God clearly had not given to pagan Romans, could have a republic that worked for the benefit of the people. To that end they needed a defender, a new Gaius Gracchus, someone to stand up to the powerful and arrogant. And as no one else was willing to step forward, then the task must fall to him.

He managed to pull it off. Having made a name for himself as an envoy to the pope in Avignon (and nearly getting him to agree to return to Rome), Cola began to attract a posse of like-minded young men equally fed up with the brutalities and excesses of the rich and their bullies. The aristocracy tolerated him as an amusing diversion, while laughing behind his back. They, however, were not his primary audience; the man in the Roman street was. The aristocracy was simply being put on notice that things were about to change.

That change came on Whitsunday in May 1347, when Cola, kitted up in bright armor—a sensible precaution as well as a striking visual statement—led his band of brothers through the streets of Rome, rousing the populace to follow him to the Capitol building, where he raised a scroll on which he said were new laws designed for the benefit of the people, people like himself, people like them. In front of hundreds if not thousands, he declared his devotion to the pope, to the city, to God and to the law; he declared he was there to serve them and no one else.

The performance was both electrifying and terrifying, but most of all, it was extremely effective. "The judges of the city came and swore fealty to him and offered themselves to the Good Estate, *buono stato.* Then the notaries came and did the same, then the merchants. In short, one by one, peacefully, unarmed, every man came to the Good Estate."[42] Their number included members of the ruling families, possibly just hedging their bets.

Cola styled himself tribune of the people, the old Roman title, defender of the plebs, and they were happy to accept that title and rejoice in his work.

The old guard may have hoped that this was a flash in the pan, that his intensity would die down, or that the execution of his vision would come to nothing. They were mistaken. Cola was now in a position to match actions to words, and the stars seemed to align in his favor. Within a month of his declaration, he had his chance to prove there was more to him than just talk. Actually, he created his chance from events that had occurred a year earlier, events that had taken place downstream at Ostia.

The Mediterranean can be as treacherous a sea as any, particularly in the autumn and winter months, to such a degree that many sailors (or rather, their shipowners) since ancient times would not send boats out after September. In late 1346, a storm arose off the coast of Ostia, threatening a cargo ship bound from Avignon and Marseilles back to its home port of Naples. Navigation around the mouth of the Tiber was treacherous for those unfamiliar with the area, and its shifting sands were a danger at the best of times, the more so in heavy weather. The captain and his crew were about to find this out the hard way. The author of the so-called *Anonimo Romano*, a contemporary chronicle written in Roman dialect, describes the events:

"Then the noxious power of the winds arose, and the sea grew angry. Such were the contrary winds that the sailing master lost all reason and forethought; black night was soon threatening. Such was the horrid darkness that you would see no greater tribulation in hell itself."[43]

They decided to head for the river.

"Ah, what dangers they encountered in that entry to the Tiber!"[44]

It was a case of frying pan to fire. After some alarming buffeting and screeching of the wooden frame against wind and water, the ship finally ran aground in the channel between Ostia and Portus, where it stuck fast. The survivors offered a prayer of thanks, and then most likely collapsed from exhaustion, grateful that they and the cargo were apparently safe.

The storm passed, the sun rose, and the survivors, shaken but safe, debarked, then approached the closed gates of Portus seeking hospitality. The locals of Portus were more interested in seeing what the storm might have tossed up. Now that the tempest was over and the ship more or less on land, the brotherhood of the sea no longer applied. No one knew this better than Martino Stefaneschi, aka Martino di Porto, aka Martin Ursini, client of the Orsini family, a former senator and nephew of two cardinals, who was living in the area at the time. He had little interest in the vessel's captain and crew, but took a great interest in the cargo—pepper and cinnamon, bales of French cloth with a value of 90,000 florins.[45] It was more than Stefaneschi could resist. The chronicler writes: "Che pericola in mare, pericola in terra."[46]

Finders keepers, in short.

In another time and place, this shameful attitude might have carried the day, and we may reasonably assume that it had worked for Stefaneschi in the past. This particular ship, however, contained the tax revenue from Provence to Queen Joanna I of Naples (1328–1382). Pope Clement VI himself got involved, writing from Avignon in February of 1347 to the senate and people of Rome that the goods must be restored.

Worse for Stefaneschi, Cola di Rienzo was in need of a known villain to prove he meant business. Stefaneschi, being well connected but also at odds with the pope and foreign powers, was perfect. The contemporary record, while referring to Stefaneschi as a tyrant and disgrace to his station, nevertheless paints an unexpectedly sad picture of an aged man, newly married to the young and beautiful widow Mascia degli Alberteschi, while effectively under house arrest at his riverside villa (*palazzo fiume de Ripa Armea*), where he had become quite ill: "His stomach was full of water, and looked like a barrel; his legs were swollen, his neck scrawny, his face thin, his thirst tremendous. He looked like a lute; he stayed quietly in his house and was treated by physicians."[47]

Justice now came quickly and without warning. One morning, Cola sent a militia to take the man from his own house (and his wife's arms—*nelle mano della soa donna*) and hustle him to the Campidoglio. Word went out that justice was about to be served, and the Roman mob came from all over the city to see this "mannifico omo," this magnificent man, stripped of his fine clothing, made to kneel, hear his death sentence, and voice his confessions before whatever remaining friends he might have could intervene. His status should have earned him the right of being beheaded, but Cola had him hanged like a common criminal, in full sight, the chronicle notes, of his wife's balcony. In case she missed the execution itself, she could gaze on his body for the following two days and one night.

Now that the price of villainy had become clear, many formerly powerful men with known histories of bad behavior began to leave town for country estates beyond Cola's reach. Others less agile found themselves hauled up on charges and punished. City life itself improved dramatically, if the chronicler is to be believed: "The streets were open; night and day travellers walked freely; no one dared to carry arms; no one injured others; masters dared not strike their servants; the Tribune watched over everything. . . . The carters who carried loads left them in the public streets and later found them again safe and sound."[48] One of Cola's own envoys to Naples, caught accepting a gratuity, was branded on the cheek, stunning proof of the new regime's high standards.

Cola could feel some grim satisfaction, and began to think in larger terms. If a cesspool as fetid as Rome could be cleansed, why not the rest of Italy? It was not as if other cities didn't have their share of overbearing crime lords in want of elimination. He sent envoys to other Italian city states in an attempt to encourage their oppressed masses to follow the example he had set in Rome, and there was a certain amount of interest in some places. The high and the mighty were less impressed, and in time the pope had doubts as well. Cola's enemies, recovered from their initial shock and willing to work together, began to fight back. His own ambitions became too large. Finally, in 1354, the Roman mob, excitable and fickle, turned on their onetime tribune and savior. They chased him up the Campidoglio and beat him, stabbed him, hanged him, and dragged his body to the Mausoleum of Augustus, where they burned the corpse and scattered the ashes—where else?—in the Tiber.

There's a bronze statue of Cola di Rienzo about halfway up the steps to the Campidoglio, marking the place where he is thought to have been killed. For a certain kind of populist, he is still something of an inspiration.

Holy Years

The year 1300 was the first holy year, a means of shriving Christians who had had a hard century of their sins. It was the brainchild of Boniface VIII, who acted, it was said, at the request of aging Romans who had a memory of hearing about something very like it from their youths the last time there was a new century. Boniface had the archives searched for anything that might confirm this story and found nothing, but on reflection considered the idea a good one and so issued a bull ordaining a plenary indulgence every hundred years for all those Romans who, over a period of thirty days, daily visited the basilicas of Saints Peter and Paul, confessed their sins, and showed contrition. Non-Romans could make do with fifteen days. (False and impious Christians (*falsos et impios Christianos*) who trade with the Saracens, along with Sicilians (then at war with the church) and members of Rome's powerful Colonna family, need not apply.)[49] Boniface was born a Caetani.

The response was extraordinary: "It was the most amazing thing that one has ever seen, that throughout the entire year, in Rome, besides the Roman people, there were 200,000 pilgrims, without counting those travelers who happened to be coming or going, and all were suitably supplied and fed, both horses and people, and with great patience, and without trouble or strife, and I can bear witness to this, and I was there and I saw it myself."[50] So said Florentine native Giovanni Villani.

There were downsides. Although bread, wine, meat, fish, and oats were cheap, "hay was very dear, and so also was lodging, so that my bed and stabling for my horse, without fodder, cost me every day a *grosso tournois*.[51] As I rode away from Rome on Christmas Eve, I found the roads encumbered with a multitude of pilgrims which no man could count, and amongst the Romans it was said that more than two millions of men and women had come to the city in all. Over and over again I saw both men and women trodden under foot in the press, and I myself more than once was hard bestead to escape the same danger."[52] Then too, a late Tiber flood damaged the local harvest that year, though all who needed feeding were apparently fed, and without much notable price gouging.

Foreign aristocracy and celebrities turned up. The painters Giotto and Cimabue, Charles Count of Valois; it is possible that Dante himself was present. Certainly he mentions some details, including the crowd's shuffling on Ponte Sant'Angelo to reach (or return from) Saint Peter's, the traffic directions separated by a wooden rail running down the middle.[53]

The question of salvation aside, there was a surprising amount for the faithful to see in Rome—fragments of the true cross, the *acheiropoeita* icon of Christ begun by Luke and completed by angels, the veil of Veronica (*vera icon*, true image, in the folk etymology), the cloth that Saint Veronica used to wipe the sweat of Christ's face as he walked the Via Dolorosa to Golgotha, and on which his face remained. Legend said that she came to Rome to present it to the emperor Tiberius, who was struck by its ability to bring sight to the blind. The Scala Pilati, or *scala sancta*, Pilate's staircase, the steps that Christ climbed to reach Pilate, taken by Saint Helena from Jerusalem and placed in the basilica of Saint John Lateran. Relics of all kinds dotted the city's churches, potent as inspiration for the faithful.

The project proved so successful that there was soon talk of a sequel. Boniface thought a hundred years was soon enough, but once he died (1303), others, including Petrarch and Bridget of Sweden, petitioned the new pope Clement V to shorten the wait. Fifty years would allow anyone allotted the proverbial three score and ten the opportunity to take part. Clement, unwilling to leave the pleasant city of Avignon, dispatched an underling to represent him at Rome.

By now, fifty years seemed too long a spell, and thirty-three was suggested, thirty-three being Christ's age when he died and nearly divisible into one hundred. The festivities came a little late, 1390. The century mark had impressed itself on pilgrims' minds, however, and the flush of visitors to Rome in 1400 caused the church to declare an ad hoc instance for that year, which nevertheless did not impact the 1423 Jubilee that marked thirty-three years after the last official jubilee. The entire schedule became hard to follow.

Then there was 1450.

"The remembrance of those days still rejoices my heart, for they made manifest the magnificence and glory of the Christian religion."[54] So recalled the Sienese diplomat Augustinus Dathus. Dathus's memory is selective. The crowds were indeed enormous, unlike anything ever before seen, and as such more than the city could reasonably cope with. Others who were there recall that "such a crowd of pilgrims came all at once to Rome that the mills and bakeries were quite insufficient to provide bread for them."[55] They couldn't find shelter either, and crowds dossed down in the streets or in vineyards: "Many perished from cold; it was dreadful to see. Still such multitudes thronged together that the city was actually famished."[56]

Predictably, there was plague that summer, which carried off massive numbers and cut down the crowds, but the disease abated somewhat by autumn, and once the harvest was in and winter still a ways off, the good Christians of Europe were well set to make the pilgrimage.

The requirements for indulgence were to visit the major churches, which meant that pilgrims had to cross the river, which stressed the bridges.

> In Holy Week the throngs coming from St. Peter's, or going there, were so enormous that they were crossing the bridge over the Tiber until the second or third hour of the night. The crowd was here so great that the soldiers of St. Angelo, together with other young men—I was often there myself—had often to haste on to the spot, and clear a passage through the throng with sticks in order to prevent serious accidents. . . .
>
> If you wanted to go to St. Peter's it was impossible to reach it on account of the masses of men that filled the streets. St. Paul's, St. John Lateran, and Santa Maria Maggiore were crowded with worshipers. All Rome was packed so full that one could not go through the streets.[57]

The year ended in tragedy. On December 19, last-minute arrivals hoping to get in under the wire swelled the crowds, particularly at Saint Peter's, where the pope was scheduled to give a benediction. At four o'clock, word came down that the event had been canceled, and so the crowd, eager to get back to their lodgings before nightfall, headed back as one to the center city, most of them by way of the Ponte Sant'Angelo. The numbers were too great. Horses and donkeys panicked, people fell off. Fearing a chain reaction, the castellan of Sant'Angelo ordered the gates closed, but by then it was a little late. Over two hundred by best estimates had been crushed or pushed over the side and drowned.

"I myself," wrote Paolo dello Mastro, "carried twelve dead bodies and it was pitiful to see there one hundred and seventy-two corpses; the weeping and lamenting of those who found fathers, mothers, sons, and brothers among the dead resounded in the streets *usque ad mediam noctem.* Truly it was a misery to see the poor people, with candles in their hands looking through the rows of dead who lay there."[58] The bridge was rebuilt and widened to avoid future accidents.[59]

Regardless, for the surviving pilgrims, the spiritual rewards were considerable. For the hostlers of Rome and for the church, the cash benefits were also, which fact was not lost on the church or on anyone else. In 1471, Paul II decreed that the Holy Year should come every twenty-five years.

By now Vatican officials had learned that a functioning infrastructure was critical to deal with the influx of visitors, and they set their hands to the task, from improving the Ponte Sant'Angelo and building the Ponte Sisto, to the renovation of the riverside and restoration of the Acqua Vergine, which feeds the Trevi Fountain, to hospitals and general sprucing up of both major and minor churches.

The year ended not only with an inadequate bridge, but a flooding Tiber, which gave pilgrims the novel experience of visiting Saint Paul's outside the Walls by boat. Word of the flood spread, as did word of the subsequent outbreak of disease, which discouraged new visitors. To make up for the short-fall, and to cater to those who were prevented from taking part, the pope conferred the benefits of indulgence on the city of Bologna from May 1461 to the end of the year. Dispensations now ran to other cities in Europe, simplifying the process for the far-flung faithful, and incidentally gathering donatives that the church might not otherwise have received.

In 1500 Alexander VI, the second Borgia pope, concerned that pilgrims might be intimidated by the highwaymen and worse who plagued Italy, had notices posted informing the local churches that they, the churches, would be responsible for the safety of those pilgrims passing through their regions. He meant business. When an ambassador of France and his entourage were robbed by highwaymen, Alexander had the band tracked down, gibbets raised on the Ponte Sant'Angelo (nine on each side), and the guilty hanged and left on display two days and one night—a comfort for the cardinals, and presumably the pilgrims.[60]

Inevitably in discussing Holy Year there comes the question of the money. Villani, writing of the 1300 Jubilee, notes only that "the Romans all became rich from the sale of their wares."[61] Other witnesses paint a more dispiriting image of the many coins dropped in front of the altars being gathered up by two monks with rakes. The impression, according to Boniface's deputy Giacomo Gaetani Stefaneschi, was misleading. He gives a brief accounting for anyone interested, noting that the greater part of the offerings was small change from various places, none of it obligatory. Of silver and gold, he claims the amount in excess of a normal year was no more than double, a sign that the richest pilgrims were the least openhanded, and that moreover most of the money gathered was eaten up by expenses.[62]

Nevertheless, the financial side of a Holy Year could not fail to look bad. What began as a spiritual and physical journey and a personal communion with dead saints and their relics devolved into the sale of indulgences for stay-at-homes. Critics were not long in coming. By 1517 Martin Luther had begun attacking the indulgence system, in which the place of Holy Year regrettably had to assume some responsibility. He had a point. The proceeds of the 1500 Jubilee were said to have funded Cesare Borgia's private interests. Of Cesare Borgia, like Nero, much calumny lards the historical record.

The modern Holy Year is on a twenty-five-year cycle, with a few additions for special occasions—1933 to commemorate the death of Jesus, 1954 as the first Marian year, 1987 as the second. Crowd control, not least of all that related to crossing the bridges, is better handled than it was in previous centuries.

Of Law and the River

In 1355, Bartolo da Sassoferrato (1314–1357), legal scholar and doctor of law at the University of Perugia, was on holiday, hiking toward "a certain villa overlooking the Tiber situated near Perugia," his mind dipping occasionally to thoughts on its legal status.[63] He had been something of a prodigy, taking a degree by age twenty, *licentia docendi*, license to teach civil law, which he did at the Universities of Pisa and of Perugia, as well as writing legal opinions for paying civilians. His portrait suggests a genial sort of man, happy in the abstractions of the law and untangling the knotty problems of such matters as transborder jurisdiction—international law, in short. No surprise that he was part of a diplomatic mission, or that the emperor Charles IV took him on as *consiliarus*. That job came with a coat of arms, which seems likely to have sparked his interest in his last work, the *Tractatus de insignis et armis* (On insignia and coats of arms), completed after his death in 1355 by his son-in-law, and received with great enthusiasm.

His most notable book was the *Tractatus de fluminibus seu Tyberiadis*—the Tiberiad, or, a treatise on rivers, a three-part study on the considerable issues concerning riparian rights, illustrated by those of the Tiber. His book covers such matters as who has rights to alluvial deposits that originate upstream, who can lay claim to an island that arises in the middle of a stream (a phenomenon that occurs more often than one might think), or what happens to an abandoned riverbed. In discussing these and other related questions, the book mixes up law and geometry in ways that would have made the ancient Egyptians proud.

The writing, to hear the author tell it, was done under compulsion. He had been on holiday, and his vacation had been proceeding nicely; he could lie back and gaze at the scenery and let the odd thought of river issues float through his head and then drift away. At one point, however, he nodded off, and a genial figure (*aspectus . . . placidus*) toting a pen, a ruler, and a compass entered his dream and told him: I have brought you a reed pen for writing, a compass to measure and draw circles, and a ruler for straight lines and marking figures.[64]

The implication was clear. The genial figure expected Bartolo to get to work. Bartolo tried to put the task off, pointing out that the proposed job was as likely to get him ridicule as praise, to which objection his visitor got a little less cheerful, a little more annoyed, pointing out that Christ and the saints put up with a good deal more than just the possibility of being laughed at.

The argument was unanswerable, and so Bartolo set about the task, and within two days he finished the maths and the explanation. He hit a snag on the third day, but fortunately, the Franciscan friar and polymath (*universalis in omnibus*) Fra Guido de Perusio happened to be walking by. Just as fortunately (God's work, according to Guido), rain kept the brother there for a full day, during which time the two men managed to get the worst of the job completed. What exactly Guido's role in the production was, Bartolo neglects to tell us—proofreading? Figure checking? Being the physical manifestation of his dream prodder?[65] No matter, the hard part was over, and the last stages of the book could be completed back at Perugia.

The final result was taken from manuscript to printing press in 1472, filled a gaping need, and enjoyed several reprintings in the coming centuries, the legal problems that arise from rivers being constant and easily recognized in any watery area. The book, among others, ensured that Bartolo's reputation among lawyers would remain high long after his death, high enough to inspire the adage "Nemo bonus íurista nisi bartolista" (The only good jurist is a follower of Bartolo). Entire university courses were devoted to his works, and only the codification of law at around the time of the French Revolution saw his influence begin to fade.[66]

Among nonlawyers, Bartolo's name entered the Italian stage as a stock label for the legal profession, much as an Einstein might stand in for a genial scientist today. Both Rossini and Mozart (their lyricists/librettists Sterbini and Da Ponte, to be more accurate) include a Dr. Bartolo in their works, respectively in *The Barber of Seville* and in *The Marriage of Figaro*. Not a bad legacy, either way. (Bartolo may be forgiven his mistaken etymology of the river, attributing it to Tyberio Romanorum Imperatore, Tiberius, emperor of the Romans; he was writing before the Renaissance, after all.)[67]

Pontius Pilate

The Tiber will endure a great deal, including dragons, but even rivers have their standards.

Consider the case of Pontius Pilate. The apocryphal Gospel of Nicodemus, and the *Mors Pilati*, a late medieval account of the procurator's wretched end, tells us that he had returned to Rome under orders from Tiberius, who had been informed of the crucifixion and been very angry. Tiberius, it seems, had recently been suffering skin disease and heard that Jesus had the power to heal. Pilate, whose mitigating circumstances did not impress the emperor, was condemned to death, and his body was flung into the Tiber.

They might as well have tossed in a human weight of potassium: "And there the devils reveled over that polluted corpse. Then the filthy carcass began to cause an overflow in the sea, and in the water, and caused storms and lightning and thunder and hail in the air [*fulgura et tempestates, tonitrua et grandines in aere*], so that all that listened were amazed."[68] The effect was so pronounced that the body had to be removed. Officials in charge ordered the body sent north to Vigenna (i.e., Via Gehenna, "being the way to hell"), where it was dropped in the Rhône, with much the same results.[69] So long as it was out of Rome, they felt the job was done and left the locals to deal with the problem or not, as they chose. The locals chose to fish out the dripping corpse and bring it to the border near Lausanne, Switzerland, for burial in a pit surrounded by mountains. Here at last Pilate was relatively quiet, though certain *diabolicae machinationes*, it was said, continued to pervade the area.[70] "And when they again were oppressed by the excessive disturbance, they brought it thence, and cast it into a well that was in a mountain, where, it is said, the snow in the wells ever bubbles. And thus it befell Pilatus."[71]

No rest for the wicked.

Alternatively, he escaped execution and ran off to Switzerland and settled near Mons Pileatus (capped mountain, misconstrued as Pilate's mountain), where he contemplated his sins for the rest of his life, ending his story by leaping into the nearby Pilatussee, Lake Pilate, apparently without any serious effect on the water supply. In medieval times, it was forbidden to climb the mountain or visit the lake, much less disturb the lake.

For the more generous minded who might think Pilate was simply an unfortunate bureaucrat who wound up in an impossible situation, there was a happier ending that had some currency in the Dark Ages. That version has the emperor Tiberius angry that darkness had fallen on Rome and specifically angry at Pilate for having brought it about. Summoned to Rome to explain himself, Pilate is condemned to death. Awaiting execution, he cries out that this is an injustice, that the consequences of his actions were unforeseeable and the actions themselves done in ignorance. He then hears a voice from heaven that informs him that he was merely part of a larger plan and that no blame attached to him. He is still beheaded, in the presence of his wife, Procula. She, however, is also aware of the situation and aware of the good that will follow, and dies of happiness and is buried alongside her husband. Or is perhaps martyred later for her new Christian faith. The details vary, but the sense of the legend was clear enough that Claudia Procula is now a saint in the Greek Orthodox Church, her saint's day being October 27. The Coptic Church goes one further and on June 25 commemorates both her and Pilate.

Hester Piozzi, Doctor Johnson's Mrs. Thrale, didn't think much of the story: "The just and zealous detestation of Christians towards Pontius Pilate, is . . . here comically expressed by their placing his palace just at the exit of the Cloaca into the Tyber; and one who pretended to doubt of its being his residence, would be thought the worse of among them."[72]

Martin and Eugenius

"He [Pope Martin V] found the city of Rome so disrupted and devastated, that it scarcely seemed to be a city at all. You could see the ruined houses, the fallen temples, deserted neighborhoods, a muddy and forlorn city, struggling with shortages and high cost of all things."[73]

Martin arrived in 1420. Soon after, the Tiber overflowed, reaching as high as the altar in the Pantheon—not a good omen. He had a lot on his agenda, between rebelling Hussites in Germany, two crusades, warfare and brigandage throughout central Italy. Charity, however, begins at home, and Rome was in need a thorough makeover. Martin appointed an official to clean the streets, put down street crime, restore the churches, and, most notablly of all, get water running back through the Acqua Vergine, bringing drinkable water to long-dry fountains some distance from the river. He also wished to establish the papal presence, but at a remove from the worst of the urban blight. Saint John Lateran, still within the walls, is somewhat a trek from the city center; Martin wanted something a little more practical and symbolic.

How to make this manifest? By crossing the river.

Martin brought the church seat across the Tiber, from Saint John Lateran to Saint Peter's Vatican, tightening the bond between the pontiff and Saint Peter. There were practical aspects as well. The Lateran was protected from the outside world by the Aurelian walls, but the location was remote, not overly imposing at the best of times. The Vatican and its Borgo neighborhood were surrounded by the more considerable Leonine wall; moreover, they had the fortress of Castel Sant'Angelo overlooking the bridge that connected to the east bank. Having survived decades of internal squabbling, and facing ambitious powers in Italy and abroad, the church would now have a physical bulwark against secular disruption.

The Papal State covered a good portion of central Italy, and Martin was of necessity in large part a secular ruler; accordingly, appointing relatives—Colonna relatives, in his case—as cardinals, a standard practice of Renaissance popes, was as much, if not more, a matter of keeping power within the trusted confines of family as it was handing out sinecures to otherwise unemployable ne'er-do-wells. The new seat of power was perhaps not coincidentally closer to the bankers who congregated just across the Ponte Sant'Angelo, easily summoned by the church when matters of finance needed discussion, and within firing range of the newly invented cannon, should discussions prove intractable. The church under Martin was no longer a part of the city proper, but a thing looming over it from the far bank, able to keep a watchful eye on its sheep, strong enough to withstand any attempts at challenging its power. The wonder is that no pope had done this earlier.

Martin's immediate successor, Eugenius IV, 1431–1447, came on strong, perhaps too strong. He saw the wealth of Martin's nephews as ill gotten and excessive and demanded it be disgorged, and when it was not, he arrested Martin's treasurer and tortured him to death. He also hanged two hundred Colonna supporters, which proved excessive, even for the mob that had no use for the Colonna.

A contemporary Florentine biographer, Vespasiano da Bistici, understates the matter nicely: "There was dissension [differenza] between [Eugenius] and the Romans, who are a contentious people [uomini iscandalosi]."[74] On May 29 of 1434 the people, backed by the Colonna, began to march, demanding that Eugenius surrender temporal power over Ostia and, more significantly, the Castel Sant'Angelo. They called for a restoration of the republic, marching in the streets shouting "The people, the people and liberty!"

Eugenius thought the better part of valor was to leave town, preferably discreetly. In the company of some loyal Benedictines, he dressed down, mounted up a mule, and his new brothers led them down to the Ripa Grande, where Valentino, a hired roughneck, was waiting to carry them away. They were less conspicuous than they might have hoped, and people were already on edge. The Ripa was not the most anonymous of places, and idlers and dockworkers took notice of this somewhat unusual parade. Some stared, others muttered, and as Eugenius, alarmed, spurred the mule forward to his rendezvous, a crowd was beginning to gather behind him.

Valentino saw this and rushed to gather up his charge, threw him over his shoulder, and hustled him onto the boat. The crowd, now aware of what was happening, started looking for stones with which to pelt the brothers, as Valentino and his men pushed their vessel out into the water. Shouts went up, word spread, and people began to appear all along the riverside as the boat headed downstream. Valentino pushed the pope down to the wet bottom of the boat and covered him with a shield as protection against the stones and, more alarmingly, the arrows now raining down from the banks. The crew-men rowed hard and were able to outdistance the missiles, and the skiffs that followed them failed to catch up with Valentino's seasoned oarsmen. Closer to Ostia—we can assume that word was carried on horseback downriver—a large fishing boat filled with armed men moved to cut Valentino off. They misjudged their man; rather than surrendering, he instead fixed his course to run straight at this new enemy, while his crew pulled out crossbows and fired. The fishermen withdrew, and from then on it was smooth sailing all the way to Ostia, where Valentino's boss the corsair Vitellius of Ischia lay at anchor, ready to take Eugenius first to Pisa, then Florence, where he remained for the next nine years, encouraging their artists and considering next steps.[75]

The absence of Eugenius did Rome no good. The mob rejoiced at the return of the republic and the assumption that power had returned to the people. It had not. A brief period of joyous anarchy ensued, which involved ransacking the papal palace in Trastevere. When the first flush of victory died down and the new government proved less than efficient, regret and second thoughts began. Eugenius was disinclined to return, but quite happy to send one of his bishops, Giovanni Vitelleschi, to take the temperature of the city. In October 1434, the crowds now called for the church to come back.

It would not be that easy. Vitelleschi might have been a bishop, but he had begun his career as a condottiere, a military man, and he was now charged with the papal armies. A strong and fearsome man by all accounts, he set to ruin Eugenius's enemies. In due course he was effectively ruling the city, at the top of his game. It did not last long. He was with his attendants riding by the Castel Sant'Angelo when his enemies ambushed him, dragged him from his horse, wounded him, and put him in a cell. His followers might have helped, but a papal warrant, real or false, was produced, and they didn't want to take any chances. In two weeks Vitelleschi was dead. The why of the whole affair is still open to question; the general feeling is that Eugenius was feeling paranoid and conspired to be rid of a now troublesome priest.

Whatever the reason, with Vitelleschi gone, anarchy reigned again, punctuated by earthquakes, eclipses, tempests, and a flooding Tiber.

In 1443, Eugenius himself returned to Rome, happily received in a city that had fallen back to destitution. Four years later he was dead, but he left the city better than he had found it, and this time the changes seemed to have taken root. The city was ready for the Renaissance.

Isola Sacra

Isola Sacra, the sacred island, was created by the construction of the canal connecting Portus to the sea. By 1450, Pius II could write that "on the island no building stands out, but wherever you dig, you will find statues and columns of considerable size."[76]

In 1451, Biondo Flavio describes the area as a wasteland:

> All over the shore of the marshy island formed by a fork in the Tiber two miles upstream of Ostia, blocks of marble can be seen scattered about, almost side by side, choked by weeds, nettles and shrubs and half buried by silt. Rough-hewn and unpolished, they were brought here by sea by traders in the prosperous days of the Republic and Empire, for whatever building use they could be cut and shaped to; and since they are there in enormous numbers (it seems a city could be built from them), some appear so massive that anyone unaware that obelisks were brought here from Egypt would scarcely believe they could have been transported by ship.[77]

As his father Cosimo picked over Ostia, Lorenzo de' Medici, "il Magnifico," turned his sights to Portus. His underling Giovanni Antonio confirmed to him what Biondo Flavio had written, that there were "many beautiful things, many marble statues and antique sepulchres, and in ancient buildings small bricks in the form of mosaic, and as regards those bricks they must be of various soils, so they have taken different colors from the firing, that are more or less red, likewise black and yellow, and off-white, such that the end results come out beautifully and quite distinct."[78]

There was a rush to reap this wealth of antiquities, with agents coming from as far off as Venice, some to preserve classical excellence, others to protect the world from pagan corruption. Cardinal Bessarion (1402–1472), notable collector and curator of Greek manuscripts and one of the greatest classical scholars of his age, was less loving of the plastic arts. While visiting Portus, he saw a louche statue of *Liber Pater Commodianus* (god of wine, plebeian rights, and male fertility) and had it thrown into the river as pagan rubbish.[79] Art can have a powerful effect on people.

Pius II Takes a Cruise

In May 1463, the cardinal of Rouen and bishop of Ostia invited Pope Pius II (1404–1464) to come visit him at Ostia, an invitation Pius accepted and a trip that he wrote up in his autobiography, the first such autobiography we have of a pope.

Pius, born of a good Sienese family (Piccolomini) fallen on hard times, was a classic story of a bright boy who rose on his merits and good nature. He studied under Francesco Filelfo in Siena and Florence, then made his way to Basel, where he attached himself to the antipope Felix V, then to Frederick III, the Holy Roman emperor, who named the young man poet laureate. His sojourn must have been a pleasant one; in his spare time he fathered a few bastards, wrote some erotic verse, and penned what some critics have styled an erotic novel, *Historia de duobus amantibus* (History of two lovers), complete with star-crossed lovers and a compelling balcony scene. An excerpt:

> "What are you doing?" said Euryalus, "Mistress of my life. What are you looking at, my heart? Here, turn your eyes here, my bulwark, for your Euryalus is here. Look—look—it is I—look at me."
>
> "You here?" cried Lucretia. "Oh, my Euryalus! Now at last I can speak to you. Oh, that I had the strength to embrace you."
>
> To which he replied, "That's easily managed. I'll bring a ladder. Lock your door. We have postponed too long the enjoyment of our love."[80]

And so forth. The book was widely read in its own time, the more so when Pius became pope, but the modern prurient may find it disappointing.

In 1445 Pius turned forty and had his Damascus moment; no more loose living and fast women, he was to dedicate his life to the church—the Roman church, not the schismatic—and offered himself to Eugenius IV to help reconcile the dueling factions. He took holy orders in 1446 and rose quickly through the ranks, getting elected pope himself in 1455.

It all seemed so easy; the hand of God was clearly present. But to what end? The answer, at least to Pius, was clear. What greater task could God want of his chosen representative on earth, after having settled the schism, than to convert the heathen Muslim? His proven skills with quill and ink were the obvious means, and he set to work writing a closely argued refutation of Islam in general and the Koran in particular, with the aim of converting the Ottoman sultan Mehmet II. That effort failed, which should come as no surprise. Mehmet had, after all, just conquered Constantinople in 1453; convincing him that Islam was the weaker religion at that point would have been difficult. Pius was forced to start work on his backup plan. He would lead a pan-European crusade. Granted, four previous crusades had failed, but those crusades had not had Pius behind them.

Before his crusade, however, Pius had time for a pleasure cruise down the Tiber.

The trip sounds idyllic: "The banks on both sides were green and the month of May clothed all the country with luxuriant grass and many-colored flowers."[81] What sorts of flowers, exactly? He does not say. Other writers over the ages referred to marsh reeds, bulrushes, grasses, iris pseudacorus, bee orchids, queen of the meadow; and the Isola Sacra was said to have been rich with roses.

Pius was a bit better on birds, observing that "swans lay eggs and rear their young on the bank and in the marsh grass and it is delightful to see and hear the flocks. . . . [The lagoon] narrows toward the sea and is like a canal hedged on the sides with trees in which birds sing sweetly."[82] Again, as with the flowers, he does not identify the songbirds in question.

He does mention lunch.

The local fishermen, imports from Dalmatia, knew he was coming and had caught no fewer than seven fish for the pope and his entourage, one of the seven weighing in at 250 pounds. He believes them to be sturgeon, the *lupi Tiberini* of the ancient texts, but is unwilling to commit himself to that.

From there it is on to the sights. He writes,

The extensive ruins show that it was once large. . . . Ruined porticoes, prostrate columns, and fragments of statues are still visible. There are also the walls of an ancient temple, stripped of their marbles, which show it was once a noble work. You may also see parts of an aqueduct which brought sweet water from a distance to the city. The older and more extensive city walls long ago fell in ruin and the circuit was narrowed to enclose only the cathedral church and a few dwelling houses, some of which were built directly on the aqueduct itself. They say that even these structures were destroyed in our time by Ladislas, King of Sicily. The walls are leveled for the most part. The church which must have been of some distinction, has been destroyed by age or violence. Only the upper part of the high altar still stands. Under the altar during the pontificate of Eugenius were found many bones of saints, among them the body of Santa Monica, mother of Aurelius Augustinus.[83]

Pius also refers to the vestiges of the tower discernible out at sea.[84] Possibly this was the same structure Richard the Lionhearted saw on his visit to Rome in 1190, referring to "a most beautiful but solitary tower" he passed by on his way upriver.[85] Possibly it was the last vestiges of Claudius's lighthouse, built in imitation of the Pharos of Alexandria, a wonder of the world, some 120 meters high. Would Rome have settled for anything less? Maybe, maybe not, though even at 50 meters it would have been visible in Rome. Pliny notes that the danger in lighthouses is "the uninterrupted burning of the beacon, in case it should be mistaken for a star, the appearance of the fire from a distance being similar."[86] (The Portus lighthouse is completely gone now, worn down by time, but it must have been a sight.)

There was the episcopal palace. Beyond that, "a sort of public tavern [*quandam tabernam*] and a high round tower built by Martin V to guard the place, that the harbor dues might not be evaded and to serve as a watch tower to prevent an enemy making a surprise landing. . . . Such today is Ostia whose fame was great in antiquity."[87]

He was also observant about the practical matters of the river's end. "The actual mouth of the Tiber is larger and admits galleys and moderate-sized freighters," which suggests that trade was picking up.[88] The whole area reeked of the melancholy romantic, which was not something one could accuse Pius of being. He also urged anyone contemplating a trip to Ostia by sea to hire the *pedota*, the pilot, on account of the shallow waters and shifting sands. "If anyone omits to do this, his stinginess is punished with a shipwreck."[89]

After his inspection of the ruins, he "returned to Ostia [and] found that fishermen had caught an enormous dolphin which the servants of the French Cardinal of Rouen had cooked in many different ways and devoured greedily, as they prize very highly this sea fish and consider it one of the sovereign's perquisites."[90]

The Italians thought it on a par with killing an albatross and complained about the foul odor. Odor was the least of their worries. Pius elaborates:

> The catching of a dolphin is said to be the sign of a coming storm. The next
> night, May 15, the sea, which during the last few days had been continuously
> disturbed and rough, became much wilder than usual. A violent tempest arose,
> a south wind churned the waters to their very depths, huge waves lashed the
> shore, and you could have heard the ocean groaning and shrieking. The force
> of the winds was such that it seemed nothing could withstand it. They fought

savagely together and seemed now to rout, now to flee from one another. They tore down forests and everything in their path. The sky flashed with repeated fires, the heavens thundered, and terrible bolts shot from the clouds. One of them struck the tower bringing down a buttress and a bell which came near crushing a monk who was lying there buried in wine and sleep. Herds of cattle were stabled nearby and heifers that had just calved bellowed horribly in their anxiety for their young, either because they were terrified at the thunder or because they were afraid that wolves might attack them in the dark. The utter blackness of the night (though there were frequent flashes of lightning) doubled the terror and such sheets of water fell that you would have said it was not rain but a deluge, as if the Creator had resolved once more to drown the human race.[91]

The storm passed; another man might have taken it as an omen, and perhaps after the fact some did. Pius was glad merely to head back home and prepare for his crusade the following year. For this he had written to the various powers across Europe, most of whom at best offered moral support and empty promises. Undaunted, certain that God was behind him, he set off upriver the following spring on the first part of his journey across the belt of Italy to Ancona on the Adriatic coast, where he expected to rendezvous with the Venetian fleet. The doge was as good as his word, but woefully short of the ships and manpower Pius had imagined. There was no chance that an expedition this small was ever going to defeat the Ottoman Turks, and Pius knew it. For the first time in his life, the grand design came crashing down. He turned his face to the wall, silent. Two days later, he died, a broken man.

Mattei and *i Soldati Rossi*

Ponte Sant'Angelo was a quick route to Saint Peter's. Normally this was a good thing. When a pope died, however, it became a concern. The Roman mob took an inordinate interest in papal conclaves, and had been known to go so far as to gather outside and threaten the College of Cardinals if they were too slow to decide or if there was any chance that they might choose poorly—if, say, the clerics chose a non-Roman, or worse still, a non-Italian.

As of 1271, to keep disruption to a minimum, the Mattei family had been given the title "guardian of bridges and shores" (among others). On the death of a pope, the Mattei brigade of a hundred *soldati rossi*, redcoats if you like, took their battle stations at key points around the Vatican and at the Tiber Island bridges until a conclave could be arranged and a new pope inducted.

This was no small thing, and at times even the *soldati* were overwhelmed. At the 1378 conclave, where the question was whether the pope would be French and live in Avignon, or Italian, and in Rome, the mob managed to reach the hall in which the cardinals were considering their next pontiff. The sound of the mob outside was bad enough, but the pounding on the floor below, and eventually the sight of lance tips breaking through, not to say the threat of the hall being burned down, concentrated their minds considerably. The crowd warned the cardinals to "consider well what you are about and give us a Roman Pope who will reside among us: otherwise we will make your heads much redder than your hats."[92] The spirit moved the cardinals to elect Urban VI, an archbishop rather than a cardinal, but Italian, and therefore acceptable. Had they met in the Castel Sant'Angelo as they had planned, with the understanding that their safety was assured in the Vatican, things might have turned out differently.

Despite the odd glitch, the Mattei family held the post as guardians for the next seven hundred years, an astonishing record, given the ups and downs of Rome's various baronial families. They served faithfully until quietly dismissed in 1823 as superfluous.[93] Any concerns are now taken care of by the full timers of the Swiss Guards, relative newcomers from 1506. The family name lives on in the small square near the Jewish ghetto, where one can find the Tartarughe, the turtle fountain. Worth a detour.

Papstesel

Papstesel is German for "the pope's ass." The Italians more gently refer to her as the *donna asino*.

The flooding Tiber washed up snakes and dragons on a regular basis; in 1495, it produced something undreamed of even in the weirdest of nightmares. A Venetian diplomat reporting back home wrote that in January the flood had washed up

> a monster that seemed to have the head of an ass, with long ears, the body
> of a human female, left arm in human form, the right [arm] at end the snout
> of an elephant. From behind, in the lower part, there was the face of an old
> man with a beard. There exited from its tail a long neck with a snake's head,

openmouthed. The right foot was that of an eagle, with talons, the left foot of an ox. The legs, from the soles on up as well as all the body, was scaled, like a fish. And these details are contained in the letters of the ambassador to the Signoria.[94]

Francesco Rococioli of Modena also wrote up some Latin verse on the matter, *Libellus de monstro Romae reperto anno Domini* MCCCCLXXXXVI, with a similarly described creature. Modena is four hundred kilometers from Rome, which speaks to just how impressive this flood and monster were, how great a warning of impending doom, and how sincere the author's desire to flatter his patron, Ercole d'Este. D'Este had been a tough man, a soldier in many Italian wars, but at sixty-four, he had reached an age at which other men had long since given up dragon slaying. He had had bad luck in recent wars, and for some time his foreign policy had been neutrality whenever possible. Rococioli seems to have had other ideas. He, Ercole, like his name-sake, was just the man to go to Rome, clear up the ruins, and kill this beastly creature for the good of all.

> In the meantime you ought to attempt to defeat such a monster
> You yourself mindful of piling up glory upon your past glory[95]

It didn't happen. Ercole chose diplomacy instead. In 1498, hoping to improve relations with the Papal States, he married his son Alfonso off to the pope's daughter, Lucrezia Borgia. He got some handsome territorial concessions out of the arrangement, if not the honor of killing a freak of nature.

Propagandists in Protestant Europe had better luck in exploiting the creature. When a verbal description wasn't enough, the German Protestant theologian Philip Melanchthon had Lucas Cranach make a woodcut of the wretched thing, giving it more animation than it appears to have had in life. The time was good for the anticlericalism then beginning to grow in parts of Europe. What could a flood be if not a sign of God's anger? What could this creature be if not a means of underscoring that displeasure? One edition of Sebastian Brand's *Ship of Fools* has a modest poem referring to the flood, echoing Pliny's take that it was less a punishment than a warning:

> You, O Tiber, have always been a dreaded augur and prophet.[96]

Twenty-seven years later, Martin Luther was still citing the wretched creature as evidence of papal corruption. There were, of course, those who blamed the Jews, whose low-lying district had been particularly hard hit by the flood. God's justice, it was said, and a means of cleaning up such a dirty people. Giuliano Dati, composer of street songs for buskers (*cantastorie*) and best known for translating into verse Columbus's first letter describing the New World, also wrote a poem about the flood, its illustrative woodcut showing a man on a raft, a man in a barrel, and three less fortunate heads just clearing the water. He left out the monster, and he and his publisher were no doubt kicking themselves that they went to press too soon.[97]

INTERLUDE

Tributary—Clitumnus

But thou, Clitumnus! in thy sweetest wave
Of the most living crystal that was e'er
The haunt of river-nymph, to gaze and lave
Her limbs where nothing hid them, thou dost rear
The grassy banks whereon the milk-white steer
Grazes,—the purest god of gentle waters![1]
Byron, Childe Harold's Pilgrimage

Byron also had a more practical attachment to the place: "I got some famous trout out of the river Clitumnus—the prettiest little stream in all po-
esy."[2]

The Clitumnus begins at a spring that could be mistaken for a pond, or
network of ponds. The water does not burble or gush, but rather rises imper-
ceptibly and fully formed at the foot of a small range of hills, some ten miles
above Assisi. In Roman times the hills were tree covered, and the soil trapped
rainwater for later dispersion. The stream in those days was wide enough to
accommodate two boats passing in opposite directions. The river wanders
slowly about the Umbrian plain, saturating the soil as it passes, and marries
the larger tributary the Topino, and later the Tiber. The Clitumnus can flood
if provoked, but is generally unhurried.

Unhurried, even idyllic. This is where Cynthia, object of the poet Sextus
Propertius's desires, chose to go for a rest from the noises, smells, and general
bustle of imperial Rome. He rejoiced as best he could, happy in the thought
that she was for the time being less likely to run into other suitors and thereby
force him to deal with the agony of jealousy. Then again, could he be sure?
It was possible that others might follow her there, with consequences too
awful to imagine. After giving the matter some thought, he decides to put
his obligations on hold for the moment and head on up himself, and finds,
to his relief, that all is well: there are no urban wolves other than himself.
Jealousy defeated, he can for the duration become a simple man of the coun-

try. While she engages with the local peasants in folk dancing, he will take up his bow and engage in the manly art of hunting—not, gods forbid, lions or boars or that sort of thing. He was thinking, perhaps—rabbits. Rabbits, or possibly ducks.[3]

Not a country boy at heart, was Propertius.

The more pragmatic Pliny was less concerned with romantic idylls than with the uniqueness of the place: "[The water is] so clear and glassy that you may count the shining pebbles and the little pieces of money which are thrown into it."[4]

The clarity was so extreme that it was once supposed to turn animals white. Certainly the area was famous for the white cattle. These animals were much prized, especially, as Juvenal noted, by the gods.[5]

> A bull high fed should fall the sacrifice,
> One of Hispulla's huge prodigious size:
> Not one of those our neighb'ring pastures feed,
> But of Clitumnus whitest sacred breed.

Virgil mentions the white cattle as well:

> Hence thy white flocks, Clitumnus, and the bull,
> Of victims mightiest, which full oft have led,
> Bathed in thy sacred stream, the triumph-pomp
> Of Romans to the temples of the gods.[6]

Silius Italicus wrote that the "Clitumnus, flowing through the spreading fields, bathes the white bulls in its cool streams."[7] Propertius (briefly turning his attention away from Cynthia) sounds a similar note: "Clitumnus . . . with his waters laves the snow-white kind."[8] The belief in the river's bleaching power was current at least as late as the eighteenth century. Addison mentions it favorably in his travels in Italy.[9]

Clear water and sacrificial-quality animals were a sign of divine presence, and the upper reaches of the area were sacred to the god Jupiter Clitumnus. The *sortes* (oracles) of the river had some prophetic power, which enticed pilgrims for whom other prophetic sites were either too far away or crowded or otherwise unsatisfactory. Caligula stopped by on his way to Germany; the emperor Honorius is said to have done so as well, though in both cases the matters under consideration were presumably personal and not shared with others. No record of history-changing prophecy has come down to us. The poet Claudian, describing Honorius's visit, refers to "the stream's strange property, flowing gently on when one approaches with silent step, but swirling and eddying should one hasten with louder utterance; and while it is the common nature of water to mirror the exact image of the body, it alone boasts the strange power that it mimics not human form but human character."[10]

The year 446 was one of earthquakes, or one long earthquake, "for it lasted six months, and without pause, but with continuous shaking, and throughout nearly the entire world."[11] The duration might be exaggerated—our source, the author Nicophorus Callistus, was writing some nine hundred years after the fact—but less credulous writers do confirm that the earth moved a good deal at that time, taking down fifty-seven wall towers in Constantinople. That the Clitumnus should have been among various springs that were either cut off entirely or reduced to a trickle is within reason. In 1694, another earthquake, this one closer to home, appears to have restored the lost flow, or rather, a good part of it, less strong, but still clear.[12]

About a mile from the stream's source is the so-called Tempietto di Clitumno, once considered an old Roman temple to Clitumnus, now recognized as an early Christian chapel built from old Roman scraps and dedicated to San Salvatore. The small building was something of a must-see object for the Grand Tour, and was much admired by the likes of Palladio and Inigo Jones.[13]

Smollett, back in a good mood, admired the area's "delightful plain, laid out into beautiful enclosures, abounding with wine, oil, corn, and cattle, and watered by the pastoral streams of the famous river Clitumnus, which takes its rise in three or four separate rivulets issuing from a rock near the highway."[14]

His delight was somewhat dampened that evening, when he stopped for the night at a local hostelry: "In choosing our beds at the inn, I perceived one chamber locked and desired it might be opened; upon which the cameriere declared with some reluctance [. . . 'Your Excellency must know that a filthy Beast died lately in that Chamber, and it is not yet purified and put in order.'] When I enquired what beast it was, he replied, 'Un eretico Inglese,' 'An English heretic.'"[15]

The idyllic land is a fraction of its former size. The immediate area is more desert than not, most obviously in high summer, but the spring itself keeps on feeding the river. It still has the power to move visitors, some more profoundly than others.

Giosuè Carducci (1835–1907) visited the springs in 1876 and was inspired to write *Alle fonti del Clitumno* (To the springs of Clitumnus), a patriotic hymn looking back on Italy's ancient past and promising future. The Nobel laureate, trained in the classics, writes of Hannibal's men and war elephants tramping through the area, various pagan gods, and protomythical heroes. He was also familiar with the arborage as described by the Latin poets, and noticed during his own visit that something was slightly off:

> Chi l'ombre indusse del piangente salcio
> su' rivi sacri? ti rapisca il vento
> de l'Appennino, o molle pianta, amore
> d'umili tempi!

> Who lured the shades of weeping willow
> To the sacred stream? Let Apennine winds
> Take you away, dismal tree,
> beloved in abject times!

Who indeed?

The local tradition was that the modern willow trees originated with the many cuttings from the tree under which Napoleon rested (and was eventually buried in 1821) on St. Helena. It is certainly true that patriotic Frenchmen took cuttings from that tree and carried them around the world, from New Zealand to Mount Vernon (in the latter case as a gift from France in 1835 for the grave of George Washington). The mania for these cuttings peaked in the 1860s, when undertakers would entwine long, thin strands of willow leaves in the hair of the newly dead for the final viewing before burial.

Easy to see how the fashion of planting these things could have reached to distant Clitumnus. In 1870 that alone would have annoyed Carducci, who had nothing good to say about Bonapartes, not so long as Napoleon III supported the pope and defied the hopes of an independent and unified Italy. Carducci was, however, a passionate man, and once he heard that German troops had surrounded Paris, he reversed himself—France was the source of liberty, Germany the home of oppression. Not that this would reconcile him to the willows of Clitumnus —they were still an offense against classical tradition.

If Bonapartists were in fact responsible for the plantings, however, they were sold a bill of goods. In later years Strasbourg botanist Dr. Julius Ritter von Wiesner (1838–1916), among others, wandering the grounds near the water, took one look at the trees and came down with the verdict—the Clitumnus willows had nothing to do with St. Helena, but were another cultivar entirely.[16] Science delivers yet another disappointing truth, disappointing enough that it is generally ignored, even in this unromantic age.

The poem, in any event, is quite good, one of Carducci's best. Italian schoolchildren are expected to memorize as much of it as possible.

Father Tiber. The Roman statue lies before the staircase
of the Palazzo Senatorio on Rome's Capitoline Hill. Author photo.

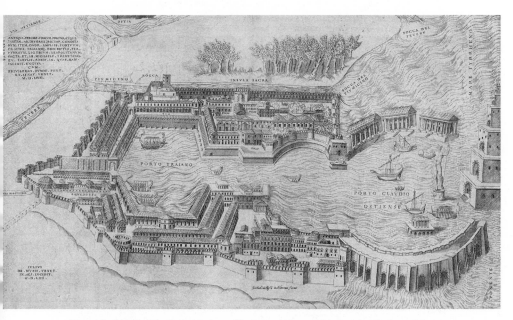

Trajan's harbor. The Tiber having no natural harbor, early Romans set about building one of their
own. The final and finest expression of their work was done by order of the emperor Trajan (AD
53–117). Metropolitan Museum of Art.

Ponte Rotto, the "broken bridge." Drawing from 1819 shows the remains
of the ancient Pons Aemilius, the oldest stone bridge in Rome, now superseded
by the Ponte Palatino. Metropolitan Museum of Art.

Ponte Rotto, 2016. Author photo.

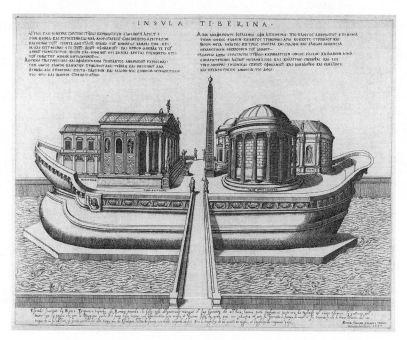

Tiber Island, depicted in a somewhat fanciful anonymous woodcut. The island was sacred to the healing god Asclepius, whose caduceus can still be seen carved on the island's old Roman cladding. The resemblance to a boat was reason enough reason to bind the land in marble and erect an obelisk (now gone) as a mast. Metropolitan Museum of Art.

Cloaca Maxima—"Great Sewer." This etching by Giovanni Battista Piranesi shows where Rome's earliest and largest drain exits into the Tiber. Wikimedia Commons.

Golden menorah and other Jewish treasure taken by the emperor Titus from the temple of Jerusalem. This rendition of the emperor's triumph is on the interior of the Arch of Titus. The treasure was rumored to have been thrown into the Tiber before the advancing Vandals could take it for themselves. Wikimedia Commons.

The 1496 flood: illustration for an epic poem by Giuliano Dati describing the worst aspects of Rome's 1496 flood. Dati is otherwise best known for putting into verse the first letters of Columbus describing the New World. Metropolitan Museum of Art.

Der Bapstesel zu Rom

LEFT *Der Papstesel*. Woodcut after Lucas Cranach of the unfortunate creature that washed up on the banks of the Tiber in the wake of the 1496 flood. Some Protestants took it as a sign of papal corruption. Wikimedia Commons.

BELOW LEFT *Il Facchino*—"the porter." Renaissance statue and fountain commissioned by the guild of water carriers, who once gathered Tiber water to sell on the city streets. Author photo.

BELOW RIGHT Hanno the elephant. He was a gift of the king of Portugal to Pope Leo X, and much prized during his unfortunately short life in Rome. The drawing is by Raphael. Wikimedia Commons.

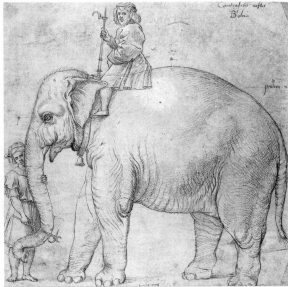

Sturgeon template: the official standard by which Tiber fishermen could ensure that their catch met with legal requirements for size. The vertical line near the gills indicates where the head should be removed. Prized for its cheek meat and use for fish stock, the head was reserved for city officials. Author photo.

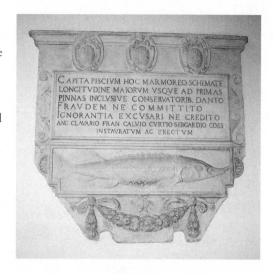

The *Barcaccia* fountain was created by Pietro Bernini in 1623, possibly with the help of his son Gian Lorenzo, and placed at the foot of the Spanish Steps to commemorate the high-water mark of the 1598 flood. The photograph dates from the early twentieth century. Courtesy Linda Lear Center for Special Collections and Archives, Connecticut College.

La Ripetta. Designed by Alessandro Specchi in 1704, these steps served as the landing spot for goods coming from upriver. The Ripetta was destroyed in 1890 to make way for retaining walls against river floods. Etching by Giovanni Battista Piranesi, Metropolitan Museum of Art.

Drago come uiueua il primo di Decembre 1691 nelle paludi fuori di Roma.

IN ROMA, Nella Stamperia di Gio: Giacomo Komarek Boëmo alla Fontana di Treui. 1696.
CON LICENZA DE SVPERIORI.

Somewhat fanciful recreation by Cornelius Meyer of a dragon said to have been found in the swamps upriver from Rome. The hard evidence of this creature, re-created by a contemporary taxidermist, proved to be fraudulent. Sotheby's.

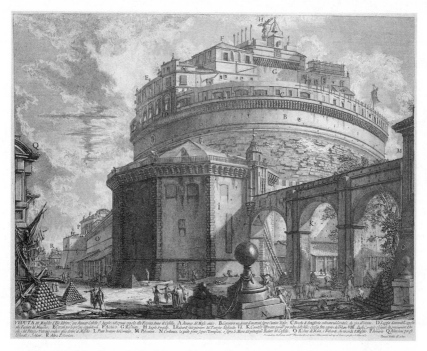

The Castel Sant'Angelo, as depicted by Giovanni Battista Piranesi. Originally the tomb of the emperor Hadrian (AD 76–138), the building, reworked, proved more useful to later generations as a fortress. On the Tiber close to the Vatican, it has occasionally served as a refuge for unpopular popes. Metropolitan Museum of Art.

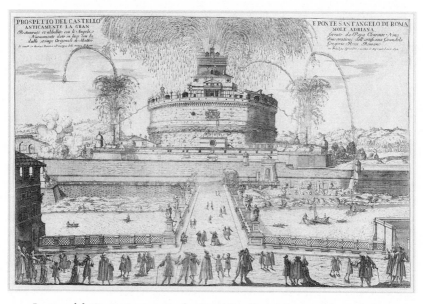

La girandola. Beginning in 1481, the Castel Sant'Angelo has served as a platform for fireworks displays. Previously these commemorated the elections of new popes; now they are an annual event celebrating the feast of Saints Peter and Paul. This etching by Giovanni Battista Falda dates from 1692. Metropolitan Museum of Art.

Olimpia Maidalchini, "La Pimpaccia." The sister-in-law of Pope Innocent X, she was said to be the power behind his throne. The papal connection made her rich, if unpopular. Courtesy Eleanor Herman.

Sophie Blanchard (1778–1819), a French balloonist who descended, unintentionally, into the Tiber. Wikimedia Commons.

The Castel Sant'Angelo and the Ponte Sant'Angelo. The statues are the work of Gian Lorenzo Bernini and his workshop. Courtesy Linda Lear Center for Special Collections and Archives, Connecticut College.

RENAISSANCE

In which a Borgia is killed, the question of whether to drink the water is addressed, a plutocrat builds his dream house, a papal charm halts a flood, Michelangelo fails to build a bridge, a pope's niece robs the Vatican, grasshoppers turn the river black, and the pope receives a white elephant.

Death of a Borgia

Nearby the Piazza Navona in downtown Rome there once lived a man named Pasquin, or Pasquino, a smart-mouthed tailor, or possibly cobbler, who could always be counted on for a sharp comment on whatever scandal was current that day. The locals mourned him his death and gave his name to a nearby statue on which were, from time to time, plastered anonymous commentaries the writers hoped were as memorable as those of the beloved tailor, or cobbler. In time the statue was goaded by questions posed by another statue, named Marforio. These witty, very public satires came to be known, after Pasquino, as pasquinades, and bad popes were a favorite target. With the election of the Spaniard Alexander VI, openly bought with Borgia family gold, the statue went to town:

> Vendit Alexander claves, altaria, Christum;
> Emerat Ille prius, vendere jure potest.[1]

> Alexander sells the keys, the altars, and even Christ:
> He paid for them first, by law he can sell them, however priced.

Other comments followed, usually assuming a literate audience with a nodding acquaintance with Rome's kings and early emperors. For the next gibe against Alexander, the reader had to recognize Tarquin as the sixth king after Romulus, and Nero as the sixth emperor (counting Julius Caesar):

Sextus Tarquinius, Sextus Nero, Sextus et iste:
Semper sub Sextis perdita Roma fuit[2]

Tarquin the sixth, Nero the sixth, and now this Sixth;
Rome always goes down when the number six comes up.

The pope's counselors suggested that he should have the Pasquino statue torn up and thrown into the Tiber. He said no. "I should fear that it should morph into a frog and that it would trouble me day and night."[3]

The commentary got worse. On the evening of Wednesday, June 14, 1497, Giovanni Borgia, allegedly the son of Pope Alexander, dined with his mother Donna Vanozza near San Pietro in Vincole along with his siblings Cesare, Lucrezia, Giovanni, and Gioffre. The party broke up late, and Giovanni and Cesare departed together, soon going their separate ways, Cesare to bed, Giovanni, it was assumed, to an assignation.

The next day Giovanni's horse came home alone, a stirrup cut. An alarmed pope sent out inquiries, and eventually a witness was found, a Sclavonian wood merchant who had brought his cargo downriver and was docked near the Piazza Giudecca. He had spent the night on board his vessel to guard against thieves. At some point he became aware of some furtive men emerging from the darkness of a nearby alley. Soon there followed the irregular clip-clop of hooves, and from that same alley a man led a horse, slung over which was a limp body, presumably dead. Some small conference between the conspirators ensued, and shortly thereafter the body was dropped into the river. It floated, to the men's clear dissatisfaction. They now gathered large stones with a view to pushing the body down, apparently with some success. The deed done, the men disappeared, never to be seen again. The Sclavonian, his lumber safe, continued his vigil.

Asked why he had not reported these events at the time, the Sclavonian replied: "In my day, I have seen as many as a hundred corpses thrown into the river at that place on different nights without anybody troubling himself about it, and so I attached no further importance to the circumstance."[4]

A grieving Alexander announced a reward for finding the body; more than three hundred men vied to win it. The body soon turned up, its hands bound, its throat slit, its torso pierced by nine knife wounds. Its expensive cloak was still present, along with a bag of gold ducats. An investigation was launched, and ten days later was abruptly halted without explanation. Rumors flew. The murderer had been Cesare. Or his cousin Gioffre. Or perhaps the Orsini family.

Whoever it was, or was not, no one was ever arrested, much less brought to trial; Cesare is the usual suspect.

The Florentine diarist Landucci was laconic: "19th June. We heard that a son of the Pope had been murdered and thrown into the Tiber."[5]

The Roman public was not overly sympathetic—quite the reverse, in fact. Within days of the body's recovery, the Neapolitan poet Jacopo Sannazaro was credited with a truly cruel pasquinade:

> Piscatorem hominum ne te non, Sexte, putemus,
> Piscaris natum retibus ecce tuum.[6]

> You're not much a fisher of men, Sextus, I think.
> Just look! You use nets to pull your own son from the drink.

Even in as insensitive an age as this, the verse was a bit much. But then, the Romans were never much taken with the Borgia family, and a good deal of the mud slung has stuck over the years. The family was able to instill fear, however, even in those who did not call Rome home. The German pilgrim Von Hafft, writing of the matter in 1497, refused to discuss the dead Borgia, "the reason for which I shall for now set aside, as well as many other unspeakable things I saw at Rome, things contrary to the Christian faith."[7]

He could well be referring to the number of bodies the Sclavonian claimed were dumped in the river. Five years after the Borgia death, we find a contemporary commenting on the death of "the Signor of Faenza [Astorre III Manfredi], a young man of about 18 years, and of such handsome figure and appearance that his like could hardly have been found among a thousand young men of his age. There were also found two young people bound to each other by the arms, one fifteen years of age and the other twenty-five years, and with them a woman, and many others."[8]

"And many others" does raise some questions, never to be answered.

Manfredi had, incidentally, inherited the lordship of the city of Faenza in Northern Italy when he was three years old. This birthright was taken from him in 1501, and he himself taken to be imprisoned at the Castel Sant'Angelo, where he was assassinated and dumped into the river. The new master of Faenza was—Cesare Borgia.

Small world, sixteenth-century Rome. Small and nasty.

Zambo

Slapstick humor with a higher quotient of cruelty than later societies might tolerate was still considered the stuff of entertainment in the Renaissance. An example appears in *Le piacevoli notti*—usually translated as "The Facetious Nights of Straparola," more accurately translated as "The Pleasing Nights of Straparola"—by Gianfrancesco Straparola, a shadowy figure who, given the at times satiric nature of the work, may have had good reason to be shadowy. The author's name itself is possibly a pseudonym (*straparlare* meaning to talk twaddle).[9] The book, first published in Venice, follows a convention established in Boccaccio's *Decameron* or Margaret of Angoulême's *Heptameron*. A group of lighthearted gentry pass thirteen nights on the island of Murano, near Venice, and while away the time by telling each other amusing or instructive stories, five a night.

The third fable of the fifth night involves three brothers, all identical, all hunchbacks, all vile. The eldest, Zambo, leaves home to seek his fortune in Rome, and eventually marries a prosperous widow, whom he proceeds to mistreat cruelly. Called away on business, he warns her that should his cunning brothers Bertaz and Santì show up, she should tell them to leave. Predictably, they do arrive, hoping to cadge money off him. She takes pity on them and gives them a meal in the kitchen. Zambo returns home, and they hide in an overturned pig trough. He is certain that mischief is afoot, but finding nothing, he departs. She checks on the two brothers, only to discover that they have died. Afraid to fess up, but eager to be rid of them, she calls a passing corpse collector (*picegamort*) to take one of them to be tossed into the river "as is the custom" (*alghe un consuet*).[10] When he comes back to be paid, she accuses him of shirking the job and points to the second corpse as proof of nonperformance. He is baffled, but takes the second corpse as well. On his way to the river, he runs into Zambo, accuses him of being a specter of some sort, and strikes him dead, and throws both into the Tiber. End of story. The audience erupts in laughter.

The church placed the title on the Index of Prohibited Books in 1624.

Papal Boats

A pope, no less than an emperor, does not ride in just any boat. The office demands that his arrivals and departures make a statement.

Gaspare Pontani, writing in 1482, refers to the Sistina Papale, a *bombarda*—a somewhat ambiguous term, likely a two-masted job—unusual enough that when it landed in town "many people came out to see it."[11]

Jacopo Gherardi, in his *Diario Romano* (November 10, 1483), mentions Giuliano della Rovere, future pope Julius II, riding down to Ostia in a *bucintoro* to see how the defense works were getting on.[12] This was basically a huge, tricked-out, expanded war galley peculiar to Venice, where each year one of these carried the doge into the lagoon to ceremoniously renew Venice's marriage to the sea, complete with spoken vows and tossing of a gold ring into the water—a one-way affair, of necessity; the hard-headed Venetians didn't even have a myth of the sea reciprocating.

Julius II was Genoese; but it was no surprise that the Venetian Cardinal Ottoboni (1667–1740) should use a bucentaur for his official travel. He called it *Stella Maris*, described by a contemporary as fitted out with "wood finely carved and richly gold leafed, adorned with beautiful crystals, and other fine trappings."[13] Nothing was too good for the cardinal to make the trip from Rome down to his new bishopric at the then dismal area of Portus. Three years later he was in the running to be pope, and might have succeeded had he not caught a fever (a serious risk near Portus) and died, surrounded by glittering prizes and deeply in debt. The ultimate fate of the bucentaur is obscure, which is a little surprising, given just how exceptional a creation it was.

The Richest Man in Rome

The richest man in Rome? That would be Agostino Chigi (1466–1520). The name tends to draw a blank. Where the Medici are a byword for plutocratic Italian Renaissance bankers, with Lorenzo de' Medici dubbed "il Magnifico"—and not without reason—Chigi, also dubbed a Magnifico, somehow gets a miss.

Chigi was a native of Siena, scion of a family of bankers in a city of bankers, the higher reaches of which trade were shared by the *mercantores senenses romanam curiam sequentes*—Sienese merchant bankers acting as agents for

Vatican business in the city of Siena. Chiefly this involved the collection of tithes; the church sold licenses to tax farmers with the mission to extract a certain amount from the areas in question. Anything the tax farmers could get above that number was theirs to keep. On their own, they exchanged currency, dealt in commodities, and, despite church disapproval, lent money.

Agostino, at age twenty, was eager to drop his formal schooling and get on with business. It was a calculated gamble in an age when a classical education was all but expected in dealings with the high and mighty. The intent was to build character, to become as noble as Cicero, but also to separate one from people who were not able to drop the apt Latin tag, the apposite quote. It was a class marker. These things oiled the wheels of bureaucracy. Young Chigi intended to substitute gumption and sheer ability.

He made the move to Rome and set up offices at the Contrada dei Banchi, the Wall Street of Renaissance Rome, and scouted for opportunity to buy low and sell high. He succeeded memorably at Foligno, which held a fair each year where every product of Italy was on offer. On the first day, Agostino appeared and bought the entire stock on credit, to be paid in three days. On the second day he rested. On the third day, he sold the goods at a hefty markup, paid his creditors, and returned to Rome.

Certainly his competitors in banking were not amused. A number of them gathered and began spreading rumors about his bank's solvency. The man was a sham, his enterprises were failing, his ships a fiction, it would be better for depositors to get out while the getting was good. Word spread, and crowds gathered, shouting outside his doors for their money. Chigi, all red hair and beard and large pale blue eyes, came down and faced his depositors calmly and courteously. Their money was perfectly safe, but should any truly wish to withdraw and not enjoy the benefits and future potential of being a partner of his, even in a small way, he would be more than happy to disburse their money. Would they prefer to be repaid in gold or silver, domestic currency or foreign? Confidence was restored; he did not have to redeem a single scudo.

Chigi was also quick to make himself known to Alexander VI, the Borgia pope. He was fortunate that Alexander was a man of considerable expenditures always in need of financing. Chigi family money spoke volumes, but even so, for the young Chigi to gain the confidence of a man as shrewd as Alexander suggests confidence and ability far beyond the common run. He was soon managing the inflows to the Curia.

He managed to snare the salt monopoly in the Papal States, along with that for alum. Alum is a fixative of dye for cloth, a huge market at the time. It was found in quantity in Anatolia, territory held by the Ottoman Turks, who kept the supply tight and the cost high. In 1461, rich deposits were found some seventy kilometers north of Rome, still within papal territory. A gift from God, clearly. The church needed secular intermediaries to exploit this resource, as indeed it did for all its income-producing resources. Chigi got the franchise.

When Alexander died, he was replaced with a stopgap pope, expected to last just long enough for ambitious cardinals to maneuver for the subsequent election, which would involve promises of future favors and payments of immediate bribes. For cash, one had to turn to the bankers. Cardinal della Rovere, old enemy to Alexander but always practical, turned to Chigi. Della Rovere won and took the name Julius II.

He was a difficult man to deal with, and far from scrupulous, as the many letters from Michelangelo complaining about unpaid bills can attest. One story goes that Julius borrowed money from Chigi using the jeweled papal crosier as collateral. The following morning, once the money was safely in his hands, he sent guards to retrieve the crosier. That particular debt went unpaid; Chigi philosophically took it as a loss leader, well aware that lending to princes is always problematic (the Bardi family of Florence, richest bankers of Europe, went bust by overgenerous lending to Edward III of England) but can pay larger dividends down the road.

His first wife died. He grieved, but he endured. His would-be second wife, Margherita Gonzaga, said of him, "He pleases me entirely except for his being a merchant and banker, which unfortunately seems to me unsuitable to our house."[14] He must have cared for her deeply, since he offered to abandon his business interests entirely, but it was still not to be. Class will tell. Of course, Margherita herself was the daughter of Francesco Gonzaga, the Marquis of Mantua . . . but not of the marquesa.

Chigi was never one to pine for lost opportunity. He consoled himself with the attentions of Imperia Cognati (aka "la Divina"), the finest courtesan of her time (and incidentally the mother of Chigi's daughter).

How rich was Chigi? Leo X once asked him. An impossible question. As with any truly rich man, Chigi confessed that he could not say. What he could do was to list his various assets. There were the legal advantages he enjoyed, courtesy of Leo and Leo's predecessors, things like his monopoly on the salt trade of Ostia, the alum trade in Latium, fishing rights to Fucine

Lake, and so forth. Of tangible goods, there were the many various houses, castles, villas about Italy, and uncounted gold and silver plate.

Then there were the business interests, the twenty thousand men on his payroll, the hundred merchant vessels based in Porto Ercole, the hundred branch banks in Italy, as well as branches in London, Lyon, Cairo, Alexandria, and Constantinople. These last three are of particular interest, as Leo was greatly concerned with the threat of spreading Islam in general and spreading Ottomans in particular. Yet here he was dining happily with a man the Ottoman sultans referred to as *magnus mercator christianus*, and from whom he received gifts of fine hunting dogs and a purebred Arabian horse.

There was the spending as well. Chigi had neglected a classical education, but he was a patron of those who had not. He bankrolled a printer to produce the first classical Greek texts in Rome: Pindar in 1515, Theocritus in 1516. He pushed the up-and-coming artists Perugino, Sodoma, and Raphael. Less successfully, he was patron to the poet, pornographer, and blackmailer Pietro Aretino—this individual became persona non grata when caught trying to walk off with a Chigi silver goblet.

Chigi's most notable possession, however, was the Villa Le Delizie. Taking advantage of Julius II's creation of the Lungara, the soon-to-be-fashionable boulevard parallel to the river's west bank, he hired the Sienese architect Baldassare Peruzzi, a student of Bramante, to design the place, said to be built on top of Julius Caesar's old summer retreat. (It isn't. Caesar's villa was outside the *pomerium*—important, as he needed a place to stash Cleopatra, who as a foreign official was not permitted to reside inside.)

Le Delizie demonstrated self-confidence in a new way. Instead of being a fortress, all grim stone outside and luxury inside, it presented the public with an elegant loggia, safe from the rain and sun, airy. Its courtyard was not enclosed by four walls but open on the northern side to a fountain and garden.

The garden! The records are scarce (though a contemporary map suggests that the architect built a retaining wall on the river, squeezing the path of water and thus affecting water flow in flood season), but we can get some idea from brief mentions by contemporaries. "We came to sport many times in the delightful garden of Agostino Chigi, to break lances, to drill horses in the lovely delightful and shady alleys in order to flee the wicked heat."[15]

His poetic sycophants mention wooden pergola vaults "over which plants creep and flowers ramble,"[16] as well as symbolic plants and a fountain. The real attraction for those fleeing the worst of Rome's wicked heat was the underground grotto hard by the river, "a cave fit for poets," *antrum aptu poetis*, with a bathing pool, bench, and small oculus in the vault for light.[17]

One of Chigi's parasites was the poet Blosius Palladius, who built a long poem extolling the beauties of this palazzo. The Tiber itself is given voice and goes on telling its own tale of history and how Chigi is bringing it back up to snuff after too many down years.

"After that Empire fell, than which no one was greater in the world, and which the idleness of the Caesars broke, I began to flow less."[18]

"Oh, how willingly I would have been with dried streams, when the Barbarian drank my waters against my will. But nevertheless it was painful to be a river god, since we streams are doomed by the law of the gods to live in perpetual running."[19]

And so on for several hundred lines. As Dr. Johnson noted, no one but a blockhead ever wrote except for money.

Or perhaps for one's supper. Chigi was famous for his dinners in the loggia overlooking the Tiber, from which vantage point the guests were invited to toss the gold and silver plate into the river. Not that he couldn't afford the loss. On another occasion, all guests who cleaned their plates found their own family crests carved into the metal, a unique souvenir of their visit. The tossed plates were, of course, caught in submerged nets and later recovered. The loggia itself, less fortunate, was destroyed by floods in the late sixteenth century.

Chigi died in bed, account books at his side, busy to the end. His fortune did not long outlast him. Le Delizie was put on the auction block and was sold in 1577 to Alexander Farnese, who renamed it Palazzo Farnesina. (Not to be confused with even grander Palazzo Farnese on the opposite bank, now the site of the French embassy. Michelangelo suggested that a private bridge be built between the two, but it never happened.)

The villa itself fell on hard times. John Evelyn visited in 1644 and declared it "famous only for the painting al fresco on the volto of the portico towards the garden; the story is the Amours of Cupid and Psyche, by the hand of the celebrated Raphael d'Urbino. . . . I must not omit that incomparable table of Galatea (as I remember), so carefully preserved in the cupboard at one of the ends of this walk to protect it from the air, being a most lively painting."[20]

John Chetwode Eustace was similarly disappointed with the interior, "unfurnished and neglected," and he knew the reason why—"it belongs to the King of Naples."[21]

Granted, the king of Naples in 1802 had a good deal on his mind, and the villa was an inheritance, one of many; nevertheless, the thought of the place being ignored does make the art lover wince. Things had not improved thirty years later. Lady Morgan writes: "Ruin and desolation are here triumphant!—the rooms are bare—time and damp are falling on the living hues of the Psyche and the Galatea. The delicious gardens, which the honest Chigi enjoyed, overgrown with weeds, command the ruinous shores of the dwindled Tiber; and the Campagna is not more melancholy than the once voluptuous pavilions of the Villa Farnesina."[22]

It has since been restored and is worth a visit.[23]

Water Carriers

Before the aqueducts came on line, early Romans drank Tiber water. Later Romans also drank Tiber water after the aqueducts failed. Without easy water, the first city to reach a population of a million collapsed to a small village surrounded by stunning architecture. Romans drifted back to the river to lessen the nuisance of gathering daily water.

Man is, however, entrepreneurial, and some were willing to do the heavy lifting, for a price. By the Middle Ages, such people created the Corporazione degli Acquaroli (or Compagnia degli Acquariciarii), the guild of the city water carriers, the *facchini* whose donkey carts carried wooden barrels throughout the city and who for a few coins would bring water to your doorstep, or, Saint Bernard–like, dispense ready water from small casks that hung around their necks. Cola di Rienzo's own mother, Maddalena, had been a guild member—modest roots for her son who would one day become the tribune of the city.

There clearly was money in the trade. Lanciani cites a 1512 contract between a water carrier and a priest, requiring the *facchino* to sell water on behalf of the priest, for which he, the *facchino*, would be provided two pairs of boots, two overcoats, and thirty silver *carlini* a year.[24] Still, change was coming.

Despite the explosion of new fountains in the sixteenth century, the trade continued for a while longer. No real surprise in that. Home water delivery is still a profitable business. The guild was flush enough to commission Jacopo del Conte (or—reaching for straws here—Michelangelo) to carve the *facchino* fountain. Set into a wall on the Via Lata, it portrays a water bearer holding a barrel from which a stream of water plays continuously for pass-ersby. Good water, too.

Various stories surround the man holding the barrel. He was Abbondio Rizio, a well-loved wine lover whose epigraph (*in publicis stillicidiis coronato*) was composed by the abbot Luigi Godard and placed over the fountain.[25] Or he was Marco Antonio de Dominici (1560–1624), heretical archbishop of Spalato, who died a prisoner in Castel Sant'Angelo (poisoned! Or maybe not) and was later burned in the Campo de' Fiori along with his books, but who, for unstated reasons, was then memorialized with this statue.[26] Or he was an unnamed wine seller who diluted his product and who, in death, was made to pay his penance by giving back the water for free.[27] Or—straws again—it might be Martin Luther, for no other reason than that it bears a squinting resemblance (perhaps more so in the past—allegedly, pious Cath-olics tossing bricks at the heretic account for the damage to the face).[28]

Whoever the fellow might be, his statue was installed at the height of the water carrier's trade. Pope Gregory XIII (1502–1585), who drank only Tiber water, restored the aqueducts at the end of the sixteenth century, and the city was soon awash in public fountains. The guild's monopoly over the Trevi Fountain water, for which members paid a few *iulii* a year, was soon a thing of the past.[29] These days, the commercial value at the Trevi is in the coins tossed by tourists, lured by the promise that those who throw in three coins will someday return to Rome. The proceeds belong to the Catholic charity Caritas, but as an open-air poor box, the fountain poses obvious temptations.

Potabile o non potabile?

Of course one *could* drink the Tiber's water—but was it wise? Opinions have differed.

Magister Gregory (c. 1250) thought it "good for horses, but unsuitable and even noxious for men."[30] Paolo Giovio advised an ailing cleric in 1527 that filtered Tiber water "was both harmless, lighter, and superior to all kinds of water, whether from springs or rain."[31] Jacques Le Saige, passing through town in 1518, claimed locals would not drink the river water while it was agitated (*tourbe*), but that in glass, it settled down nicely.[32] The poet Ariosto (1474–1533), conscious of his delicate health, had his brother draw river water to settle for a few days before he, Ariosto, arrived:

Fa ch'io truovi de l'aqua, non di fonte
Di fiume si, che già sei di veduto
Non abbia Sisto, né alcun altre ponte.[33]

Fetch me water, not from springs
But from the river, which for six days
Ponte Sisto, nor any other bridge, should see.

The question came to a head in 1556, when Giovanni Battista Modio wrote: "It is not many days past, that a writer friend of mine, who was suffering from kidney stones, and side pains, told me that to become healthy, he had done nothing more than to refrain from the water of the Tiber, and to drink that of the Trevi Fountain."[34]

Anyone who has ever had kidney stones will sympathize, and if Modio was particularly insistent, it is because he too had suffered from the ailment, and rather more so than most. His had been serious enough to block urination, leading him to think he was about to die. Modio was fortunate enough to be friendly with Saint Philip Neri (1515–1595), who, distressed by his friend's discomfort, stepped into a nearby church and prayed for him. At the moment the first tear of compassion fell from Neri's eye, the stone passed.[35] Of course, not everyone has access to living saints. (Morever, the Hippocratic oath enjoins doctors not to take the knife to kidney stones. The operation at the time was a specialist's task, something best left to barbers.)

Modio was a respected man in Rome. A qualified physician, he wrote widely, as educated Italians of the time did, and among his works was a short treatise on the Tiber, in which he included the anecdote of his friend helped by the Trevi water. Modio thought Tiber water a poor substitute for spring water, such as was piped in on the Acqua Vergine aqueduct. That the ancient Romans went to the trouble of building aqueducts at all was proof enough that they saw the advantages.

Modio went to Hippocrates himself, fountain of all medical thinking. Hippocrates had much to say on the subject of water, its sources, and the qualities good or bad that depend on those various sources. Swamp water was to be avoided. He was somewhat guarded about spring water; hot springs carried too many minerals, while cold springs could be good or bad, depending whether they came from rocky soil (bad) or loam (good). River water was a little trickier. The quality depended on a number of variables, such as the orientation of the river flow, the size of the stream, the nature of the ground it ran over, and the various tributaries. Each tributary, each rivulet, had its own character, dependent on its origins, and the more of these rivulets that gathered into one large stream, the more mixed and therefore unpredictable the final product. Bad water was, in fact, liable to cause—kidney stones.[36]

Modio's claims ran straight against the opinion of the personal physician of the pope.

Alessandro Traiano Petroni had written a treatise of his own in 1552, *De aqua Tiberina*, in which he declared that Tiber water was not only safe, but positively invigorating. He, moreover, dedicated *his* book to the pontiff.

Modio wasn't impressed. "If our doctors had told the sainted Pope Paul III the truth, he never would have stooped to believe that Tiber water was perfect, as he did."[37]

Strong words, somewhat undercut by Paul's surviving to a vigorous age eighty-two. Petroni's allies in debate included M. Andrea Bacci ("medico et filosofo"), who wrote no fewer than three editions of his own *Del Tevere*, in which he contested Hippocrates. The Tiber and the Nile, he said, were exceptions to the rules, since they had few tributaries. As to aqueducts, far from being a sign of Rome's greatness, they were in fact evidence of its notorious decadence. The hardy early Romans satisfied their practical water needs with river water. The Rome of the emperors piped in absurd amounts of water for useless, not to say morally questionable, ends. Baths, for example.

Moreover, did not some popes insist on carrying Tiber water with them when traveling, among them Clement VII and Paul III (and later Clement XIII)?[38] Each edition expanded as Bacci found more to talk about, adding chapters on how to store water, what health effects it brought, how Rome might avoid floods—the river was something of an obsession for the man.

Modio, having fired his one shot, had moved on. He gave up medicine and followed the kidney stone expert Philip Neri in preaching the lives of the saints to the city's faithful. He died in 1560, five years after his book on the Tiber, five years before Bacci's (first) rebuttal. That same year, the pope began renovations on the Acqua Vergine.[39] Renaissance Rome, like imperial Rome, was growing. The Tiber couldn't fulfill those needs, however healthful its waters might be. The work on the Acqua Vergine, along with the Acqua Felice (1587) and the Acqua Paola (1612), all of them papal operations, allowed the church to favor friends and snub enemies.[40]

Life went on.

By 1685, Gilbert Burnet, DD, could state confidently that "almost every private house hath a fountain that runs continually."[41] We can only guess how low down the social ladder the good doctor went to corroborate this claim, or how he defined private houses. Restored aqueducts should have made Tiber water superfluous, but did not. Maximilien Misson, visiting Rome in 1688, was of the settled-down-nicely school; he wrote of Tiber water that "if it be suffer'd to stand one or two days, more or less, it grows clear and limpid, and they assure that 'tis very good."[42] It sounds as if he did not put their assurance to the test.

Half a century later, Pascoli claimed that as of 1740, drinking river water was a thing of the past ("si son bevute fin quasi ai nostri tempi"), but he was mistaken.[43] The French traveler Joseph-Jérôme de Lalande, in 1765, saw a case for patience: "When one allows Tiber water to rest, it settles, becomes clear and becomes very good to drink."[44] Nor is that just the word of an ignorant foreign tourist. The nineteenth-century professor Antonio Clemente considered Tiber water not only potable, but superior to that of the Thames and the Seine.[45] Nor was this all just talk. In 1811, the Theresians of la Scala, the Benedictines of the Monastery of Caliso, and the Philippines of the Chiesa Nuova still made daily treks to the river for drinking water.[46]

In 1877, the English Tiber enthusiast Strother Smith put the matter to the test, scientifically, if amateurishly. "To form an opinion as to the time within which [Tiber water] might be drunk, I filled a large flagon with it at a time when it was greatly discoloured by a sudden flood. At the end of five hours I found that it had deposited its yellow mud, but still retained a slightly milky hue. . . . [Five days later] it had become as clear as crystal and in no way distinguishable from the water of the Acqua Vergine." So far, so good. "I drank a portion, used another portion for making tea, and found it excellent. A trial of it with soap showed it to be of a medium decree of hardness. . . . A bottle of it well corked was left at Rome during the summer, to see whether it would undergo fermentation owing to the presence of organic matter, and develop any unpleasant taste or smell. On my return, after an interval of four months, the water was found to be perfectly sweet to the taste, and free from any disagreeable odour."[47]

Rodolfo Lanciani was not impressed. Referring to the popes Clement VII, Paul III, and Gregory XIII and their taste for Tiber water, he argued that their experience "simply proves that the three pontiffs were proof against typhoid."[48]

That was in 1900. The debate, given latter-day chemicals and sewage, is now moot. Certainly Smith's is no longer an experiment one would care to repeat.

Paolo Giovio and His Book of Fish

On an evening in 1523, Paolo Giovio (1483–1552) was a guest at a banquet thrown for François Louis, cardinal of Bourbon. The food was good, the conversation sophisticated, the spirits high. Course followed course, and high on the menu was fish. All present being good Latin scholars, the question was raised what the ancients would have called the various dishes they were eating. The cardinal suggested in passing that such a large question would make for an interesting study.

Giovio, trained in medicine and natural history, was one of those Renaissance polymaths ready to turn his hand to almost anything, and this sounded like a challenge well suited to his talents. For him, as for all good hacks, it was a matter of money, or at least the promise of money. Within a year he presented the cardinal with *De romanis piscibus libellus*.

The book was the first work since ancient times dedicated entirely to fish. Forty different kinds of fish. He fulfilled the original mandate, giving contemporary Roman names as well as Latin, and even on occasion adding terms from other languages or other dialects, notably those of Spain and Venice. That would have been good for a few pages, and hardly worth the effort. Giovio decided to expand the work, drawing on his medical and scientific training to discuss the health benefits and threats of given species, in particular as they applied to the sedentary scholar of the kind that might actually read his book.

He scoured the ancient works, Pliny mostly, but also did legwork among the living professionals, tracking down the local fisherman and fishmongers for their observations. Topping the fish scale was the sturgeon, then still plentiful in the Tiber and found as far away as the Black Sea, by the Dnieper River, where the locals maintained fishponds and workshops devoted exclusively to harvesting sturgeon eggs, which he informs us are salted and called caviar and considered a great delicacy. Less desirable was the torpedo, a kind of electric eel, or some such, that if touched when netted, numbs the fisherman's hand (*piscatorum manus stupefaciat*). Only poor people, he said, bother to eat that fish.

We get cooking tips, chiefly involving rosemary and olive oil, to bring out the best in any given fish. (Footnote on how to cook lamprey eel: "One usually kills lamprey in Cretan wine, and closes up their mouths with nutmeg, and plugs the gill holes with a like amount of cloves, rolls it into a coil, covers it with minced hazelnuts, bread crumbs, olive oil, Cretan wine, and spices and cooks it with care over hot coals for a specific period of time.")[49]

We learn how Roman fishmongers overcharged the abstemious and widely despised Dutch pope Adrian VI for third-rate fish, and laughed in contempt at the crabbed old bumpkin while doing so. Indifference to the quality of food is, rightly, an unforgivable sin for Italians past and present. We read about porpoises and dolphins and how they differ, and how they resemble sharks, and how they can trouble sharks. He tells of a beached whale so immense that men on horseback on either side cannot see each other, one whose fat can serve as fuel for lamps.

He tells the story of the notorious Renaissance parasite and glutton Tito Tamisio, who, learning of a particularly fine umbrine fish bought at market by city magistrates on the Capitoline Hill, inveigles his way into the magistrates' quarters on some weak pretext and in anticipation of dinner. Alas, the fish has been given to Cardinal Riario, their patron. Tamisio chases the fish down there, only to find that it has been given away again to Cardinal Frederick Sanseverino. The cardinal, in debt to the banker Agostino Chigi, and in a gesture of goodwill, passed the catch on to him. Chigi had it dressed up with flowers and sent to his mistress Imperia Cognati. Tamisio, not the most physically fit of men, now nearly exhausted and always shameless, invites himself to dine with her, much to her surprise.

The book was a modest thing, some eighty-four pages, a short read intended to wheedle a quick gratuity from a specific cardinal in want of light diversion and heavy flattery. Moreover, it sparked the imagination of other natural historians, serious ichthyologists who improved on the science of the book by expanding the variety of fishes described and adding woodcuts of the creatures under discussion.[50]

For Giovio, however, his own work, done with such high hopes of preferment or money, or some kind of material advantage, was a bust. That it was popular as these things went is unquestioned—reprints came out in Rome and Basel (1527), Antwerp (1528), Basel again (1531), and Strasbourg (1534); we can only hope that the author got residuals for his work. The only reward the French cardinal gave Giovio, or so Giovio said in later life, was a "fictitious benefice situated on the island of Thule, beyond the Orkneys."[51]

Put not your faith in princes, even princes of the church, least of all on the basis of casual remarks made over dinner conversation.

Julius II and Urban Renewal

In 1508, Pope Julius II decreed that a palazzo belonging to a Borgia enemy was to be razed to the ground and the Palazzo dei Tribunali, a central office building, put in its place, consolidating the various bureaucratic functions that even then troubled city life.[52]

The church had not fully consolidated its power in opposition to the leading families of Rome. Julius wanted to change that. One way to do so was to create a street parallel to the Tiber, the Via Giulia, named after himself, and make it a desirable address. To be desirable, however, it needed a view of the other bank that was more than just warehouses and slums. The answer was to revive the Via della Lungara, stretching from the Vatican down to the Ponte Sisto (the work of his uncle). This, he thought, would encourage the rich to come out from behind their fortresslike bunkers and to replace them with buildings more suitable to the civilized setting: urban villas, all light and air and sunshine and gardens and river views.

There was protest, of course. Eminent domain never goes down well at the donor's end. Still, in a year, the riversides had been subdivided into building lots, and those who could afford to do so, bought and built. (Or, even more ostentatiously, did not build. The odd vineyard was to be found on the odd lot.) Not all the buildings were as grand as Julius might have hoped; the Palazzo Farnese was to come some years after his death. Other names are mostly forgotten.

Julius did much to improve the aesthetics of the area. He did not, however, address the perennial problem of the Tiber's excesses.

Bartolomeo Brandano

In 1527, Rome was visited by a monk who arrived from Siena and demanded to see the pope. He passed through the streets up to the Castel Sant'Angelo shouting of visions of catastrophe. A contemporary takes up the story.

Brandano went to Rome and ran through the streets shouting, "Repent! that the city is to be sacked and put to the sword by men from beyond the Alps"; he spoke ill of the pope, without any respect, and with such force that the pontiff with indignation ordered him taken and imprisoned [at the Castel Sant'Angelo], and kept there for several days. Having finally released him, he had the man escorted out of Rome and warned him that should he ever return, he would have him thrown into the Tiber. Disdaining this threat, the man returned to Rome again, speaking against the pope even more forcefully than before, and repeating that he and all of Rome would suffer badly, that God would punish him for causing the death of so many people with the war he was making; that the good Shepherds should prevent war, not foment it, and he said that the wicked life of the clerics would be the reason that Rome was to be sacked and burned. These things he said with such ardor that he was believed by many and the words frightened the foolish and they took him to be a Prophet because his speaking was not unknowing; indeed it seemed that his words were uttered by the Holy Spirit and all that he said was merely repetition, just as with a Prophet; and following him through Rome spouting these things, Pope Clement VII again had him seized and thrown from the Ponte Sant'Angelo into the Tiber, that he should drown; but when he emerged without any injury, and again went about shouting thoughout Rome, the pope, because of his marvelous recovery, resolved to leave him alone, saying that if he was mad, the madness had made him sick, but if he was a righteous man, and beloved by God, it was worse to punish him. And so the pope let him have his say.[53]

Brandano would return to Siena and live until 1555. He may or may not have been mad, but his words were prophetic.

Cellini, the Sack of Rome, a Flood, and Prison

Clement VII became pope in 1523 and might well have regretted it. His term coincided with the power struggle between two great European sovereigns: Francis I of France and Charles V of the Holy Roman Empire. Charles had too much power, and Francis too little—at least that was Francis's thinking, he having lost the election as Holy Roman emperor for no other reason than Charles had paid the electors bigger bribes. Even though Charles was chiefly interested in maintaining the considerable European real estate he had and taking the fight to Islam, others—particularly the republics of Venice, Genoa, and Florence, and the Duchy of Milan—had come to see him, rather than the Muslim world, as the clearer and more present danger. In 1526 they cobbled together the so-called League of Cognac to preserve their interests against a presumably rapacious Charles, fearing that otherwise "Charles will inevitably become *signor dil mondo*, king of the world."[54] Clement opted to join them.

The league never got beyond the planning stage. Charles, by contrast, had gathered a considerable force made up of German Lutherans—men who despised the Catholic Church—and others, nominally good Catholics, who liked adventure. While Charles tried to hammer out things diplomatically, his soldiers, camped in Northern Italy, unpaid for months, grew restless. With the natural instincts of predators, the army, more a mob than a disciplined military force, roused itself and embarked on the very invasion that the league had sought to prevent. Their target was Rome.

The troops trudged down the spine of Italy, their numbers swollen by adventurers and bandits and opportunists until, when they arrived at Rome, they were some forty thousand strong.[55] Word of their movement and target spread before them and to the citizens of Rome. Note that there had been portents. The Tiber had produced a particularly bad flood in 1526. A mule gave birth in the Cancelleria. A statue spontaneously broke apart without reason.

Some took note, if not of the portents, then of the political situation. Those who could quietly left the city for safer places in the country. Clement was not among them, nor did he approve of their passion for self-interest. So tied was he to the city that in February he posted guards at the city gates to keep anyone else from leaving. He made similar edicts against merchants who might try to move goods out of the city. Common citizens, apolitical by nature, seemed to see no great difference in one ruler over another and were sanguine about any upcoming changes.

The imperial army was coming south to the right bank, from the north. Good walls, built in the time of Leo and as a consequence of the Saracen raids, now surrounded Saint Peter's. Good, but capable of improvement. The greater part of the city was on the left bank. Breaking the walls would be difficult and time-consuming, and the Duke de Bourbon (confusingly also named Charles), head of the imperial army, was disinclined to try.

Bourbon knew that the Vatican and Trastevere were not the real goal; the real goal was across the river. The bridges were vital. He knew that the citizens on the far side would not hesitate to destroy them. The Romans were confident that, absent guns, the army could not take the city.

Renzo da Ceri, in charge of the defenses, was not so sanguine. He argued for the destruction of the bridges. The city fathers refused. The walls were strong; that should be good enough.

When the imperial army arrived at the walls, Bourbon demanded entry, so as to avoid the horrors of a sacking. Da Ceri refused "with angry words" (*palabras descompuestas*).[56] A fight was now inevitable.

Among Rome's inhabitants at this time was Benvenuto Cellini (1500–1571), court musician and goldsmith to Pope Clement. A good Florentine serving a Florentine pope, and a man always happy for a fight (street brawls in Florence had forced him to flee his native city disguised as a monk), Cellini, along with fifty other youths—*ben pagati e ben trattati*, well paid and well treated—was persuaded to take up arms and safeguard the personal property of the Florentine merchant Alessandro del Bene, at risk since the pope had declared no foreigners might leave with their goods. The job was reasonable enough, at least until the sound of gunfire from the east suggested that the real fighting was going on on the other side of the river, by the Vatican. Alessandro decided that a few of his hired men should see what help they could offer.

One was Cellini, who arrived at the high ramparts overlooking the so-called Campo Santo, ramparts the enemy hoped to scale. Early morning mist had drifted in from the Tiber, obscuring much of what was going on below. The approaching German troops could be heard, but the defenders were unable to see through the mist. Nevertheless, seemingly random shots had made their marks, and Cellini reports bodies of the dead lying on the ramparts. The attackers attempted to place scaling ladders against the wall, but with little success, as these laid them open to gunfire from above, or were simply being tipped backward. Finally, to inspire his men, the Duke de Bourbon himself, distinct in polished silver mail, got off his horse and set up a ladder for himself, waving others to follow. It was an inspiring gesture, but a fatal one—he was gut shot, and carried to a nearby chapel to die.

Cellini adds detail to the story: "Directing my arquebuse where I saw the thickest and most serried troop of fighting men, I aimed exactly at one whom I remarked to be higher than the rest; the fog prevented me from being certain whether he was on horseback or on foot."[57] He directed his two companions to fire in that general direction as well (after he had shown them "how to avoid being hit by the besiegers").[58] He goes on: "When we had fired two rounds apiece, I crept cautiously up to the wall, and observing among the enemy a most extraordinary confusion, I discovered afterwards that one of our shots had killed the Constable of Bourbon, and from what I subsequently learned, he was the man whom I had first noticed above the heads of the rest."[59]

True? Not true? Who can say? Others have other versions, and in the event it scarcely mattered. The general was dead, and in such cases, one of two things can happen. Confusion leads to dismay and attacks fail, or dismay leads to fury and attacks are redoubled. In this case fury prevailed. More ladders hit the walls, and the besiegers too numerous to counter began to enter the Vatican and Rome itself.

Cellini and his companions were already heading back to Del Bene's property, and barely made it into the Castel Sant'Angelo before the portcullis came down. His was not the only hairbreadth escape. Clement VII, still trusting to God and the Leonine walls, was at this time celebrating Mass in Saint Peter's. Paolo Giovio, the author of the fish book, accompanied the pope from Mass to the relative safety of the Castel Sant'Angelo, via the Passetto di Borgo. All now climbed to the roof, where the artillery was located, and watched. From the safety of the building, their chief task now was to support their comrades on the far bank in keeping imperial troops from crossing the river, at least long enough that a proper defense could be mounted. Doing so entailed firing into residential areas, even the soldiers' own homes.

Other lesser men, overcome by sentiment and unwilling to risk collateral damage to their city, froze. Cellini was made of sterner stuff.

I took one of the matches, and got the assistance of a few men who were not overcome by their emotions. I aimed some swivels and falconets at points where I saw it would be useful, and killed with them a good number of the enemy. Had it not been for this, the troops who poured into Rome that morning, and were marching straight upon the castle, might possibly have entered it with ease, because the artillery was doing them no damage. I went on firing under the eyes of several cardinals and lords, who kept blessing me and giving me the heartiest encouragement. In my enthusiasm I strove to achieve the impossible; let it suffice that it was I who saved the castle that morning, and brought the other bombardiers back to their duty.[60]

He could not, however, save Rome. He, the pope, some fortunate cardinals, and other retainers, spent the remainder of the day and night listening and watching. Across the river, the city had become a scene out of Dante's *Inferno* as civilians were attacked, robbed, murdered, and churches and houses ransacked. As night fell, Cellini, honest if appalling ("[I] have always taken pleasure in extraordinary sights") watched the sky turn orange as the city burned.[61]

What followed was the stuff of horror. Protestant troops were no respecters of Catholic beliefs. Nuns were raped, priests disemboweled, reliquaries seized, papal tombs—thought to have gold—smashed open. Frescoes were covered with graffiti; there was a mock election of a pope, and Masses officiated by drunken prostitutes. Nominal Catholics satisfied themselves with plundering the secular side of the city.

The violence, like all violence, would eventually peter out, but not before a long night of terror, cries so bad that not a man among them, least of all Cellini, was willing to leave the safety of Castel Sant'Angelo. With dawn came the sight of rising smoke, collapsed roofs, battered civilians.

And then there were the dead. A single Spanish sapper claimed to have buried nearly ten thousand corpses and to have thrown another two thousand into the Tiber.[62]

The pope remained prudently in the castle for weeks, helpless, but safe.

He called upon Cellini's other skills; the craftsman was to dig the jewels from and melt down the papal tiaras (two hundred pounds of gold), in order to coin the ransom demanded by the surrounding army, a task he completed in his quarters with a quickly constructed brick kiln. The ransom paid, the jewels safely sewn into the pope's clothing, Clement left for Orvieto, Cellini for Florence. The work Cellini did in service of the pope would eventually come back to haunt him, but for now he was happy enough simply to leave the devastated city and resume his preferred employment in less contentious surroundings.

Months passed, and the imperialists realized that holding Rome was more trouble than it was worth. By February, the pope's French allies managed to rouse themselves enough to see Charles's imperial troops evacuating the city, and in a relatively orderly manner. Pillaging at this point was strictly forbidden, and violators were hanged in conspicuous places to enforce the edict. The better part of Charles's forces were soon gone, with a few leftover personnel arranging for the removal of property and the sick and wounded.

The French forces, led by the Orsini, now entered the city and were looking for blood. Imperial stragglers were attacked, and the last Spanish barges moored at the Ripa, and stacked high with booty, were seized (one sunk), the crews condemned to slavery. This new outburst of violence also frightened off fourteen ships that had been carrying relief supplies of grain and wine to the city.

Previous sackings of Rome had lasted a few days, and in the case of Gaiseric, two weeks. The sack of 1527 lasted nine months.

In time, the city began to recover, and two years after the sack, Cellini, busy in his studio, received a letter from Rome, explaining that the pope had returned and was asking for him. He was reluctant—hard to blame him—but an invitation from the pope is not easily dismissed. He headed back to Rome.

A brief digression is in order here. Rome, it seemed, had recovered at least somewhat from its misfortunes, and Cellini in discussing his own return gives a brief glimpse of river infrastructure at that time. The city had three bridges across the Tiber, all of which cost money to build and maintain. Someone has to pay, and by this time control of the bridges had been inherited by those strong enough or connected enough to manage the job. The new owners demanded tolls. This was met by competition in the form of ferrymen. It was one of these, by the name of Giacopo della Sciorina, who had written to Cellini.

Della Sciorina had been a Florentine pattern maker for cloth weavers, but in Rome he was referred to as Giacopino della Barca because he kept a ferryboat that made the crossing somewhere between the Ponte Sisto and the Ponte Sant'Angelo.[63] "He was a person of considerable talent, distinguished by his pleasantries and a striking conversation. . . . He was intimate with the Pope, who took great pleasure in hearing him talk."[64] One has to wonder what brought him to leave a highly skilled trade in Florence for such an unlikely second trade in Rome, while still having friends in very high places.

Giacopino's name crops up in a poem by the Swiss writer Conrad Ferdinand Meyer (1825–1898), who combined obscure scholarship with an oddly upbeat Romanticism:

> Sweet is the darkness after the heat of the day! On the twilit bridge
> I see the shores along of this immortal city.
> Castles and temples joined in one mighty legend!
> Beneath me, the river shelters some lost treasure.
>
> There, in the flood, the specter of a boat! Is it a fleeing emperor?
> Is that "Iacopino della Barca" who ferried Buonarotti?
> Piercing, a song rises from the boat to the glory of the loved one.
> Listen! A lively tongue calls out for living happiness.[65]

The poem raises more questions. Did he really ferry Michelangelo? It's possible. Meyer was well known as a Michelangelo aficionado and was possibly referring to the sculptor's disinclination to cross the Pons Aemilius. But even among nineteenth-century scholars, how many are going to get the allusions? And what about the boat (or perhaps boats)? Did Giacopino man the craft himself, or did he rent it out to willing and able oarsmen, as taxicab owners do? Cellini does not enlighten us, preferring as usual to make himself the center of attention in any anecdote. Archival spelunking might turn up a further clue.

Back to Cellini. Having arrived in Rome, the goldsmith came to an agreement with Clement and set up an atelier where he got down to work on a medallion. He was still in town in 1530 when the river began to rise.

The water rose, and he kept on working. It gathered around his ankles, and higher, enough that it could no longer be ignored, putting the goldsmith in a quandary over what exactly he should do. Eventually the water level seemed to stabilize, but who could say whether it would go down, or go up again? His life and his work were at stake; so was a pile of jewels Pope Clement had left with him to be reset. Cellini followed his conscience: "Bethinking me first of my own safety and in the next place of my honour, I filled my pockets with the jewels, and gave the gold-piece into the custody of my workmen, and then descended barefoot from the back-windows, and waded as well as I could until I reached Monte Cavallo."[66]

Jeweler and jewels were safe, at least for the moment. About the journeymen, we hear nothing more. Cellini was well known as a paragon of egocentricity.

Still the water rose. The Venetian envoy Antonio Suriano, a man who knew a thing or two about water, had to abandon his host's palace when the water reached the ceiling of the first floor. The water eventually reached the steps of the Campidoglio, a thing unheard of. In the aftermath, three palazzi on the Via Giulia collapsed.[67]

The flood is commemorated by a marker (one of many) on the side of Santa Maria sopra Minerva, giving thanks to the intervention of the Virgin Mary, "without whose swift aid, all Rome would have been overwhelmed."[68] The plaque, like Cellini, tells only part of the story, and not that of the human consequences. A visiting Spanish dignitary tells the rest: "By sunrise on Saturday morning, October 8, the Tiber had risen from its normal bed and begun to spill mountains of water, to the great shock of everyone. . . . Thus having begun to flood the city by midday, the troubled river rose to flush the sewers, the cellars, and the lower-lying areas; a little later one could see the water overcome houses, and rising as if in betrayal, and flowing with great force, which seemed to undercut the city's very foundation."[69]

Floods, like sackings, eventually pass, and this one passed; the filth was cleaned, the disease spent, and life returned to normal. Cellini himself would continue his work, more or less out of trouble, until his patron Clement died and was succeeded by Paul III (Alessandro Farnese), a Roman, a man less cordial to Cellini. In short order, the goldsmith found himself hauled before the papal court and charged with having stolen the papal jewels that Clement had taken to Orvieto and that were now missing. He denied the charge, to no avail, and was imprisoned in the Castel Sant'Angelo that eleven years earlier he had worked so hard to protect.

His situation wasn't so bad at first. His cell was a gentleman's apartment in the upper floors of the fortress overlooking the Cortile del Pozzo. The worst of it was a jailer, who, each year, went quite mad. "One time he thought he was an oil-jar; another time he thought he was a frog, and hopped about as frogs do. Another time he thought he was dead and then they had to bury him."[70] During Cellini's stay, the man thought he was a bat, emitted high-pitched screeches and flapped his arms as if ready to fly. His doctors dragooned Cellini to keep him company. Some months of this injustice proved too much for the craftsman, and he contrived to escape, in as clichéd a fashion as possible—he tied bedsheets together to form a rope and rappelled himself from the rooftop toward the ground below. Unfortunately the bedsheet rope broke before he reached the bottom. He fell and broke his leg, and fainted from the pain. In agony he crawled across the city, inviting pity and talking a few night workers into helping him, until he finally reached the house of a powerful cardinal who would take up his cause.

All efforts on his behalf were in vain, and this time he was placed in more squalid quarters deeper inside the castle, where he passed the time drawing the features of the resurrecting Jesus and God the father on the walls of his cell, until his family back in Tuscany was able to come up with the money to get him out. (It could have been worse—a 1495 diary notes that when the river had overflowed, "many cattle perished, and also men, especially those who were imprisoned in the vaults of towers.")[71] With that, he left Rome for good and headed for France, for whose king he made the famous saltcellar now in Kunsthistorisches Museum, and eventually made his way back to Florence, there to dictate his memoirs, which are rich in self-serving stories that highlight aspects of his talents, bravery, ingenuity, and overall superiority.

The drawings he left on the walls are still there, albeit faded from time, but evidence that not everything he wrote in his memoirs is necessarily a fable.

Two Popes, Three Bridges, Four Heads

Bridges have a life, and over the years, those built by the Romans dropped out one by one, as floods and traffic wore them down to uselessness. Between the expense and expertise needed to rebuild them and the ease with which boats could handle most jobs, the number of bridges in the early Renaissance was down to four, with two of those serving as a single crossing at Tiber Island.

Boat rides are fun but time consuming, and boats do not always take carts. Once Rome had recovered from its several stumbles and begun to pick up population and pilgrims, the need for reliable bridges became pressing. Sixtus IV (1414–1484), mindful of the 1450 Jubilee tragedy (too many pilgrims on too narrow a bridge, a panicky donkey, pedestrians fatally pushed over the sides of the Ponte Sant'Angelo) and planning a better outcome for the 1475 Jubilee, hired Baccio Pontelli, designer of the Sistine Chapel, to take some stone from the Colosseum and resurrect the Aurelius bridge. He did not resurrect its ancient name.

The resulting Ponte Sisto was the first new bridge since antiquity, in consequence of which, as a contemporary noted, "all that part of Trastevere, which had been a filthy wasteland, became vibrant and cultured."[72] Renaissance gentrification, as it were. More to the point, the bridge provided a direct line between the quays and granaries of the Ripa Grande on left bank and the marketplaces of the Campo de' Fiori on the right, useful for the largely Genoese merchants who lived in that area.[73] Sixtus himself was from near Genoa.

The enterprise was undertaken with a good deal of pomp and circumstance. Popes no less than politicos prefer that their good deeds not be anonymous, and by any measure the erection of the Ponte Sisto was an extremely good deed. A Roman diarist, Stefano Infessura (c. 1430–1500), records the numerous cardinals, prelates, and gawkers who headed down to the riverside to witness the pontiff lay a cornerstone on which was inscribed:

SIXTUS QUARTUS PONT. MAX. FECIT FIERI SUB ANNO DOMINI 1473
(Sixtus IV Pontifex Maximus caused this to be built in the Year of Our Lord 1473)

The diarist goes on: "The pope placed some gold medallions with his head on that stone, and in the doing, banished the name Ponte Rotto to use for that other broken bridge."[74] (The diarist is possibly referring to the Pons Aemilius, severely damaged in 1230 and restored several times over the centuries.)

The bridge features in Platina's series of frescoes on the life of Sixtus IV at the Ospedale di Santo Spirito in Sassia. One panel depicts Sixtus blessing the men working on his unfinished bridge, some of whom, kneeling, are taking full advantage of his presence, while others are farther back, hard at work, lifting a stone block by crane, holding hammers above their heads, not goofing off. These men took six years to finish the project, and to make sure that no one should forget who was responsible for this boon, not one but two plaques were attached to the sides.

XYSTUS IIII PONT MAX

AD UTILITATEM PRO PEREGRINAEQUE

MULTITUDINIS AD IUBILEUM VENTURAE

PONTEM HUNC QUEM MERITO RUPTUM VOCABANT

A FUNDAMENTIS MAGNA CURA ET IMPENSA RESTITUIT

XYSTUMQUE SUO DE NOMINE APPELLARI VOLUIT

Sixtus IV, Supreme Pontiff, for the benefit of the Roman people and of the multitude of pilgrims who will be coming to the jubilee, with great care and expense, restored from the foundations this bridge which they properly were calling "Broken," and he willed that it be called "Sisto" after his own name.

In a matter of decades, the bridge became notorious as a red-light district for the cheapest of Rome's streetwalkers. Celio Secondo Curione (1503–1569) alludes to them cruelly as "Roman Vestals, who work the neighborhood of Ponte Sisto."[75] So notorious was its reputation that as far off as Venice the writer Lorenzo Veniero (1510–1550) knew enough to have the fallen heroine of his *La puttana errante* (The wandering whore), ravaged by syphilis, carted up and jeered at, while carried via the Ponte Sisto to the nearby lazaretto hospice to die.

The streetwalkers have moved on, and there are happier associations with the bridge. Some say that anyone who chances to see a loaded ass, a priest, and a soldier crossing Ponte Sisto is assured of good luck.[76] Loaded asses are, for better or worse, not a common sight in Rome these days. Soldiers, alas, are rather more so.

The medallions Sixtus placed on the foundation stone are presumably still there.

Downriver, the one bridge that had survived from antiquity was the Pons Fabricius, which led from the left bank to Tiber Island. The island had never been enough of a draw in its own right to warrant a bridge—taboo, perhaps—until 63 BC, when the *curator viarum* Lucius Fabricius decided to put one in. It is the oldest bridge in Rome standing in its original form.

The bridge was a convenience for those Romans who wanted to take advantage of the healing powers available in the Temple of Asclepius. Perhaps ferry service was too much for the gravely ill, just the sort of persons who would want to go to Tiber Island. A large number of ex-votos have been dredged from the river bottom in later years, tokens of thanks given to the gods for their help, wished for or attained, in the curing of various illnesses that afflicted the ancient Romans. Possibly street vendors lined the structure, offering these objects for sale.[77]

In the Middle Ages the bridge became known as the Pons Judaeus for being near the ghetto, and by the Renaissance it was called the Ponte dei Quattro Capi—the Four Heads Bridge—in recognition of the four-faced head that now graces one end of the bridge wall (there used to be two, but things disappear). The head is a Janus, the god of doors and gateways and the new year, looking forward and back, and perfectly suitable for ancient bridges.

Time robbed them of meaning, and later Romans, presumably asked by their children who these men might be, needed a new explanation; fabulists delivered one. Giggi Zanazzo (1860–1911), Roman folklorist, reports the local story that the carved heads dated from the pontificate of Sixtus V (1585–1590) and that they represented four architects working on the bridge. The men had fallen out, fought, with the result that one was killed. Sixtus, as hard-boiled a pope as ever wore a tiara, had the survivors arrested, beheaded, and their heads spiked on the bridge. To keep the warning alive, he had the stones carved and placed where all could see them.[78]

It's not a bad story, but it sounds somewhat off. Four architects for one already built bridge? The number seems excessive. Possibly we are hearing a garbled nineteenth-century retelling of the half-remembered scandal of four young men, followers of the Sforza clan, who happened to be in Rome at the time of the 1585 election of Sixtus V. Their story, however, has nothing to do with the Pons Fabricius, but rather, as we shall see, with the Pons Aelius—the Aelian bridge—farther upstream again.

To return to the pope: the College of Cardinals elected Sixtus V in the knowledge that he was a serious man. (Or possibly not. Another account claims that prior to the election he hobbled about bent over, supported by a cane, to all appearances a safe bet for a short life and elected under that assumption, only to stand bolt upright and cast away his crutch the moment the votes were announced.)

Sixtus, like others before him, inherited a Rome that was about as degraded as possible. Crime was rampant, and God-fearing citizens were at risk from bands of young thugs. The city needed change, and with the election of Sixtus, they got it, good and hard. Even before his formal investiture, the pope had begun issuing edicts, one of which banned civilians from carrying arms. The Sforza supporters were caught with arquebuses, and, despite pleadings from sympathetic cardinals, including an offer to pay 4,000 scudi and to have the offenders spend time rowing galleys (a job normally reserved for slaves), Sixtus was adamant. The four were executed, beheaded, their heads stuck on spikes on the Ponte Sant'Angelo.[79] Hard-boiled, and if the Sforza family grieved, the man in the street was ecstatic. The talking statue of Pasquino harked back to a previous and equally stern pontiff. The comment was short and to the point: "Pius V has arisen again alleluia, alleluia!" For once we can believe that the writer was not being sarcastic, an indication of just how bad things had become in Rome.[80]

Sixtus was just getting started. Roman patricians and, sad to say, church officials, had been providing shelter and sanctuary to the more useful or intimidating of bandits, on occasion even joining in their activities. Sixtus was determined to put a stop to this, and the positive results were not long in coming. On May 24, 1585, Romans approaching the Ponte Sant'Angelo were treated to the sight of a new head, and one familiar to them. It belonged to Guercino, self-styled "King of the Campagna," appropriately sporting a gilt crown. This onetime priest was well known in and about Rome as a brigand and a murderer, and his death was applauded by all honest citizens.

The timing was exquisite—the following day, Sixtus marked the beginning of a papal jubilee dedicated to the ushering in of good times.[81]

As part of this new law-and-order regime, Sixtus declared that any bandit who could supply the church with another bandit, dead or alive, would gain absolution for past crimes and a cash reward for present snitching. Call it the ultimate prisoner's dilemma, made the more compelling by the thought of an eternity in hell. In short order, criminal bands started to fall out among themselves, and the bodies began piling up in Rome, their heads popped onto the spikes of the bridge, more numerous, it was said, than the melons in the marketplace.[82] Come the hot summer months, the more fastidious cardinals objected that the smell of the dead sinners was getting to be too much, to which Sixtus replied that it was nothing near so bad as the stench of living sin.[83]

Snaffling bandits was all well and good, but Sixtus soon made it clear that he had no patience with sinners of any kind, be they astrologers, card sharps, blasphemers, graffiti artists, or journalists (*menanti*) who leaked official secrets or slandered innocent civilians.[84] Death was not necessarily the default punishment, but there were instances that seemed excessive even at the time. A Venetian ambassador writes of a woman hanged on the Ponte Sant'Angelo for the crime of pimping her daughter, while the daughter, dressed in the rich clothes her lover had bought, was forced to watch. Then there was the group of young Roman nobles who thought to make a joke of the situation, and put cats' heads on pikes on the bridge.[85] The pope was not amused, and the young men barely escaped with their own heads.

Law and order are an undisputed good, as was Sixtus's initial work (abandoned at his death) of draining the malarial Pontine marshes; public works throughout the city of Rome—fountains, churches, roads, and bridges—are in large part due to his efforts. His taxes, however, were high, and his Catholicism severe—he wanted to punish adultery by death. No surprise that, despite all the considerable good he had done, Romans found his death easy to bear.

Bandit heads on the Ponte Sant'Angelo have long since given way to the stone angels that began to appear, first in 1527 under Clement VII (Peter and Paul), the rest under Pope Clement IX (1669–1671), carved by Bernini and his atelier. Opinion has been mixed. Charles Dickens had a room with a view of the bridge and its statues. His verdict—"execrable work."[86] Only slightly more generous was William Wetmore Story: "Sculptured saints of Bernini, fantastic in their draperies and grotesque in their attitude, but picturesque in their general effect."[87]

Rome does not always bring out the best in people.

Agnus Dei

That medallion placed under the Ponte Sisto—it was more than symbolic; it was intended to confer special protection for the intended structure. A less lasting but also potent version was the so-called Agnus Dei, Lamb of God, small discs of white beeswax taken from the gutterings of candles blessed in Easter ceremonies and imprinted with the Lamb of God on one side and other identifying marks on the reverse. They were given as papal gifts and prized as such, not least of all those associated with Pius V. (They are mentioned at least as early as 1204.)[88]

Among the various miracles Pius's particular Agni Dei are credited with is that of the Spanish soldier taken prisoner by soldiers under William of Orange in 1568. The war in question had been vicious, and pity played small part. The Dutchmen tied their prisoner to a tree, lined up, and began to fire on him with arquebuses and small cannon (*sclopetis vel bombardis*).[89] When the smoke cleared, the tree was seen to have been well shaken, but the Spaniard himself was untouched, his only protection being the Agnus Dei strung around his neck. No names, no follow-up, and no other details trouble the anecdote, but that is beside the point.

Saving one soldier is impressive. Saving an entire city is even more so.

A notice in the Florentine state archives dating from 1570 states: "Two nights passed in which Rome was completely upset for fear of the Tiber, which did not come out as it had begun, but Our Lord (Pius V) quickly remedied the situation by sending for one of his chamberlains to put an Agnus Dei blessed by his Holiness in the Tiber, at which a miracle was seen, that immediately began to return the Tiber in its bed."[90]

Michelangelo and His Bridge

By the middle of the sixteenth century, it was clear that the second-century Pons Aemilius needed a makeover. The pope had declared it so, and Roman guilds and communities—bakers, millers, the Jews—who also benefited from the structure, chipped in according to their ability and sense of civic-mindedness to pay the carpenters, stonemasons, bricklayers, and casual labor needed to repair the thing.[91] What was most needed was an architect.

Enter Michelangelo. Besides carving marble and painting ceilings, he was an accomplished architect—indeed, the chief architect of the Vatican since 1546. He had also sketched out plans for a bridge by the Palazzo Farnese. That never happened, but Pope Paul III did tap him for the job of bridge refurbishment, which commission he accepted.

Politics, however, is everything. Paul died in 1550 and was replaced by Julius III. Julius did not like to be bothered with trivia, making him a perfect foil for determined men. A cabal of high-ranking clerics suggested that the bridge work would go more quickly—and cheaply—with a fresh architect. Michelangelo was an old man, with great accomplishments, it was true—but the dome of Saint Peter's was still not complete. Was the bridge perhaps not a bit much for one of his age? Julius, who spent most of his time in semiretirement at the Villa Giulia (for which Michelangelo was also doing some work), agreed, and his underlings lost no time in replacing Michelangelo with their favored candidate, Nanni di Baccio Bigio.

Bigio was a Florentine like Michelangelo, but there the resemblance ends. Bigio cut corners—bad cement rather than stone, more attention to decoration than to structural integrity. His backers were happy with the results, but Michelangelo had only scorn. Giorgio Vasari recalls his comment when circumstance forced the two men to cross Bigio's work: "Giorgio, the bridge is shaking. Let us proceed with caution in case it should collapse while we're on it."[92]

Sour grapes? Not at all. Within five years an autumn deluge washed the better part of the bridge away, much as Michelangelo had predicted. (Bigio himself had long since moved on, to Ancona, where, having contracted to clear the port on the cheap, he was said to have done more damage in one day that the sea had in ten years.)[93]

Six years after Michelangelo's death, Matteo Bartolani da Città di Castel was hired to do the job right. He failed. Floods of 1575 and 1598 broke off most of the eastern parts, leaving a bridge to nowhere, suitable only for idlers to perch on and watch the passing scene, perhaps drop a fishing line. Pius IX in 1853 had an iron footbridge complete the crossing, but in 1887, the better part of the bridge was demolished to make way for the new Ponte Palatino. Two lone piers remain, covered in vegetation, called without irony the Ponte Rotto, Broken Bridge.

It's a striking ruin, but in hindsight, it is a stark reminder that you get what you pay for. For a few extra florins, they could have had a Michelangelo.

Grasshoppers

The Roman diarist Giacinti Gigli in May of 1653 reported that the peasants of Formello and environs had applied to Pope Innocent X to "excommunicate and curse" (*scommunicare e maledire*) a plague of grasshoppers that year. The pope dispatched three bishops to investigate the matter. They found the claims to be with merit and demanded that the grasshoppers desist and disperse. In short order, the entire swarm had leaped into the Tiber, filling it to such an extent that it became "*negra come l'inchiostro*"—black as ink.[94]

Sport and Spectacle

With the Renaissance having spread the appeal of a classical education, and Italy having become calm, relative to the past, Rome and environs became a destination for pure entertainment. The river inspired art. In 1638 Bernini built stage settings for a Carnevale production that simulated a flooding of the Tiber so realistic that spectators, all too familiar with the real thing, nearly stampeded. More-static renderings—statues of Father Tiber, say, or paintings by various foreigners—caused less of a ruckus, but still could find an audience.

But to really excite a crowd, nothing can compare to a good joust.

The taste for, and mention of, mock naval combat was revived in the Renaissance, that age of all things classical. Water jousting is mentioned in an eleventh-century English manuscript, and depicted in fourteenth- and fifteenth-century illuminated manuscripts.[95] In 1549, the French cardinal Guillaume du Bellay, then at Rome, arranged to celebrate, on the Tiber, the birth of the second son of Henry II and Catherine de' Medici. François Rabelais described the festivities in *La Sciomachie et festins faits à Rome*:

> Fifty small vessels, such as little galleys, galliots, gondolas, and armed frigates [*fustes, galiotes, gondoles et frégates armées*] attacked a great monster galleon put together from the two biggest vessels there were in this navy, which they had towed up from Ostia and Porto by the power of wild oxen.
>
> And after many feints, assaults, repulses, and other customary features of a naval battle, in the evening they set a fire inside the said galleon. There was a terrible bonfire of celebration, in view of the great number and quantity of

fireworks they had placed inside. Already that galleon was set for a fight, the little vessels ready to attack, and painted to match the liveries of the attacking captains, with a very gallant-looking target-fence [*pavesade*] and crew.[96]

And then?

But this combat was canceled because of a horrible rise of the Tiber—and much too dangerous whirlwinds (or waterspouts).[97]

Disappointing. Still, there were other shows in following years. Pompilio Totti refers to the *pallii delle barchette e de' notatori*, celebrating the August 25 feast of Saint Rocco, and that of Saint George *Decollato* on August 29.[98]

Johan Sprenger wrote in 1660: "Each year, boat-owners [*navicularii*] engage in mutual combat on the Tiber, just as Parisians play [the board game] *le jeu de l'oie*, the game of the goose, by the Seine."[99] (Romans, apparently, were prohibited from playing at cards and dice, *chartam et fritillos*, under threat of prison, and so had to content themselves with potentially lethal seminaval combat.) Michele Giustiniani writes of the riverine festivities of 1670 as involving various martial contests (undescribed) that involve cleverly (*ingegnosamente*) killing various land animals and birds.[100]

Officially, Innocent XI outlawed these spectacles in 1686 (the same year he founded the riverside hospital for foundling children). The ukase appears to have fallen away by 1750, when the French painter Claude-Joseph Vernet produced his *Sporting Contest on the Tiber at Rome*.[101] It is a cinematic piece of work. The picture centers on the river near the Castel Sant'Angelo and its bridge, where we see what appears to be a jousting match between two bare-chested champions equipped with buckler and lance, and standing on the prows of two modest boats, each propelled by six oarsmen clothed respectively in red and blue, heads bundled in white. At ground level, all social classes from milords and miladies to urchins, soldiers, and monks to blue-coated trumpeters (are those redcoats on the far bank?) are present, only some of whom are paying much attention to the contest, which appears to be at a climactic stage, advantage team red. On one side a high terrace, decorated with bunting, holds a number of toffs intent on the action below. Perhaps they had money riding on the outcome. In the far background, laborers continue with their own affairs, oblivious to the duel taking place not a few meters away.

The Tiber has not hosted this kind of sport for some time. The curious can get a taste of it at the August Festival de Saint Louis in Sète, Languedoc. Ten oarsmen, one point man.

Two French Poets

Joachim Du Bellay (1522–1560) wrote on the ephemeral nature of man-made glory against the eternal indifference of the river.

> Rome de Rome est le seul monument,
> Et Rome Rome a vaincu seulement.
> Le Tibre seul, qui vers la mer s'enfuit,
> Reste de Rome. Ô mondaine inconstance!
> Ce qui est ferme, est par le temps détruit,
> Et ce qui fuit, au temps fait résistance.

> Rome now of Rome is th'onely funerall,
> And onely Rome of Rome hath victorie;
> Ne ought save Tyber hastning to his fall
> Remaines of all: O worlds inconstancie!
> That which is firme doth flit and fall away
> And that is flitting doth abide and stay.[102]

Bellay's fellow Frenchman Marc-Antoine Girard de Saint-Amant (1594–1661) worked from personal disappointment. He was one among the five hundred French diplomatists sent to Rome to petition Pope Urban VIII to annul the marriage of Gaston d'Orléans and Marguerite de Lorraine. The real work was done by his superiors, and it took time, as matters of this size and importance and, we may presume, cost, generally do. With time to kill, the mission's underlings visited the brothels and hells of Rome. Saint-Amant, higher-minded than his fellows, sought out and spent time with Galileo, discussing science.

As to Rome—he didn't much like it. He despised the ruins, the fountains, Romans' cruelty and greed, the food, drink, and lodging, the jealously of Italian husbands. He took the opportunity to compose (anonymously) a pamphlet so insulting that it was soon banned and the publisher imprisoned. Saint-Amant later had official duties in England, and wrote an even more savage diatribe against that green and pleasant land. It is worth noting that he had risen from the working classes, and was ignorant not only of Greek, but also of Latin, a shortcoming for a diplomat even at that time. The sad truth was that Saint-Amant was simply one of those people who will never be happy outside their own country. To each his own, but was it absolutely necessary to take down the poor Tiber itself?

Il vous sied bien, Monsieur le Tibre,
De faire ainsi tant de façon,
Vous dans qui le moindre poisson
A peine a le mouvement libre:
Il vous sied bien de vous vanter
D'avoir de quoi le disputer
A tous les fleuves de la terre;
Vous qui, comblé de trois moulins,
N'oseriez défier en guerre
La rivière des Gobelins.

It suits you well, Master Tiber,
To gad about in this manner,
You in whom the smallest fish
Can scarcely move freely:
It suits you well to brag
About having something to argue over
With all the rivers of the world;
You who, packed with three whole mills,
Would not dare declare war
On the Gobelin's River.

The last line is foolish bravado. But then, he had not experienced a Tiber flood.

Floods

The sixteenth century was a record period for Tiber floods. Let François Rabelais explain why: "As you know, it's one of the most dangerous rivers in the world and rises unexpectedly, not only by flooding from the waters pouring down from the mountains from the melting snows or other rains, or by overflows from the lakes that drain into it, but also in a stranger way by the southerly winds which, blowing straight into its mouth near Ostia, suspend its flow, and keeping it from running out into the Etruscan Sea, force it to swell and turn back on itself, with miserable calamity and devastation of the adjacent land."[103]

Climate was in part to blame. The years of the Roman Republic were cool and humid; for the Roman Empire, it turned warmer and drier, a state that lasted until 1200. The decade of 1310–1320 was a bad one for floods, and as Europe cooled again after 1500, rain tended to fall and floods to follow.

There were also two ill-advised human causes. Pope Alexander VI built out towers in front of the Castel Sant'Angelo at the end of the fifteenth century, which constricted river flow. In 1510, the architects of the Villa Farnesina built up an embankment for the riverside garden above the Ponte Sisto. The unintended consequences followed in 1530, described above by Cellini, and commemorated by a marker on the side of Santa Maria sopra Minerva.

A generation passed, long enough for memories to fade at least a bit, before the next cataclysmic rise. The flood of 1557 was so strong that it cut though an oxbow and set a new, shorter course to the sea near Fiumicino. At a stroke, the riverside castle that Julius II had built to guard the ocean approaches to the Tiber, an imposing heavy brick structure designed to intimidate anyone who might try coming upriver—was rendered militarily useless. (In time, it was repurposed as a prison.)

The troubles began on September 15:

At midnight, the Tiber broke its banks and inundated a great part of the unfortunate city. The catastrophe took place quite suddenly, so that no one had time to save their possessions. In the vineyards near the Castle of Sant'Angelo, many houses, the inhabitants of which had taken refuge on the roofs, were carried away by the rush of the river. Very little more was needed to raise the inundation to the level of that of 1530; in St Peter's Square, the people were getting about in boats. After 24 hours the water began to subside, and then the damage done could be estimated. The Ponte S. Maria (Ponte Rotto) and nine of the mills on the Tiber were completely destroyed. The Ponte Fabricio, the passage leading from the castle of St Angelo to the Vatican, and the new fortifications of the city had also suffered greatly. . . . such quantities of grain, wine and oil had been destroyed that famine was to be feared. The streets and squares were full of mud and filth, in many places the water was standing, a pestilential stench poisoned the air, and disease of all kinds was rife. The Venetian ambassador thought that the catastrophe would hardly have been greater had the city been sacked.[104]

In 1598, the century was capped off with the worst flood on record, described by its marker as

REDUX RECEPTA PONTIFEX FERRARIA

NON ANTE TAM SUPERBI

HUC USQUE TYBRIDIS

INSANIENTES EXECRATUR VORTICES

ANNO DNI M.D.C.VIII

VIIII KAL JANUARII

The pontiff, returned from the conquest of Ferrara
Curses the mad vortices of the Tiber
Which never before exhibited such arrogance
In the year of our Lord 1598, December 25

Cardinal Pietro Aldobrandini (1571–1621) did more than just curse the river. On the afternoon of December 24, he crossed the Pons Aemilius to rescue some families trapped by the water. Seconds after he passed, two arches on the bridge collapsed.[105]

An anonymous witness goes into more detail:

The evening of the 23rd, the month of December past, the Tiber began to rise out of its bed, no longer below the city, rising continuously till 10 o'clock the following night, putting the city under water, outside the seven mountains and the summits of some places higher in the middle of the city, surpassing the riverbanks and signs of flooding in ancient and modern times, particularly, the plain, more than that which came in the time of Pope Clement VII. . . . [The waters caused] the ruin of the Bridge of Santa Maria, the two arches outside parts of the Ponte Molle[;] and that of Sant'Angelo, even though it remained, the fury of the water struck the shacks and workshops, this directed at the Castle which fell in places and was ruined—Submerging forty valuable places that were in Torre di Nona and the countryside—drowned many persons and animals, large and small. This horrendous spectacle was finished by 4 p.m. and in this hour, which was the birth of our Lord Jesus Christ, began to go down, and by Christmas Day, was down three levels. It was said that the sudden flood drowned in this city and surrounding areas 1,400 people.[106]

The flood was source material for the poet Giuseppe Castiglio, who used the tragedy as a basis for praising the pope and his disaster-relief efforts; Clement is noted for having lifted his eyes to heaven and praying, making the sign of the cross, after which the water backed down.[107] Castiglio claimed that the flood was a sign of God's displeasure, which is a backhanded compliment to the pope who successfully intervened. The poem is not well remembered (nor is the author, for that matter) and does not appear in anthologies.

By contrast, the Barcaccia fountain in the Piazza di Spagna, another memorial to the 1598 flood, is one of Rome's more charming and well-visited landmarks. This low-lying structure at the foot of the Spanish Steps, some five hundred meters from the river—a stone memorial to an actual boat that was left behind after that flood receded—is said to mark the high point of the floodwaters, a perennial reminder of just how far afield the river can rise. Allegedly, Pietro Bernini, father of Gian Lorenzo Bernini, was given a commission for a fountain in that square in 1623 and was faced with the problem of its having faint water pressure, and consequently few options for anything terribly dramatic. He had been in Naples at the time of the flood, and so someone would have had to tell him about the original boat, assuming it existed. Certainly the concept solved the pressure problem. He, possibly with help from his son, crafted a copy out of marble, and equipped it with a pleasing, slow-burbling fountain, which serves as a nice counterpoint to the murderous force of the flood.

The poet Keats had the burbling as white noise during his last days, wasting away in his lodgings just feet from the fountain. When asked what he would like on his tombstone, he said, "Here lies one whose name was writ in water." Possibly inspired by the constant burble, but who can say for sure?

La Pimpaccia di Piazza Navona

"Naughty Olimpia of Piazza Navona," more formally, Donna Olimpia Pamphili, née Maidalchini, had her chief residence on the Piazza Navona and her secondary in a villa fronting the Tiber. She was a strong-willed woman who had married young and rich and, widowed after three years, married again, to the brother of Giovanni Battista Pamphili, a midcareer cleric with a bright future. A son was born, the husband died, and Donna Olimpia devoted herself to maintaining and expanding the family fortunes, political and financial, by whatever means necessary. Her task was made easier by the election (aided with some judiciously applied family money) of her brother-in-law to the papacy, as Pope Innocent X (1574–1655).

She was more than equal to the politics of the church and made herself the *consigliera* for his eminence, much to the annoyance of long-serving cardinals and to the scandal of the mob. Human nature being what it is, she used her position to advance her now fatherless son and other Maidalchini family members, including, incidentally, herself.

The Roman street picks up on things like this, and soon they began to refer to her as "the papess"—and not with affection. They also gave her the moniker Pimpaccia, a reference to the commedia character Pimpa, sometime spouse of Pulchinello.[108] She did nothing to curry their favor or change her image. Quite the opposite. The riverside garden viridarium, near Ripa Grande and the customs house, was hers. From there, it was said, she would swim the river, to the scandal of the locals.[109] In due course, the talking statue of Pasquino gave his take on the woman:

> Chi dice donna, dice danno—
> Chi dice femmina, dice malanno—
> Chi dice Olimpia Maidalchina,
> Dice donna, danno e rovina
>
> You talk about a lady, you're talking about problems
> You talk about a woman, you're talking about headaches
> You talk about Olimpia Maidalchina,
> You're talking about a lady, problems, and ruin

Among the Latin-speaking elite, the humor was lapidary, if less suggestive:

> Olim pia, nunc impia
>
> She who was once pious, is now impious

One more example for those who like their jokes earthy: She had a lover named, oddly, Conte Fiume, Count River. Rome had gotten used to the practice of flood markers put on public buildings, marble plaques with fingers pointing to the high-water points of the more excessive floods. An imaginative caricaturist placed a red chalk drawing of a naked Donna Olimpia by Pasquino, her hand pointing at her crotch, with the caption

Fin qui arrivò Fiume.

The River got this high.

The story sounds too good to be true, but comes on the authority of German historian and longtime Roman resident Ferdinand Gregorovius; moreover, Fernando Raggi, Roman agent of the Republic of Genoa, refers in his writing to a *conte* Fiume, a lively man, possibly assassinated (*con 17 coltellate*, with seventeen knife blows) by a jealous husband in 1664.[110] Perhaps it is the same man? Or his son?

Back to the pope: he could not live forever. In the weeks leading up to his death, Donna Olimpia was said to have stolen into his private chambers and absconded with two chests of gold hidden under his bed. The treasure was quickly spirited to the family palace across the river, leaving his eventual, and modest, burial to his butler. The truth of this story is open to a good deal of skepticism, as are good many stories concerning Donna Olimpia. What is certain is that she lost power once he was dead, and had no choice but to face up to the abuse from the mob. Hopeful rumors that she would be tried and executed, and her head stuck on the Ponte Sant'Angelo, were never realized; the official inquiries into her alleged mischief became moot when she died, alone, of plague in 1657. When the body was shifted from her deathbed to her coffin, three diamonds were said to have fallen from her cheek—the last place a light-fingered servant would dare to look.

It is said that each year on the anniversary of her death, if you happen to be strolling the late-night streets of downtown Rome, you can see a shiny black carriage, fitted with brass lamps and drawn by black horses, its interior dark except for the glint of gold scudi. The whole arrangement is urged on by a woman of a certain age, from the Pamphili palazzo at Piazza Navona through the streets to the midpoint of the Ponte Sisto, from where it flies into the river, into which it sinks, brought down by the weight of ill-gotten gold.[111]

Or so it is said.

Pope Leo's Elephant

An Indian elephant, Hanno by name, was a gift to Pope Leo X in 1510 from Manuel I, king of Portugal. A white elephant, in fact, arguably the original white elephant. Almost certainly Hanno was the first elephant to reach Italy since the empire had brought elephants from Africa for warfare and entertainment.

Hanno came from India, at the time on Portugal's trade route east. The task of getting the creature from Cochin to Italy fell to Tristão da Cunha, and it is testament to both Portuguese ships and the elephant's constitution that Hanno was able to survive the trip at all. The Portuguese had been running the line around Africa since 1488, and had good sailors, but even so, the trip must have been grueling.

A brief stop in Lisbon, and the journey nearly stopped there when Hanno, back on terra firma, utterly refused to return to the ship. Frustrating for the king, but it soon turned out that the mahout who had come along with the elephant had fallen in love with a local girl and had no interest in going all the way to Rome. The mahout had whispered to Hanno that the ship was going to take man and elephant to a dry and nasty land that he, Hanno, would not like at all. Manuel threatened the mahout with beheading if the elephant was not on the ship in three days. It took some coaxing, but in the end, Hanno reluctantly did as he was asked. Not long after, master and elephant debarked at Porto Ercole and walked the seventy miles to Rome, astonishing the locals all the way.

Hanno's entrance and presentation were to be the grand finale to a long ceremony for the pope involving rich gifts from the Orient (silk, gold, unusual animals). Crowds of locals rushed to see this remarkable creature, the dejected mahout on its back, as it lumbered through the narrow streets and through the piazzas of Rome on its way to the Vatican. The onlookers shouted and pointed, the more daring perhaps coming forward to test its hide. As if all that were not stressful enough, Hanno was then expected to cross the river at the Ponte Sant'Angelo and be presented to the pope himself.

On approaching the pope on the far side, the elephant genuflected three times in respect.[112] The mahout then had Hanno hoover a trough of water and spray it over the cardinals and Leo himself, fortunately to his delight. (Renaissance princes liked practical jokes involving water.)

What does one do with a white elephant? As well ask what does a white elephant do with you. Hanno had a spot in the gardens and was brought out on special occasions. In one of the age's crueler practical jokes, the *abate* of Gaeta, Giacomo Baraballo, "an old man of sixty from an honest family" but vain about his verse and notably bad at writing it, was told he was to be honored for his skill.[113] He was given a Roman toga and set on Hanno's back and led from the Campidoglio across town toward the Ponte Sant'Angelo, where increasing noise of fifers and drummers and even cannon fire unnerved the elephant. Hanno stopped, refusing to cross the bridge, and kneeling down to let Baraballo—by now aware that he was being mocked—dismount. Leo had the incident immortalized in an intarsia panel in a door of the Stanza della Segnatura.

Despite a soft life, Hanno did not take to the eternal city. He died within two years. Leo himself wrote an epitaph, bemoaning the quinsy that did him in (*Obiit anginie morbo*).[114]

More sober records suggest that Hanno died from complications arising from the several gallons of gold-laced laxative the local veterinarians used to treat his constipation. He was mourned by elephant lovers throughout the city, then buried in the Cortile del Belvedere.

Elephants do seem to have been loved and respected by the Romans. A century and a half later, when a small obelisk was uncovered in the city, no less an artist than Bernini was commissioned to design a marble elephant, again white, for the object to rest on. Elephant and obelisk grace the piazza in front of Santa Maria sopra Minerva; below them a plaque reads:

SAPIENTIS AEGYPTI

INSCULPTAS OBELISCO FIGURAS

AB ELEPHANTO

BELLUARUM FORTISSIMA

GESTARI QUISQUIS HIC VIDES,

DOCUMENTUM INTELLIGE

ROBUSTAE MENTIS ESSE

SOLIDAM SAPIENTIAM SUSTINERE.

(Whoever sees here the markings of wise Egypt carved on the obelisk and borne by an elephant, strongest of beasts, take these as a metaphor that a strong mind supports genuine wisdom.)

As to Hanno—his bones lay forgotten until 1964, when construction workers digging a foundation chanced upon them.

He was not replaced. No matter—Bernini's statue does nicely.[115]

—————

Tributary—Chiana

If the Clitumnus is a source of white, clear water, then water from the Chiana (ancient Clanis, allegedly from the Etruscan *glánis*, meaning "muddy water") was black. This presented a hydrological problem that was recognized but unsolved for millennia. The Chiana has been called the Lethe of Tuscany.

To start at the beginning:

The basin of the Val di Chiana was once the agricultural heartland of the Etruscans, a plateau so perfectly level that it had no preferred outlet. By AD 15, the area was fully Roman, and the Etruscan drainage channels were neglected. Water began to arise, and the land turned to marsh. Push came to shove that year when an exceptional flood reached the city of Rome. Tiberius wanted something done about it. He appointed Lucius Arruntius and Ateius Capito to consider the matter.

That proved a curious pairing. Capito was a respected jurist and chief commissioner of the *curatores aquarum*, though the Roman historian Tacitus claims that he had "dishonored the good name of his house."[1] Perhaps so—Tacitus does not elaborate—but Capito's legal writings were still in use as late as the sixth century. Arruntius was considered upstanding to a fault (and finally committed suicide when it appeared that Tiberius intended to execute him regardless).

The two-man commission (later expanded to a five-man board and renamed the *curatores riparum*)[2] realized that high up in the hills, the waters had split into two, one branch feeding the Arno, the other feeding the Clanis (modern Chiana), which fed the Paglia, which fed the Tiber. Pliny wrote of boats carrying produce down to Rome from this most fertile area—he also notes that the slow-moving river was navigable only if water was blocked for a period of nine days and then allowed to flush down to the Paglia.

As their mandate was limited to solving the problem of flooding, the commission suggested that a canal be dug to divert more water into the Arno and thus save Rome from times of excess. The suggestion did not go over well in Florence. Perhaps the river could be constricted and a lake formed? The cost would be to those who owned the riverside land. Moreover, the religiously inclined reminded the senators once again that water is sacred and must be allowed to do whatever it thinks best.[3]

No action was taken.

Centuries passed. Silt was piling up in the mouths of the tributaries, and channels were becoming clogged. By the late fifteenth century, the natives of Chiusi had become accustomed to the rising waters, going so far as to ape the Venetians and climb aboard skiffs on Whitsunday, head out to watery border of Montepulciano, where, to the accompaniment of trumpets, a magistrate would solemnly toss a wedding ring into the marsh—*desponare Clanas et consuetum est.*[4] Their goodwill was not always reciprocated. The bishop of Chiusi noted in 1195 that many of his flock had moved to higher ground in Montepulciano to avoid malaria.[5] The area was notorious enough that Dante singled it out for attention in his *Inferno*:

> What pain would be, if from the hospitals
> Of Valdichiana, 'twixt July and September
> And of Maremma and Sardinia
> All the diseases in one moat were gathered.[6]

The hospitals, according to fourteenth-century commentator Benvenuto Rambaldi da Imola, were specific to paupers, and tended to fill up in August.[7]

By 1500 the valley was a no-man's-land, a dismal buffer zone between the Papal States and Florence. There had been half-hearted attempts at land reclamation, mostly by Florence, but they came to little. In 1502 Leonardo da Vinci enters the picture, and the wet sponge of the Val di Chiana was once more addressed. He proposed the lake option, imagining a stable reservoir and solid land all around it, from which a canal would lead to Florence and Pisa, serving both as a drain and a means of transporting food. It might have worked, too, but the Pisans already had an established role as transport hub and saw the canal as a threat. Navvies who had been digging were attacked and the project abandoned. Happily, Leonardo's drawings for this plan have survived, and are now part of the Windsor collection.

Things change. As the decades passed, political peace between most of the concerned parties was sufficient to revive the canal project, along with plans to reclaim the lost land. The slight slant of the valley floor toward the south, away from the Arno, presented a major difficulty. Learned men including

Galileo were consulted, and disagreed over what could be done. The obvious solution was to cut the channel even deeper. But the obvious solution was mistaken, according to the engineer Evangelista Torricelli. The slope was too high, the amount of water that could be diverted too small. Until the lower-lying southern parts of the valley could be raised, nothing of any value could be done with a larger drain. He was ridiculed by other scientists, but he had the ear of Leopoldo de' Medici, and his view was adopted.

Torricelli was not, however, a simple naysayer. He also proposed the snagging of sediments. Let the small creeks and streams carry sediment into *colmate*, wide flat areas surrounded by levees. Let the water be cut off, grow still, and the sediments drop to the bottom. Let the clear water be decanted and the process repeated. Torricelli died young, too young to see the enterprise begun. It took centuries, and progress was piecemeal, but the plan worked. The land gradually rose, hardened, and became suitable once more for agriculture.

By the middle of the eighteenth century, a concordat was reached between Tuscany and the Papal States agreeing on how the final solution to the hydraulic problem would be arranged. Count Vittorio Fossombroni (1756–1844), the governor of Tuscany and a capable engineer in his own right, put the final stamp on the centuries-long project to bring together the disparate *colmate* and an updated canal system into one coordinated plan. By 1823, 1,260 square kilometers had been recovered, and the area, once a river basin for the Tiber, had become a source for the Arno.[8] By 1844, a year of a serious flood on the Arno, the engineers were able to prove that the work on the Valdichiana had had little effect on the matter.

6

MODERN TIMES

———

In which a bigamous duchess sails up the river, French painters paint the river,

prospectors search for treasure in the river, tourists watch fireworks across the

river, monks bury the dead dragged from the river, a balloonist floats over the

river, a frogman floats on the river, and World War II provides two stories, one

tragic, one hopeful, relating to the river.

Ostia and Portus Redux

Ostia would start another down cycle with the election of Paul V, who in 1612 cleared the old channel between the Tiber and Portus and so diverted to Portus what maritime traffic still existed. Ostia declined, its country reverted to swamp, the population fell off.

What could the intrepid tourist expect? Gavin Hamilton, a Scottish painter who visited in the 1770s, wrote to his patron Lord Townsend that he had found "fine Antinous in the character of Abundance, perhaps the finest of that subject in the world" and a little ways away "a fine Torso of a young man of which most of the other parts were found much broke, excepting the Head."[1]

It was a nice place for antiquarians and aesthetes and romantics to visit, but not very many people wanted to live there year round. By the early eighteenth century, not even the local vicar lived in the place; rather, he came only on feast days and Sundays to conduct Mass and administer sacraments to "shepherds, buffalo tenders, fishermen, salters, and a small number of others who gather and who resemble specters from the grave more than living men, such is their yellow pale pallor, thinness, and feebleness."[2] The mere presence of travelers at that time and place was an odd enough sight that the night sentinel woke residents regularly to meet with *des curieux*.[3]

Edward Gibbon (1737–1794) visited while writing his *Decline and Fall of the Roman Empire*, and his take was gloomy: "Porto and Ostia, the two keys to the Tiber, are still vacant and desolate: the marshy and unwholesome banks are peopled with herds of buffaloes, and the river lost to every purpose of navigation and trade."[4]

The situation had not improved fifty years later, when in 1819 Mrs. Eaton and her companions traveled down to investigate Ostia old and new. The old ruins they never reached; the new, they might as well have not. A ghost town, until they finally rustled up one old woman:

" 'Where are the people of this town?' we inquired.

" 'Dead!' was the brief reply."

She numbered the population of Ostia at twelve men, four women, and two priests. Those eighteen, and the convicts "whose lives it is found convenient to shorten are also kept there."[5]

Malaria again, of course.

If Mrs. Eaton did not have a very good time, the anonymous writer for the *Cornhill Magazine* was able to paint a sunnier picture some thirty years later. He describes the bumpy carriage ride out from Rome, after which the traveler is left to wander at will:

> The day is young and one wants to walk and to have as little company as possible while prowling among the ruins and excavations. A malaria-stricken peasant emerges from a massive stone doorway and helps to stable the horses. A priest, dirty and unshaven, is amusing himself by feeding with coarse oatmeal the litter of a wild boar, which he has tamed to be his companion in this solitary place. The old sow, in spite of her fierce appearance and shaggy bristles, is very friendly; and but for his cassock the padre would look far more like a professional swineherd than a servant of the altar. Once upon a time the bishopric of Ostia was the most famous in the world.[6]

The population seems not to have recovered in the seventy years since Mrs. Eaton paid it a visit. Our *Cornhill* correspondent continues: "I am told the population of the *paese*, or neighborhood, is sometimes as high as one hundred souls, though in the season of malaria it sinks below this figure. I can only speak of it as I found it, and I saw only one priest and one peasant. To make the population larger I must count the wild sow's litter."[7]

Yet the river trade continued under the watchful eyes of the church.

The tedium of customs extended for centuries. An English visitor in 1855 explains the process once freighters reached Ostia:

> There their vessels require to be lightened, or partly discharged into barges, there not being sufficient water in the Tiber to allow them to ascend to Rome; the average depth of water throughout the year being from four to five feet, which is only sufficient for the Pope's navy force, employed in tugging barges from Fuma-Cina [Fiumicino] to Rome. It is not the least important part of the Roman merchant's business to know that their long-expected goods have entered the river. This is ascertained at the custom house at Ripa Grande, where the intelligence is chronicled every evening, on return of the navy force.
>
> That navy consists of three small steamers. . . . Two of the steamers are kept for the traffic between Fuma-Cina and the custom-house at Rome. The other is employed on the upper part of the river, starting from the Ripetta in Rome for the Sabina country, going up about forty miles, and returning with wine, oil, Indian corn and wood for fuel, green and charred. The dredging boat is scarcely ever used. The constantly filthy state of the river causes so much deposit that the machine is unable to overcome it.[8]

And the customs house? "A very respectable amount of bribery is done in these places."[9]

Pompeii was wholly immersed in dust in a matter of hours. Ostia took some centuries. This slow death and the general awareness that the city still existed allowed later ages to rummage through and carry off a large amount of material (marble from Ostia can be seen in fourteenth-century Pisa, Florence, Amalfi, and Orvieto). Not just building material, either. Archaeologists digging through the wreckage centuries later found columbaria with significant amounts of gold and silver. So long as there are people who have things to trade, port cities have a remarkable tenacity.

Despite the gloom and dismalness of the place in the nineteenth century, it seems to have maintained both commercial and even recreational functions. Thomas Hodgkin notes—this in 1898—that in the town of Fiumicino one finds "a small wooden pier projecting into the sea, a few ships discharging their cargoes, a row of tall lodging houses, all filled during a few weeks in spring by the crowd of bathers from Rome, all empty and deserted in September from fear of the everywhere brooding malaria."[10]

Also present was a modernized church, evidence, one might infer, of a quiet seaside town. He also notes, however, that "the frogs fill the air with their harsh melody: other signs of life there are none."[11]

> The sacred island surround by the two arms of the Tiber was sold in 1830 to the Marchese Guglielmi, of Civita Vecchia, with no stipulation whatever, except the payment, once and for ever, of a fixed amount of money. It was only two years ago that the fiscal authorities opened their eyes to the irregularity of the bargain. It has been ascertained that since the day the property was bought, fifty-six years ago, its surface has been nearly doubled by the addition of 648 acres of ground, which should have been added, of course, not to the patrimony of the Marchese Guglielmi, but to that of the nation.[12]

You could do that sort of thing in those days. In 1856 Prince Alessandro Torlonia bought the neighboring lot that included all of Trajan's harbor at Portus.

What exactly was the prince buying? A British traveler of 1872 describes a "dreary desert of marshy ground overgrown with the ash-pale asphodel, rampant reeds and lean bristling rushes; roamed by herds of half-wild oxen with enormous horns, which eyed us menacingly as we passed, as if resenting our intrusion on their territory. Here and there a lonely tower or wall rises, forlorn witness of the desolation around."[13] To say nothing of the malaria. Small wonder the price was cheap.

The recently ennobled Torlonia family of bankers, however, had a taste for ancient artworks, and the prince might have had treasure in mind. If so, he struck pay dirt when one of his groundskeepers chased a badger to what appeared to be a simple bolt hole. The man began to poke at the area with a stick, and soon discovered brickwork. Old brickwork. He pulled away at the crumbling material and soon found himself in the first gallery of a vast imperial Roman suite, quietly waiting over the centuries while history had passed on by. The prince was informed, and in short order a secret examination and excavation of the forgotten building were under way. Soon laborers were hauling out dozens of ancient marbles, both statuary and relief work. The operation was an amateurish affair, the prince being primarily interested in decoration rather than the mundane detritus that excites scholars. Eventually, almost as an afterthought, he hired a young engineer, Rodolfo Lanciani, to take a look at his new holdings.

For someone just staring out on an archaeological career, this was a considerable coup, and Lanciani attacked it with energy. He drafted plans for a full and proper measurement of the place and began proper scientific examination of the findings. His efforts came to nothing. Without warning, the "great lord," in the words of an annoyed French archaeologist, "clumsily enamoured of antiquities," decided he was satisfied with his haul and closed down the operation.[14]

The site itself quickly reverted to nature, presumably safe for badgers, if not welcoming of academics. Briefly, during the 1970s and 1980s, the owner stocked the area with more dangerous and exotic animals and charged admission to drive through. Lanciani went on to be one of the great modern archaeologists, his many works in both Italian and English (his wife was American) readily available and to be read with pleasure. As to the treasures, a few can be seen in the Museo Torlonia at Ostia, including the so-called Torlonia relief. It's worth a look if you're in the area.

Since Lanciani's time, scientific digging has been irregular. Happily, in recent decades, archaeologists from the British School of Rome have been able to take up where Torlonia left off on southern portions now owned by the Italian state. The northern side is still in private hands, and the owners display a more generous attitude toward scholarship than the previous ones.

What have the archaeologists found? Wonderful things, if not much gold or silver. A larger canal than they had expected between the harbor and the Tiber, for one, causing yet another upward reconsideration of the scale of Roman trade. Archaeologists have an admirably mundane view of what constitutes treasure.

Porto di Ripetta

Rome also had a small port upriver of its bridges, dedicated to cargo traffic coming down instead of up the river.

Boniface IX (1389–1404) was the first we know of to use the word *ripetta*. Among the problems he faced was a sudden influx of Illyrian Christians, survivors and refugees of the battle of Kosovo (1389). He had his underlings settle them upriver in an ill-populated area near the modern Piazza del Popolo, where they restored an aging church (San Girolamo degli Schiavoni) and made the place their own.

A 1577 map of the area shows the riverbanks lined by inelegant buildings that were lapped by the river itself, commercial warehouses into which contracted material could be offloaded directly. For those reaching an inner market, the mud bank would have to do. The mud bank was unsightly and, given its frequent use as a place to tip rubbish, hard on the nose (which presumably interfered with the merchants who tried to offload goods there). Worse, the practicalities of the area as wharfage were steadily being diminished by rain, flood, and the attendant erosion. Various popes made various improvements in the area—paving the road between it and the Piazza del Popolo—and laid out plans that were never executed, such as the trading floor for lumber that was otherwise dealt with in front of San Girolamo, an ongoing affront to the church's dignity.

In 1703, Clement XI (1700–1721) authorized and funded the creation of proper docks. By happy coincidence, an earthquake had shaken loose a good deal of travertine from the Colosseum, which cut down on the material costs.

The docks could have been purely utilitarian, all square steps and ramps up a steep incline, a quick move from ship to shore to city. Clement wanted more than that. He wanted it to be beautiful, and taking a look at contemporary etchings and drawings of the river, one can see why. The riverfront was overwhelmingly flat, uninspiring—even grim—on both sides. As one traveler put it, "With few exceptions, the houses rise out of the water, leaving no passage along the margin. This arrangement brings the rear of the buildings to the river, and as they are uniformly shattered, gloomy, and dirty, the borders appear bleak and ruinous."[15] Tall warehouses, flat-faced walls, some walkways and quays, and muddy banks. There were a few villas on the river, even inside the city walls, but held back, the gardens filling in a space between water and structure, and high walls to keep out water and other uninvited nuisances.

The Porto di Ripetta was to be something else entirely. Open to water and to anyone, it was meant to be used, and to be seen. Clement hired Alessandro Specchi, with a directive to make the thing attractive. And there is no question but that he did. (Specchi later submitted a design for the Spanish Steps, but lost that commission to Francesco de Sanctis.)

The steps' focus was San Girolamo, now Saint Jerome of the Croats. The steps themselves followed sweeping curves common to that time, and there was fountain for man and beast at the top, useful for carters and such who had to move cargo off the landing. In honor of the river, two columns marked the flood levels since 1495 (and would continue to do so until 1750). Iron lamps illuminated late-night work—an interesting comedown from the ancient days, when nightfall meant all traffic came to a standstill. The entire design was intended to make the area functional, beautiful.

What to call the thing? The obvious answer would be to honor the patron, and some did call it Clement's Harbor. Others had their own ideas—"porto della Legna" (Lumber harbor), "porto delle Posterule" (Postern wharf), "porto degli Acquaroli" (Waterman's quay)—none of which lasted. Ripetta, "Small riverbank port," it would be.

We can get an imaginative glimpse of the steps in action in a print by Piranesi. The artist shows high-masted vessels weighed down by outsize barrels, stevedores considering the job before them, tricorned gentry presumably discussing trade, and on the far bank, a lone man with a fishing pole. A very alive place, the Ripetta of Piranesi's time.[16]

As to aesthetics, not everyone was impressed. French writer Charles de Brosses (1709–1777) reported that "the port of Tiber, called the Ripetta, has recently been upgraded by Clement XI, and the results are not as attractive as they might have been."[17] This could be said of just about any creative work, or any work at all, for that matter. (Admittedly, de Brosses was using the fountains and gardens of Versailles as a benchmark, but even so, he is bit harsh.)

Smollett disagreed. He called it "a handsome quay by the new custom-house . . . provided with stairs on each side, and adorned with an elegant fountain, that yields abundance of excellent water."[18]

The steps are gone now, sadly. The 1870 flood required that the great embankment (*muraglione*) be built. One of the eggs sacrificed to this particular omelet was the Ripetta. Some consciences were salved by the knowledge that it had become run-down in its later years and that it was no longer the hub of traffic it had once been. Regardless, the pictures of the steps taken on their deathbed have to make a traditionalist cringe.[19]

The original is gone, but upriver, by the modern Ponte Pietro Nenni, is a substitute dating from the late nineteenth century, the *muraglione del porto fluviale* conceived and built with the intention of serving the artisans and craftsmen of the area, an intention squelched in 1909 when city regulators rezoned the neighborhood as residential. What would de Brosses have made of this ersatz creation? Not much, at a guess. The structure itself, a simpler amalgam of ramps and steps, is not gorgeous, and it serves little practical use. It gives access to a dozen or so barges tied a ways away, and is now a setting for a 1974 monument, a stylized sixteen-meter flower ready to bloom in honor of Giacomo Matteotti, socialist politician kidnapped and killed by Fascists in 1924. The following year, the steps were renamed the Scalo de Pinedo in honor of Francesco de Pinedo, "the Italian Lindbergh," who landed his airplane there after a record-breaking trip of fifty-five thousand miles. For tourists, it is low on the list of must-see sights.

Four French Painters

The Tiber seems not to have sparked the imagination of Italian painters as much as one might expect. Bernardo Bellotto (1722–1780), nephew of the more famous Canaletto (1679–1768), traveled the cities of Italy and elsewhere and produced a few canvases featuring the Tiber, predictably using the river as a foreground to the Castel Sant'Angelo and Saint Peter's. Where his uncle gloried in light, Bellotto was interested in shadow. His attachment to Rome and the Roman Campagna is, however, somewhat fleeting. Piranesi includes the river in a few of his etchings, but his focus is always on architecture. It was the French who seem to have really taken to the river as integral to the landscape and worthy of equal billing to whatever else is being painted. The fascination begins with Nicolas Poussin.

Poussin (1594–1665) spent the better part of his working life in Rome, first in making religious paintings to fill the baroque churches, and classical themes to satisfy the classically educated, and finally, inspired by the Roman Campagna, landscapes, often featuring religious or classical themes, but notable for nature. He had lodgings on the Via Paolina (modern Via del Babuino), from which he could walk north to the Piazza del Popolo and along the banks of the Tiber up to the Ponte Milvio and beyond into the Roman Campagna. The landscapes provided background for many of his religious works—*Baby Moses Saved from the River*, *Landscape with Matthew and the Angel*, that sort of thing.

His friend and colleague and fellow Italophile Claude Lorraine, master of landscape painting, also exploited the Tiber, chiefly through drawing and ink wash.

The two, Poussin in particular, remained an inspiration for other (mostly French) painters for years to come. Corot (1796–1875) emulated Poussin to the point of literally following his footsteps in what was he came to refer to as *La promenade du Poussin*, Poussin's Promenade, hoping to absorb a touch of the older man's genius. He went so far as to name one of his pictures after this route. The result is a decidedly somber and brown rendering of the river and its banks and a frankly melancholy painting, one lone, misshapen tree in a dismal landscape and a strong disincentive to make a trip to Italy. His *Bridge at Narni* (1826), a gray and ochre job that now hangs in the Louvre, is not much more inviting. Granted, these were early on in his career, and he did improve, but these works do not live up to his inspiration.

The apotheosis of Poussin worship came with Léon Benouville's 1856 work *Nicolas Poussin on the Banks of the Tiber*, a study of three washerwomen doing laundry, one distressed infant being dunked in the water, and Poussin himself sitting back a ways, looking somewhat annoyed that these people are interfering with his view. There is more than a faint touch of the absurd in the painting, however heartfelt the sentiment, and we can only be charitable to the changing nature of taste.

The Tiber inspired more blatantly dramatic work as well. Claude-Joseph Vernet (1714–1789), mentioned above in connection with his sports painting, and much admired among the English residents in Rome, has left a number of river-and-ruin paintings. His *Ponte Rotto*, now in the Louvre, was done while the bridge still reached the river's left bank, if not its right, with Santa Maria de Cosmedin visible in the background, fishermen in the fore. His was the stuff of dramatic light and dark, moon or sun illuminating clouds and reflecting off water, sometimes Tiber water.

Most dramatic is his *Fire on the Tiber*, a picture straight out of Hollywood. The center shows a blaze of orange light on the far side of the river. A warehouse? A church? A boat? Impossible to say. The fire illuminates and may be threatening a three-masted ship that appears to be displacing no water at all and yet is not keeling over. Small boats in the middle distance seem to be ferrying people away from the blaze. In the foreground, men are carrying an exhausted body from yet another small boat to the riverbank, where a crowd of people in various stages of dress are engaged in uncertain activity. On the far left of the foreground, two gentlemen in long coats, one with a tricorn hat, seem to be oblivious of everything other than their own conversation.

It is all very confusing, but nonetheless compelling. Ship fires are always a concern, and ship fires on the Tiber had peculiar problems associated with them, as we have seen. Still, one has to wonder what prompted this particular vision. The painting is at odds with his other works, where natural light provides drama, and only rarely does there seem any risk to life and limb.

Academic painters of the 1800s were drawn to historical themes to inspire the viewers' spirits or break their hearts. Paul Delaroche (1797–1856), a painter of such dramatic subjects as *The Execution of Lady Jane Gray* and *The Princes in the Tower*, was much praised for his 1855 painting *The Young Martyr*, which could as well be the dead Ophelia. We see a pale woman floating supine on a body of (blue) water said to be the Tiber, and said to represent all the Christian martyrs of the emperor Diocletian. Her hands are tied, her body clothed in white, and she has an awkward-looking halo floating above her face, but is otherwise unmarked. The painting is dark for the most part, the better to concentrate white light on her upper body and face; in the far background, the orange of either dusk or dawn marks the outline of presumably grieving parents on shore. The picture takes on an even more somber note when one learns that the model was his wife, who had died ten years earlier.

The Duchess of Kingston

In 1775, Elizabeth Chudleigh, Countess of Bristol, Duchess of Kingston, newly widowed after a short marriage, coped with her grief on a European tour:

> In gratitude for these favours so flattering to the pride and vanity of the
> duchess, notwithstanding her avarice, she treated the Romans with a public
> spectacle. She had built an elegant yacht in England, which she had brought
> into Italy under the direction of a gentleman who had served in the British
> Navy; and this vessel, with considerable labour and an immense expense,
> was conveyed up the Tiber. To the degenerate Italians, an English yacht was
> as great a curiosity as the ancient vessels of the Carthaginians were to their
> renowned and virtuous ancestors.[20]

So wrote the English author of a contemporary biography of the woman. It is not how the Italians saw the matter. To them, the boat was a trifling affair, "only a model, & . . . a pretty thing to put upon the Lake of Albano, & be a pleasure boat for the late Pope."[21] The boat was the *Minerva*, captained by a former Royal Navy captain, and just one of various indulgences with which the duchess soothed her widowhood.

She had come a long way in her life. Her family was old, good, and poor; her father was an army colonel who had invested unfortunately in the South Sea Bubble and died while she was young, forcing her mother to send her out on short term to various better-off relatives. When she was twenty-two, a family friend got her a position as maid of honor to Augusta, Princess of Wales. Effervescent and said to be pretty, she attracted her share of attention, most particularly from Augustus John Hervey, second son of the Earl of Bristol. As second son, he was without prospects, but he did have a commission in the navy. The pair enjoyed a whirlwind romance, a secret wedding, after which he was off to the West Indies. Secret because there was a good chance his father the earl would not approve, and because a married woman would have to give up her two hundred pounds per annum as lady in waiting.

The wonder is that Augustus married her at all—in general he preferred other men's wives.

Absence did not make the heart grow fonder. Quite the contrary. While he was enduring the grueling trials of eighteenth-century shipboard life (his career was in fact distinguished), she was making the rounds of London parties, flirting shamelessly, and making friends among male peers. She neglected to mention that she was married, and given the mortality rate of Englishmen sent to the West Indies, it seemed even odds at any time that she was in fact not. Men caught all manner of disease in the West Indies.

Her husband did not, although by the time of his return, their initial ardor had cooled. Still, discretion on both their parts enabled both parties to keep up their extramarital affairs. She reached a new peak of notoriety at a masquerade ball thrown in honor of George II's Jubilee, at which she appeared in the person of Iphigenia. Her costume, variously described (near naked, they said; topless, if engravings carved after the fact are to be believed), was upstaging enough to prompt the other women there to refuse to speak to her. This was no hardship for Elizabeth—women were not her intended audience. She was soon mistress to the Duke of Kingston-upon-Hull, ten years her senior, who proposed marriage.

This was pleasing, but difficult. Her husband was content to remain married, and now that his father was dead, to say so publicly. What the civil courts would not do, the ecclesiastical courts of the time would. She was able to lay a charge of jactitation, the putting forward of oneself as married to someone who denied it, which put the onus of proving marriage on the soon-to-be earl. He had no proof; he gave in, and she was legally declared a spinster and therefore free to marry the Duke of Kingston-upon-Hull.

The ruling was a farce, and all London knew it, though the duke appeared not to mind. Four years of wedded bliss followed, after which he died, leaving her everything, so long as she did not remarry.

And so her trip to Rome, where she was very much the thing. Pope Clement XIV, an amiable man and not at all put out by her lack of Catholic faith, became something of a protector, waiving various fees and duties on her considerable property brought into the city on the *Minerva*.

Alas for Elizabeth, while she was entertaining in Rome, the family of the duke's sister, the Meadowses, disinherited for poor behavior and convinced that Elizabeth was to blame, was challenging the will, and worse, digging through the records to find proof of felonious bigamy. As a duchess, Elizabeth demanded, and got, a trial in the House of Lords. It proved magnificent entertainment. Special admission was by ticket, of which only 350 were printed, while some four thousand extras filled the galleries. She was found guilty. Duchess no more; now only wife to an earl.

Popular accounts were pitiless: "Here was cunning, despicable cunning, enveloping the possessor in a net of her own fabricating. No wonder, when her hour of degradation arrived, that she fell unpitied." Worse still, the Meadowses were now able to reopen the chancery court proceedings, which in the best traditions of the bar dragged on endlessly, providing a new pastime for the Meadowses, an ongoing trial for Elizabeth. There was nothing for the duchess (she refused to relinquish the title) but to leave the country with some considerable sums and live out the rest of her days in Calais, Saint Petersburg, Estonia, Paris, and Rome, dying in 1788 in France as the Countess of Bristol. At least one member of the Meadows family showed up, only to sneak inside the dead woman's house to abscond with the family silver.

Yet as late as 1905, the official reports of the Royal Commission of Historical Documents referred to her as "Elizabeth (so called) Duchess of Kingston."[22]

Treasure

But the great magazine of all kinds of treasure, is supposed to be the bed of the Tiber.
We may be sure, when the Romans lay under the apprehensions of seeing their city
sacked by a barbarous enemy, as they have done more than once, that they would take
care to bestow such of their riches this way as could best bear the water: besides what
the insolence of a brutish Conqueror may be supposed to have contributed, who had
an ambition to waste and destroy all the beauties of so celebrated a city.[23]
Joseph Addison, Remarks on Several Parts of Italy

Rome is notorious for the wealth of the ages under its soil. In part inertia, in part deliberate fill to rise above the flood levels, the modern city is in places tens of meters higher than the city the ancient Romans knew. Digging the city subway lines has been retarded by example after example of historically interesting material that archaeologists must examine before work can continue. Forgotten treasures are simply too plentiful.

What about the Tiber? The idle mind of one who leans over the bridge rails or riverside walls and gazes on the river is easily crowded with thoughts of ancient arts and artifacts. Stories passed down through the ages fuel that imagination. Small coins, of course, must inevitably find their way down inclines and into streams, and join the loose change that the sentimental, superstitious, and hopeful give to the Tiber voluntarily (or at least did give, before the Trevi Fountain siphoned off that line of business).

Among the more spectacular of these donations is that of Georgius Trapezuntius (1396–1486), a Renaissance scholar, to whom the pope gave a hundred gold ducats for his translation of Aristotle into Latin. Not enough! Offended at such a poor reward, he marched straight to the Aelian bridge and in a *grand geste* tossed the lot into the Tiber, declaiming "Periere labores, pereat et eorum ingrata merces!"—"The works are gone, let their poor purchase die as well!"[24] One can just imagine a flock of street urchins hesitating only briefly before diving in and hoping for a windfall.

Cassiodorus (AD 485–c. 585) describes his Rome as having more bronze and marble statues than live human beings.[25] Granted, he was writing after the great population collapse, which had begun even before the third century (Constantine had moved the capital to Constantinople in 330; and Attila sacked the city in AD 410), but where had all the statues gone? Josephus refers to the statue of Isis thrown into the river.[26] Gregory the Great was also singled out as an enemy of the plastic arts, at least when they were of pagan origin. Stories about his intolerance circulated for years and became a matter of record in 1506, when Raphael Maffei wrote that the pope "caused outstanding Roman statues and other remarkable works to be thrown into the Tiber."[27] Distressing to art lovers, but the evidence is weak, and none of it contemporary. Gregory's opinions of paganism did not prevent him from admiring the likes of Trajan, whose forum he hoped to restore, and whom he got out of hell by the power of prayer. (He was informed in a dream that this was a one-time thing, and he should not ask such favors in future.)

Still, we are talking about treasure, and whether the story of the statuary is a later invention by zealous friends or contemptuous enemies, one cannot say, only that it is compelling and that there is always the off chance that it is true, and if so, is surely worth a look. After all, Rome was said to have more statues than people, and given that the human population was over a million, well, that's a lot of statuary unaccounted for. And this is to say nothing of the smaller bits and bobs that are lost in the daily course of life, coins and jewels and artifacts that fall to the ground and are tugged riverward by rain or flood. Loot too hot to hold on to that can be acquitted with forever by a single toss. The possibilities grow and grow.

Some did think to leave well enough alone. A Dutch journal of trivia reports in 1699 that "a certain farmer in Ostia, having found an old gold coin, was jailed so that the authorities could determine if he had found anything more. Unhappy in his luck! Ever since then, no one was willing to dig or delve there. The louts [*Kinkels*] flee from it, like Satan from the Cross."[28]

It was presumably the gold that made the coin interesting, and the assumption was that gold coins tend to flock together more than other metals, at least if all the fairy tales are true.

Along with the stories of what has wound up in the Tiber are stories about what has been drawn out.

The sixteenth-century sculptor Flaminio Vacco (1538–1605), looking back on a long life in the thick of the Roman Renaissance art world, dictated a brief pamphlet outlining various antiquities of ancient Rome that had come to light in his time, from the trivial ("a great quantity of brass arrows near the foot of the arch of the Horatian bridge . . . as would have filled a number of boats")[29] to the more substantial: "A certain man, employed in getting up boats and wrecks from the Tiber, was searching for a sunken wherry, and diving between the Flaminian Gate and the Ripetta brought up a consul in a sitting position with a scroll in his hands; his head was lost to ravages of time."[30] The kicker—"He [the certain man] told me that there were a number of marble pieces which he was afraid to bring up without authorization." Clearly a savvier operator than the farmer from Ostia.

Bureaucrats stifle enterprise yet again. But mining the Tiber is a beguiling idea that seems to arise every few hundred years. The French Benedictine monk Bernard de Montfaucon, commenting on Vacco in 1702, takes that Renaissance writer at his word, though though he cites no observations of his own: "It is clear from the endless stories and the personal experience of many that not only that there are statues and marbles in the Tiber, but that treasures, cast in at the same time long ago, also rest [beneath the surface]."[31]

Cardinal Melchior de Polignac, the French minister to Rome in 1724, "a man of the world, and most agreeable; who knows everything, discusses everything, yet has all the sweetness, the liveliness, and geniality that one could wish for in one's society," had his own designs on the river.[32] A fervid collector of coins and medals and suchlike knickknacks, he spent a good deal of time and money in digging up whatever Roman land he could get access to, unearthing some decent treasures in the process. His dream, however, was that chance to spend even just two weeks mucking about in a drained riverbed. "In all the civil wars, the party that prevailed threw the statues of the opposite party into the Tiber. They must still remain there. I have never heard that any of them have ever been taken out, and they are too heavy to be carried away by the flow of the river."[33] He went so far as to have a survey drawn up, the idea being to reroute the Tiber and rake through the mud at leisure. It never happened, of course. Another dream deferred.

Don Alfonso Bruzzi and friends made their own attempt in 1773, with some sort of dredge and filter apparatus, with disappointing results.[34] Don Alfonso did, however, find some marble pilasters that wound up in the Vatican Sacristy: "All the pillars are plastered with a superb African green, and taken from a large drum of an ancient column, fourteen palms long, five palms in diameter, extracted from the Tiber, near Marmorata in 1772 by P. Alfonso Bruzzi . . . on the basis of which he desired to petition Clement XIV, to execute the plan, attempted many other times, to cleanse the bed of the river, and to extract the ancient monuments of all kinds, which must be hidden there."[35]

His failure, like all failed treasure hunts, seems not to have put people off the scent. Prince Alessandro Torlonia, the pope's banker and a man who liked his antiquities, was another said to have toyed with the idea of diverting the river and poking about the mud to see what might turn up.[36] There was, after all, one stupendous prize that kept hope alive.

In Search of Jewish Gold

Before becoming emperor, Titus was most noted for his conquest and destruction of Jerusalem in AD 72; the razing was so complete that only the Wailing Wall was left standing after he departed with the treasures of the temple in tow. The gold and silver booty was considerable, the most striking example being the golden menorah—you can see a carving of it on the inside of his triumphal arch near the Colosseum, a small part of the piles and piles of trophies brought back to Rome after that ghastly war. Vespasian, Titus's father, had had it housed in the newly constructed Temple of Peace, where it remained along with other examples of Jewish gold, more prized as an artifact than for its melt value.

And if the stories are true, it was still there in 455 when Gaiseric (aka Genseric) the Vandal, in exchange for sparing the lives of Rome's inhabitants, took the city down to its studs, the temple's plunder to be shipped off to Carthage, where it presumably served a similar function in Gaiseric's treasury. As Gibbon recapped it: "The holy instruments of the Jewish worship, the gold table, and the gold candlestick with seven branches, originally framed according to the particular instructions of God himself, and which were placed in the sanctuary of his temple, had been ostentatiously displayed to the Roman people in the triumph of Titus. They were afterwards deposited in the temple of Peace; and at the end of four hundred years, the spoils of Jerusalem were transferred from Rome to Carthage, by a barbarian who derived his origin from the shores of the Baltic."[37] The menorah figures prominently in Karl Pavlovich's 1833 painting of "Genseric Sacking Rome."

The story did not end there, however. Some eighty years later, in 534, Belisarius, the Byzantine general under Justinian who wanted to reclaim the western empire for Constantinople, landed in Carthage and found the temple treasures intact. Of course he brought the pieces back to Justinian, who soon received a petition from the local Jewish community seeking their return. A Jewish adviser pointed out that custody of the sacred objects did not bring anything good to those gentiles who controlled them: "These treasures I think it inexpedient to carry into the palace in Byzantium. Indeed, it is not possible for them to be elsewhere than in the place where Solomon, the king of the Jews, formerly placed them. For it is because of these that Gaiseric captured the palace of the Romans, and that now the Roman army has captured that of the Vandals."[38]

The argument worked, and Justinian had the goods sent to Jerusalem, albeit to the care of a Christian church. And there they disappear from the record yet again. Sober historians might assume that these treasures were lost to the Persian sack of Jerusalem in 614. Unless, of course, Procopius got it wrong. Procopius is at times an uncertain source, responsible for the unutterably salacious *Secret History*, which seems to take as its model the most eyebrow-raising passages of Suetonius writing about the twelve Caesars. The book is a hatchet job, principally on Justinian and Theodora, perhaps the product of a courtier disillusioned, perhaps written as a potential gift for any new emperor who wanted evidence that that a fresh start was desirable. So perhaps Procopius is less than fastidious in other stories as well.

In any event, the menorah is clearly not in Jerusalem, and given that gold is easily converted from the sacred to the profane, and given that the Persian sack of AD 614 was thorough, one might easily conclude that it was melted down centuries ago. Occam's razor shaves off other narratives, which might be an end to the matter, but for whatever reason—hope, suspicion, uncertainty, hope again—the nagging thought persisted that maybe, just *maybe*, the treasure was still around.

So if it is not in Jerusalem, the candlestick hunters are forced to retrace the menorah's known history, which leads them back to Rome. Benjamin of Tudela, the twelfth-century Jewish traveler and writer, who briefly stopped at Rome to visit his coreligionists on his way from Spain to the Holy Lands, had a version that cut out Carthage entirely: "There is a cave in which Titus son of Vespasian hid the temple vessels that he brought back from Jerusalem. And there is [another] cave in a hill, on the side along the banks of the Tiber River, where the righteous ones are buried, the ten martyrs."[39]

All traces of the cave, the martyrs, and the temple vessels were gone by the time he got there, of course, so we need to dial time forward a bit, to Gaiseric's raid.

Imagine you are an observant Jew (or backsliding Christian, for that matter) and have heard that the pope is negotiating the lives of the locals in exchange for all the city's material goods. Time is short. As one of the quick and the pious, hearing that Gaiseric had agreed to this deal, you might wish to remove the most valuable objects and put them in a place of greater safety.[40] A place within Rome itself.

Some have thought (some think to this day) that the temple treasures—not only the menorah, but the Ark of the Covenant, the staffs of Moses and Aaron, the golden censer and golden urn filled with manna, and the table of the showbread as well—were secured beneath the high altar at Saint John Lateran.[41] The Vatican periodically gets letters asking that this be proved false.

The other, more beguiling theory is that the Jewish goods wound up in the Tiber. That, at least, was the hope, and in the late seventeenth century a Jewish consortium was willing to lay good money on the prospect. The pope turned them down, the official story being that he feared that while the river water was temporarily diverted to another outlet, "the Heats [*sic*] might advance too far before they had finished their Work and produce a Pestilence among his People."[42] So said Joseph Addison (1672–1719), and anyone familiar with a low-lying estuary in high summer can appreciate the thinking.

De Brosses (1709–1777) has a less generous explanation: "This is a bigoted nation and not the wiser for being so. I have also heard that the Jews offered to dredge and deepen the bed of the Tiber at their own cost, and to make quays as far as the Island of St. Bartholomew [Tiber Island], where a quay is most wanted, if they were allowed to retain all the antiquities found in the river during the work."[43]

No doubt a quay and a deeper Tiber would have been a good thing for the city. On the other hand, what if they were on to something? Did the Jews know something the church did not? Best not to risk it. Petition denied.

The advent of Napoleon was a further reason to do nothing. John Chetwode Eustace discussed the prospect in 1802 with various respectable and deep-pocketed Romans. They demurred:

> The fatal experience of French power and malignity, and the fearful obscurity in which the intentions of that infernal government are enveloped, must of course act as a drawback upon the benevolent plans of the Pontiff, and keep the resources of the country almost in a state of stagnation. . . . If a project of cleansing the bed of the Tiber is proposed, and about to be adopted, for whom, it is asked, shall we draw up these long neglected treasures? for our greatest enemies. Is a palace to be repaired or new furnished; what! they exclaim, shall we spend our fortunes to prepare lodging for a French general?[44]

Clearly not. But with the end of Napoleon in 1814 and the departure of the French menace, the dream awoke, and ambitious men got busy. In 1818, Cardinal Benedetto Naro (1744–1832) founded a company to dredge the Tiber and had Cardinal Consalvi present the application to Pope Pius VII. Permission granted. Naro was able to sell 120 shares for 36,000 scudi for a summer excavation of 1819. A ship, a barge—the details are not recorded—named the *Medusa*, was covered by the license and was floated in the area between the Ponte Milvio and Porta Ostiense (modern Porta San Paolo).[45]

The enterprise excited British investors more than Italian, and was in fact undersubscribed.[46] Among the punters, the most notable was Lady Elizabeth, Duchess of Devonshire, the duke's second wife after Georgiana. Beau Brummell slightly exaggerated her role in the whole operation: "She was the duchess who, at her own expense, caused a machine to be fabricated for dragging the Tiber, in the vain hope of redeeming some of the statues which it is well ascertained had been thrown into it at different periods during the civil wars, and the first invasion of Clovis."[47] Reports from Rome came back to England on a regular basis.

August 7—"Nothing has yet been found in the river."[48]

August 23—"The famous scheme for fishing for statues appears to have failed."[49]

August 26—"The search in the Tiber affords ample material for the inexhaustible raillery of the Romans. The machine has turned out to be a wretched piece of work, so that the wheels have not the power of two horses. Nothing has been found."[50]

September 5—"The river has risen five or six feet, and the machine cannot touch the bottom."[51]

By October—"The machine is already broken."[52]

In the end, only fifteen artifacts were thought worth mentioning.[53] The best piece was a sarcophagus created for one Cornelia, and *that*, according to Roman authorities, was found not in the river but on the banks, and as such was outside the scope of the dredging permit. Rome's *commissario delle antichità*, Carlo Fea, claimed the piece was a known object, and so took it for the Vatican museum, leaving the investors high and dry.

Beau Brummell condoled the duchess on tossing this investment into the river and noted, "I allude to her mode of writing merely the initial and final letters of words, an affectation which often cost me considerable trouble in guessing at her meaning. Thus in referring to her repeated disappointments on this subject, she writes: 'My l—t like my f—t at —s have failed!'"[54]

The whole affair, and particularly the hope of finding the menorah, were enough of an embarrassment that twenty years later Giuseppe Gioachino Belli, poet of the Roman dialect, was still able to mock the investors' ambition in his sonnet "Campo Vaccino":

> Mo nnun c'é ppiú sto Cannellabbro ar monno.
> Per èsse sc'è; ma nun lo gode un cane
> Perché sta ggiú in ner fiume a ffonno a ffonno.
> Lo voi sapé lo voi dov'arimane?
> Viscino a pponte Rotto: e ssi lo vonno
> Se tira sú per un tozzo de pane.[55]

> But the candelabra is not on earth anymore
> Though it's still around, no good even to a dog,
> because it's down in the river, deep, deep as you like.
> You want to know, do you really want to know where to find it?
> Near the Ponte Rotto, and if they want to
> Pull it up, it will set them back a penny or two.

Faith springs eternal, it would seem—Mrs. Hawthorne writes in 1871: "We crossed the Ponte Molle, very memorable for the battle between Constantine and Maxentius, fought upon and near it, when it was the Milvian bridge. Hereabouts in the Tiber, still lies imbedded the seven-branched golden candlestick brought by Titus from Jerusalem."[56]

Her more famous kinsman Nathaniel mined a similar vein, albeit of trivial quality. He describes his young friend J—, who "had a fever for marbles, just on the edge of its muddy waters."[57]

Marbles. Presumably small bits and chips. This is what mudlarking had come to on the Tiber.

And yet, and yet! Our Renaissance memoirist Vacco had clearly been on to something. Just under two hundred years before the Hawthornes, Bernard de Montfaucon did just tell us on the good authority of genuine Romans that "all manner of coins are pulled up on a daily basis."[58]

It took the Italian government until 1877 to order the dredging of the river, and that for the practical purpose of establishing a uniform depth of three meters. In digging foundations for the Ponte Garibaldi and Ponte Sisto, they reached down nearly eleven meters. Vacco and the others, it turns out, were to be vindicated.

Lanciani discusses the finds, noting that the higher strata are contemporary with the 1857 siege and capture of the city by General Charles Oudinot, as street weapons were abandoned once resistance proved punishable.[59] Beneath these came material from the 1831 disturbances, followed by the Napoleonic War—artifacts and curiosities of various sorts. Then the sack of Rome in 1527, a rich tragedy. The total number of coins found worked out to an average dump rate of twelve hundred a month. Some at least must have been attached to prayers and wishes; how many of these, one wonders, were fulfilled?

Deeper digging around the Ponte Sisto in 1878 turned up even older material. Finds of interest to archaeologists include inscriptions commemorating the AD 71 surveying of the Tiber riverbanks under Vespasian, and an inscription on how the city prefect L. Aurelius Avianius Symmachus rebuilt the Ponte Sisto's predecessor in 366–367, during the reigns of Valentinian and Valens. Dating from that time as well were the tops of a triumphal arch—how on earth, why on earth, would anyone take the trouble to lug that to the river? Or perhaps it graced one of the destroyed bridges?

In 1885, air caissons, similar to the ones used to lay the foundations of the Brooklyn Bridge in the 1870s, descended down to anchor the Ponte Garibaldi. From an archaeological standpoint, the chosen spot was almost miraculous. Eight meters below the water surface, five more meters into the mud, the diggers found a life-size bronze statue of Bacchus. Also a gilt bronze *patera*, a Roman dish used to pour libations, some two feet in diameter (pagan, ergo suspect to Christian minds, perhaps). Also a land survey inscription, and "the usual prodigious mass of smaller objects."[60] "Usual prodigious mass" is a nice touch, given that the length of the bank so dug was only a few meters long, a small fraction of the length within Rome.

Workmen at this time also hauled up a number of small bronze statuettes of Caligula, popular when he was alive, less so once he was assassinated. The senate wanted to put an official *damnatio memoriae* on him; his uncle Claudius the Stammerer met them halfway. Official statues and images were to be destroyed, but no official action taken. These smaller figures would have been for personal use, something to put in *privata sacra*, household *lararia*, wall niches dedicated to family gods and, in imperial times, the family gods of the emperor. Difficult to know what to do with them once Caligula himself was dead. Assuming he was dead. In life he had claimed to be a god, and who could say for sure that he was not? Certainly he was related to gods. What to do? Tossing his figures into the river turned the problem over to his fellow gods. His spirit would be either washed away, or assumed by the Olympians.[61]

Digging the Tiber bed expressly to find antiquities has not been attempted since the eighteenth century, and now that the banks are clad with stone, future excavation seems unlikely anytime soon. Just as well. Let later generations have the thrill of discovery. Perhaps the river could be diverted, the earth dug at leisure. Perhaps. Who knows what might be found?

Lanciani can tell us of one item that might not come immediately to mind. In 1866,

a freight train having been carelessly coupled on the gradient which leads from the railway bridge at S. Paolo to the station of Porta Portese, fourteen trucks [railcars] began to descend the steep incline towards the bridge with such velocity that the central span, which was open for the passage of a steamer, could not be closed in time, in spite of the desperate efforts of the guardsmen. The fourteen trucks fell through the gap in mid-stream and were heaped up to the height of some twenty feet above water. It took the government engineers a little more than two weeks to make the necessary arrangements for the removal of the wreck; but they had scarcely completed these when they found, much to their astonishment, that the whole mass had disappeared without leaving a single trace of the catastrophe. The fourteen cars had been swallowed, as it were, by the quicksands which fill the bed to a depth of some thirty feet.[62]

They're still there, if newspaper silence is any indication.

Fireworks

At the end of his 1540 treatise on gunpowder and its destructive uses, Vannoccio Biringuccio gives us a chapter on how fireworks can brighten up any special occasion.[63] His example is the Girandola at the Castel Sant'Angelo.

The tradition dates back to 1481, to celebrate the election and coronation of a pope, or Easter Monday, or the feasts of Saints Peter and Paul, or whatever other good excuse could be cobbled together. On the day in question, artillery men rigged up thousands of pyrotechnics to the stoneworks of the Castel Sant'Angelo and, by night, oversaw the setting them off.

The accounts written by people not yet jaded by television and computers were ecstatic. A seventeenth-century French tourist claimed that "one can see on all sides the girandole created from 4,500 rockets which fly at once, and gather in a circle in the form of a parasol, the most beautiful man-made creations I have ever seen."[64]

Robert Adam, in town in 1755 to soak up classical architecture, was similarly bowled over. The spectacle

exceeded for beauty, invention, and grandeur anything I had ever seen or indeed could conceive. What was the grandest part of the operations they call the Girandola, being thousands of rockets which are sent up at one time, which spread out like a wheat sheaf in the air, each one of which gives a crack and sends out a dozen burning balls like stars, which fall gently downwards till they die out. They, to appearance, spread a mile, and the light balls occasioned, illuminating the landscape, showed the Castle of Sant'Angelo, the river Tiber, and the crowds of people, coaches and horses which swarmed on all sides and appeared to me the most romantic and picturesque sight I have ever seen.[65]

Charlotte Eaton, not a woman easily impressed, went on at some length over Easter Sunday 1818:

Red sheets of fire seemed to blaze upwards into the glowing heavens, and then to pour down their liquid streams upon the earth. . . . Hundreds of immense wheels turned round with a velocity that almost seemed as if demons were whirling them, letting fall thousand of hissing dragons and scorpions and fiery snakes. . . . Fountains and jets of fire threw up their blazing cascades into the skies. The whole vault of heaven shone with the vivid fires. . . . The reflection in the depth of the calm clear waters of the Tiber were scarcely less beautiful than the spectacle itself.[66]

And so forth.

Likewise Dickens, twenty-six years later:

The show began with a tremendous discharge of cannon, and then, for twenty minutes or half an hour, the whole castle was one incessant sheet of fire and labyrinth of blazing wheels of every color, size, and speed, while rockets streamed into the sky, not by ones or twos, or scores, but hundreds at a time. The concluding burst—the Girandola was like the blowing up into the air of the whole massive castle, without smoke or dust.[67]

Gloriously vulgar, as the best fireworks should be. Goethe in 1787 liked the Girandola well enough, but his taste was refined—he preferred the nearby Saint Peter's sideshow, the *Luminaria di San Pietro*, where a small army of *Sanpietrini*, Vatican caretakers turned lamplighters for the day, contrived to set alight a few thousand lanterns and torches more or less simultaneously, clambering over the dome, the facade, and the colonnade to make the effect work. As far as Goethe was concerned, the main event "did not compare with the illuminations."[68]

Today, the Luminaria is not part of the spectacle—floodlights have made it superfluous—but the fireworks show, inimitable, is an annual event and a worthwhile attraction if you happen to be in town.

Beware of pickpockets.

Airborne

In 1783, the Montgolfier brothers sent up the first hot-air balloon, making the dreams of Icarus real. It influenced dress, wall decoration, hairstyles, and much else besides. One can see why. The earth took on a perspective that previously was available only from mountaintops, which limited both choice and maneuverability. How could one not be thrilled?

Jean-Pierre Blanchard was so inspired that he quit his job, left his wife, and devoted the rest of his life to ballooning. He was the first to fly in Belgium, the Netherlands, Poland, and the United States, crossing the Delaware River from Philadelphia to New Jersey. He crossed the English Channel. In 1785 he demonstrated an early parachute, initially with a dog, later (when one of his balloons sprang a leak), with himself.

Early in the new century he met Marie Madeleine-Sophie Armant, a shy, petite woman twenty-five years his junior. She seems an unlikely candidate for this emerging and still dangerous novelty, and yet, from the moment of their first flight together, she was hooked. Just as well. He had been doing this for two decades, and the show was perhaps getting a little old. Sophie could rejuvenate it. They married in 1804.

Their time together was short. In 1808 he suffered a heart attack while flying over The Hague. He fell from the balloon, was more or less paralyzed, and died a year later.

The show must go on. Her sex, her widowhood, her own possible death were already draws, and the novelty of ballooning was still unnatural enough to bring out a crowd, but she would soon need new gimmicks.

In 1811 she brought her act to Rome. Her time there coincided with the birth of Napoleon's son, the performance a celebration of it. The crowds gathered at the Corea Amphitheater, at the Mausoleum of Augustus.

Bad weather prevented takeoff on the assigned day, and the next. On day three, she grew impatient. Weather was still bad, but she went off regardless. The carriage swung about the arena. Audience members tried to catch the anchor ropes to pull her down, but failed. The balloon cleared the arena and disappeared from sight. From the arena it was a short flight, more or less straight into the river, and she might have died had not locals come to her rescue. (Alternatively, she was swept downriver and grabbed a branch and thereby dragged herself ashore.) Undeterred, she made a more successful attempt a few days later, taking off from the Piazza Navona and landing safely outside the city.

As careers go, hers was bound to end badly. Ballooning was already highly risky. For the sake of her art, she took unnecessary chances—she introduced pyrotechnics into her act. On the night of July 6, 1819, the balloon cloth itself caught fire. A witness wrote, "There was an awful pause. In a few seconds, the poor creature, enveloped and entangled in the netting of her machine, fell with a frightful crash upon the slanting roof of a house in the Rue de

Provence (not a hundred yards from where I was standing), and thence into the street,—and Madame Blanchard was taken up a shattered corpse!"[69]

Mastro Titta, *Er dilettante de Ponte*

Mastro Titta—a slurred pronunciation of *maestro di Giustizia*, or Master of Justice—the dilettante of the bridge. The name he got from Romanesco poet Giuseppe Gioachino Belli, the bridge being the Ponte Sant'Angelo, which connects the Castel Sant'Angelo with the left bank. Titta's real name was Giovanni Battista Bugatti. He was a short, round man who, with his wife, made a living by making umbrellas, painting them with portraits and Roman scenes, and selling them to tourists near the Vatican. Quirky, as jobs go, and seasonal, leaving Bugatti in need of a second income stream. At age seventeen, he found one.

He was, in the years between 1796 and 1864, Rome's official executioner. Five hundred and sixteen in the course of his career, and the bridge in his unofficial title was the one he crossed on those occasions when he was called on to execute his job, which was on average more than seven times a year. Mastro Titta is the source of the Italian proverb "Boia nun passa Ponte"—The executioner isn't crossing the river, or, loosely, All's right in the world. (Roman wits joked that he also provided a good cure for headache.)

Dickens, who attended one of his executions, said, "He dare not, for his life, cross the Bridge of St. Angelo but to do his work." The fear was of excitable relatives of those he had dispatched, perhaps. Other accounts say he was forbidden because his appearance on the left bank was invariably noticed and crowds would come out to see if there was going to be a killing that day. Justice was, after all, a public affair. Tradesmen (Dickens mentions cigar sellers and pastry merchants) wandered the crowd, hawking their goods. The superstitious jockeyed for the best positions to see how many gouts of blood would spurt out, and factor that number into their choice of future lottery tickets. Children were escorted to the event as a warning against wicked living, and clouted on the neck as the blade came down, to underscore the lesson. Children, being children, soon incorporated the man into rhyme:

> Sega, sega, Mastro Titta,
> 'na pagnotta e 'na sarciccia.
> Un' a mme, un' a tte,
> un'a mmàmmeta che sso'ttre.[70]

Slice, slice, Mastro Titta,
A loaf of bread and salami.
One for me, one for thee,
One for Mama, that makes three.

Not that he minded his celebrity. On the contrary, he eschewed the traditional head cover that ensured the executioner's anonymity. It was a part-time job, one he did with professionalism and even compassion. To those about to die, he offered snuff, and promised a quick end. Off duty, when not in his red-robed executioner's gown (or, according to Lord Byron, who saw him in 1817, half naked), he dressed with some flair and style, making up in dress what he lacked in height and slimness. The job done, he was back across the river until the next criminal was condemned to die.

He retired at the age of eighty-five on a papal pension, and lived a further five years, just short of seeing the Unification of Italy and the abolition of his secondary trade. A fly-by-night publisher published his autobiography in 1891, mixing the ghoulish with the anticlerical, all of it utterly fraudulent, Titta having had nothing to do with it.[71] More genuine are the red robe and his white high-pointed capirote hood and face mask (familiar from Spanish Holy Week celebrations, or Ku Klux Klan meetings), now on display at Rome's Museum of Criminology, along with some tools of his trade, including the guillotine that replaced him, machinery demanding less skill to operate than a mere ax.

Some Italian Poets

If the French poet Saint-Amant disliked Rome, the Neapolitan Domenico D'Aquino (1650–1697) seems to have been fond of it, at least as a subject for dark humor. Heir to the title of Prince of Caramanico, D'Aquino as a young man was a student at the Seminario Romano. While there, he was beguiled by *poesia volgare*, Italian verse rather than Latin poetry, and composed a number of poems that he declaimed in public performances (*commedie publiche*), as well as in the seminary itself.

Among his works was the heroic epic *Il Tebro incoronato* (The Tiber crowned). This lengthy piece goes over the many major rivers of the world, giving each one its due, but in the end crowns the Tiber above all others. He awards the river such epithets as *l'irrigator delle latine arene*, irrigator of

Latin sands, and, more disquieting, *il valoroso innondator Latino*, valorous Latin flooder.[72]

The poem is possibly a takeoff on the similarly titled *Il Tevere incatenato* (The Tiber enchained), a serious study published thirteen years earlier on how the river's flooding might be restrained. As jokes go, this was pretty obscure, and we have to wonder how it went down with D'Aquino's fellow students, in particular those who had endured Tiber floods. He was probably on safer ground with his ongoing crusade to get the Italian alphabet to accept the letter *H*.[73]

More strictly lyrical is the work of Tuscan poet (and Nobel laureate) Giosuè Carducci (1835–1907). *Sul Monte Mario* is a standard for Italian schoolchildren. The first two stanzas of twelve:

> Solenni in vetta a Monte Mario stanno
> nel luminoso cheto aere i cipressi,
> e scorrer muto per i grigi campi
> mirano il Tebro,
>
> mirano al basso nel silenzio Roma
> stendersi, e, in atto di pastor gigante
> su grande armento vigile, davanti
> sorger San Pietro.

> Cypresses solemn stand on Monte Mario;
> Luminous, quiet is the air around them;
> They watch the Tiber through the misty meadow
> Wandering voiceless.
>
> They gaze beneath them where, a silent city,
> Rome lies extended: like a giant shepherd,
> O'er flocks unnumbered vigilant and watchful,
> Rises St. Peter's.[74]

A more melancholic view comes from Giuseppe Ungaretti (1888–1970). Born and raised in Alexandria, Egypt, Ungaretti moved to Paris in 1912 to soak up the culture. He fought for Italy in World War I, an experience that seemed as much a source for his poetry as it was for the Owenses and Sassoons and Graveses further up the trench line. He was an Italian nationalist and early supporter of Mussolini, but also a cosmopolite who lived abroad for many years and appears devoid of race prejudice; in later life he was a strong Catholic. Written in 1947, after the death of his brother and of his young son, the poem is both an antiwar statement and a meditation on grief. It begins,

> Mio fiume anche tu, Tevere fatale,
> Ora che notte già turbata scorre;
> Ora che persistente
> E come a stento erotto dalla pietra
> Un gemito d'agnelli si propaga
> Smarrito per le strade esterrefatte;
>
> You too are my river, fateful Tiber
> Now that night already troubled flows;
> Now that insistent
> And like in pain erupted from the stone
> A wail of lambs echoes
> Bewildered through terror-river streets;[75]

The river appears in popular song, in one of the bigger hits of the Trastevere native Romolo Balzani (1892–1962), who as a boy spent so much time swimming the river that his skin turned dark, earning him the name *Tizzo Nero*, Coal Black. The song in Roman dialect was "Barcarola Romana."

> Quanta pena stasera
> c'è sur fiume che fiotta così,
> disgrazziato chi sogna e chi spera,
> tutti ar monno devemo soffrì,
> ma si n'anima che cerca la pace,
> può trovalla sortanto di quì.
>
> Er barcarolo va contro corente
> e quanno canta, l'eco s'arisente.
> Si è vero, fiume, che tu dai la pace,
> fiume affatato, nun me la nega'.
>
> How much sorrow there is tonight
> That floats here on the river.
> Unhappy he who dreams and hopes,
> All of us in the world must suffer.
> But if some poor souls seeks peace,
> He can find it only here

The boatman pulls against the current
And when he sings, the echo refrains.
If it is true, river, that you bring peace,
Enchanted river, don't deny it to me.

Boy meets girl, boy dumps girl, boy regrets his loss and goes to the river to find her. He fails, and confronts the slow-running Tiber where it seems that Ninetta (her name) has been swallowed, and consequently his desire to go on.

Whether it's the nature of the subject or the nature of the writers, the Tiber doesn't seem to bring out much cheer in the poetical fraternity.

French Polish

In 1796 Napoleon first crossed the border into Italy, where his troops were to be a diversion, while the better part of the French army was to attack the Rhine. The main attack bogged down, but then the relatively unknown Napoleon managed to pull off a stunning victory against greater forces and so make a name for himself. Peace terms were settled, which lasted until 1799, when he invaded a second time (David's picture of the general on a rearing horse crossing the Alps dates from this campaign). Again, the victories were stunning (Marengo) but cut short at Rome, courtesy of Britain's Royal Navy.

The failure of 1799 did not deter Napoleon, by then emperor, and in 1809 he was back, this time expelling the pope and installing his own brother Joseph as king of Rome. The French meant to stay. On May 17, Napoleon declared that the Papal States were henceforth a part of the French Empire, and his brother was now its secular king. In an attempt to make a French presence more palatable, Napoleon married the Duchess of Parma, and a year later, in 1811, made their son king of Rome. What he had in mind for Italy was to make the country rational, modern, all through the judicious application of rational and modern laws and directives.

His initial focus would be Rome, a second Paris, but a second Paris rather the worse for wear. In a sense, Rome was the perfect subject for his ambitions, for the new empire reveled in all things modern, while respecting all things classical. Whatever monuments the Italians of past ages had left to ruin, or exploited for personal gain, France would accord a deserved dignity. (Much of the Louvre is still devoted to this proposition.) To address this goal, and the goal of modernization, the French emperor created the office of *préfet de Rome et du Tibre*, and to fill this post he chose the thirty-year-old Comte Camille de Tournon-Simiane.

Tournon, "a gentleman by character as well as by birth," was born in 1778 in Apt, Vaucluse.[76] If his portrait is to be believed, he was remarkably un-threatening. Entitled by rank and office to wear a uniform, he chose to be painted in loose shirt and pants more reminiscent of a Byron or a Shelley than a French bureaucrat. Well read in classics, he found his appointment an exciting opportunity to do good. Revolution is a messy business, and even in France itself, the more levelheaded had to create the Commission tem-poraire des arts in 1793 to stop the more excitable firebrands from breaking nice things. Under the new rules, there would be no more contempt for the treasures of France, be they books, paintings, museums, statues, antiquities. Everything was now under government protection.

The same, it was hoped, would be the case in Italy, with Tournon as point man: "May I be so happy as to be able to plant some seeds of prosperity in this soil which is so poetic, but so wretched."[77]

Well intentioned or not, Tournon was French, and alien rule is rarely com-fortable, even less so when enforced at the tip of bayonets, less so still when the outsiders clearly think they know better than locals. Among the first ukases was one against swimming in the Tiber, at least without underwear, at least if you were a man. Women had no business enjoying the river at all, nor even the fountains of Rome, "on pain of penalties appropriate to their station."[78]

In the summer of 1811, the Commission des embellissements issued a de-cree designed to improve the general layout of the city, chiefly involving the tearing down of crowded areas, much as had been done in Paris, to be re-placed by wider boulevards. (Napoleon also knew the value of long straight streets; as commander of the Royalist artillery on the 13 Vendémiaire Year 4 [October 5, 1795], he found that wide boulevards simplified the matter of turning artillery on rioting Parisians.) This was a tall order, but Tournon's Commission des monuments et bâtiments civils was accorded a million francs for the restoration of Roman antiquities and the general improvement of the city. Ten percent was allotted for the refurbishment of the Tiber River, at the time not the most utilitarian of waterways.[79]

Tournon hired numbers of Roman citizens, many previously relying on church charity, to make his projects a reality. He, and they, are responsible for digging out and removing four meters and more of dirt that had accu-mulated over the centuries, and so brought the Roman Forum down to its original level. Anticipating Mussolini by over a century, Tournon bought up medieval houses surrounding the site and set his crews to knocking them down, creating much of the vista familiar to tourists today. He had buildings that had latched on to ancient structures scraped off, revealing their ancient origins and restoring less cramped roads and walkways.

His plans for the Tiber were similarly ambitious. He wished to extend the reach of heavy river traffic as far upstream as Perugia. He also intended to enclose the banks. He took aim at the bridge situation as well. Rome by now had only three effective crossings: the Ponte Sant'Angelo, the Ponte Sisto, and the twin island bridges Ponte San Bartolomeo and Ponte dei Quattro Capi (Ponte Fabricius). The slack was taken up by ferries. He would revive the Oratius Cocles bridge (Ponte Sublicio) and improve the Ponte Sisto.

By March 1813, only 63,000 of the original million francs had been spent. The river had been dredged to a degree, but much remained to be done. The retaining walls, designed to imitate those that constrain the Seine, had not yet been started. Rome was not to be restored in a day.

Tournon's days ran out in 1814 with the return of Neapolitan forces and the restoration of the pope. He took his records with him, fodder for his Études. He was done with Napoleon, in any event, and after the emperor's failure following the Hundred Days, was rewarded by the king by being made prefect of the Gironde, and then of the Rhône.

There would, however, be more French soldiers in Rome. In 1849, Napoleon III would send a garrison to support Pope Pius IX against the forces of Italian reunification.

These French were not universally loved. Too arrogant, too drunk, and too forward with respectable women. The Roman folklorist Giggi Zanazzo (1860–1911) writes casually of Roman youth dressing up like women to put French soldiers, whether those of Napoleon I or Napoleon III, off their guard. The disrespectful would end up with a knife in the gut, a stone around the neck, and a watery grave in the river. The arrangement was hard on French morale: "Every now and then you would see a soiled, drunk Frenchman, sword unsheathed, wandering the streets of Rome, abusing and insulting everyone he met."[80] The last assassination Zanazzo could recall occurred in 1870, when the last of Napoleon III's French garrison was pulled from Rome to fight the Germans in the Franco-Prussian War. They did not return.

But to get back to and finish off the first Napoleonic story, and the role of the British navy:

In 1798, Admiral Nelson had defeated Napoleon's fleet at the battle of the Nile. Within a year, French forces were in temporary retreat, not least of all from Italy. Sir Thomas Troubridge landed sailors and marines in Civitavecchia north of Rome in September 1799 and effected the surrender of the French forces in the Roman states. Not all were happy to leave, fearing the reaction they would get in France, but this was none of Troubridge's affair. His only regret, laid out in his official report, was that he could not be harsher: "As I knew the French had all the valuables of the Roman State packed up ready for embarking, and the coast at Civita Vecchia forming a deep bay with hard W.S.W. gales and heavy seas, which prevented the blockade from being so close as was necessary to prevent the enemy from carrying off those truly valuable articles, I therefore thought it best to grant the liberal terms I have to get them out of this country, where they have committed every excess possible."[81]

To expedite the French departure, British captain Thomas Louis took a squadron of marines down the coast to Ostia and a barge up the Tiber to Rome, where he climbed the steps of the Capitoline and hoisted British colors. Or perhaps British colors and the papal flag over the Castel Sant'Angelo. Possibly both. Regardless of which story is exactly true, the message was clear—the French were gone. For as long as it took to evacuate French personnel, Captain Louis was in effect the governor of the city, much to the locals' relief. In short order, control (along with some of the artwork looted by the French) was returned to the Vatican, in gratitude for which, it is said, the pope granted an area outside the city walls for the Protestant Cemetery, last resting place of Keats, Shelley, and other non-Catholic expatriates of note.

As for Captain (later Admiral) Louis, how did this British naval officer come by such an un-English name? The family tradition is that his grandfather was an illegitimate son of France's Louis XIV.

English Rose

"The stone erected to the fair, the young, the much-loved Rose Bathurst, recalled a tragedy that I rarely look upon the Tiber without remembering."[82]

So writes Trollope in 1842.

The Rosa (rather than Rose) Bathurst in question, niece of Lord Aylmer, had been the headline story eighteen years earlier, one that was clearly impressed on the minds of all good Englishmen.

> She was the belle of Rome—at least, she was so considered by all except the
> rival Miss Gent and her admirers. She was a good horsewoman, and on the
> 16th of March, 1824, rode out as usual with her relations and a gay party. They
> crossed the Ponte Molle and turned to the right; when finding a gate shut
> through which they had intended to pass, the old Duc de Montmorenci, the
> French ambassador, who was as blind as a bat, assured them that he could
> guide them along a path beside the river which he had often passed himself;
> without—thanks to his blindness—being aware of its danger.[83]

Miss Bathurst's horse slipped on the steep bank, and both horse and rider went into the river. Her uncle tried to save her, but he was a bad swimmer. He tried twice, failed, and would have gone a third time had not the horse now been clearly riderless. Miss Bathurst had utterly disappeared.

The following year, Mr. Charles Mills had occasion to revisit Rome. In a suitably melancholy mood, he took a stroll by the riverside, contemplating the fate of the missing woman. He glanced up at the other side of the river and saw two peasants pulling a bit of blue cloth from the mud. He corralled some men to bring spades and start digging, and soon found Rosa Bathurst, seemingly untouched except for a small blow to her forehead, stone dead but otherwise—they say—perfectly preserved.[84]

(Alternatively, a letter to Dr. H. Bathurst, bishop of Norwich, claims that "two carters saw the body as they crossed over the Melvino [Milvian] bridge, perfectly visible and recognized not so much by the countenance as by the dress and jewels." The accounts do concur that sand or mud had preserved her from the ravages of six months in the water.)[85]

Her sister expressed grief in poetry:

> Oh! who can tell, at that sad hour of awe,
> That form divine, that soul-subduing grace
> The heaven that beam'd from thy expressive face
> Float for a moment upon Tiber's wave
> Then sink forever in a watery grave.[86]

Strangers who found her story affecting also tried to render their sentiments in verse, not only English, but Italian as well. Alessandro Poerio's poem was titled "In morte di una giovinetta inglese, caduta nel Tevere" (On the death of a young Englishwoman, lost in the Tiber):

Oh quanto le giovava
Errar col fiume, accompagnar le sponde!
Qui tutta nel pensar s'abbandonava;
Qui dal suon cupo delle torbid'onde
Mirabile diletto ricevea;
Ma con l'onde seguenti ahi l'immaturo
Suo Fato si volvea!

E ruinò veloce,
E'l bel corpo con l'acque si confuse;
Gli occhi alzarsi e le braccia, uscì la voce,
Ma il flutto e'l mondo sovra lei si chiuse;
E muto il suo perir fu d'ogni traccia.
Raggio di Sol non venne in sull'eterno
Pallor della sua faccia.

Oh how she took her delight
In wandering by the river, escorting the bank!
Here she lost herself in thought
Here she enjoyed wondrous delight
To the somber sound of turbid currents;
But with ensuing waves alas! her untimely fate
Was sealed.

She was quickly undone
Her beautiful body became confused with the waters
Her eyes and arms reached up, her voice escaped,
But the flood and the world closed over her
Her death was silent and without a trace;
No ray of sun came to warm the
Pallor of her face.[87]

Giuseppe Gioachino Belli wrote an elegy for her, "In morte di Rosa Bathurst."

Per veder come il sole italo rida
Di Britannia venìa nobil donzella,
E la vedova madre erale guida:
Tanto del volto e delle membra bella
Che, alla fama di lei, di stupor piena
La gente si movea, dicendo: è quella.

To see the laughter of the Italian sun
The noble damsel from Albion comes,
With widowed mother as her guide:
Such beauty of face and limb allied
that, by her repute, the crowd struck dumb
Passes by, saying: She's the one.

The enthusiasm, not to say fad, became faintly ludicrous once a Signor Gentili set his hand to the subject. He described old Tiber's "calling all his nymphs and naiads and tributary courtiers around him and announcing to them the coming of a visitor from the far lands of the barbarous north."[88]

Gentili wrote one canto, which he shared with an English friend, who later noted only: "I do not remember whether I had any hand in preventing the completion and the publication of the work."[89]

The events inspired other artistic ventures as well. One, at least, produced a plaster cameo, framed in gold, a grim Grand Tour souvenir presumably commercial in origin. (If that cameo wasn't enough, there was also a companion piece of Mrs. Hunt, killed that same year by rural bandits while returning from a visit to the old Greek temples at Paestum.)[90]

The drowning was doubly tragic for Rosa's mother, who had already lost her husband, Benjamin Bathurst, a junior diplomat, in 1809. He had disappeared while on a confidential mission to Vienna on behalf of the British Foreign Office. For weeks, all Europe buzzed with talk of it. Misadventure? Murder? Mrs. Bathurst wandered much of Europe to find out what had really happened, but failed. Some blamed France, which took exception to the accusation. Only the British, they claimed, used assassins, and moreover Britain hired lightweights for diplomatic missions, men of whom anything could be expected. There were no answers, at any rate, either then or later. As with Rosa, the truth was likely mundane, that he had fallen victim to brigands, or army deserters, of which there were many at the time.

Mountains, like rivers, keep their secrets.

I Sacconi Rossi

*Our attention is taken by a remarkable procession of people who walk
solemnly two by two and seem to be as much out of the Middle Ages as anyone
painted by Giotto or Ghirlandaio or Sandro Botticelli. These men are dressed from
head to toe in long red robes, their heads covered by pointed hoods which also cover
their faces, with two slits for their eyes. All are barefoot, and rope girds their loins.
Some carry crosses, but the two spectres who lead the procession hold before
them human skulls and bones, murmuring prayers as they walk.
They are the Brotherhood of the Rossi Sacconi.*

Ferdinand Gregorovius wrote this in 1863, in *Wanderjahre in Italien*.

The order in question is the Confraternita dei devoti di Gesù al Calvario e
di Maria ss Addolorata in sollievo delle anime sante del Purgatorio—more
commonly, the *Sacconi Rossi*, the Red Sacks, after their garb and the cloth
receptacles in which they once accepted alms for the poor.

The order was created in 1643 and tasked with gathering those who died
in the gutter and hauling out the bodies of those drowned in the Tiber, and,
in the event the bodies went unclaimed, to ensure them proper burial in the
order's crypt. Important work, and it was as well that they did it.

Bodies take up space, even buried, and the church took a practical view of
disposal. Once the flesh had rotted, the bones could be dug up and placed on
display in suitable manner, as a memento mori for the living.

The nineteenth century was difficult for the order, as modern views on
biohazards began to take hold. The practice of arranging the bones as art
came to an end in 1836, when Pope Gregory XVI decreed that the dead
should be buried in Verano Cemetery. There had been a recent outbreak of
cholera, and so . . .

The new government of a unified Italy in 1870 laid down further restric-
tions governing the disposal of the dead, and the order diminished almost
to the point of extinction.

Since 1983, however, the processional has been revived. Red-hooded religious brothers (or lay parishioners of Santa Maria dell'Orto) carrying oil
lamps can be seen walking from the San Giovanni Calibita Hospital at
Fatebenefratelli around Tiber Island, culminating at one end, where a priest
throws a wreath of white flowers into the water to commemorate the dead.
The parade then crosses the river to Santa Maria dell'Orto to visit the crypt,
where the bones of the dead are sprinkled with holy water and blessed.

The bones, the few that remain, can still be seen there on request, or more generally, on November 2.

Fishing for Wood

One unlikely job goes unmentioned in classical or Renaissance texts. Strother Smith describes men who stand on the banks or the bridges at autumn flood-water, waiting for the river to carry down trees, or parts of trees. These men carry *rampicone*, which he describes as "a piece of wood, from which project two or three long and crooked teeth formed by the smaller branches growing out of the trunk from which the piece of wood is cut."[91]

Grappling hooks, in short. Grappling hooks tied to ropes. The point of the exercise is to snag the passing tree. In the late nineteenth century, raw wood, firewood, was a salable commodity, and it was worth these men's while to cast a line.

Nathaniel Hawthorne saw the practice as well, in 1858: "As I approached the bridge of St. Angelo, I saw several persons engaged, as I thought, in fishing the Tiber, with very strong lines; but on drawing nearer, I found that they were trying to hook up the branches, and twigs, and other drift-wood, which the recent rains might have swept into the river. There was a little heap of what looked like willow twigs, the poor result of their labor. The hook was a knot of wood, with the lopped-off branches projecting in three or four prongs."[92]

In the case of larger logs, when anglers wrapped their rope around their wrists, tragedy could follow, and did.

Serious log reapers went down to the water itself, piloting small boats from which they could, like riverine whalers, come alongside their prey to strike up close. This carried risk as well, and boats could be gored and sunk, their passengers forced to swim to shore in heavy current. Success, however, allowed the men to add their catch to piles on the steps of the Ripetta, where they were sold as firewood.

Pius IX

Pope Pius IX (1792–1878), *Crux de Cruce*, Cross from the Cross in Malachy's list, gave the world papal infallibility, a contentious issue now and at the time. Pius was a contentious pope, for that matter. Some questioned his sanity. The

German historian Ferdinand Gregorovius: "A short time ago the Pope put his infallibility to the test, as the French their new *Chassepots* [rifles]. On one of his walks, he called to a man afflicted with paralysis, 'Arise and walk.' The poor devil attempted to obey him and fell down. This greatly perturbed the vice-god. The anecdote is already discussed in the papers. I really believe that the Pope is insane."[93]

Insanity does not preclude cunning, and on the question of papal infallibility, Pius was able to arrange a political outcome to his favor. Threats and bribes and other ploys got him what prior popes had declared off-limits. The rule remains. The lasting image for traditionalists before the rigged vote came from the bishop of Montpellier, François Lecourtier, so dismayed by the proceeding that just before he left town, in a gesture far milder than that of previous malcontents, he threw his copies of the council documents into the Tiber.

As to Pius himself—he died in 1881, and was not universally mourned. The Curia, all too aware of popular sentiment, thought it best to move his body from Saint Peter's to San Lorenzo Fuori le Mura by night. Word got out regardless, and anticlerical zealots on the Ponte Sant'Angelo cried out: "Abbasso le carogne!" and "A fiume il Papa porco!"—"Down with the swine!" and "Into the river with the pig Pope!"[94] Darkness emboldened the mob, stones flew, and the hearse driver, unnerved, brought the horses up to an undignified gallop. The body arrived at San Lorenzo, and the interment proceeded behind locked doors.

The whole affair was a scandal made worse by a weak trial for the protesters resulting in five of six possible convictions, and those given trivial penalties. The gallery cheered, and Freemasons struck a medal in honor of the guilty. Innocent's successor, Leo XIII, kept a lower profile.

Toto Bigio

The unification of Italy brought about a renaissance of bridge building, starting with the Ponte Ripetta, a steel pedestrian structure just north of the Ponte Sant'Angelo. The papers covered the grand opening in 1870 with suitable fanfare, even as they saw that it marked the beginning of the end of a tradition passing back to an age before the Romans. One popular journal reported as follows:

> And yet in the midst of this general approval there was a person who looked at
> the new bridge with a jaundiced eye. That would be Toto Bigio. Who is Toto

Bigio? He is an old ferryman who, for the last forty years, has ferried people from one shore to the other on his boat. It was his right, a privilege which no one would ever dare contest. And when he understood that they wanted to connect the shores with a bridge, the old boatman was ready to die: he turned half of Rome upside down to avert the danger, but in vain.

But there was sympathy for that good old man, who was appointed guardian of the bridge. He can therefore still live on the banks of that river which is his, which he loves, and from which he could not live far away. There is therefore reason to hope that time will diminish his grudge against the new iron giant, which came to steal his livelihood.[95]

The Ponte Ripetta would be replaced in 1901 by the Ponte Cavour, which had the advantage that it could support two-way cart traffic. Old Roman hands remembered Toto Bigio as late as the 1950s.[96]

Waterborne

Captain Paul Boyton, aka the Fearless Frogman (1848–1924), made a point of visiting Rome during his world tour of 1877. Crowds flocked to see him.

Boyton was one of those nineteenth-century men who craved adventure, whether with the Union navy in the US Civil War, the Mexican Navy under Benito Juárez, or the French franc-tireurs during the Franco-Prussian War. Finished with military service, he turned inventor, creating an inflatable rubber suit, which he tried to market as personal life preserver. Commercially, the device went nowhere, but once Boyton managed to cross the English Channel while wearing one, he, and it, became a global sensation. He began traveling the world, floating down every major river he could find, including those of Italy. He describes the adventure in his third-person autobiography:

> While in the ancient city, Paul determined to make a voyage down the Tiber. He went up the river as far as he could get, to Orte. The distance from that town to Rome is about one hundred and ninety miles by river. News of his determination to try the Tiber having preceded him to Orte, he was royally received by the authorities and populace. When the start was made, the mayor escorted him to the river, lustily blowing a horn all the way, like a fish peddler trying to attract attention. The Tiber is an uninteresting stream, running through the Roman Campagna, and is made up of great bends. He left Orte in the afternoon, and night came on terribly cold. Now and then he would get a cheer from people along the banks; but in a moment it was

lost. He drove rapidly along all night without an adventure worth recording. About six o'clock next morning he was caught in an awkward manner in the branches of a tree that had washed into the stream and he only freed himself by cutting away the limbs with his knife, causing considerable delay. All day he drove energetically along, and the stream turned and twisted so much that he frequently passed the same village twice in swinging around great bends. At nightfall he came near frightening the life out of a shepherd. Not knowing where he was and hearing the bark of a dog he climbed up the bank to ascertain, if possible, his locality. He met the shepherd on top of the bank, who looked at him a moment and then scampered away across the plain as fast as his legs would carry him.

That night Paul was met by the Canottiere del Tevere, the leading boat club of Rome, and was accompanied by them for the rest of the journey. Next morning, when they neared Rome, they hauled up at a clubhouse for breakfast. For some miles before they reached the city, people came out on horseback and on foot, saluting them with vivas. At three o'clock they pulled into Rome and were welcomed by thousands of people, and Paul was agreeably astonished at hearing a band play Yankee Doodle in a house which was profusely decorated with American flags. In fact, the reception was something indescribable. People were crowded into every available space. A barge upset in the river, but all the occupants were saved. Boyton landed at Ripetta Grande and so great was the pressure of the throng that the iron band about the waist of his dress was crushed like an eggshell. No end of fêtes followed, the citizens seeming to vie with one another as to which could give the most splendid entertainment.[97]

He would later appear in P. T. Barnum's circus and open a seaside park that would become New York's Coney Island. His memoirs make for entertaining reading.

Airborne Two

A happier Tiber landing than Sophie Blanchard's came nearly a hundred years later, in the person of Francesco de Pinedo (1890–1933), the Neapolitan Lindbergh. A marquis by birth, he was in the Italian Air Force in World War I. He continued flying after the peace, making the first westward crossing of the Atlantic (via the Cape Verde Islands and the Caribbean). He made no fewer than three round-the-world flights in a two-seater hydroplane, the *Gennariello*, in homage to San Gennaro, patron saint of Naples.

In 1925 he made a Rome–Australia–Tokyo–Rome circuit; the Pacific was an ocean too large, but the fifteen-thousand-mile trip was still no mean feat, longer than anything previously attempted. It ended with an impressive river landing on November 7, where he and his copilot were greeted by Mussolini and crowds of proud Italians.

The imperfect technology would eventually undo him, just as it had Sophie. Attempting to take off from New York's Floyd Bennett Field in an airplane weighted down with fuel, he crashed into a building and died by fire.

All Italy mourned.

Two War Stories

The last political execution—a lynching, really—by Tiber water was in 1944, soon after liberation and coincident with the trial of Pietro Caruso, former *questura* of Rome. Under the Fascists, Caruso had delivered fifty partisans to the Germans, partisans who were later shot in the Ardeatine caves. With the fall of Mussolini came the call for retribution. The courts were handling the matter, Caruso was arrested and set to be tried in open court, and the public's blood was up. On the morning of the trial a crowd had gathered outside the Palace of Justice. When the doors opened for the people's business, the people began to push their way into the building and were disappointed to discover that Caruso had not yet arrived.

They did find, however, Donato Carretta, warden of the Regina Coeli prison under Caruso. Despite efforts of the Carabinieri, the mob fell on this man and dragged him from the courtroom, hustled him outside, beat him, then pinned him to tram tracks. The tram driver they hoped would finish the job refused to take part, and indeed walked off with the hand crank needed to operate the train. The mob then frog-marched Carretta to the Tiber and threw him in. (Some claim he jumped.)[98] He managed to flail his way to shore, but the mob, now spread along the bank, pushed back. Still foundering, he managed to grab onto a riverboat, and was struck with an oar. With that, his grip failed and he slipped beneath the water. Not long after, his corpse was recovered and, like Mussolini, hung upside down from the bars of the prison he had overseen.

The full story came out later. In the period leading up to the Ardeatine massacre, whether from conscience or a weather eye on which way the wind was blowing, Caretta, in his capacity as jailer, had been aiding the prisoners, insisting to his superior the *questura* that a number of them were far too ill to be moved. He was in court that day as a witness for the prosecution.

His testimony would have been superfluous. Caruso was found guilty two days later and killed by firing squad the next morning.[99]

The war years do offer at least one happier story, this one from Tiber Island. The island has never lost its medical associations, and in 1944 that fact and the island's proximity to the Jewish ghetto area proved fortuitous. In charge of the Benefrati Hospital was Dr. Giovanni Borromeo, who as such had to deal with whatever government held power for the moment. When Mussolini fell and the Nazis arrived in Rome and set about rounding up Jews, Dr. Borromeo set about his own gathering. Inevitably the SS came to inspect the hospital for candidates for departure, whereupon the doctor regretted to have to inform those inquisitors that the wards were at capacity with patients suffering from the highly contagious and highly deadly "*morbo di K.*"

His bluff was never called.[100]

EPILOGUE

Tevere incatenato

Tevere incatenato—Tiber Enchained.

The haphazard flood markers of the Renaissance gave way to the more scientific recording of the early moderns in the 1704 erection of a marble column at the Ripetta to mark levels. So it continued until 1821, when an improved hydrometer was installed and measurements were taken on a daily basis, rather than just when the river grew frisky. The floods continued, but the Romans had other things on their minds, and after the withdrawal of the forward-looking French, resignation seems to have been the order of the day.

Indeed, for a certain kind of foreigner, the floods had a perverse attraction. Just as some jaded tourists make a point of visiting Venice during the *acqua alta* to get a novel perspective on the city, these were people who found a similar appeal in Rome when the Tiber overtopped the banks.

Sir Richard Burton, contemplating the Pantheon, saw an upside to the floods, "which not unfrequently rise so high as to come into the church." He advised tourists to take advantage of the unique experience: "A beautiful effect is produced by visiting the building on these occasions at night, when the moon is reflected upon the water through the aperture of the dome."[1]

The English curate the Reverend Thomas Mozley (1806–1893), a some-time correspondent of the *Times* of London, came to the city in 1870s to cover the Vatican Council, the Concilium Vaticanum Primum, the first such gathering since the Council of Trent. His letters home are collected in two volumes, which chiefly cover the doings of the various clerics from across the Catholic world; but for those readers whose liturgical interests are limited, he throws in a good amount of local color. Concerning the Tiber's rising and falling just after the new year, he was remarkably insouciant: "This afternoon all the people are going to see the Pantheon under water. By getting admission at the side door they can stand on an altar and see the vast dome perfectly reflected, upside down, in the water."[2]

Stendhal suggests that the popular draw was more than just the novelty of an interior reflecting pool: "As soon as the Tiber floods Rome, all the rats in the quarter take refuge on the paved section of the Pantheon, which is beneath the skylight, where they are attacked by an army of cats."[3]

Elsewhere in Italy, however, politics were brewing. By the middle of the nineteenth century, serious men were determined that Italy would become one nation. The Tiber played its minor part in a few battles between the unification forces of Garibaldi and his opponents (in part French again, defending the doomed Papal States), but for the most part, the river was a silent observer.

By 1870 the bloodshed had ended, and despite a truculent pope who refused to acknowledge the changing times, secular politicians were setting up a unified Italy with Rome as its capital and Victor Emmanuel of Savoy as its crowned head. He was preparing to move south from his ancestral home when the weather took a turn for the worse.

Dark clouds gathered over the midsection of Italy in mid-December 1870. On Monday the twenty-sixth, the rains began. Thunder shook houses. Lightning struck the Vatican, snaking its way into the pope's own chapel, destroying a picture on the altar.[4] On December 27, the river began to rise.

Long-term residents of Rome were initially not overly concerned, any more than Venetians are excited by the *acqua alta*. Ugo Pesce, a non-Roman veteran of Garibaldi's campaigns to unify Italy, wrote in 1870 to describe how, after a presentation at the Teatro Apollo, the audience was informed that the river had reached the theater and that they were invited to exit a side door on an improvised wooden causeway that would lead them to the Piazzetta di San Salvatore in Lauro) where their carriages would be waiting.[5] When in Rome ...

Pesce was staying at the house of a friend who downplayed the matter. The river, yes, it does this from time to time. Nothing to be alarmed over. There will likely be boats floating between the Palazzo Borghese and the Palazzo Valdambrini—something to see! But nothing to be alarmed over. It rises quickly, it departs quickly. Pesce was still uneasy. At about two in the morning, he turned into bed, but not before noting that the streetlamps reflected on the black surface of the water on the via del Corso. The next morning, he could not open his front door.

The German historian Gregorovius reported much the same thing: "The river rose suddenly at 5:00 AM, soon covered the Corso, and advanced through the Via Babuino as far as the Piazza di Spagna. Since 1805 no inundation has reached such a height."[6] Water spread through the low-lying streets of the Jewish ghetto, seeping under doorways into houses and shops, filling basements, pushing down doors and walls. Mail from the north was suspended as the train lines were covered. Gasworks flooded, and the city, only recently lighted, went dark the night of the twenty-eighth.[7] Candles appeared in windows above streets that had become canals, navigation points for national guardsmen, only recently established as a government service, who themselves carried red lanterns. In the ghetto, the water had reached the height of a man.[8]

On December 28 the rain stopped. National guardsmen, prowling the streets by boat, delivered bread to people trapped in upper stories, "drawing attention on themselves by their practical services."[9] The pope claimed the flood was a judgment from heaven, but left things at that. His failure to make any material contribution to the well-being of his flock earned him no credit.

Victor Emmanuel, who had planned to enter his new capital after the New Year with a suitable display of pomp and circumstance, now wondered if he should push up his schedule and tone down the pageantry.[10] His advisers urged him on, pointing out that coming to the city in its time of crisis would suit the image of a benevolent monarch and demonstrate his concern for the people of Italy. Anything less would seem callous.

Accordingly, he and his small entourage entered Rome from the north at 3 AM on December 31. The sights and smells unnerved the king. The water had receded but left behind a slimy coating of yellow mud, ankle deep in some places, on everything it had touched. The populace, recovering from shock, had begun to fill the streets with household goods beyond salvaging—rugs, clothing, and furniture, for the most part. There was little the king could do other than wander the city, survey the damage, express sympathy, and distribute alms. He left before nightfall. Ceremonies and spectacles were canceled, the official inauguration of Rome as capital over for now.

Death figures were low, perhaps seventeen souls, though rumors of floating corpses were making the rounds, an indictment against whichever party, clerical or secular, one found more negligent in responding to the flood.

If the tally of dead was low, the number of displaced would eventually reach an estimated total of twenty thousand.[11] Forty-seven flood markers commemorate the event: 17.22 meters above sea level at the Ripetta station hydrometer. Red lines marked the level on buildings, for engineers to get data to consider the next steps.

The king would eventually settle on the left bank in the Quirinal Palace, while the pope remained on the right in the Vatican, the two staring metaphorically across the waters at each other as the king set about administering the city for the new age. The river was, no surprise, a high priority.

A commission was appointed to find a solution, and hopes ran high. Science and engineering had achieved marvels of hydrology in recent decades. Just a year earlier, the French had opened the Suez Canal. Creditable men were discussing the possibility of connecting the Atlantic and Pacific Oceans across the isthmus of Colombia. Paris had lined the Seine with stone embankments in 1827, London the Thames in 1864. Rome had considered its own projects along these lines for two millennia. Now it was in a position and had the impetus to do something about it.

Garibaldi, hero of the unification, stepped forward as a leading figure in the debates. For the general, it was personal. His wife had died of malaria. As a military man, he took a direct view of things; he wanted nothing less than total surrender. Expel the river from Rome. Shunt it aside to another area, possibly the Anio, fill in the ditch, and reclaim the area for the people. Let it be paved over and become Rome's own Champs-Élysées, its Fifth Avenue, without the rigid insistence of straight lines.

"The winds of change in Rome now include the world of science. Thousands of Italians deny the charge [*reputazione*] that they are holding back the country."[12]

Nor was it just Italians who took a direct interest. No less a figure than Sir Richard Burton noted that Mr. Thomas Page, the acting engineer for the Thames Tunnel and in 1842 the winning designer of the Thames Embankment from Westminster to Blackfriars, "purposes gigantic measures, but measures of no difficulty, and the sooner they are begun and the more promptly they are erected, the more satisfactory will be their results and the more economical their execution."[13] His plan was an elaboration on the Marquis Raffaelle Pareto's, which would redirect the course of the river and "give the opportunity and the means of training the Campagna into one of the most productive and salubrious districts in Italy. With an extent of 311,550 hectares of valuable land, with a new channel for drainage, and with improved means of irrigation, the suburban district of Rome will soon become worthy of her greatness, past and present."[14]

Nothing came of it, of course, and the scarcity of records suggests that without any Italian interest, Page shifted his attentions to more promising enterprises, bridges primarily. The holdups, at least according to Burton, were national pride, both Italian and English, hindrances that Burton thought could be overcome: "There should be no difficulty in raising a 'City of Rome Improvements Company,' directed by a board which would combine southern thrift with northern energy and capital, a combination hitherto found wanting."[15] Then, too, Page himself died in 1877.

In the end, the plan to redirect the Tiber was scrapped in favor of building embankments.

Not that the path for these was by any means smooth. A flood in November 1878 was a bit of a setback, though some took it in stride:

> The recent flood of the Tiber, which gave us the unexpected pleasure of a sailing match in the Corso, has shaken the works of embankment on each side of the river which were executed during the summer. These works have been compared by Pasquino to the web of Penelope, not without reason when we consider that four months were scarcely sufficient to cement together a few hundred bricks in a wall, which, they say, will be in the course of centuries, nine miles long. A good round sum of money was washed away on Saturday the 16th of November, by the overflowing stream, and the loss would be complete had not the headless statue of Valentinian the elder been left in our hands.[16]

The area around Tiber Island presented an unforeseen problem of hydraulic engineering: uneven water flow around Tiber Island. What to do? One idea was to fill in the space between the island and Trastevere and avoid having the water flow split. The plan failed. The alternative plan, which involved making the branch between Tiber Island and the right bank wider than the corresponding side, failed as well, at least at first. The engineers had not considered how the embankments would alter the river flow around the island. Ideally, the two branches should have been equal. In fact, the right branch was ten meters wider than the left. More and swifter water ran through the right branch, with the result that the left branch's current was too weak to flush out the silt from upstream.[17] By 1900, the left branch was blocked completely. A rising river that year destabilized the bank on the Trastevere side, resulting in the collapse of 150 meters of the new embankment.

The solution was severalfold. The silted bed was dredged, returning the river to the prior state, which meant that the problem, if not addressed, would eventually recur. Engineers installed sills under the arches of the

Ponte Cestio, retarding water flow through the arches and forcing more to the Ponte Fabricius. Further tweaking farther upstream and downstream had also been done to limit erosion as much as possible. The results precluded the kind of river traffic familiar to earlier centuries, but the Tiber hadn't seen that sort of thing in years.

The plan failed. In 1902, high water washed out the newly build Lungotevere degli Anguillara embankment, sending the engineers back to the drawing board. Luigi Cozza determined that the bend in the river would see a repetition of this problem—best to maintain the island as it was and build embankments around it.

There are some pieces of clever engineering, as one would expect from the Italians. A small waterfall was arranged to put the brakes on the floodwater. Force is proportional to velocity squared; slow down the river's velocity—which a waterfall will do—and the force behind the water is proportionally lessened.

"As regards inundations, the Tiber ranks among the proudest rivers in the world. That of December, 1870, will never fade from the memory of the living generation; and I fear that this impressive and picturesque spectacle will never be seen again, since civilization has taken up the matter, and by means of lofty embankments, of locks and gates, will succeed, I am sure, in keeping the river confined hereafter within its two parallel walls."[18]

So said Lanciani in 1888. He was being optimistic.

Item 1900: "London, Dec. 5. A serious catastrophe is reported from Rome. Owing to the floods about 1000 ft of the great Tiber embankment collapsed, and the waters now cover a large area of country."[19]

Item 1915: "Rome, Feb. 14. The river Tiber is over fifty feet out of its normal banks and has flooded the lower parts of the town, especially the quarters around the Vatican. . . . Soldiers in boats are going about taking food to marooned persons, ladders, ropes and other paraphernalia to be used in rescue work and timbers for shoring up the walls of houses. The Sublicius bridge is entirely under water."[20]

Item 1937: "The River Tiber is still rising and has caused floods which are the worst experienced for a century. Several people have been drowned and it is estimated that in Rome alone 7,000 people have been rendered homeless. . . . Firemen and Black Shirts are carrying out salvage work."[21]

High water struck again in 2005, 2008, 2009, and 2010 and caused concern and at least one highway closure on the Via Tiburtina. The river rose enough in 2012 to pass through the eyelets on the 1850 Milvian bridge, forcing authorities to close the bridge to traffic. The city avoided serious harm; the countryside did not. Upward of 100 million euros in damage was estimated.

The price tag was doubtless less than if the water had inundated the city, but even so, the modern bulwarks against the Tiber have had other, less tangible costs. Rome now has the river level, as measured by the opening of the Cloaca Maxima, a height of some ten meters to the streets above.

Lanciani revisited the matter of the Tiber embankment in 1900 when he and Rome had had time to get used to it. "The huge walls between which we have imprisoned the stream have transformed it into a deep and unsightly channel, with nothing to relieve the monotony of its banks."[22] It's hard to disagree.

They have also held back much in the way of human imagination. The river, once vital to the people of Rome, is now cut off from easy access, and largely from view. The mills are gone, barges largely gone, fishermen fish at their peril, and members of the Tiber swim club confine themselves to playing cards on a riverboat all but permanently anchored at its spot.

The embankments took thirty-five years to build and have largely succeeded, but at a cost in river traffic and melancholy beauty. The stonework is imitative of Paris, but smaller in scale and less charming, less inviting. Views of Roman river life, a staple of Romantic painters, are gone. The riverside patches where people could lounge on a sweltering July afternoon are gone. The ships have stopped calling. The tourists find little of interest there, never mind something to write home about. The walkways are left to the down-and-outers who traditionally reside under bridges. The river, securely locked between two walls, is generally unthreatening but not inviting. Fishermen drop their lines into the river from time to time, and they can land sizable fish (though how good the fish are to eat is open to question). The waterfront has been ceded to the city's marginal residents, mostly to poor immigrants. City planners, whose unenviable task it is to put some kind of order to this space, have imagined a stretch of river transformed into a piazza along the lines of the Piazza Navona—the water acting as a picturesque divide.

The American artist Kristin Jones has done interesting work in this area, creating outlines of Roman themes by cleaning away grime from the walls, contrasting the clean and the filthy to quite good effect. Light shows have been occasioned, and there are further projects in mind.

As to the river's utility, it appears to have none now, beyond a bit of fishing and sculling and, lately, tourist boats and the odd water bus. Ostia is now a bedroom community to the city, and a beach. Trains traverse the distance in about an hour, faster and safer than the trip Stendhal describes: "We took a large boat because the course of the Tiber at Rome passes through some dangerous waters."

The Romans seem to have been happy enough to give it up. The relationship had always been problematic, the benefits balancing out the downsides, but the benefits began decreasing as the modern age made the river both less useful and, in the twentieth century, less obviously imposing. Its bounty is of a previous time, its entertainment value minimal, its beauty in the eyes of few beholders. Leave it to the no-hopers and oddballs; it has nothing to do with the modern Roman. The bridges are secure.

It has not, however, given up its claim as portal to the greater world. The Claudian harbor is now covered over by the tarmac and concrete and steel that make up Leonardo da Vinci airport, more familiarly referred to by its geographical setting at the mouth of the river as Fiumicino.

Tevere incatenato, locked away more or less safely at the bottom of a long narrow pit, out of sight, out of mind, its ancient spirits, once feared, honored, sometimes loved, always respected, are seemingly gone.

Or perhaps simply biding their time.

ACKNOWLEDGMENTS

Capturing the life of an entity that measures its age in millennia, whose pulse runs from diastolic to systolic in the course of a twelve-month cycle, is necessarily a challenge. The river has touched the lives of more rich and famous and poor and obscure than could fill a library, much less a book the size of the present one.

To shift metaphors, the writer is an attentive idler leaning over a bridge, gazing across the flowing water and grabbing at half-submerged curiosities and oddities, some explicable, some not, some tangible, some illusory, some easily snagged, some just a hairsbreadth out of reach. The longer you wait and the harder you look, the more goods make themselves apparent, but eventually there comes a point where even previous objects have to be allowed to drift away, or tossed back into the stream.

In the gazing and grabbing and making sense of it all, I have had much welcome help from others who have pointed out bits of flotsam and jetsam I would otherwise have missed, facilitated the snaffling of obscure bits of information, explained the significance of some curiosities, helped clarify clotted phrasings in old-source sources, and generally encouraged the enterprise. Without their help, the book would never have made it to completion.

Among these people are, in alphabetic order:

Susan Abel (University Press of New England)

Gregory Aldrete (University of Wisconsin)

Marie-Jose Bodoy

Giovanni Bonello (Fondazzjoni Patrimonju Malti)

Gilbert Borrego (University of Texas)

James Cheney (Getty Museum)

William Connell (Seton Hall)

Lorenzo Fabbri (University of Minnesota)

Clara Flath (Madison, Connecticut, library)

Maria-Antonia Garces (Cornell University)

Denise Gavio (American Academy in Rome)

Valérie Guillot (Archives, Order of Malta)

Eleanor Herman

Stephen Hull (University Press of New England)

Anne-Marie Laidlaw

Marilyn Miguiel (Cornell University)

Charlotte Miller (Sotheby's)

Glenn Novak

Rose Oliveira (Linda Lear Special Collections, Connecticut College)

Katherine Rinne (California College of the Arts)

John Rudolph (Dystel, Goderich & Bourret)

Valerie Scott (British School at Rome)

Phillip Tanswell (Cornish Sea Salt)

Maria Vella (University of Malta)

Many thanks to the various academic and university libraries in America that have granted me access or shared their works by mail. They bear no responsibility for any errors of fact or translation that may have seeped into the text (any and all of which errors I would be grateful to hear about from attentive readers).

Finally, thanks to Mrs. Allen, aka Blacknall Allen, who has lived with this project longer and more intimately than anyone ought, who read the rough manuscript and made countless improvements.

NOTES

INTRODUCTION

1. Henry James, *Selected Letters*, ed. Leon Edel (Cambridge, MA: Harvard University Press, 1974), 55.

2. Pliny, *Natural History* 3.9, trans. H. Rackham (Cambridge, MA: Harvard University Press, 1938).

3. Richard Lassels, *The Voyage Of Italy, Or A Compleat Journey Through Italy: The Second Part* (Paris: Vincent du Moutier, 1670), 318.

4. David Garrick, *The Letters of David Garrick*, vol. 1 (Cambridge, MA: Harvard University Press, 1963), 396.

5. Tobias Smollett, *Travels in France and Italy*, in *The Works of Tobias Smollett*, vol. 8 (London: Bickers, 1872), 284.

6. Theodore Edward Hook, *The Ramsbottom Letters* (London: Richard Bentley & Son, 1872), 47.

7. Henry Hazlitt, *Notes of a Journey through France and Italy* (London: Hunt and Clar, 1826), 280. (Hazlitt went on to say that "St. Peter's is not equal to St. Paul's" in London, for what it's worth.)

8. Nathaniel Hawthorne, *Notes of Travel by Nathaniel Hawthorne in Four Volumes*, vol. 3 (Boston: Houghton Mifflin, 1900), 197.

9. Robert Burn, *Rome and the Campagna* (Cambridge: Deighton Bell, 1871), 8.

10. M. Andrea Bacci, *Del Tevere* (Venice, 1576). 4, "il Tevere a Roma, fiume grande, navigabile, & utilissimo, cognominato però meritamente Padre, & almo Tevere, coronato d'imperio, di religione, & di mille vittorie."

11. Tacitus, *Annales* 14.22. See also Statius (40–96) *Silvae* i. 5, 26, "Marsas nives et frigora ducens" ("Marcia carrying cold and snow").

12. Virgil, *Aeneid* 8.31, "Huic deus ipse loci fluvio Tiberinus amoeno" ("The very god of the place Tiberinus of the pleasant stream").

13. Mussolini was perhaps overstepping his bounds. The epithet "Tuscus" was the most widely used among the Roman poets in describing the river.

1 | GODS, KINGS, AND MEN

1. Virgil, *Aeneid* 8, 330–333, trans. H. Rushton Fairclough (London: Heineman, 1926), 83.

2. Livy, *Ab urbe condita* i.3.8.

3. Varro, *De lingua latina* 5.30.

4. Virgil, *Aeneid* 8.62–65, trans. Stanley Lombardo, *Virgil: The Essential Aeneid* (Indianapolis: Hackett, 2006), 119.

5. Ovid, *Fasti* 5.646.

6. Sophocles, *Trachiniae* 9–18, trans. Francis Storr (London: Heineman, 1913), 258. (The after story of Deianira was predictably tragic. She married Hercules, but as she aged and doubted her hold on the hero, she was tricked by the centaur Nessus into providing Hercules a jacket treated with a caustic material so painful that he was forced to suicide.)

7. Ovid, *Metamorphoses* 9.1, trans. Brooks More (Boston: Cornhill, 1922), 397.

8. *The Aeneid of Virgil*, trans. Rolfe Humphries (New York: Scribners, 1951), 178.

9. Otto Rank, *The Myth of the Birth of the Hero* (New York: Journal of Nervous and Mental Disease Publishing Co., 1914), trans. Gregory C. Richter (Baltimore: Johns Hopkins University Press, 2004) deals with a number of these stories.

10. For the various takes on this myth see Timothy Peter Wiseman, *Remus: A Roman Myth* (Cambridge: Cambridge University Press, 1995).

11. This observation is noted in passing in the anonymous historiographical tract *Origo gentis Romanae* 23.6, the dating of which (fourth century AD?) is as uncertain as the dates of Egnatius himself.

12. Livy, *Ab urbe condita* 1.45, trans. Aubrey de Sélincourt, *Early History of Rome* (London: Penguin Classics, 1960), 84.

13. Valerius Maximus, *Facta et dicta memorabilia* 3.1.

14. Livy, *Ab urbe condita* 1.45.

15. Hesiod, *Works and Days* 737.

16. Livy, *Ab urbe condita* 1.32, trans. Aubrey de Sélincourt, *Early History of Rome* (London: Penguin Classics, 1960), 69.

17. Dionysius of Halicarnassus, *Roman Antiquities* 3.45.2, 9.68.2; Pliny, *Natural History* 36.100; Servius, *Commentary on Aeneid* 8.646. Julius Caesar left a detailed description of building his Rhine bridge in his *Gallic Wars* 4.17. The basics are likely the same as those for the Sublicius.

18. A long disquisition on the subject can be found in Fritz Graf, "The Rite of the Argei—Once Again," *Museum Helveticum* 57, no. 2 (2000): 94–103.

19. Plutarch, *Moralia, Roman Questions* 32; Dionysius of Halicarnassus, *Roman Antiquities* 1.38.2; Ovid, *Fasti* 5, 621; Varro, *De lingua latina* 7.44; Macrobius, *Saturnalia* 1.11.46; Festus, *De significatione verborum* 1.15.

20. Dionysius of Halicarnassus, *Roman Antiquities* 4.44.1, cf. Livy, *Ab urbe condita* 1.56.3.

21. Livy, *Ab urbe condita* 1.37.

22. A. J. Ammerman, "On the Origins of the Forum Romanum," *American Journal of Archaeology* 94 (1990): 636.

23. Ibid., 634–635.

24. Ibid., 634–638; A. J. Ammerman and D. Filippi, "Dal Tevere al Argelito," *Bullettino della Commissione Archeologica Communale di Roma* 105 (2005): 7–28.

25. Ammerman, "On the Origins," 641–645.

26. Gregory Aldrete, *Floods of the Tiber in Ancient Rome* (Baltimore: Johns Hopkins University Press, 2007), 219.

27. H. Bauer, "Die Cloaca Maxima in Rom," *Mitteilungen des Leichtweiss-Institutes für Wasserbau der Technischen Universität Braunschweig* 103 (1989): 49.

28. Pliny, *Natural History* 36.24.106 records this as a *memorabile exemplum*. On suicides see Pliny, *Natural History* 36.107; Cassius Hemina, *Historicorum Romanorum fragmenta* fr. 15P.

29. Pliny, *Natural History* 36.24.105.

30. Livy, *Ab urbe condita* 5.55, trans. Rev. Canon Roberts (London: J. M. Dent & Sons, 1905).

31. Dionysius of Halicarnassus, *Roman Antiquities* 3.67.5.

32. Strabo, *Geography* 5.3.8 A.

33. Cassiodorus, *Variae* III.30.1–2, S. J. B. Barnish, *The Variae of Magnus Aurelius Cassiodorus Senator* (Liverpool: Liverpool University Press, 1992), 61.

34. Johannes Goethe, Rome, August 1, 1787, in Johann Wolfgang von Goethe, *Italian Journey, 1786–1788*, trans. W. H. Auden (London: Penguin, 1962), 492.

35. Henry James, *Letters*, ed. Leon Edel, vol. 1, *1843–1875* (Cambridge, MA: Belknap Press of Harvard University Press, 1974), 175.

36. Rodolfo Lanciani, *Ancient Rome in the Light of Recent Discoveries* (New York: Harcourt Brace, 1888), 54–56.

37. A. Scobie, "Slums, Sanitation, and Mortality in the Roman World," *Klio* 68 (1986): 413.

38. "Nec pudeat pabula praebere novali / immundis quaecumque vomit latrina cloacis," Columella, *De re rustica* 10.85.

39. Agrippa's voyage is described in Cassius Dio 49.31; Pliny, *Natural History* 36.28.104.

40. R. Reynolds, *Cleanliness and Godliness* (New York: Doubleday, 1946), 305. The Byron attribution crops up repeatedly, but never with citations.

41. John Gay, "Trivia: Or, the Art of Walking the Streets of London," in *Poetical Works of John Gay with a Memoir* (Cambridge: Houghton, Osgood, 1879), 220.

42. Ibid., 223.

43. Fabio Barry, "The Mouth of Truth and the Forum Boarium: Oceanus, Hercules, and Hadrian," *Art Bulletin* 93, no. 1 (March 2011): 7.

44. Edward Wright, *Some Observations Made in Travelling Through France, Italy, Etc. in the years 1720, 1721, and 1722* (London: Tho. Ward and E. Wicksteed, 1730), 253.

45. Francesco de Ficoroni, *Le vestigia e rarità di Roma antica* (Rome: Girolamo Mainardi, 1744), 1.74.

46. Samuel Platner, *A Topographical Dictionary of Ancient Rome* (London: Oxford University Press, 1929), 127.

47. Livy, *Ab urbe condita* 2.10, trans. Sélincourt, 116.

48. Livy, *Ab urbe condita* 2.10, trans. Roberts.

49. Ibid. 2.12, trans. Sélincourt, 118.

50. Valerius Maximus, *Factorum ac dictorum memorabilium* 3.2.2.

51. Ibid. 4.5. More on the story can be found in C. Bennett Pascal, "Fire on the Tarentum," *American Journal of Philology* 100, no. 4 (Winter 1979): 532–537.

52. Livy, *Ab urbe condita* 10.47.1.

53. Ibid., 10.32.

54. Virgil, *Aeneid* 7.123ff; Horace, *Carmina* 1.4.

55. Cicero, *De deorum natura* 3.37.

56. "Mater delira necabit in gelida fixum ripa, febrimque reducet," Horace, *Sermones* 2, 3, 293–294.

57. Livy, *Ab urbe condita* 1.33.

58. Ibid., 2:11.

59. Rutilis Namatianus, *De reditu suo* 476–482, trans. J. Wright Duff and Arnold M. Duff (Cambridge, MA: Harvard University Press, 1934), 148.

60. The process is described nicely in Georgius Agricola, *De re metallica, Translated from the First Latin Edition of 1556* (New York: Dover, 1950), 546.

61. Biondo Flavio, *Roma instaurata* (Turin, 1527), 40r-v, "Salinas in locum quo sal populo vendendum conservaretur fuisse ei in Tyberis ripa / quae a Ponte nunc Sanctae Mariae in Aventinum pertinet."

62. Pliny, *Natural History* 31.7.41.

63. Ovid, *Fasti* 4, 337, *The Fasti, Tristia, Ponti Epistles, Ibis and Halieuticon of Ovid*, trans. Henry T. Riley (London: H. G. Bohn, 1851), 148.

64. Ibid., 255ff. A more sober version in which the stone is simply taken off the boat and transported by land is in Livy, *Ab urbe condita* 29.14.10–14.

65. Herodian, *Roman History* 1.11; Ovid, *Fasti* 4.291–344; Suetonius, *Tiberius* 2; Augustine, *City of God* 10.16. For a modern discussion of this incident see Sarolta Takacs, *Vestal Virgins, Sibyls, and Matrons: Women in Roman Religion* (Austin: University of Texas Press, 2008).

66. Ovid, *Fasti* 4, 337–340, *The Fasti, Tristia, Pontic Epistles, Ibis and Halieuticon of Ovid*, trans. Henry Riley (London: Bohns, 1851).

There is a place where swift Almo flows into the sea
And the secondary river loses its name primary
There with the aged priest in purple robes
Washes the goddess and her sacred tools in its waters

Est locus in Tiberim qua lubricus influit Almo
Et nomen mango perdit ab amne minor
Illic purpurea canus cum veste sacerdos
Almonis dominam sacraque lavit aquis
—Lucan, *Pharsalia* 1.600

And they carry Cybele back, cleansed in the small Almo
Where the Almo bathes the iron of the Phrygian mother

Et parvo lotam revocant Almone Cybelem
Phrygiumque Matris Almo qua lavat ferrum
—Martial, *Epigrams* 2,47, 2

See also Cicero, *De natura deorum* 3.20, and Varro, *De lingua latina*, vol. 71. As late as the 1830s, Richard Burgess writes that the water there is good for unspecified "maladies." Richard Burgess, *The Topography and Antiquities of Rome*, vol. 1 (London: Longman, 1831), 106.

67. Quoted in Rodolfo Lanciani, *The Ruins and Excavations of Ancient Rome* (New York: Harcourt Brace, 1897), 134.

68. Livy, *Ab urbe condita* 39.14, *The History of Rome*, vol. 3, trans. William A. M'Devitte (London: Bell & Daldy, 1873), 1804.

69. Josephus, *Jewish Antiquities* 18.3.4.65–80.

70. For Nero as persecutor of Isis see Stephen Dando-Collins, *The Great Fire of Rome* (New York: Da Capo, 2010), 107.

71. Juvenal, *Satires* 6.521–526, *Juvenal & Persius*, trans. G. G. Ramsey, Loeb ed. (Cambridge, MA: Harvard University Press, 1918), 125, 127. By the time Juvenal was writing, Isis was well established in Rome. He nevertheless gives a good notion of how a stodgier sort of Roman might have viewed the whole thing.

72. Livy, *Periochae* 67. Publicius Malleolus, a matricide, was first sewn into a sack and then thrown into the sea.

73. Cicero, *Pro Roscio Amerino: Defense Speeches by Cicero*, trans. D. H. Berry (Oxford: Oxford University Press, 2000), 71.

74. Seneca, *Controversiae* 5.4.

75. Juvenal, *Satires* 1.214.

76. Dositheus the Grammarian, fourth century, *Corpus glossariorum Latinorum*, Gustaff Loew (Leipzig: Teubner, 1887), 38, "In culleum missus conscriberetur cum vipera et simiam et gallu et cane impiis animalibus impius homo." Cf. also Herennius Modestinus in Justinian's *Digest of Roman Law* 48.9.9. A German scholar, Gustav Landgraf (*Ciceros Rede für Sex Roscius* [Erlangen, Germany: A. Deichert, 1906], 268–269), explains the animals as being despised (dog), lacking in familial affection (rooster), responsible for their mothers' deaths (snake; the snake legend comes from Aristotle, *History of Animals* 2.8), and being an alarming imitation of a human being (ape). Landgraf is silent on the matter of the scorpion.

77. Suetonius, *Life of Augustus* 33.1.

78. Seneca, *On Clemency* 1.23.

79. Cassius Dio, *Epitome* of bk. 62, 15, trans. Earnest Cary (Cambridge, MA: Harvard University Press, 1925), 69.

80. Cassius Dio, *Roman History* 62.15.

81. Cicero, *Pro Caelio* 15(36).

82. Cicero, *Letters to Atticus* 12.38a. See also D. R. Shackleton-Bailey, *Cicero Letters to Atticus*, vol. 5 (Cambridge: Cambridge University Press, 1966), appendix 3, 410–413.

83. See, e.g., Marilyn B. Skinner, *Clodia Metelli: The Tribune's Sister* (Oxford: Oxford University Press, 2011).

84. Appian, *Civil Wars* 2.102.424; Cassius Dio, *Roman History* 51.22.3.

85. Cicero, *Letters to Atticus* 15.15.

86. Cassius Dio, *Roman History* 43.27.3.

1. Biondo Flavio, *Italy Illuminated*, vol. 1, trans. Jeffrey A. White (Cambridge, MA: Harvard University Press, 2005), 115.

2. Dionysius of Halicarnassus, *Roman Antiquities* 12.frag 21, in William Gell, *The Topography of Rome and Its Vicinities* (London: Henry G. Bohn, 1846), 456.

2 | RIVER OF EMPIRE

1. Suetonius, *Life of Julius Caesar* 39.4; Cassius Dio, *Roman History* 43.23.4; Appian, *Civil Wars* 2.102; Plutarch, *Life of Julius Caesar* 55.4.

2. Cassius Dio, *Roman History* 45.17 (cf. Joël Le Gall, *Le Tibre, fleuve de Rome, dans l'antiquité*, 116).

3. Augustus, *Res gestae* 23.

4. Pliny, *Natural History* 16, 200.

5. Tacitus, *Annals* 14.15.

6. Ovid, *Ars amatoria* 1.171.

7. Cassius Dio, *Roman History* 61.33.3; Suetonius, *Life of Claudius* 21.6. Dio says fifty ships on each side, Suetonius, twelve triremes each.

8. Tacitus, *Annals* 12.56.1.

9. Cassius Dio, *Roman History* 61.33.4; Suetonius, *Life of Claudius* 21.6 has it as "they who are about to die," for what it's worth.

10. Suetonius, *Life of Claudius* 21.6.

11. Ibid., trans. J. C. Rolfe (Cambridge, MA: Harvard University Press, 1919), 45.

12. Tacitus, *Annals* 12.56, trans. John Jackson, *Tacitus: Annals, Books IV–VI, XI–XII* (Cambridge, MA: Harvard University Press, 1937), 399.

13. Pliny, *Natural History* 36.124.

14. Tacitus, *Annals* 12.31.

15. Pliny, *Natural History* 19.24.

16. Suetonius, *Life of Claudius* 12.1.

17. Ibid.

18. Seneca, *Epistle* 70.26.

19. Cassius Dio, *Roman History* 62.15.1.

20. Martial, *On the Spectacles* 28, 11–12, trans. Walter C. A. Kerr (Cambridge, MA: Harvard University Press, 1929), 43.

21. Suetonius, *Life of Domitian* 4.1–2, trans. J. C. Rolfe (Cambridge, MA: Harvard University Press, 1919), 347.

22. Ibid., 4.

23. Sidonius Apollinaris, *Letters* 1.5.6–9, trans. O. M. Dalton (Oxford: Clarendon, 1915), 11.

24. Pliny, *Letters*, vol. 1, trans. William Melmoth (Cambridge, MA: Harvard University Press, 1915), Letter 4.2 to Attius Clemens, 277.

25. Ibid., 379, 381.

26. Suetonius, *Life of Galba*, 1.

27. Cassius Dio, *Roman History* 48.53.

28. *Corpus inscriptionum Latinarum* 6.17985a, trans. Mary Beard et al., *Religions of Rome*, vol. 2, *A Sourcebook* (Cambridge: Cambridge University Press, 1998), 236.

29. Strabo, *Geography* 5.3.8, *Geography of Strabo*, vol. 2, trans. Horace Leonard Jones (Cambridge, MA: Harvard University Press, 1923), 409.

30. Elizabeth S. Cohen, "Seen and Known: Prostitutes in the Cityscape of Late-Sixteenth-Century Rome," *Renaissance Studies* 12, no. 3 (1998): 392–409.

31. Martial, *Epigrams* 5.64, trans. A. S. Kline (online).

32. Aulus Gellius, *Attic Nights* 15, 1, 2–3.

33. Livy, *Ab urbe condita* 21.63.

34. Plutarch, *Life of Cato* 21.5, trans. Bernadotte Perrin (Cambridge, MA: Harvard University Press, 1914), 367.

35. Ibid.

36. Peter Temin, *The Roman Market Economy* (Princeton, NJ: Princeton University Press, 2013), 170.

37. John Anthony Crook, *Law and Life of Rome, 90 BC to AD 212* (Ithaca, NY: Cornell University Press, 1976), 223.

38. Petronius, *Satyricon of Petronius* (Paris: Charles Carrington, 1902), 208–209, 211. (The translation was reprinted in 1930 by New York's Panurge Press, in which the translator Alfred R. Allinson was given credit).

39. *Corpus inscriptionum Graecarum*, 3920.

40. D. J. Mattingly and G. Aldrete, "The Feeding of Imperial Rome: The Mechanics of the Food Supply System," in *Ancient Rome: The Archaeology of the Eternal City*, ed. Jon Coulston and Hazel Dodge (Oxford University School of Archaeology, Monograph 54, 2000), 142–165.

41. Geoffrey Rickman, *The Corn Supply of Ancient Rome* (Oxford: Clarendon, 1980), 121.

42. *Codex Theodosi* 14.4.9 (AD 417).

43. O. Guéraud, "Un vase ayant contenu un échantillon de blé," *Journal of Juristic Papyrology* 4 (1950): 107–115.

44. Acts of the Apostles 27.36.

45. Lucian, *Navigium*, trans. H. W. Fowler, *The Works of Lucian of Samosata* (Oxford: Clarendon, 1905), 5.45.

46. Lionel Casson, "The Isis and Her Voyage," *Transactions and Proceedings of the American Philological Association* 81 (1950): 43–56.

47. Seneca, *On Taking One's Own Life—Moral Letter to Lucilius*, trans. Richard Mott Gummere (London: Heinemann, 1961), 169.

48. Juvenal, *Satire* 14, 275–274, trans. G. G. Ramsey (Cambridge, MA: Harvard University Press, 1914), 185.

49. Procopius, *De bello Gothico* 5.26.9.

50. *Select Papyri (Non-literary Papyri)*, ed. A. S. Hunt and C. C. Edgar (Berlin Papyrus no. 27 [=Select Papyri no 113]).

51. Tacitus, *Annals* 15.18.

52. Procopius, *De bello Gothico* 5.26.

53. Gregory Aldrete, *Floods of the Tiber in Ancient Rome* (Baltimore: Johns Hopkins University Press, 2007), 235–236.

54. Seneca, *De brevitate vitae* 19.1, trans. John W. Basore, *Seneca Moral Essays*, vol. 2 (Cambridge, MA: Harvard University Press, 1931), 349.

55. Juvenal, *Satire* 10.77–88, trans. A. S. Kline (online).

56. Livy, *Ab urbe condita* 4.10., trans. Sélincourt, 303.

57. Ibid. 4.13.

58. Cicero, *Tusculan Disputations* 3.48.

59. Sallust, *Catilinarian Conspiracy* 37.7.

60. Cicero, *Ad Atticus* 2.19.

61. Cicero, *Pro Sestio* 25.55.

62. Suetonius, *Life of Julius Caesar* 41.3.

63. Charles de Brosses, *Selections from the Letters of de Brosses*, trans. Lord Ronald Sutherland Gower (London: Kegan Paul, Trench, Trübner, 1897), 248.

64. *Chronicle of Adam of Usk*, trans. Edward Maunde Thompson (London: Henry Frowde, 1904), 98 (Latin), 270 (English).

65. Aelius Aristides, Oratio 26, *The Complete Works II: Orationes 17–53* (Leiden: Brill, 1981), 75.

66. Lionel Casson, "New Light on Maritime Loans: P Vindob G.40822," *Zeitschrift für Papyrologie und Epigraphik* 84 (1990): 195–206; Lionel Casson, "P Vindob G.40822 and the Shipping of Goods from India," *Bulletin of the American Society of Papyrologists* 23, nos. 3–4 (1986): 73–79.

67. Pliny, *Natural History* 36.8.

68. Catullus, *Carmina* 57 (but also 29, 114, 115).

69. Ibid. 105.

70. Pliny, *Natural History* 36.11, trans. D. E. Eichholz (vol. 10) (Cambridge, MA: Harvard University Press, 1954), 43.

71. Ibid. 36.16.

72. Ibid.

73. Ibid.

74. Ibid. 13.4.14.

75. Ibid. 17.4.12.

76. Ibid. 18.4.15. (It was replaced with a bronze also plated with gold—to look as if the torch were fully alight.)

77. "Navis, quom obeliscus maximus Romam esset advectus, quod audisset carinas Aeneae, ut primum solvissent a portu, deas maris fuisse effectas, ea spe in altum sese perditum excessit," Leon Battista Alberti, *Apologi centum* no. 65. See David Marsh, *Renaissance Fables: Aesopic Prose by Leon Battista Alberti, Bartolomeo Scala, Leonardo da Vinci, Bernardino Baldi* (Tempe: Arizona Center for Medieval and Renaissance Studies, 2004), 65. The ships that brought Aeneas to Rome morphed into sea goddesses. *Aeneid* 9.107–122.

78. Plutarch, *Life of Julius Caesar* 58.9–10, trans. Bernadotte Perrin (Cambridge, MA: Harvard University Press, 1919), 579.

79. Cicero, *Letters to Atticus* 13.33a, trans. E. O. Winsted (Cambridge, MA: Harvard University Press, 1921), 181.

80. "Fossis ductis a Tiberi operis portus caussa emissisque in mare urbem inundationis periculo liberavit," *Corpus inscriptionum Latinarum*, vol. 14, n85.

81. Tacitus, *Annals* 15.42, trans. Alfred John Church (London: Macmillan, 1895), 303.

82. Suetonius, *Life of Nero* 31.3.16.

83. Tacitus, *Annals* 15.42, trans. Church, 303.

84. "Canna Micipsarum prora subvexit acuta." Juvenal, *Satire* 5, 89.

85. Martial, *Epigrams* 4.64.23–24, trans. Bohn (London: George Bell & Sons, 1904), 208.

86. Propertius 1.14.3–4.

87. Seneca, *De beneficiis* 7.20.3, trans. Miriam Griffin, *On Benefits* (Chicago: University of Chicago Press, 2011), 183.

88. Giuseppe Marquis Melchiorri, *Guida metodica di Roma e suoi contorni* (Rome: Tipografia Tiberina, 1856), 99.

89. Livy, *Ab urbe condita* 45.35.3–4.

90. Plutarch, *Life of Cato the Younger* 39.1–3, trans. Bernadotte Perrin (Cambridge, MA: Harvard University Press, 1919), 329.

91. Tacitus, *Annals* 3.9.

92. Juvenal, *Satire* 6 (30–33), in *Juvenal and Persius*, trans. G. G. Ramsay (Cambridge, MA: Harvard University Press, 1940), 85, 87.

93. Suetonius, *Life of Nero* 47.3.

94. Suetonius, *Life of Vespasian* 19.2.

95. John Chetwode Eustace, *A Classical Tour through Italy in 1802*, 7th ed., vol. 3 (London: Thomas Tegg, 1841), 446.

96. *Die Kaiserchronik*, 4128–4164, 4108–13.

97. *Nero's Son, the Toad, Escaping in the Tiber*, J. Paul Getty Museum, http://www.getty.edu/art/collection/objects/2006/unknown-maker-nero's-son-the-toad-escaping-in-the-tiber-german-about-1400–1410.

98. Suetonius, *Life of Nero* 21; Cassius Dio, *Roman History* 63.10; R. M. Frazer, "Nero the Singing Animal," *Arethusa* 4, no. 2 (Fall 1971): 2.

99. Classicist Albin Lesky (1897–1981) notes that this belief was common in his Austrian childhood. Albin Lesky, *Neroniana Annuaire de l'Institut de Philologie et d'Histoire Orientale* 9 (1949): 385–407.

100. Pliny, *Natural History* 2.37; Aristotle, *History of Animals* 2.8.

101. Plutarch, *Moralia, De sera numinis vindicta* 22 Moralis 567e.

102. Tacitus, *Annals* 15.36.

103. Cassius Dio, *Roman History* 62.15.6.

104. Simon Keay, Martin Millett, and Kristian Strutt, "Recent Archaeological Survey at Portus," *Memoirs of the American Academy in Rome: Supplementary Volumes*, vol. 6, *The Maritime World of Ancient Rome* (2008), 102.

105. Jerome, *Epistles* 66, 77.

106. Edward Gibbon, *Decline and Fall of the Roman Empire*, ed. J. B. Bury, vol. 1 (London: Methuen, 1909), 85–86.

107. *The Complete Works of Liudprand of Cremona*, trans. Paolo Squatriti (Washington, DC: Catholic University of America Press, 2007), 134.

108. "Fecit et sui nominis pontem et sepulchrum iuxta Tiberim," *Historia Augusta*: Hadrianus 19, 11.

109. Cassius Dio, *Roman History* 69.23.1.

110. Cassius Dio, *Epitome of Book 69*, trans. Earnest Cary (Cambridge, MA: Harvard University Press, 1925), 469; cf. John of Antioch, *Fragmenta historicum Graecorum*, vol. 4 (Paris: Ambrosius Firmin Didot, 1851), frag. 114, 581.

111. Richardson does not. L. Richardson Jr., *A New Topographical Dictionary of Ancient Rome* (Baltimore: Johns Hopkins University Press, 1992), 296.

112. "Item penes veteres quisque se homicidio infecerat purgatrices aquas explorabat," Tertullian, *De baptismo* 5.1–2.

113. Cassius Dio, *Roman History* 79.21.3; *Historia Augusta* Elagabalus 17.5.

114. Henry A. Myers, *The Book of Emperors: A Translation of the Middle High German Kaiserchronik* (Morgantown: West Virginia University Press, 2013), 204.

INTERLUDE | TRIBUTARY—ANIO

1. Pliny, *Epistolae* 8.17, trans. William Melmoth (Cambridge, MA: Harvard University Press, 1922).

2. Ibid.

3. Livy, *Ab urbe condita* 5.46.

4. Frontinus, *De aquaeductu urbis Romae* 92.

5. Pliny, *Natural History* 21.24. The Aqua Marcia was named not for Martius but for the Marsi hills from where it is tapped.

6. Frontinus, *De aquaeductu urbis Romae* 91.5, *Frontinus: The Stratagems, and the Aqueducts of Rome*, trans. Charles E. Bennett (Cambridge, MA: Harvard University Press, 1925), 65.

3 | CHRISTIAN TIBER

1. *Historiae Augustae scriptores*, vol. 3, trans. David Magie (Cambridge, MA: Harvard University Press, 1932), 135.

2. Ibid.

3. Ibid., 141.

4. Ibid., 137.

5. Ibid., 141.

6. Zosimus, *Nova historia* 2, 16.

7. Eusebius, *Vita Constantini* 1.28.

8. C. E. V. Nixon and Barbara Saylor Rodgers, *In Praise of Later Roman Emperors: The Panegyrici Latin* (Berkeley: University of California Press, 1994), 321–322.

9. Ammianus Marcellinus, *Rerum gestarum* 19.10.1, trans. John C. Rolfe (Cambridge, MA: Harvard University Press, 1935), 521.

10. Ibid. 19.10.3.

11. Ibid. 19.10.2.

12. Ibid. 27.3.3–4.

13. Symmachus, *Relationes* 9.7, 18.3.

14. Ibid., trans. R. H. Barrow, *Prefect and Emperor: The Relationes of* Symmachus, *A.D. 384* (Oxford: Clarendon, 1973).

15. Pliny, *Natural History* 32.2–6.

16. Symmachus, *Relationes* 26.5, trans. Barrow.

17. *Kaiserchronik* 10688–10819.

18. Claudian, *De consulatu Stilichonis*, 30.24, trans. Maurice Platnauer, *Claudian*, vol. 2 (Cambridge, MA: Harvard University Press, 1922), 49.

19. Claudian, *De sexto consulatu Honorii Augusti*, 555–558, trans. Maurice Platnauer *Claudian*, vol. 2 (Cambridge, MA: Harvard University Press, 1922), 113.

20. Jordanes, *De origine actibusque Gotarum* 30.158.

21. Procopius, *De bello Vandalico* 1.2.

22. Alexander Donatus, *De urbe Roma* 4.7.

23. See Carlo Fea, *Dissertazione sulle rovine di Roma*, in G. G. Winckelmann, *Storia dell'arte di disegno*, vol. 3 (Rome: Pagliarini, 1783), 389.

24. He did not exercise Huneric's right to take the throne; it went to a senior senator, Avitus, who held on for two years.

25. Gregory Aldrete, *Floods of the Tiber in Ancient Rome* (Baltimore: Johns Hopkins University Press, 2009), 144.

26. Sidonius Apollinaris, *Letters* 1.5.6–9, trans. O. M. Dalton (Oxford: Clarendon, 1915), 11.

27. Procopius, *History of the Wars* 5.19. 20–22, trans. Henry Bronson Dewing, Loeb ed. (Cambridge, MA: Harvard University Press, 1919), 190–191.

28. J. von Pflugk-Harttung, *Acta pontificum Romanorum*, inedita 2 (Stuttgart: W. Kohlhammer, 1884), 57–58.

29. Oretta Zanini DeVita, *Popes, Peasants, and Shepherds: Recipes and Lore from Rome and Lazio*, trans. Maureen B. Fant (Berkeley: University of California Press, 2013), 20.

30. Paul Bairoch, Jean Batou, and Pierre Chèvre, *La population des villes européennes de 800 à 1850* (Geneva: Droz, 1988).

31. Crescenzo Del Monte, *Sonetti giudaico-romaneschi, sonetti romaneschi, prose e versioni* (Florence: Giuntina, 2007), 250.

32. Procopius, *De bello Gothico*, in *History of the Wars*, vol. 5, bks. 7.36 and 8, Loeb ed. (Cambridge, MA: Harvard University Press, 1928), 278.

33. Ibid.

34. Procopius, *De bello Gothico* (in 4.21.11–17), 217.

35. Ibid., 279.

36. Ibid., 281.

37. Norman Douglas, *Old Calabria* (London: Martin Secker, 1915), 99.

38. Gregory of Tours, *Historia Francorum*, bk. 10.1.

39. "Cum magno dracone in modo trabis," in Gregory of Tours, *Historia Francorum*, bk. 10.1.

40. Johannes Hymonides, *Vita S. Gregorii papae*, in Henricus Canisius, *Thesaurus monumentorum ecclesiasticorum et historicorum, sive Henrici Canisii lectiones antiquae 2* (Amsterdam: Apud Rudolphum & Gerhardum Wetstenios, 1725), 257.

41. Ibid.

42. Paulus Diaconus, *De gestis Langobardorum* 3.23.

43. Lorena Battistoni, *Il tempio di Santa Maria della Consolazione in Todi, 1508–1607* (Todi, Italy: Associazione pro Todi Editrice, 2007).

44. Anna Esposito, "Le inondazioni del Tevere tra tardo medioevo e prima età moderna: Leggende, racconti, testimonianze," *Mélanges de l'École Française de Rome* (Rome: École Française de Rome, 2006), 7–12. See also *Bollettino Storico della Svizzera Italiana Emilio Motta*, anno 10 (Bellinzona, Switzerland: Carlo Colombi, 1888), 147; see also *Memorie della Società medico-chirurgica di Bologna*, vol. 6, fasc. 9 (Bologna: Gamberini e Parmeggiani, 1892), 3699. The two differ on spelling, the former *ale*, the latter *alle*, or possibly *alie*.

45. See also David O. Patterson, "*Adversos paganos*: Disaster, Dragons, and Episcopal Authority in Gregory of Tours," *Comitatus: A Journal of Medieval and Renaissance Studies* 44 (2013): 1.28 (Center for Medieval and Renaissance Studies, UCLA).

46. Esposito, "Le inondazioni del Tevere," 8.

47. "So ein junger Drach, so gross als ein grosser Hund," " 'Disputatio V' De Dracone," in G. C. Kirchmaier, *Disputationum zoologicarum* (Wittenberg, Germany: Johannis Berger, 1661).

48. Cornelio Meyer, *Nuovi ritrovamenti divisi in due parti* (Rome: G. G. Komarek, 1696).

49. "Late-Surviving Pterosaur?," Palaeontologia Electronica, http://palaeo-electronica.org/content/2013/384-late-surviving-pterosaur.

50. Caesar Baronius, *Annales ecclesiastici*, Tomus Decimus 546–559 (Barri-Ducis, 1867), 463. There are various sources for the life of Gregory the Great.

51. *Liber pontificalis*, ed. L. Duchesne (Paris: Ernest Thorin, 1886), 72, Vita Honorii, c. 1.

52. Ibid., 86, Vita Sergii 1, c. 11.

53. Ibid., Vita Gregorii III.

54. Ibid., Vita Pauli.

55. Ibid., Vita Hadriani, 46, 45, 84, 87.

56. Ibid., 98, Vita Leonis III, 28, 53, 54, 64, 86, 87.

57. Rodolfo Lanciani, *The Destruction of Ancient Rome* (New York: Macmillan, 1899), 129.

58. *Liber pontificalis*, quoted in *Travelling through Time: Essays in Honour of Kaj Öhrnberg*, ed. Sylvia Akar, Jaakko Hämeen-Anttila, and Inka Nokso-Koivisto, vol. 114 in Studia Orientalia (Helsinki, 2013), 100. See also Barbara M. Kreutz, *Before the Normans: Southern Italy in the Ninth Century* (Philadelphia: University of Pennsylvania Press, 2011), 25–27.

59. For a full account of ancient sources see Tommi P. Lankila, "The Saracen Raid of Rome in 846—an Example of Maritime *ghazw*," in Akar, Hämeen-Anttila, and Nokso-Koivisto, *Travelling through Time*, 93–120.

60. Richard Krautheimer, *Rome: Profile of a City* (Princeton, NJ: Princeton University Press, 1980), 118–119.

61. His doubts might have arisen from the willingness of Naples to hire Saracen mercenaries in prior years.

62. Edward Gibbon, *Decline and Fall of the Roman Empire*, ed. J. B. Bury, vol. 6 (London: Methuen, 1909), 45.

63. "Deo odibilis Aggarenorum gens," *Liber pontificalis*, vol. 2, ed. Louis Duchesne (Paris: E. Thorin, 1892), 81.

64. G. A. Knott, "The Historical Sources of 'Fierabras,'" *Modern Language Review* 52, no. 4 (October 1957): 504–509.

65. *Fierabras and Floripas: A French Epic Allegory*, ed. and trans. Michael A. H. Newth (New York: Italica, 2010), 29.

66. Liutprand of Cremona, *Antapodosis, seu rerum per Europam gestarum, Libri VI*, bk. 1, 31.

67. "Johannes . . . ex patre Sergio papa." *Liber pontificalis*, ed. Louis Duchesne (Paris: E. Thorin, 1892), 2.243, though some modern scholars think the relationship unlikely. See Peter Llewellyn, *Rome in the Dark Ages* (New York: Praeger, 1970), 300.

68. "Non quasi uxor in consuetudinem malignam." *Il chronicon di Benedetto, monaco di S. Andrea del Soratte*, ed. Giuseppe Zucchetti, vol. 20, Fonti per la storia d'Italia pubblicate dall'Istituto storico (Rome: Tipografia del Senato, 1920), 158–159.

69. Liutprand of Cremona, *Antapodosis* bk. 2, 48.

70. "Johannes papa, dum a quadam potenti femina, cognomine Marocia, principatu privatus sub custodia detineretur, ut quidam vi, ut plures astruunt actus angore defungitur."

Les annales de Flodoard, ed. Ph. Lauer (Paris: Alphonse Picard et Fils, 1905), 44; see also *The "Annals" of Flodoard of Reims, 919–966*, ed. and trans. Bernard S. Bachrach and Steven Fanning (Peterborough, ON: Broadview, 2004).

71. *The Complete Works of Liudprand of Cremona* (Medieval Texts in Translation), trans. Paolo Squatriti (Washington, DC: Catholic University of America Press, 2007), 132.

72. Zucchetti, *Il chronicon di Benedetto*, 161.3–5, "Subiugatus est Romam potestative in manu femine, sicut in propheta legimus; Femini dominabunt Hierusalem."

73. *Complete Works of Liudprand of Cremona*, 134.

74. Zucchetti, *Il chronicon di Benedetto*, 165.10. Many historians do not consider Benedict to be a reliable source.

INTERLUDE | TRIBUTARY—NERA

1. "Sulfureas posuit spiramina Naris ad undas." Q. Ennius, *Annalium* 1.6; "Sulferea Nar albus aqua." Virgil, *Aeneid* 7.516.

2. Maurus Servius Honoratus, *Commentary on the Aeneid of Virgil* A.7.511.

3. Biondo Flavio, *Italy Illuminated*, vol. 1, trans. Jeffrey A. White (Cambridge, MA: Harvard University Press, 2005), 220.

4. G. Forni, "Manio Curio Dentato uomo democratico," *Athenaeum* 31 (1953): 170–240; C. Pietrangeli, "La Sabina nell'antichità," in *Rieti e il suo territorio* (Milan, 1976), 9–164; M. R. Torelli, "La conquista romana della Sabina," *Dialoghi di Archeologia* 5, no 1 (1987): 43–51.

5. Maurus Servius Honoratus, *Commentary on the Aeneid of Virgil* 7.712.

6. Virgil, *Aeneid* 7.712.

7. Varro, *Saturae Menippeae* 2.1.17 ("Muli e Rose campestri aestate exiguntur in burbures altos montes"); 3.2.10.

8. Pliny, *Natural History* 17.32.

9. Cicero, *Ad Atticum* 6.15, trans. E. O. Winstedt (Cambridge, MA: Harvard University Press, 1918).

10. For the flood, see T. Leggio, "Ermanno Di Reichenau, l'alluvione del 1053, i laghi reatini e Giulio Cesare," *Territorio* 2, no. 3 (September–December 1986): 275–277. For the lakes, E. Dupré-Theseider, "La rivolta di Perugia nel 1375 contro l'abate di Monmaggiore ed i suoi precedenti politici," *Bollettino della Deputazione di Storia Patria per l'Umbria*, 1938: 60–63; E. Dupré Theseider, *Il lago Velino: Saggio storico-geografico* (Rieti, Italy: Nobili, 1939).

11. Tobias Smollett, *The Miscellaneous Works of Tobias Smollett, M.D.: In Six Volumes, volume the fifth* (Edinburgh: David Ramsay, 1790), 513.

12. R. Lorenzetti, *Studi e materiali per una storia sociale e economica della Sabina* (Rieti, Italy: Istituto E. Cirese, 1989), 98–114.

13. *The Works of Lord Byron*, vol. 1 (London: John Murray, 1819), 441.

4 | DARKNESS AND LIGHT

1. "Item Romae in publica platea est monumentum lapideum erectum illius papae, qui fuit femina et peperit puerum in eo loco. Illum lapidem ego vidi, et miror papase fosse ferre." Martin Luther, *Martin Luthers Werke Kritische Gesamtausgabe, Tischreden*, vol. 5 (Weimar: Hermann Boehlays Nachfolger, 1919), 667 (entry 6447). He expatiates further on page 669 (entry 6452).

2. *Chronica universalis Mettensis*, ed. G. Wait, *Monumenta Germaniae historica, scriptorum tomus XXIV* (Hanover, Germany: Impensis Bibliopolii Hahniani, 1879), 514.

3. Martin Polonus, "Chronicon pontificum et imperatum," in *Monumenta Germaniae historica: Scriptores XXII* (Hanover, Germany: Impensis Bibliopolii Hahniani, 1872), 428.

4. Ibid.

5. Bartolomeo Platina, *Lives of the Popes*, trans. W. Benham, vol. 1 (London: Griffith, Farran, Okeden & Welsh, 1888). Cf. *Vitae pontificum* (Nuremberg: Anton Koberger, 1481), 49 v 225.

6. "Ad destestacionem tamen pape Agnetis, cujus ymago de petra cum filio suo prope Sanctum Xlementem in via recta existit." *Chronicle of Adam of Usk*, trans. Edward Maunde Thompson (London: Henry Frowde, 1904), 263, 90.

7. Maximilien Misson, *Nouveau voyage d'Italie, fait en l'année 1688* (The Hague: Marchand Libraire, 1731), 306.

8. Elias Hasenmüller, *Historia Jesuitici ordinis* (Frankfurt: Johannes Spies, 1595), 577.

9. "Filius eiusdem episcopus Hostiensis effectus est." Martin Polonus, "Chronicon pontificum et imperatum," in *Monumenta Germaniae historica: Scriptores XXII*, 428–429.

10. For the curious, Rosemary Pardoe and Darroll Pardoe, *The Female Pope: The Mystery of Pope Joan; The First Complete Documentation of the Facts behind the Legend* (Wellingborough, UK: Crucible, 1988), is a good place to start.

11. G. Levi Della Vida, "The 'Bronze Era' in Moslem Spain," *Journal of the American Oriental Society*, no. 3 (1943): 187.

12. *Kitab al-masalik wa'l-mamalik* (The book of roads and kingdoms of Abu'l Qasim Ubayd Alla b. Abd Allah bin Hurradadbih [820–885 or 826–913]), quoted in Marco Di Branco, *L'Immagine de Costantino nelle fonti Arabe*, in *Costantino I: Enciclopedia costantiniana sulle figura e l'immagine dell'imperatore del cosidetto editto di Milano, 313–2013*, vol. 2 (Rome: Instituto della Enciclopedia Italiana, 2013), 374. See also "Le livre des routes et des provinces par Ibn Khordebdeh," trans. C. Barbier de Meynard, *Journal Asiatique, Sixième Série, Tome V* (Paris: Imprimerie Impériale, 1865), 482–483.

13. Bernard Lewis, *A Middle East Mosaic: Fragments of Life, Letters and History* (New York: Random House, 2000), 29. (He gives the year as AD 886. As he traveled to Rome after his sojourn in Constantinople in AD 911, this seems off.)

14. "Un fleuve dont le fond est pavé en lames de cuivre, en sorte qu'aucun navire ne peut y jeter l'ancre." *Géographie d'Édrisi, traduite de l'arabe en français d'après deux manuscrits de la Bibliothèque du Roi et accompagnée de notes par P. Amédée Jaubert* (Paris: Imprimerie Royale, 1840), 251. Cf. Nicola Cariello, *I Saraceni nel Lazio (VIII–X secolo)* (Rome: Edilazio, 2001), 86.

15. G. Levi Della Vida, "The 'Bronze Era' in Moslem Spain," *Journal of the American Oriental Society*, no. 3 (1943): 187. The translator may have been working from a corrupt text. See also Mayte Penelas, "A Possible Author of the Arabic Translation of Orosius' Historiae," *Al-Mas āq: Islam and the Medieval Mediterranean 13* (2001): 113–135, http://digital.csic.es/bitstream/10261/4112/1/Penelas_Possible%20author_pre.pdf. The date of the MS is subject to desperate debate, but no later than the thirteenth century. See Ann Rosemary Christys, *Christians in Al-Andalus, 711–1000* (London: Routledge, 2002), 148.

16. Grünbaum translates: "Man sagt, er habe über die ganze Welt geherrscht; im vierten Jahre seiner Regierung legte er dem ganzen Lande (oder der ganzen Erde) einen Tribut an Kupfer auf und belegte den Fluss Tiberis . . . mit sehr dicken Kupferplatten . . . und nach Kupferzeitrechnung zählen sie noch heute in ihren Urkunden." M. Grünbaum, "Nachträge zu den 'Bemerkungen über die Samaritaner,'" *Zeitschrift der Deutschen Morgenländischen Gesellschaft* 23, no. 4 (1869): 626, ft 2 (cf. Markus Katz, "Abraham Ibn Dauds Sepher Hak-Kabbala: Übersetzung, Quellennachweis nebst kritschen Bemerkungen," inaugural diss., Universität Bern, 1907).

17. Quoted in *The Chronicles of Jerahmeel*, trans. M. Gaster (London: Royal Asiatic Society, 1899), 101.

18. Filippo Maria Bonini, *Il Tevere incatenato* (Rome: F. Moneta, 1663), 136.

19. Theodore Mommson, *Monumenta Germaniae historica edidit Societas Aperiendis Fontibus rerum Germanicarum Medii Aevi, auctorum antiquissimorum tomus XI Chronicorum Minorum Saec IV, V VI VII*, vol. 2 (Berlin: Weidmann, 1844), Historia PseudoIsodorian Isidori Iunioris episcopi Hispalensis chronica maiora ed primum a DCXV chronicorum epitor ed a DCXXVII p 380. Historia Pseudoisidoriana Cod. Parisini 6113 (ed. Theodor Mommsen, MGH AA 11, Berlin 1894), 377–388. For a discussion of the MS see Ann Christys, "'How can I trust you, since you are a Christian and I am a Moor?' The multiple identities of the Chronicle of Pseudo-Isidore," Austrian Academy of Sciences, *Forschungen zur Geschichte des Mittelalters*, vol. 12, *Texts and Identities in the Early Middle Ages*, January 2006.

20. *The Book of Good Love of the Archpriest of Hita, Juan Ruiz*, trans. Elisha Kent Kane (Newark, DE: William Edwin Rudge, 1933).

Todo el suelo del río de la cibdad de Roma
Tiberio agua cabdal que muchas aguas toma,
físole suelo de cobre, reluse más que goma,
a dueñas tu loxuria d'esta guisa las doma.

21. Pero Tafur, *Travels and Adventures, 1435–1439*, trans. Malcolm Letts (New York: Harper, 1926), 35; Pero Tafur, "Andanças é viajes de Pero Tafur por diversas partes del mundo avidos (1435–1439)," *Colección de libros españoles raros ó curiosos*, t.8 (Madrid: Impr. De M. Ginestra, 1874), 23.

22. Aḥmad ibn Muḥammad al-Maqqarī, *The History of the Mohammedan Dynasties in Spain*, trans. Pascual de Gayangos, vol. 1 (London: Oriental Translation Fund, 1840), 202.

23. "Un lungo canale overo condotto di piombo." BAV, Urb. Lat. 1058, quoted in Johannes Albertus Franciscus Orbaan, *La Roma di Sisto V negli avvisi* (Rome: Società Romana di Storia Patria, 1910), 311.

24. Cariello, *I Saraceni nel Lazio*, 85.

25. Ibid. He also claims that every Good Friday "the king" opens the tombs of Saints Peter and Paul to shave Paul's head and beard and cut his nails and distributes these relics to all the people, then closes the tomb up for another year.

26. Lorenzo Comensoli Antonini, "Profezie e alchimia alla corte di Gregorio XIII e Sisto V: Un carteggio dall'Accademia Carrara di Bergamo" (*Aevum* 89 [2015]: fasc 3 721–744 [737]).

27. Arnold de Wyon, *Lignum vitae* (Venice: Georgius Angelerius, 1595), 3027.

28. Ibid. "Fuit archiepiscopus Rossanensis in Calabria, ubi manna colligitur."

29. *British Pharmacopeia* 1867 (London: Spottiswoode, 1880).

30. Claude-François Ménestrier, *La philosophie des images énigmatiques* (Lyon: Hilaire Baritel, 1694), 345ff.

31. Peter Bander, *The Prophecies of Malachy* (New York: Alba House, 1970).

32. Ibid.

33. Ritter Arnold von Harff, *Die Pilgerfahrt des Ritters Arnold von Harff* (Cologne: J. M. Heberle, 1860), 27–28; Iacobo de Albericis, *Historiarum sanctissimae et gloriosis. Virginis deiparae de populo almae urbis compendium* (Rome: Nicolai Mutii, 1599), 1–10.

See also *The Pilgrimage of Arnold von Harff Knight*, trans. Malcolm Letts (London: Hakluyt Society, 1946), 34–35. See also Kai-Michael Sprenger, "The Tiara in the Tiber: An Essay on the damnatio in memoria of Clement III (1084–1100) and Rome's River as a Place of Oblivion and Memory," *Reti Medievali Rivista* 13, no. 1 (2012).

34. "Vita Barbati episcopi Beneventani," in *Monumenta Germaniae historica / Scriptores rerum Langobardicarum et Italicarum saec. VI–IX* (Hanover, Germany: Hahn, 1878), 560.

35. Pliny, *Natural History* 3.12.2:81.

36. *Chronicon Sublacens del P. D. Cherubino Mirzio da Treveri* (Rome: A. Befani, 1885), 363.

37. For more see Norman A. F. Smith, "The Roman Dams of Subiaco," *Technology and Culture* 11, no. 1 (January 1970): 58–68.

38. Chris Wickham, *Medieval Rome: Stability and Crisis of a City, 900–1150* (Oxford: Oxford University Press, 2015), 106.

39. Dante, *Divine Comedy*, *Purgatory*, canto 2, 101.

40. Biondo Flavio, *Italy Illuminated*, vol. 2, trans. Jeffrey A. White (Cambridge, MA: Harvard University Press, 2004), 121.

41. "Cum ivimus ad videndum portum Cosmus et ego, nulla invenimus epigrammata, nam templum illud, quod isti pro calce demoliuntur est sino epigrammate: epigramma vero quod est in via Hostiensi iuxta ripam fluminis, alias ad ti misi." Poggio Bracciolini, *Poggii epistolae*, ed. T. Tonelli, vol. 1 (Florence, 1832), 209–210.

42. *Life of Cola di Rienzo*, trans. John Wright (Toronto: Pontifical Institute of Mediaeval Studies, 1975), bk. 1, chap. 11, p. 45 (trans. of bk. 18 of *Anonimo Romano* 18.2, 473–478).

43. Ludovico Antonio Muratorio, *Antiquitates Italicae Medii Aevi*, vol. 3 (Milan: Societatis Palatinae, 1740), 396.

44. Ibid. 3:395–396, "Ahi quanto pericolo passaro in quella intrata!"

45. Ibid. 3:398.

46. Ibid. "What's at hazard at sea is likewise at hazard on land."

47. "Sio ventre era pieno de acqua. Como votticiello pareva, piene le gamme e llo cuollo sottile e lla faccia macra, la sete grannissima. Leguto da sonare pareva. Stavase in soa casa quetamente renchiuso e facevase medicare dalli fisichi." *Life of Cola di Rienzo*, trans. Wright, bk. 1, chap. 11, p. 49.

48. Ibid., 50.

49. Conte Luigi Tosti, *History of Pope Boniface VIII and His Times*, trans. Eugene J. Donnelly (New York: Christian Press Association, 1911), 522–523.

50. Giovanni Villani, *Cronica*, ed. G. Porta (Parma: Fondazione Pietro Bembo, 1991), vol. 2, bk. 9, chap. 36, p. 563. Guglielmo Ventura gives a figure of two million; we may assume a misplaced comma. See Arsenio Frugoni, *Pellegrini a Roma nel 1300. Cronache del primo giubilo* (Casale Monferrato, Italy: Piemme, 1999), 55–56.

51. *Gros tournois*, a groat of Tours, four and a half grams of silver stamped into a coin. At the time of writing, it was as universally recognized and accepted as a Maria Theresa thaler would be several centuries later.

52. Guglielmo Ventura, aka the Chronicler of Asti, quoted in Herbert Thurston, *The*

Holy Year of the Jubilee: An Account of the History and Ceremonial of the Roman Jubilee (St. Louis: B. Herder, 1900), 19. Ancient and medieval crowd numbers must always be taken with considerable salt. Assuming the two hundred thousand visitors at any given time, and a two-week stay per pilgrim, and a rolling arrival and departure schedule, the figure of two million visitors in total sounds short. Italy alone is estimated at over eleven million souls at this time, so the total figure could easily be higher.

53. Dante, *Inferno*, canto 18.28–33.

54. Paolo di Benedetto di Cola dello Mastro, *Cronache Romane*, quoted in Ludwig von Pastor, *The History of the Popes, from the Close of the Middle Ages*, vol. 2, ed. Frederick Ignatius Antrobus, 3rd ed. (London: Kegan Paul, Trench, Trübner, 1906), 103.

55. Quoted ibid., 83.

56. Quoted ibid., 89.

57. Quoted ibid.

58. Quoted in Thurston, *Holy Year of the Jubilee*, 69–70, "until midnight."

59. Bk. 1, letter 16, April 19, 1472, Bartolomeo Fonzio to Battista Guarini, *Bartolomeo Fonzio Letters to His Friends*, trans. Martin Davies (Cambridge, MA: Harvard University Press, 2011), 32–33.

60. Johannis Burckardi, *Liber notarum, ab anno MCCCCLXXXIII usque ad annum MDVI*, vol. 2 (Città di Castello, Italy: S. Lapi, 1914), 220.

61. Villani, *Cronica*, vol. 2, bk. 9, chap. 36, 563.

62. A fuller explanation by a sympathetic biographer can be found in Tosti, *History of Pope Boniface VIII*, 525.

63. Osvaldo Cavallar, "River of Law: Bartolus's *Tiberiade (De alluvione)*," in *A Renaissance of Conflicts: Visions and Revisions of Law and Society in Italy and Spain*, ed. John A. Marino and Thomas Kuehn (Toronto: Centre for Reformation and Renaissance Studies, 2004), 31.

64. "Hec que cogitare cepisti scribe et, quia oculorum inspectione indiget per figuras singna [*sic*]. Ecce aportavi tibi calamum quo scribas, circinum quo mensures et figuras fatias circulares, et lineam qua lineas ducas figuras formes." Bartolo de Sassoferrata, *De fluminibus seu Tiberiadis* (1355), quoted in Cavallar, "River of Law," in Marino and Kuehn, *Renaissance of Conflicts*, 84.

65. Cavallar plans to address this issue in a forthcoming edition of the *Tiberiadis (De alluvione)*. See "River of Law" in Marino and Kuehn, *Renaissance of Conflicts*, 45, fn 62.

66. Bartolo de Sassoferrata, *Tyberiadis (De alluvione)*, quoted in Marino and Kuehn, *Renaissance of Conflicts*, 72.

67. Ibid., 72.

68. "The History of Pilate," from *Selections from the Hengwrt Mss.*, vol. 2, trans. Robert Williams (London: T. Richards, 1876), 623.

69. *Gospel of Nicodemus and Kindred Documents*, trans. Arthur Westcott (London: Heath, Cranton & Ouseley, 1915), 35.

70. Tibor Grüll, "The Legendary Fate of Pontius Pilate," *Classica et Mediaevalia* 61 (2010): 151–176.

71. "The History of Pilate," from *Selections from the Hengwrt Mss.*, trans. Robert Williams, 2:624.

72. Hester Lynch Piozzi, *Observations and Reflections Made in the Course of a Journey through France, Italy, and Germany*, vol. 1 (London: A. Straham, 1789), 382.

73. "Urbem Romam adeo diruptam et vastam invenit, ut nulla civitatis facies in ea videretur. Collabentes vidisses domos, collapsa templa, desertos vicos, coenosam et oblitam urbem, laborantem rerum omnium caritate et inopia. Quid plura? Nulla urbis facies, nullum urbanitatis indicium in ea videbatur." Bartholomæus Sacchi de Platina, *Historia B. Platinae de vitis pontificum Romanorum* (Cologne: Agrippinae 1626), 292.

74. "Chi sono uomini iscandalosi" (the editor interprets *iscandalosi* as *rissosi, faziosi*—turbulent, factious). Vaspasiano da Bistecci, *Virorum illustrium CIII qui saeculo XV extiterunt vitae* (Florence, 1859), 7.

75. "Affievoliti erano i manigoldi non soddisfatti: chè in quel di furono in venti sottoposti a tal forma di disamina. All'ultimo vengo io chiamato alla punizione; si apprestano all'ufficio loro i carnefici; dispongono gl'ingegni crucciosi; mi svestono, mi graffiano, e qual ladro rapinatore mi bistrattano; intanto che il Vianisio—un consacrato—altro Minosse e in sembiante di partecipe alle cene di Atreo e di Tantalo, sedeva su preziosi tappeti." Biondo Flavio, *Historiarum ab inclinatione Romanorum*, bk. 31 (Basel: Frobeniana, 1531), 481ff. Ferdinand Gregorovius, *History of the City of Rome in the Middle Ages*, vol. 7, pt. 1 (London: G. Bell, 1900), 45.

Stefano Bissolati, *Le vite di due illustri Cremonesi descritte da Stefano Bissolati* (Milan: Gaetano Brigola Librajo, 1856), 41.

76. Pius II, *Pii Secundi pontificis max. commentarii rerum memorabilium*, bk. 101 (Frankfurt: Officina Aubriana, 1614), 302. In insula nullum eminet aliud aedificium; verum ubicunque effoderis, marmora invenies, et statuas, et columnas ingentis magnitudinis.

77. Biondo Flavio, *Italy Illuminated*, 1:63.

78. "Assai cose et belle, molte statue marmoree et sepulture antique, et in edifitii antichi opere di mattoni minuti in forma di musaico, e secondo che quelli mattoni dovevono essere di varie terre, così havevono preso diversi colori dal fuoco, chi un poco più et mancho rosso, simile nero et giallo et presso al biancho, tale che lopera tornavano belle et bene distinte." Johann Wilhelm Gaye and Alfred von Reumont, *Carteggio inedito d'artisti dei secoli XIV, XV, XVI*, vol. 1 (Florence: Presso G. Molini, 1839), 286.

79. "Hanc statuam Bessarion Trapezuntius cardinalis Nicaenus, cum sui iuris fecisset, profani cultus impietatem detestatus in mare demergi iussit." Volpi, *Vetus Latium* xi.c.2, cited in Lily Ross Taylor, *The Cults of Ostia* (Bryn Mawr, PA: Bryn Mawr College, 1912), 30.

80. Aeneas Sylvius Piccolomini, *The Tale of the Two Lovers*, trans. Flora Grierson (London: Constable, 1929), 54.

81. *The Commentaries of Pius II*, bks. 10–13, trans. Florence Alden Gragg, with historical introduction and notes by Leona C. Gabel (Northampton, MA: Smith College, 1957), 750.

82. Ibid., 751.

83. Pius II, *Pii Secundi*, 301.

84. Ibid, 751.

85. "Et postea intravit Tyberim: ad cuius introitum est turris pulcerrima sed solitaria."

Roger of Hoveden, in *Monumenta Germaniae historica* (SS.27), ed. Pertz (Hanover, Germany: Impensis Bibliopolii Hahniani, 1885), 114–115.

86. "Periculum in continuatione ignium, ne sidus existimeretur, quoniam e longinquo similis flammarum aspectus est." Pliny, *Natural History* 36.8.83, trans. H. Rackham, vol. 10 (Cambridge, MA: Harvard University Press, 1938), 67.

87. Pius II, *Pii Secundi*, 301.

88. *Commentaries of Pius II*, bks. 10–13, 751.

89. "Si quis neglexerit avaritiam naufragio punit." Pius II, *Pii Secundi*, 302.

90. *Commentaries of Pius II*, bks. 10–13, 753.

91. Ibid.

92. *Sir John Froissart's Chronicles of England*, bk. 2, trans. Thomas Johnes (London: Longman, Hurst, Rees and Orme, 1808), 162.

93. Luigi Huetter, "I Mattei, custodi dei ponti," *Capitolium* 5 (1929): 347–352.

94. "Un mostro che par che habbia la testa d'aseno, con le rechie longhe, e 'l corpo de femena humana; el brazzo zanco de forma humana, el destra ha in cima un muso de elefante; da drio, in la parte posterior, un viso da vechio, con barba de forma humana; ghe esce per la coa un colo longo, con una teste de serpe con la boca averta; el pè destro de aquila con le griffe, el pè zanco de bo; le gambe, dalla pianta in su, con tutta la persona squamosa, a similitudine de pesche. E questi particolari se contien in le lettere dell'Ambassador alla Signoria." *Archivio storico Italiano: Periodico trimestriale: Ossia raccolta di opere e documenti finora inediti o divenuti rarissimi risguardanti la storia d'Italia*, vol. 7, pt. 1 (Rome: Olschki, 1943), 422.

95. "Interea tantum coneris vincere monstrum, Tu memor ipse tui famaequae adiungere famam." *Ad illustrissimum ac excellentissimum principem divum Erculem Estensem Francisci Rococcioli mutinensis libellus de monstro Romae in Tyberi reperto anno dmi. M.CCCC.LXXXXVI.*

96. *De inundatione Tybridis anno domini millesimo quater centesimo nonagesimo quinto*. See Anna Esposito, "Le inondazioni del Tevere tra tardo medioevo e prima età moderna: Leggende, racconti, testimonianze," *Mélanges de l'École Française de Rome* (Rome: École Française de Rome, 2006), 10.

97. Giuliano Dati, *Del diluvio di Roma del M.CCCC.lxxxv*, ed. Anna Esposito and Paula Farenga (Rome: Roma nel Rinascimento, 2011).

INTERLUDE | TRIBUTARY—CLITUMNUS

1. George Gordon Byron, *Childe Harold*, canto 4, v 66ff.

2. George Gordon Byron, letter to Murray, Venice, June 4, 1817, in *Letters and Journals of Lord Byron: With Notices of His Life*, vol. 2 (London: John Murray, 1830), 122.

3. Propertius 2.19.

4. Pliny, *Epistolae* 8, 8, trans. William Melmoth (Cambridge, MA: Harvard University Press, 1922), 115.

5. Juvenal, *Satires* 12.11–14, trans. in *The Satires of Decimus Junius Juvenalis translated into English verse by Mr [John] Dryden. . . .* There are numerous editions.

6. Virgil, *Georgics* 2.146–148, trans. J. B. Greenough, *The Bucolics, Aeneid, and Georgics of Virgil* (Boston: Ginn, 1883).

7. "Et patulis Clitumnus in arvis candentes gelido perfundit flumine tauros." Silius Italicus, *Punica* 4.545–546, trans. J. D. Duff, *Silius Italicus Punica*, vol. 1 (Cambridge, MA: Harvard University Press, 1922), 209.

8. "Et niveos abluit unda boves." Propertius 2.19.26, trans. H. E. Butler, *Propertius* (Cambridge, MA: Harvard University Press 1929), 119. Propertius then turns back to sex, and he writes to his beloved Cynthia that he will be with her soon enough, after he has finished bagging some rabbits and birds near the riverside. No word if they were white.

9. J. Addison, *Remarks on Several Parts of Italy* (London: Tenson, 1705), 150–151.

10. *C. Claudiani de sexto consulatu Honorii Augusti*, trans. Maurice Platnauer (Cambridge, MA: Harvard University Press, 1922), lines 543–548.

11. "Nam ad menses sex maxime duravit, et non ex intervallo, sed motu continue omnia concussit, idque per orbem fere universum . . . alicubi fontes non exigui subito exaruere." Nicephorus Callistus, *Historia ecclesiastica* 14.46.927, in *Patrologiae cursus completus*, vol. 146 (Paris: J. P. Migne, 1865). See also Cesare Baronius, *Annales ecclesiastici*, vol. 6 (Rome: S. Mariam Vallicella, 1595), 37.

12. *Report of the Annual Meeting, vol. 22, British Association for the Advancement of Science* (London: John Murray, 1853), 102.

13. Judson J. Emerick, *The Tempietto del Clitunno near Spoleto*, vol. 2 (State College, PA: Penn State University Press, 1998).

14. Tobias Smollett, *The Works of Tobias Smollett*, vol. 8 (London: Bickers, 1872), 337.

15. Ibid., 8:295. The inkeeper had apparantly taken them for German Catholics. "Bisogna dire a su'eccellenza, poco fa, che una bestia e morta in questa camera, e non e ancora lustrate." Smollett failed to translate the Italian here.

16. Giulio Locatelli, "Alle sorgete di Clitunno," *Giornale d'Italia*, May 31, 1940, p. 3. Science delivers yet another disappointing truth, disappointing enough that it is generally ignored, even in this unromantic age.

5 | RENAISSANCE

1. Celio Secondo Curione, *Pasquillorum tomi duo* (Basel: Johannes Oporinus, 1544), 24.

2. Ibid., 24, 81.

3. Maximilien Misson, *Nouveau voyage d'Italie*, 4th ed., vol. 2 (The Hague, 1702), 158. Misson also claims that the same comment is ascribed to Adrian IV.

4. *Pope Alexander VI and His Court: Extracts from the Latin Diary of Johannes Burchardus*, ed. F. L. Glaser (New York: N. L. Brown, 1921), 91 (cf. *Archivio Storico Italiano: Periodico trimestriale: Ossia raccolta di opere e documenti finora inediti o divenuti rarissimi risguardanti la storia d'Italia*, part 1, vol. 7 (Florence: Gio. Pietro Vieusseux, 1843), 489ff.

5. Luca Landucci, *A Florentine Diary from 1450 to 1516*, trans. Alice de Rosen Jervis (London: J. M. Dent & Sons, 1927), 123.

6. Jacopo Sannazaro, *Opera omnia latine scripta* (Venice: Aldi Manutii et Andreae Asulani, 1535), fol. 41a.

7. Arnold Von Hafft, *Rom, Jerusalem, Santiago: Das Pilgertagebuch des Ritters Arnold von Harff, 1496–1498*, ed. Helmut Brall-Tuche (Cologne: Böhlau, 2007), 66.

8. *Pope Alexander VI and His Court: Extracts from the Latin Diary of Johannes Burchardus*, ed. F. L. Glaser (New York: Nicholas L. Brown, 1921), 161.

9. Ruth B. Bottigheimer, *Fairy Godfather: Straparola, Venice, and the Fairy Tale Tradition* (Philadelphia: University of Pennsylvania Press, 2002).

10. Giovanfrancesco Straparola da Caravaggio, *Le piacevoli notti* (Venice: Francesco Lorenzini da Turino, 1560), 155v.

11. "Venne la bombarda, chiamata la Sistina Papale, da Fuligni, et passo lo Tevere sotto de Orte [i.e., Sant'Angelo] a guazzo su li carri et fu posata nello campo de Castello et molta gente ando a vederla." *Il diario romano di Gaspare Pontani, già riferito al "Notaio del Nantiporto," 30 gennaio 1481–25 luglio 1492* (Città di Castello, Italy: S. Lapi, 1907–1908), 9.

12. *Il diario romano di Jacopo Gherardi da Volterra*, September 7, 1479, to August 9, 1484, ed. Enrico Carusi (Città di Castello, Italy: S. Lapi, 1904), vol. 23, pt. 3, p. 502.

13. *Diario ordinario*, num. 3070, April 6, 1737 (Rome: Stamperia del Chracas, 1737); cf. Francesco Valesio, *Diario di Roma*, ed. G. Scano, vol. 6 (Milan: Longanesi, 1977–1979), 6, March 30, 1737, 32.

14. "Piaceme interamente, salvo che l'essere mercante et banchiere, il che purtroppo mi pare sconvenevole alla casa nostra." Michael Hirst, *Sebastiano del Piombo* (Oxford: Oxford University Press, 1981), 31.

15. D. Coffin, *Gardens and Gardening in Papal Rome* (Princeton, NJ: Princeton University Press, 1991), 227 (55).

16. Blosio Palladio, quoted in *The Villa in the Life of Renaissance Rome* (Princeton, NJ: Princeton University Press, 1979), 178 (41).

17. Egidio Gallo, *De viridario Augustini Chigii vera libellus*, in D. Coffin, *The Villa in the Life of Renaissance Rome* (Princeton, NJ: Princeton University Press, 1979), 188 (38).

18. Mary Quinlan-McGrath, "Blosius Palladius, 'Suburbanum Augustini Chisii': Introduction, Latin Text and English Translation," *Humanistica Lovaniensia: Journal of Neo-Latin Studies* 39 (1990): 134.

19. Ibid., 136.

20. *The Diary of John Evelyn*, ed. Austin Dobson, vol. 1 (Cambridge: Cambridge University Press, 1906), 201.

21. John Chetwode Eustace, *A Classical Tour through Italy in 1802*, 7th ed., vol. 1 (London: Thomas Tegg, 1841), 327.

22. Lady Sydney Owenson Morgan, *Italy*, vol. 2 (London: Henry Colburn, 1824), 223.

23. For more on Chigi see Ingrid Rowland, *The Culture of the High Renaissance* (Cambridge: Cambridge University Press, 1998).

24. Rodolfo Lanciani, *The Golden Days of the Renaissance in Rome* (Boston: Houghton Mifflin, 1901), 80.

25. "Abondi Rizio—in publicis stillicidiis coronato—in ligandis superilligandisque sarcinis—expertissimo—qui vexit quantum voluit—vixit quantum potuit—et dum

vini cadum intus—et extra portabat—nolens obiit"; that is: "To Abondi Rizio, crowned (king) on the public pavement, greatest expert in binding and carrying bundles, who carried as much as he chose, who lived as much as he could, but who, while carrying a barrel of wine inside and (another) outside, died against his will." *Il Buonarroti: Scritti sopra le arti e le lettere di Benvenuto Gasparoni continuati per cura di Enrico Narducci*, vol. 7 (Rome: Tipografia delle Scienza Matematiche e Fisiche, 1872), 231.

26. Luigi De Sanctis, *Roma papale* (Florence: Tipografia Claudiana, 1865), 320.

27. Giovanni Michele Silos, *Pinacotheca, sive Romana pictura et sculptura*, bk. 2 (Rome: Philippus Marai Mancini, 1673).

28. Margherita Naval, *A Roma si racconta che . . . Leggende, aneddoti, curiosità* (Rome: Hoepli, 1937).

29. Marvin Pulvers, *Roman Fountains: 2000 Fountains in Rome; A Complete Collection* (Rome: L'Erma di Bretschneider, 2002), 17. See also Rodolfo Lanciani, *Storia degli scavi di Roma e notizie intorno le collezioni romane di antichità*, vol. 4 (Rome: E. Loescher, 1912), 15, in which he quotes the following placard near the Trevi Fountain: "Item che qualunque aquarolo che piglia aqua alla fontana [Trevi] de continovo tutto lanno [*sic*], paghi in tutto iulii cinque: item che tutti i cavalli et muli che charichino aqua dalla fontana, paghi bol. [i.e., baiocchi] cinque per ciasche bestia."

30. "Fluvius etenim Tiberis, qui urbem perlabitur, equis utilis est, set hominibus inutilis et nocuus habetur." (An alternative reading is: "Fluvius namque Tiberis equis est salubris, sed hominibus noxius.") Gregorius (Magister), and Robert B. C. Huygens, *Narracio de mirabilibus urbis Romae* (Leiden: Brill, 1970), 18.

31. "Eam enim supra omne genus aquae, fontanae vel pluvialis, et levissimam et innoxiam experimur." Paolo Giovio, *De optima victus ratione* (Rome, 1527), 144–145.

32. Jacques Le Saige, *Voyage de Jacques Le Saige* (Douai, France: Adam D'Aubers, 1851), 29.

33. Ariosto, *Satire* 2, 46–48.

34. Giovanni Battista Modio, *Il Tevere* (Rome: Vincenzo Luchini, 1556), 58v, "Non sono anchora molti giorni passati, che un letterato mio amico, il quale pativa di renelle, et di dolor di fianchi, m'ha detto d'esser divenuto sano, solamente con l'astenersi dall'acque del Tevere, et col ber quelle, della Fontana di Trievi."

35. Antonio Gallonio, *Vita beati P. Philippi Neri* (Rome: Aloysium Zanettum, 1600), 56. Cf. Pietro Giacomo Bacci, *Vita S. Philippi Nerii Florentini* (Rome: Vitalis Mascardi, 1645), 24.

36. Also hernias, but mostly kidney stones, something of a scourge at the time.

37. Modio, *Il Tevere*, 8v.

38. Alessandro Traiano Petronio, *De aqua Tiberina opus quidem nouum* (Rome: Valerium, 1552). Cf. Andrea Bacci, *Del Tevere di M. Andrea Bacci, medico et filosofo*, bk. 3, *Ne' quali si tratta della natura, & bontà dell'acque, & specialmente del Tevere* (Venice: Manuzio, 1576), 211, 212.

39. See Katherine W. Rinne, "Between Precedent and Experiment: Restoring the Acqua Vergine in Rome (1560–70)," in *The Mindful Hand: Inquiry and Invention from the Late Renaissance to Early Industrialization*, ed. L. Roberts, S. Shaffer, and P. Dear (Amsterdam: Edita, 2007), 94–115.

40. Katherine W. Rinne, "Water: The Currency of Cardinals in Late Renaissance Rome," in *La civiltà delle acque tra Medioevo e Rinascimento*, ed. A. Calzona and D. Lamberini (Florence: Olshki, 2010), 367–387.

41. Gilbert Burnet, *Burnet's Travels: Or, a Collection of Letters to the Hon. Robert Boyle Esq* (London: Ward and Chandler, 1738), 194.

42. Maximilien Misson, *A New Voyage to Italy*, vol. 2, pt. 1 (London, 1714), 72 (translation of his *Nouveau voyage d'Italie* [The Hague: Henri van Bulderen, 1702], 177).

43. Lione Pascoli, *Il Tevere navigato e navigabile* (Rome: Antonio de' Rossi, 1740), 53.

44. "Son eau est toujours trouble et jaune, et dans cet état elle n'est point salutaire; mais quand on l'a laissé reposer, elle dépose, se clarifie e devient très-bonne à boire." Joseph-Jérôme de Lalande, *Voyage d'un françois en Italie: Fait dans les années 1765 & 1766*, vol. 3 (Paris: Chez Desaint, 1769), 301.

45. Strother A. Smith, *The Tiber and Its Tributaries: Their Natural History and Classical Associations* (London: Longmans, Green, 1877), 40.

46. Francesco Cancillieri, *Il mercato, il lago dell'Acqua Vergine ed il palazzo Panfiliano nel circo Agonale detto volgarmente Piazza Navona* (Rome: Francesco Bourli, 1811), 287.

47. Smith, *Tiber and Its Tributaries*, 41.

48. Rodolfo Lanciani, *The Ruins and Excavations of Ancient Rome* (New York: Harcourt Brace, 1897), 15.

49. Paolo Giovio, *Pauli Iovii opera, dialogi et descriptiones*, ed. Ernesto Travi and Maria Grazia Penco (Rome: Instituto Poligrafico e Zecca dello Stato Libreria dello Stato, 1984), 51–52.

50. Notable among these men were Pierre Belon, Guillaume Rondelet, Ippolito Salviani, Conrad Gessner, and Ulisse Aldrovandi. Gessner is kind enough to acknowledge his debt to Giovio, calling him "vir doctus et elegans." *Conradi Gesneri medici Tigurini Historiae animalium* (Frankfurt: Andreas Cambier, 1604), 1030. Aldrovandi simply plagiarizes him.

51. Quoted in T. P. Zimmerman, *Paolo Giovio: The Historian and the Crisis of Sixteenth-Century Italy* (Princeton, NJ: Princeton University Press, 1996), 64.

52. For more on this subject see Luigi Salerno, Luigi Spezzaferro, and Manfredo Tafuri, *Via Giulia: Una utopia urbanistica del 500* (Rome: Staderini, 1973).

53. Giovanni Antonio Pecci and Valenti Gonzaga, *Vita di Bartolommeo da Petrojo chiamato dal volgo Brandano* (Siena: Fran. Quinza, 1746), 30–31.

54. Pietro Bragadino, Pera, December 29, 1525, in Marino Sanuto, *I Diarii di Marino Sanuto*, vol. 40 (Venice: F. Visentini, 1894), 824.

55. Judith Hook, *The Sack of Rome, 1527* (New York: Macmillan, 1972), 155.

56. *Calendar of Letters, Despatches, and State Papers Relating to the Negotiations between England and Spain Preserved in the Archives at Simancas and Elsewhere*, vol. 3, pt. 2, 1527–1529, Great Britain Public Record Office (London: Longman, Green, Longman, & Roberts, 1877), 196.

57. *Autobiography of Benvenuto Cellini*, trans. John Addington Symonds (New York: P. F. Collier & Son, 1910), 72.

58. Ibid.

59. Ibid., 72–73.

60. Ibid., 74.

61. Ibid.

62. Hook, *Sack of Rome*, 177.

63. "Teneva una barca che passava il Tevere infra Ponte Sisto e Ponte Santo Agniolo." Benvenuto Cellini, *Opere: vita, trattati, rime, lettere* (Rome: Rizzoli, 1968), 155–157.

64. Cellini, *Autobiography,* 90.

65.

Süß ist das Dunkel nach Gluten des Tags! Auf dämmernder Brücke

Schau' ich die Ufer entlang dieser unsterblichen Stadt.

Burgen und Tempel verwachsen zu *einer* gewaltigen Sage!

Unter mir hütet der Strom manchen verschollenen Hort.

Dort in der Flut eines Nachens Gespenst! Ist's ein flüchtiger Kaiser?

Ist es der "Jakob von Kahn," der Buonarotti geführt?

Gellend erhebt sich Gesang in dem Boot zum Ruhme des Liebchens.

Horch! Ein lebendiger Mund fordert lebendiges Glück.

Conrad Ferdinand Meyer, Gedichte: Ausgabe 1892 (Berlin: Verlag der Contumax, 2015), 198.

66. Cellini, *Autobiography*, 116. See also Benvenuto Cellini, *Vita*, bk. 1.54, in *Opere a cura di Bruno Maier* (Milan: Rizzoli, 1968), 187.

67. Kenneth Setton, *Papacy and the Levant, 1240–1571*, vol. 3 (Philadelphia: American Philosophical Society, 1983), 353.

68. HUC TIBER ASCENDIT IAMQ[ue] OBRUTA TOTA FUISSET ROMAN, NISI HUIC CELEREM VIRGO TULISSET OPEM.

69. "Era già sul levar del sole il sabato mattina, dell'8 del mese di Ottobre, quando il Tevere mossosi fuor del solito letto, cominciò a versare montagne d'acqua con grande ammirazione di ognuno . . . haveva cominciato il travagliato fiume a inondare per la città innanzi al mezzogiorno, e crescendo tuttavia impiendo le chiaviche, le cantine et i luoghi più bassi, poco dopo si vedevano le acque soverchiare le case, e crescendo come a tradimento, e di nascosto con maggior impeto e come torrenti cominciarono a pigliare i passi, e scorrere per tutte le strade con tanta furia, che pareva dovesse subissare la città fondamenti." Lodovico Gomez, *De prodigiosis Tiberis inundationibus ab urbe condita ad annum MDXXXI* (Rome: F. Minitium, 1531), quoted in M. Bencivenga, E. Di Loreto, and L. Liperi, "Il regime idrologico del Tevere con particolare riguardo alle piene nella città di Roma," in *La geologia di Roma: Il centro storico*, 2 vols., ed. Renato Funiciello, vol. 60 of Memorie descrittive della Carta Geologica d'Italia (Rome: Istituto Poligrafico e Zecca dello Stato, 1995), 159.

70. Cellini, *Autobiography,* 224.

71. Luca Landucci, *A Florentine Diary from 1450 to 1516*, trans. Alice de Rosen Jervis (London: J. M. Dent & Sons, 1927), 98.

72. Sigismondo dei Conti da Foligno, *Le storie de' suoi tempi: dal 1475 al 1510*, vol. I (Rome: 1883), 206. "Tota regio illa transtyberina, quae inanissima, et immundissima erat, frequentissima et cultissima reddita est."

73. Carla Keyvanian, *Hospitals and Urbanism in Rome, 1200–1500* (Leiden: Brill, 2015), 370.

74. Stephani Infessura, *Diario della città di Roma di Stephano Infessura scribasenato*, ed. Oreste Rommasini (Rome: Forzani E. C. Tipografi del Senato, 1890), 76.

75. "Vestales romanae, quae regionem pontis Sixti colunt." Celio Secondo Curione, *Pasquillus ecstaticus* (Geneva: Ioannes Girardus, 1544), 163.

76. Johannes Albertus Franciscus Orbaan, *Sixtine Rome* (New York: Baker and Taylor, 1911), 117.

77. Rodolfo Lanciani, *Pagan and Christian Rome* (London: Macmillan, 1895), 62.

78. Giggi Zanazzo, *Tradizioni popolari romane*, vol. 2, *Usi, costumi e pregiudizi del popolo di Roma* (Turin: Società Tipografico-Editrice Nazionale, 1908), 284–285.

79. Baron Hübner, *The Life and Times of Sixtus the Fifth*, trans. Hubert E. H. Jerningham, vol. 1 (London: Longmans, Green, 1872), 257. Cf. Pastor, *History of the Popes*, 21:73–74.

80. Pastor, *History of the Popes,* 21:74. In his time Pius V (1528–1572) was roundly disliked.

81. Ibid., 21:77.

82. "E quest'anno si può dire, che quasi più son state le teste in Ponte, ch'i meloni in Banchi." Johannes Albertus Franciscus Orbaan, *La Roma di Sisto V negli avvisi* (Rome: Società Romana di Storia Patria, 1910), 284.

83. Gregorio Leti, *Vita di Sisto V., pontefice romano*, vol. 2 (Amsterdam: Giovanni & Egidio Jansson à Waesberge, 1698), 366. In all fairness, Leti is not taken seriously by serious scholars.

84. Hübner, *Life and Times of Sixtus the Fifth*, 1:276.

85. Ibid.

86. Charles Dickens, *Pictures from Italy* (London: Bradbury and Evans, 1846), 230.

87. William Wetmore Story, *Castle St. Angelo and the Evil Eye* (London: Chapman and Hall, 1877), 2.

88. *Chronicle of Adam of Usk*, trans. Edward Maunde Thompson (London: Henry Frowde, 1904), 275, 101.

89. Johannes Molanus, *De historia SS. imaginum et picturarum pro vero earum usu contra abusus* (Leuven, Belgium: Typis Academicis, 1771), 607.

90. Archivio di Stato Florence, Mediceo del Principato vol. 3080, fol. 887, Avviso da Roma, December 23, 1570, quoted in Minou Schraven, "Beyond the Studiolo: Ritual and Talismanic Handling of Portrait Medals in Early Modern Italy," *Vienna: Numismatische Zeitschrift Wien* 128 (2016): 80, fn 66.

91. "Dai Pasticceri in Torre Sanguigna . . . dalli Molinari . . . dalla Comunità delli Iudei," quoted in Roberta Morelli, "Gli uomini del Tevere: Fonti per la storia degli edili Romani tra 1450 e 1550," in *Le technicien dans la cité en Europe occidental, 1250–1650*, ed. De Mathieu Arnoux et Pierre Monnet (Rome: École Française de Rome, 2004), 77–92.

92. "Giorgio, questo ponte ci triema sotto; sollecitiamo il cavalcare, che non rovini in mentre ci siàn su." Giorgio Vasari, *Le vite de' più eccellenti pittori, scultori ed architettori*, bk. 7, ed. Gaetano Milanesi and Cornelius von Fabriczy (Florence: G. C. Sansoni, 1881), 235.

93. Ibid., 266.

94. Giacinto Gigli, *Diario romano, 1608–1670* (Rome: Tumminelli, 1958), 418.

95. Paul B. Newman, *Daily Life in the Middle Ages* (London: McFarland, 2001), 163.

96. *The Complete Works of François Rabelais*, trans. Donald M. Frame (Berkeley: University of California Press, 1991), 790. Cf. *Oeuvres de Rabelais*, vol. 2 (Paris: P. Deffis, 1872), 464.

97. *Complete Works of François Rabelais*, 790.

98. Pompilio Totti, *Ritratto di Roma* (Rome: Il Mascardi, 1638), 352.

99. Johan Theodor Sprenger, *Roma Nova* (Frankfurt: Sebastian Rohneri, 1660), 295.

100. "Si tien corso di barchette, e nell'istesso fiume si fanno diversi giochi di lotta, e s'uccidono ingegnosamente varii animali terrestri, e volatili." Michele Giustiniani, *Lettere memorabili dell'abbate Michele Giustiniani, patritio genovese, de' signori di Scio, e d'altri*, pt. 1, vol. 3 (Rome: per Nicolò Angelo Tinassi, 1667–1675), 400.

101. Now in Britain's National Gallery.

102. *Les antiquités de Rome*, trans. Edmund Spenser, *Yale Edition of the Shorter Poems of Edmund Spenser* (New Haven, CT: Yale University Press, 1989), 387.

103. *Complete Works of François Rabelais*, 790.

104. Pastor, *History of the Popes*, 14:169.

105. Lanciani, *Ruins and Excavations*, 11.

106. Anonymous, quoted in Bencivenga, Di Loreto, and Liperi, "Il regime idrologico del Tevere," in Funiciello, *La geologica di Roma*, quoted in G. Heiken, *The Seven Hills of Rome: A Geological Tour of the Eternal City* (Princeton, NJ: Princeton University Press, 2005), 64.

107. Giuseppe Castaglione, *Tiberis inundatio anni MDIIC* (Rome: Nicolai Mutii, 1599), 13.

108. In Neapolitan commedia dell'arte, Pimpa is the wife to Pulcinello and appears in such works as Carlo Sigismondo Capece's *La locanda di Pimpa e Pulcinello*. See Benedetto Croce, *I teatri di Napoli: Secolo XV–XVIII* (Naples: Luigi Pierro, 1891), 688ff.

109. Giggi Zanazzo, *Usi, costumi e pregiudizi del popolo di Roma* (Torino: Società Tipografico-Editrice Nazionale, 1908), 115–116.

110. Ferdinand Gregorovius, *Sulla storia delle inondazioni del Tevere*, trans. Raffaele Ambrosi (Rome: Tipografia delle Scienze Mathematiche e Fisiche, 1877), 16. For Raggi see A. Neri, "Saggio della corrispondenza di Ferdinando Raggi, agente della repubblica Genovese a Roma," *Rivista Europea*, Florence Ufficio della rivista Europea–Rivista Internazionale, 1878, p. 667.

111. Giggi Zanazzo, *Novelle, favole, e leggende romanesche* (Turin: Società Tipografico-Editrice Nazionale, 1907), 359–361. There is in Rome a housing project for workers built under Mussolini; clearly someone in his government had a sense of irony.

112. Planned, no doubt. Martial, in an obsequious poem to the emperor Domitian, describes an elephant that bows down to him without being prompted. Martial, *On the Spectacles* 17.

113. "Sexagenarius senex honesta ortus familia." Paolo Giovio, *Vita Leonis Decimi, pontifici maximi* (Florence: Laurentii Torrentini, 1551), 98, says only that he was able to descend before crossing the bridge.

114. Achilles Pellizzari, *Portogallo e Italia nel secolo XVI: Studi e ricerche storiche e letterarie* (Naples: Società Editrice F. Perrella, 1914), 154.

115. For more on Hanno see Silvio A. Bedini, *The Pope's Elephant: An Elephant's Journey from Deep in India to the Heart of Rome* (Nashville, TN: J. S. Sanders Books, 1997).

INTERLUDE | TRIBUTARY—CHIANA

1. "Bonas domi artes dehonestavisset." Tacitus, *Annales* 3.70.

2. "Curatores riparum qui primi terminaver(unt)." *Corpus inscriptionum Latinarum*, 6, 31541g,h,o,r,s,u, 31542s; Dess. 5922c, 5923d, 5924d.

3. Tacitus, *Annales* 1.79.

4. F. Morozzi, *Dello stato antico e moderno del fiume Arno, e delle cause e dei rimedi delle sue inondazioni* (Florence: G. B. Stecchi, 1768).

5. Henry Edward Napier, *Florentine History* (London: E. Moxon, 1847), 399.

6. Dante, *Inferno*, canto 29.46, trans. Longfellow (Boston: Ticknor & Fields, 1868).

7. "Iuxta autem vallem istam erat illo tempore hospitale de Altopassu, ubi solebant esse multi pauperes infirmantes, et per consequens magnus dolor, tra 'l luglio e 'l settembre. Idest, de mense augusti." Benvenuto da Imola, *Benevenuti de Rambaldis de Imola comentum super Dantis Aldigherij comoediam*, ed. J. P. Lacaita, vol. 2 (Florence: G. Barbèrta, 1887), 394.

8. David Alexander, "The Reclamation of Val-di-Chiana (Tuscany)," *Annals of the Association of American Geographers* 74, no. 4 (1984): 527–550.

6 | MODERN TIMES

1. G. J. Hamilton and A. H. Smith, "Gavin Hamilton's Letters to Charles Townley," *Journal of Hellenic Studies* 21 (1901): 315.

2. "Pastres, Gardiens de Buffles, Pêcheurs, Saulniers, & autres gens en petit nombre, qui s'y assemblent, & qui ressemblent plûtôt à des spectres fortans de sépulchres, qu'à des hommes vivans, tant ils sont jaunes, livides, maigres & décharnés." Jean-Baptiste Labat, *Voyages du P. Labat en Espagne et en Italie*, vol. 8 (Saint Paul, 1720), 91.

3. Labat, *Voyages du P. Labat*, 8:85.

4. Edward Gibbon, *Decline and Fall of the Roman Empire*, vol. 7, ed. J. B. Bury (London: Methuen, 1909), chap. 69, 247.

5. Charlotte Eaton, *Rome in the Nineteenth Century*, vol. 3 (London: Bohn, 1852), 439.

6. "A Port to the Past," *Cornhill Magazine*, May 13, 1882, 476.

7. Ibid., 477.

8. James Aitken Wylie, *Pilgrimage from the Alps to the Tiber; or the Influence of Romanism on Trade, Justice, and Knowledge* (Edinburgh: Sheapherd and Elliot, 1855), 348.

9. Ibid.

10. Thomas Hodgkin, *Italy and Her Invaders: The Imperial Restoration, 535–553*, vol. 4 (Oxford: Oxford University Press, 1896), 481.

11. Ibid., 481–482.

12. Rodolfo Lanciani, *Ancient Rome in the Light of Recent Discoveries* (New York: Harcourt Brace, 1888), 235.

13. William Davies, *The Pilgrimage of the Tiber*, 2nd ed. (London: Sampson Low, 1875), 6.

14. Gaston Boissier, *Rome and Pompeii: Archaeological Rambles*, trans. D. Havelock Fisher (New York: G. P. Putnam's Sons, 1896), 322.

15. Nathaniel Hazeltine Carter, *Letters from Europe* (New York: G. & C. & H. Carvill, 1925), 175.

16. Neither Specchi nor Piranesi shows rafts, which at an earlier time were certainly a logical means of moving goods. Artistic license? Boats are more readily understood by viewers, and rafts are so utilitarian. This is not life on the Mississippi.

17. Letter to Mesdames de Blancey and de Neuilly, *Lettres historiques et critiques sur l'Italie, de Charles de Brosses*, vol. 2 (Paris: Ponthieu, 1797), 263.

18. Tobias Smollett, *The Works of Tobias Smollett*, vol. 8 (London: Bickers, 1872), 284.

19. For more see Tod A. Marder, "The Porto di Ripetta in Rome," *Journal of the Society of Architectural Historians* 39, no. 1 (March 1980): 28–56.

20. Elizabeth Chudleigh, *The Life and Memoirs of Elizabeth Chudleigh afterwards Mrs. Hervey and Countess of Bristol, commonly called Duchess of Kingston* (London: Randall, 1788), 13. "The Duke's nephew's persecution, and all the malicious gossip that, thank God, I do not in the least deserve, has given me a feeling of distaste for everything in England."

21. January 28, 1775, letter from Rome of Father John Thorpe, quoted in Claire Gervat, *Elizabeth: The Scandalous Life of an 18th Century Duchess* (London: Century, 2003), 126.

22. *The Manuscripts of his Grace the Duke of Rutland, K.G., Preserved at Belvoir Castle*, vol. 4 (London: Mackie, 1905), 237.

23. Joseph Addison, *The Works of the Right Honourable Joseph Addison*, vol. 1 (Chicago: George Bell, 1881), 471.

24. Humphrey Hody, *De graecis illustribus linguae graecae literarumque humaniorum* (London: Carol Davis, 1742), 108. The story is so good that Paolo Giovio ascribed it (absent the Tiber reference) to Theodore Gaza (c. 1398–c. 1475), another translator of Greek: "'Effugere hinc lubet,' inquit, "'postquam optima segetes in olfactu praepinguibus asini sordescunt.'" "It is fine time to leave here," he said, "since the best fruits grow foul in the noses of gross asses." Paolo Giovio, *Gli elogi degli uomini illustri*, in *Pauli Iovii opera*, vol. 8, ed. R. Meregazzi (Rome: Istituto Poligrafico dello Stato, 1972), 60.

25. Cassiodorus, *Variorum* 7.105.

26. Josephus, *Jewish Antiquities* 18.7.

27. Raphael Volaterranus, *Commentaria urbana*, bk. 22, fol. 305 (Rome, 1506), quoted

in Tilmann Buddensieg, "Gregory the Great, the Destroyer of Pagan Idols: The History of a Medieval Legend concerning the Decline of Ancient Art and Literature," *Journal of the Warburg and Courtauld Institutes* 28 (1965): 57.

28. "Zeekere Boer van Ostia, een oude Madaille van goud gevonden hebbende, is in hegtenis genomen, om te weeten, of hy'er niet meer heeft gevonden. Zoo werd men ongelukkig door zyn geluk. Zedert heeft 'er niemand meer willen graven of delven; De Kinkels vlugten 'er voor als de Drommel voor 't Kruis." Hendrik Doedyns, *Haagsche Mercurius*, April 29, 1699, no. 77, in *Haagsche Mercurius*, part 2 (Amsterdam: J. Ratelband, 1735), 541.

29. "Ho sentito dire, che vicino quelli speroni antichi del Ponte d'Orazio, che si vedono nel Tevere dritto S. Gio. de' Fiorentini incontro S. Spirito vi fu trovata tanta quantità di metallo, che ne furono empiti li schifi." Flaminio Vacco, *Memorie di varie antichità trovate in diversi luoghi della città di Roma* (Rome: Stamperia De Romanis, 1820), 20.

30. Ibid., 19–20.

31. Bernardo de Montfaucon, *Diarium italicum* (Paris: Joannem Anisson, 1702), 232.

32. Madame de Sévigné, March 18, 1690, in *Lettres de Madame de Sévigné de sa famille et de ses amis*, vol. 9 (Paris: Hachette, 1862), 489.

33. Quoted in Chrysostome Faucher, *Histoire du Cardinal de Polignac* (Paris: D'Houry, 1778), 236.

34. *Impresa privilegiata Tiberina, documenti legali ed autentici inservienti di pubblico ragguaglio* (Rome: Paolo Salviucci e figlio, 1819), 16.

35. Francesco Cancellieri, *Sagrestia Vaticana eretta dal regnante pontefice Pio Sesto* (Rome: Arcangelo Cassaletti nel Palazzo Massimi, 1784), 117.

36. Eraldo Pistoni, *Villa Torlonia e Mussolini* (Rome, 2009), 57. The author does not, alas, cite this point or give a date.

37. Gibbon, *Decline and Fall*, vol. 4, 36, 6.

38. Procopius, *Vandalic War* 4.9.5, trans. H. B. Dewing, Loeb ed. (Cambridge, MA: Harvard University Press, 1916).

39. Marcus Nathan Adler, *The Itinerary of Benjamin of Tudela* (London: Oxford University Press, 1907), 8.

40. Marie Thérèse Champagne and Ra'anan S. Boustan, "Walking in the Shadows of the Past: The Jewish Experience of Rome in the Twelfth Century," *Medieval Encounters* 17 (2011): 464–494.

41. Ibid.

42. Joseph Addison, *Remarks on Several parts of Italy, &c: in the years 1701, 1702, 1703*, in *The Works of the Late Right Honorable Joseph Addison, Esq*, vol. 2 (Birmingham, UK, 1761), 111.

43. Letter to Mesdames de Blancey and de Neuilly, trans. Lord Ronald Sutherland Gowers, from *Selections from the Letters of de Brosses* (London: Kegan Paul, Trench, Trübner, 1897), 143.

44. John Chetwode Eustace, *A Classical Tour through Italy in 1802*, 7th ed., vol. 3 (London: Thomas Tegg, 1841), 427.

45. Ronald T. Ridley, *The Pope's Archaeologist: The Life and Times of Carlo Fea* (Rome: Quasar, 2000), 207.

46. Ibid.

47. William Jesse, *The Life of George Brummell, Esq., Commonly Called Beau Brummell*, vol. 1 (Philadelphia: Carey and Hart, 1844), 45.

48. *Literary Gazette and Journal of Belles Lettres, Arts, Science, etc.*, October 16, 1819, no 143.

49. *Annual Register or a View of the History, Politics, and Literature for the Year 1819*, vol. 61 (London: Baldwin, Cradock, and Joy, 1820), 59.

50. *Literary Gazette and Journal of Belles Lettres, Arts, Science, etc.*, October 16, 1819, no. 143.

51. Ibid.

52. Ibid.

53. *Documenti legali ed autentici inservienti di pubblico ragguaglio delle operazioni eseguitesi nell'estate dell'anno 1819 per la prima stagione delle escavazioni nel fiume Tevere della società denominata Impresa Privilegiata Tiberina* (Rome: Paolo Salviucci e Figlio, 1819), 41, 14.

54. William Jesse, *The Life of George Brummell Commonly Called Beau Brummell*, vol. 1 (London: Sunders and Otley, 1844), 197. James Cheney of the Getty Museum suggests a possible interpolation is "My last like my first attempts have failed." The only argument against this is that the printed text clearly marks "at" as a separate word from "—s." The original manuscript, wherever that may be, might clear up the matter.

55. Giuseppe Gioachino Belli, *I sonetti romaneschi*, vol. 1 (Città di Castello, Italy: S. Lapi, 1906), 59.

56. Mrs. Hawthorne, *Notes in England and Italy* (New York: Putnam & Son, 1871), 545.

57. Nathaniel Hawthorne, *Passages from the French and Italian Note-Books of Nathaniel Hawthorne*, vol. 1 (Boston: James R. Osgood, 1872), 136.

58. "Numismata omnis generis educi in dies," Bernard De Montfaucon, *Diarium Italicum* (Paris: Joannem Amesson, 1702), 232.

59. Rodolfo Lanciani, *Ruins and Excavations of Ancient Rome* (New York: Harcourt Brace, 1897), 27.

60. Lanciani, *Ancient Rome in the Light of Recent Discoveries*, 258.

61. See Eric R. Varner, *Mutilation and Transformation: Damnatio Memoriae and Roman Imperial Portraiture* (Leiden: Brill, 2004), for more on individual portraits.

62. Lanciani, *Ancient Rome in the Light of Recent Discoveries*, 255–256.

63. Vannoccio Biringuccio, *De la pirotechnia* (C. Navo, 1540), 166.

64. Joseph-Jérôme de Lalande, *Voyage d'un françois en Italie: Fait dans les années 1765 & 1766*, vol. 4 (Paris: Chez Desaint, 1769), 544, "On ne peut pas imaginer une situation plus heureuse pour un spectacle de cette espèce; on le voit de tous côtés, la girandole formée par 4,500 fusées qui partent à la fois, et se répandent circulairement en forme de parasol, est la plus belle chose que j'aie vu en fait d'artifice."

65. Quoted in J. Fleming, *Robert Adam and His Circle in Edinburgh and Rome* (London: John Murray, 1978), 177.

66. Charlotte Anne Waldie Eaton, *Rome in the Nineteenth Century: Containing a Complete Account of the Ruins of the Ancient City, the Remains of the Middle Ages, and the Monuments of Modern Times* (1820; London: G. Bell 1892), 3:179.

67. Charles Dickens, *Pictures from Italy* (London: Penguin Classics, 1998), 160.

68. Johann Wolfgang von Goethe, *Italian Journey, 1786–1788*, trans. W. H. Auden (London: Penguin, 1962), 348. Robert Southey (1784–1843) also has a few words on the subject. See his *Letters from England: By Don Manuel Alvarez Espriella* (1807).

69. John Poole, *Crotchets in the Air; or an (Un)scientific Account of a Balloon-Trip: In a Familiar Letter to a Friend* (London: Henry Colburn, 1838), 80.

70. Amerindo Camilli, *Filastrocche fanciullesche di Roma*, in *Archivio per lo studio delle tradizioni popolari*, diretta da G. Pitrè e S. Salomone–Marino, vol. 23 (Nologna: Forni Editore Bologna, 1907), 191. The author collected this among other verse in the area of Porta Trionfale in November 1905, well within memory of the man being discussed. On Roman street games he refers to Acchiapparèlla, in which two boys pull a stretched rope in imitation of a saw, while reciting the poem. In recent years, Mastro Titto has been replaced by the anonymous Mastro Ciccio, "Master Fatty," a name more suitable to a grocer than a hangman. See Giggi Zanazzo, *Usi, costumi e pregiudizi del popolo di Roma* (Turin: Società Tipografico-Editrice Nazionale, 1908), 329.

71. *Mastro Titta, il boia di Roma: Memorie di un carnefice scritte da lui stesso* (Rome: Edoardo Perino, 1891). The real author is believed to be Ernesto Mezzabotta, one of the publisher's known hacks.

72. D. Domenico D'Aquino, *Il Tebro incoronato* (Naples: Antonio Bulifon, 1680), *l'irrigator delle latine arene*, p. 61; *il valoroso Innondator Latino*, p. 121.

73. Giammaria Mazzuchelli, *Gli scrittori d'Italia*, vol. 2, pt. 1 (Brescia: Giambatista Bossini, 1753), 911–912.

74. George Arthur Greene, *Italian Lyrists of Today: Translation from Contemporary Italian Poetry* (London: Elkin Mathew and John Lane, 1893), 78–79.

75. Giuseppe Ungaretti, *A Major Selection of the Poetry of Giuseppe Ungaretti*, trans. Diego Bastianutti (Toronto: Exile Editions, 1997), 309.

76. Basic biographical details can be found in Camille de Tournon, *Études statistiques sur Rome et la partie occidentale des états romains*, vol. 1 (Paris: Firman Didot Frères, 1855), avant propos.

77. Quoted in Susan Vandiver Nicassio, *Imperial City: Rome under Napoleon* (Chicago: University of Chicago Press, 2005), 188.

78. Giuliano Friz, "La popolazione di Roma dal 1770 al 1900," *Archivio Economico dell'Unificazione Italiana*, series 2, vol. 19 (1974), IRI Rome, in Susan Vandiver Nicassio, *Imperial City: Rome, Romans, and Napoleon, 1796–1815* (Chicago: University of Chicago Press, 2005), 101–102.

79. Robert Ridley, *The Eagle and the Spade* (Cambridge: Cambridge University Press, 2009), 64.

80. Zanazzo, *Usi, costumi e pregiudizi*, 210–211, "Ogni tanto vedevio un sordato francese imbriaco, co' la sciabbola sfoderata, ggirà ppe' le strade de Roma, bbaccajanno e insurtanno chiunque incontrava."

81. *The Naval Chronicle*, vol. 3, ed. James Stanier Clarke (London: Bunney & Gold, 1800), 223.

82. Frances Milton Trollope, *A Visit to Italy*, vol. 2 (London: R. Bentley, 1842), 329.

83. *Catholic Register and Magazine*, no. 61 (March 1850), vol. 11, 20.

84. Edward Arnold, in Augustus Hare, *Story of My Life* (London, 1900), 6:146.

85. H. Bathurst, *Memoirs and Correspondence of Dr. H. Bathurst, Bishop of Norwich*, ed. Tryphena Thistlethwayte (London: Richard Bently, 1853), 287.

86. H. de Crespigny, in Constance Charlotte Elisa Lennox, Lady Russell, *The Rose Goddess and Other Sketches of Mystery & Romance* (London: Longmans, 1910), 112–113.

87. Mariano D'Ayala, *Poesie edite e postume di Alessandro Poerio: La prima volta raccolte con cenni intorno alla sua vita* (Florence: Le Monnier, 1852), 75–76.

88. *Catholic Register and Magazine*, no. 61 (March 1850), vol. 11, 20.

89. Ibid.

90. See also "The Macabre Mystery of the Deathly Cameos," Order of the Good Death, http://www.orderofthegooddeath.com/macabre-mystery-deathly-cameos#.VxvsXTrDfFk.

91. Strother A. Smith, *The Tiber and Its Tributaries: Their Natural History and Classical Associations* (London: Longmans, Green, 1877), 80.

92. Nathaniel Hawthorne, *Passages of French and Italian Notebooks of Nathaniel Hawthorne*, vol. 10 of *Complete Works* (Boston: Houghton Mifflin, 1871), 65.

93. Ferdinand Gregorovius, *The Roman Journals of Ferdinand Gregorovius, 1852–1874* (London: George Bell & Sons, 1907), 367.

94. G. Spadolini, *I Repubblicani dopo l'unità* (Florence, 1980), 161–163.

95. *Rivista Illustrata Settimanale* (Milan: Stabilimento F. Garbini, March 1870), 2.

96. *Strenna dei Romanisti, Natale di Roma*, 1952 (Rome: Straderini, 1952), 115–116.

97. Paul Boyton, *The Story of Paul Boyton: Voyages on All the Great Rivers of the World* (Boyton, 1892), 173–174.

98. Alessandro Portelli, *The Order Has Been Carried Out: History, Memory, and Meaning of a Nazi Massacre in Rome* (New York: Palgrave Macmillan, 2015), 234.

99. Robert Katz, *The Battle for Rome: The Germans, the Allies, the Partisans, and the Pope* (New York: Simon & Schuster, 2003), 331.

100. Adriano Ossicini, *Un'isola sul Tevere: Il Fascismo al di là del ponte* (Rome: Editori riuniti, 2005).

EPILOGUE

1. Edward Burton, *A Description of the Antiquities and Other Curiosities of Rome*, 2nd ed., vol. 1 (London: C. & J. Rivington, 1828), 180.

2. Robert Mozley, *Letters from Rome on the Occasion of the Œcumenical Council, 1869–1870*, vol. 1 (London: Longmans, Green, 1891), 301–302.

3. "Lorsque le Tibre inonde Rome, tous les rats du quartier se réfugient sur la partie du pavé du Panthéon, qui est placée au-dessous de la lanterne, où on les fait attaquer par des troupes de chats." M. de Stendhal, *Promenades dans Rome*, vol. 1 (Paris: Delaunay, 1829), 350.

4. Strother A. Smith, *The Tiber and Its Tributaries: Their Natural History and Classical Associations* (London: Longmans, Green, 1877), 81.

5. Ugo Pesce, *Come siamo entrati in Roma* (Milan: Fratelli Treves, 1895), 277–278.

6. Ferdinand Gregorovius, *The Roman Journals of Ferdinand Gregorovius, 1852–1874* (London: George Bell & Sons, 1907), 393.

7. Smith, *Tiber and Its Tributaries*, 81.

8. Pesce, *Come siamo entrati in Roma*, 280.

9. Gregorovius, *Roman Journals*, 393.

10. Daniel Pick, *Rome or Death* (London: Pimlico, 2006), 71.

11. Smith, *Tiber and Its Tributaries*, 121.

12. G. Heiken, *The Seven Hills of Rome: A Geological Tour of the Eternal City* (Princeton, NJ: Princeton University Press, 2005), 77.

13. Lady Isabel Burton, *The Life of Captain Sir Richard F. Burton*, vol. 2 (New York: Appleton, 1893), 22.

14. *Tablet: The International Catholic News Weekly*, November 2, 1872, 15. Pareto was the father of economist and sociologist Vilfredo Pareto.

15. Isabel Burton, *Life of Captain Sir Richard F. Burton*, 2:23.

16. Rodolfo Lanciani, *Notes from Rome* (Rome: British School at Rome, 1988), 56–57.

17. A. Ronna, *Le Tibre et les travaux du Tibre* (Paris: Chamerot et Renouard, 1898), 126S.

18. Rodolfo Lanciani, *Ancient Rome in the Light of Recent Discoveries* (New York: Harcourt Brace, 1888), 234.

19. *Launceston (Australia) Examiner*, December 7, 1900, 6.

20. *Sacramento Union*, February 15, 1915.

21. *Canberra Times*, December 20, 1937, 1.

22. Rodolfo Lanciani, *Ruins and Excavations of Ancient Rome*, 14.

SELECT BIBLIOGRAPHY

The source material for the Tiber is diffuse enough to warrant a book of its own.
Space does not permit a full accounting of everything that went into this book,
but the following were among the more useful in the research.

Adam of Usk. *Chronicle of Adam of Usk*. Translated by Sir Edward Maunde Thompson.
London: Henry Frowde, 1904.

Addison, Joseph. *The Works of the Right Honourable Joseph Addison*. Vol 1. Chicago:
George Bell, 1881.

Adler, Marcus Nathan. *The Itinerary of Benjamin of Tudela*. London: Oxford University
Press, 1907.

Albericis, Iacobo de. *Historiarum sanctissimae et gloriosiss. Virginis Deiparae de populo
almae urbis compendium*. Rome: Nicolai Muti, 1599.

Aldrete, Gregory S. *Floods of the Tiber in Ancient Rome*. Baltimore: Johns Hopkins
University Press, 2007.

Alexander, David. "The Reclamation of Val-di-Chiana, Tuscany." *Annals of the
Association of American Geographers* 74, no. 4 (1984): 527–550.

Al-Maqqarī, Aḥmad ibn Muḥammad. *The History of the Mohammedan Dynasties in
Spain*. Translated by Pascual de Gayangos. London: Oriental Translation Fund, 1840.

Ammianus Macellinus. *The Roman History of Ammianus Marcellinus*. Translated by C.
D. Yonge. London: G. Bell & Sons, 1911.

Anonymous. *Cronica dell'anonimo Romano*. In *Antiquitates Italicae Medii Aevi*, vol. 3,
edited by Ludovico Muratori. Milan: Typographia Societatis Palatinae, 1740.

Bacci, Pietro Giacomo. *Vita S. Philippi Nerii Florentini*. Rome: Vitalis Mascardi, 1645.

Bander, Peter. *The Prophecies of Malachy*. New York: Alba House, 1970.

Bathurst, Henry. *Memoirs and Correspondence of Dr. H. Bathurst, Bishop of Norwich*.
Edited by Tryphena Thistlethwayte. London: Richard Bentley, 1853.

Beard, Mary, John North, and Simon Price. *Religions of Rome: A Sourcebook*. Cambridge:
Cambridge University Press, 1998.

Bedini, Silvio A. *The Pope's Elephant: An Elephant's Journey from Deep in India to the
Heart of Rome*. Nashville, TN: J. S. Sanders, 1997.

Belli, Giuseppe Gioachino. *I sonetti romaneschi*. Vol. 1. Città di Castello, Italy: S. Lapi,
1906.

Benedict (monk of St. Andrew). *Il chronicon di Benedetto, monaco di S. Andrea
del Soratte*. Edited by Giuseppe Zucchetti. Fonti per la storia d'Italia pubblicate
dall'Istituto Storico, vol. 20. Rome: Tipografia del Senato, 1920.

Biondo Flavio. *Italy Illuminated*. Vol. 1. Translated by Jeffrey A. White. Cambridge, MA:
Harvard University Press, 2005.

Bonini, Filippo Maria. *Il Tevere incatenato*. Rome: F. Moneta, 1663.

Borgatti, Mariano. *The Castle of St. Angelo*. Rome: Gaecanot Garzoni Provenzani, 1911.

Bottigheimer, Ruth B. *Fairy Godfather: Straparola, Venice, and the Fairy Tale Tradition*. Philadelphia: University of Pennsylvania Press, 2002.

Boyton, Paul. *The Story of Paul Boyton: Voyages on All the Great Rivers of the World*. New York: Boyton, 1892.

Brosses, Charles de. *Lettres historiques et critiques sur l'Italie, de Charles de Brosses*. Paris: Ponthieu, 1797.

——. *Selections from the Letters of de Brosses*. Translated by Ronald Sutherland Gower. London: Kegan Paul, Trench, Trübner, 1897.

Burchard, Johannes. *Pope Alexander VI and His Court: Extracts from the Latin Diary of Johannes Burchardus*. Edited by F. L. Glaser. New York: N. L. Brown, 1921.

Burnet, Gilbert. *Burnet's Travels: Or, a Collection of Letters to the Hon. Robert Boyle Esq.* London: P. Savouret and W. Fenner, 1738.

Burton, Edward. *A Description of the Antiquities and Other Curiosities of Rome*. 2nd ed. London: C. & J. Rivington, 1828.

Burton, Lady Isabel. *The Life of Captain Sir Richard F. Burton*. New York: Appleton, 1893.

Byron, George Gordon. *Letters and Journals of Lord Byron: With Notices of His Life*. London: John Murray, 1830.

Callistus, Nicephorus. *Historia ecclesiastica*. Frankfurt: Oporinus & Hervagius, 1561.

Carducci, Giosuè. *Carducci: A Selection of His Poems, with Verse Translations Notes and Three Introductory Essays*. London: Longmans, Green, 1913.

Cariello, Nicola. *I Saraceni nel Lazio, VIII–X secolo*. Rome: Edilazio, 2001.

Carter, Nathaniel Hazeltine. *Letters from Europe*. New York: G. & C. & H. Carvill, 1925.

Cassiodorus. *The Variae of Cassiodorus Senator*. Translated by S. J. B. Barnish. Liverpool: Liverpool University Press, 1992.

Catullus, Tibullus, and Pervigilium Veneris. Translated by F. W. Cornish. Cambridge, MA: Harvard University Press, 1921.

Cellini, Benvenuto. *The Autobiography of Benvenuto Cellini*. Translated by J. Addington Symonds. New York: P. F. Collier and Son, 1910.

——. *Opere: Vita, trattati, rime, lettere*. Rome: Rizzoli, 1968.

Champagne, Marie Thérèse, and Ra'anan S. Boustan. "Walking in the Shadows of the Past: The Jewish Experience of Rome in the Twelfth Century." *Medieval Encounters* 17 (2011): 464–496.

Christys, Ann Rosemary. *Christians in Al-Andalus, 711–1000*. London: Routledge, 2002.

Chudleigh, Elizabeth. *The Life and Memoirs of Elizabeth Chudleigh afterwards Mrs. Hervey and Countess of Bristol, commonly called Duchess of Kingston*. London: Randall, 1788.

Cicero. *Ad Atticum*. Translated by E. O. Winstedt. Cambridge, MA: Harvard University Press, 1912.

——. *Pro Roscio Amerino: Defense Speeches by Cicero*. Translated by D. H. Berry. Oxford: Oxford University Press, 2000.

Coffin, David. *Gardens and Gardening in Papal Rome*. Princeton, NJ: Princeton University Press, 1991.

———. *The Villa in the Life of Renaissance Rome*. Princeton, NJ: Princeton University Press, 1979.

Crook, John Anthony. *Law and Life of Rome, 90 BC to AD 212*. Ithaca, NY: Cornell University Press, 1976.

Curione, Celio Secondo. *Pasquillorum tomi duo*. Basel: Johannes Oporinus, 1544.

D'Aquino, Domenico. *Il Tebro incoronato*. Naples: Antonio Bulifon, 1680.

Davies, William. *The Pilgrimage of the Tiber*. 2nd ed. London: Sampson Low, 1875.

Della Vida, G. Levi. "The 'Bronze Era' in Moslem Spain." *Journal of the American Oriental Society*, no. 3 (1943).

Del Monte, Crescenzo. *Sonetti iudaico-romaneschi, sonetti romaneschi, prose e versioni*. Florence: Giuntina, 2007.

De Sanctis, Luigi. *Roma papale*. Florence: Tipofrafia Claudiana, 1865.

DeVita, Oretta Zanini. *Popes, Peasants, and Shepherds: Recipes and Lore from Rome and Lazio*. Translated by Maureen B. Fant. Berkeley: University of California Press, 2013.

Dickens, Charles. *Pictures from Italy*. London: Penguin, 1998.

Dionysius of Halicarnassus. *Roman Antiquities*. Translated by Earnest Cary. Cambridge, MA: Harvard University Press, 1950.

Donatus, Alexander. *De urbe Roma*. Rome, 1638.

D'Onofrio, Cesare. *Il Tevere e Roma: Con documenti e disegni inediti*. Rome: Staderini, 1957.

Duchesne, Louis, ed. *Liber pontificalis*. Paris: Ernest Thorin, 1892.

Eaton, Charlotte Anne Waldie. *Rome in the Nineteenth Century: Containing a Complete Account of the Ruins of the Ancient City, the Remains of the Middle Ages, and the Monuments of Modern Times*. London: G. Bell, 1892.

Emerick, Judson J. *The Tempietto del Clitunno near Spoleto*. State College, PA: Penn State University Press, 1998.

Esposito, Anne. "Le inondazioni del Tevere tra tardo medioevo e prima età moderna: Leggende, racconti, testimonianze." *Mélanges de l'École Française de Rome*. Rome: École Française de Rome, 2006, 7–12.

Espriella, Don Manuel Alvarez [Robert Southey]. *Letters from England by Don Manuel Alvarez Espriella*. London: Longman, Hurst, Rees, Orme and Brown, 1807.

Eustace, John Chetwode. *A Classical Tour through Italy in 1802*. 7th ed. Vol 3. London: Thomas Tegg, 1841.

Evelyn, John. *The Diary of John Evelyn*. Edited by Austin Dobson. Cambridge: Cambridge University Press, 1906.

Faucher, Chrysostome. *Histoire du Cardinal de Polignac*. Paris: D'Houry, 1778.

Fea, Carlo. *Dissertazione sulle rovine di Roma*. 1784.

Fleming, John. *Robert Adam and His Circle in Edinburgh and Rome*. London: John Murray, 1978.

Flodoard of Reims. *The "Annals" of Flodoard of Reims, 919–966*. Edited and translated by Bernard S. Bachrach and Steven Fanning. Peterborough, ON: Broadview, 2004.

Fonzio, Bartolomeo. *Letters to His Friends.* Translated by Martin Davies. Cambridge, MA: Harvard University Press. 2011.

Froissart, John. *Sir John Froissart's Chronicles of England, Bk II.* Translated by Thomas Johnes. London: Longman Hurst, Rees and Orme, 1806.

Gallonio, Antonio. *Vita beati Neri.* Rome: L. Zannetti, 1600.

Gaster, Mose. *The Chronicles of Jerahmeel.* London: Royal Asiatic Society, 1899.

Gellius, Aulus. *Attic Nights.* Translated by J. C. Rolfe. Cambridge, MA: Harvard University Press, 1927.

Gervat, Claire. *Elizabeth: The Scandalous Life of an 18th Century Duchess.* London: Century, 2003.

Gherardi, Jacopo. *Il diario romano di Jacopo Gherardi da Volterra dal VII settembre MCCCCLXXIX al XI agosto MCCCCLXXXIV.* Edited by Enrico Carusi. Città di Castello, Italy: S. Lapi, 1904.

Gibbon, Edward. *Decline and Fall of the Roman Empire.* Edited by J. B. Bury. London: Methuen, 1909.

Gigli, Giacinto. *Diario romano, 1608–1670.* Rome: Tumminelli, 1958.

Giovio, Paolo. *De optima victus ratione.* Rome, 1527.

———. *De romanis piscibus libellus ad Ludovicum Borbonium Cardinalem amplissimum.* Rome: Francesco Minuzio Calvo, 1524.

———. *Pauli Iovii opera, dialogi et descriptiones.* Edited by Ernesto Travi and Maria Grazia Penco. Rome: Instituto Poligrafico e Zecca dello Stato Libreria dello Stato, 1984.

Goethe, Johann Wolfgang von. *Italian Journey, 1786–1788.* Translated by W. H. Auden. London: Penguin, 1962.

Gowers, Emily. "The Anatomy of Rome from Capitol to Cloaca." *Journal of Roman Studies* 85 (1995).

Gregorius, Magister, and Robert B. C. Huygens. *Narracio de mirabilibus urbis Romae.* Leiden: Brill, 1970.

Gregorovius, Ferdinand. *The Roman Journals of Ferdinand Gregorovius, 1852–1874.* London: George Bell & Sons, 1907.

———. *Wanderjahre in Italien.* Vienna: Bernina, 1957.

Gregory of Tours. *History of the Franks.* Translated by L. Thorpe. London: Penguin, 1974.

Grüll, Tibor. "The Legendary Fate of Pontius Pilate." *Classica et Mediaevalia* 61 (2010): 151–176.

Guéraud, O. "Un vase ayant contenu un échantillon de blé." *Journal of Juristic Papyrology* 4 (1950): 107–115.

Hare, Augustus C. J. *Story of My Life.* London: G. Allen, 1900.

Harff, Arnold Ritter von. *Die Pilgerfahrt des Ritters Arnold von Harff.* Cologne: J. M. Heberle, 1860.

Harff, Arnold Ritter von, and Helmut Brall-Tuche. *Rom, Jerusalem, Santiago: Das Pilgertagebuch des Ritters Arnold von Harff, 1996–1498.* Cologne: Böhlau, 2007.

Hawthorne, Nathaniel. *Passages of French and Italian Notebooks of Nathaniel Hawthorne.* Vol. 10 of *Complete Works.* Boston: Houghton Mifflin, 1871.

Heiken, G. *The Seven Hills of Rome: A Geological Tour of the Eternal City*. Princeton, NJ: Princeton University Press, 2005.

Herman, Eleanor. *Mistress of the Vatican: The True Story of Olimpia Maidalchini, the Secret Female Pope*. New York: William Morrow, 2008.

Hodgkin, Thomas. *Italy and Her Invaders: The Imperial Restoration, 535–553*. Vol. 4. Oxford: Oxford University Press, 1896.

Holland, L. A. *Janus and the Bridge*. Rome: Memoirs of the American Academy in Rome, 1961.

Holland, L. A., and L. B. Holland. "Down the Tiber on a Raft." *Archaeology* 3 (1950): 87–94.

———. 1950. "The Tiber in Primitive Commerce." *American Journal of Archaeology* 54:261–262.

Hook, Judith. *The Sack of Rome, 1527*. New York: Macmillan, 1972.

Hopkins, John. "The Cloaca Maxima and the Monumental Manipulation of Water in Archaic Rome." *Waters of Rome*, no. 4 (March 2007).

Hübner, Baron. *The Life and Times of Sixtus the Fifth*. Vol. 1. Translated by Hubert E. H. Jerningham. London: Longmans, Green, 1872.

Hunt, A. S., and C. C. Edgarm, eds. *Select Papyri: Non-literary Papyri*. Cambridge, MA: Harvard University Press, 1937.

Infessura, Stephani. *Diario della città di Roma di Stephano Infessura scribasenato*. Edited by Oreste Rommasini. Rome: Forzani E. C. Tipografi del Senato, 1890.

Josephus. *Jewish Antiquities*. Translated by H. St. J. Thackeray. Cambridge, MA: Harvard University Press, 1927.

Juvenal. *Juvenal and Persius*. Translated by G. G. Ramsey. Cambridge, MA: Harvard University Press, 1918.

———. *A Literal Translation of the Satires of Juvenal and Persius*. Translated by Martin Madan. Dublin: A. Watson, 1822.

Katz, Robert. *The Battle for Rome: The Germans, the Allies, the Partisans, and the Pope*. New York: Simon & Schuster, 2003.

Keay, Simon, Martin Millett, and Kristian Strutt. "Recent Archaeological Survey at Portus." *Memoirs of the American Academy in Rome*. Supplementary Volumes. Vol. 6. Rome, 2008.

Krautheimer, Richard. *Rome: Profile of a City*. Princeton, NJ: Princeton University Press, 1980.

Kreutz, Barbara M. *Before the Normans: Southern Italy in the Ninth Century*. Philadelphia: University of Pennsylvania Press, 2011.

Labat, Jean-Baptiste. *Voyages du P. Labat en Espagne et en Italie*. Paris: Saint Paul, 1720.

Lagunes, Laria Margarita Segarra. *Il Tevere e Roma: Storia di una simbiosi*. Rome: Gangerni, 2016.

Lalande, Joseph-Jérôme de. *Voyage d'un françois en Italie: Fait dans les années 1765 & 1766*. Paris: Chez Desaint, 1769.

Lanciani, Rodolfo Amadeo. *Pagan and Christian Rome*. London: Macmillan, 1895.

———. *The Ruins and Excavations of Ancient Rome*. Boston: Houghton Mifflin, 1897.

Landucci, Luca. *A Florentine Diary from 1450 to 1516*. Translated by by Alice de Rosen Jervis. London: J. M. Dent & Sons, 1927.

Lankila, Tommi P. "The Saracen Raid of Rome in 846: An Example of Maritime *ghazw*." In *Travelling through Time: Essays in Honour of Kaj Öhrnberg*, edited by Sylvia Akar, Jaakko Hämeen-Anttila, and Inka Nokso-Koivisto, 93–120. *Studia Orientalia*, vol. 114. Helsinki, 2013.

Le Gall, Joël. *Le Tibre: Fleuve de Rome dans l'antiquité*. Paris: Presses universitaires de France, 1953.

——— . *Recherches sur le culte du Tibre*. Paris: Presses universitaires de France, 1953.

Le Saige, Jacques. *Voyage de Jacques Le Saige*. Douai, France: Adam d'Aubers, 1851.

Liudprand of Cremona. *The Complete Works of Liudprand of Cremona*. Translated by Paolo Squatriti. Washington, DC: Catholic University of America Press, 2007.

Lorenzetti, Roberto. *Studi e materiali per una storia sociale e economica della Sabina*. Rieti, Italy: Cerbara di Città di Castello, 1989.

Lucian of Samosata. Translated by H. W. Fowler. Oxford: Henry Frowde, 1905.

Marder, Tod A. "The Porto di Ripetta in Rome." *Journal of the Society of Architectural Historians* 39, no. 1 (March 1980): 28–56.

Marsh, David, trans. *Renaissance Fables: Aesopic Prose by Leon Battista Alberti, Bartolomeo Scala, Leonardo da Vinci, Bernardino Baldi*. Tempe: Arizona Center for Medieval and Renaissance Studies, 2004.

Martial. *Epigrams*. Translated by Walter C. A. Ker. Cambridge, MA: Harvard University Press, 1919.

Mattingly, D. J. "The Feeding of Imperial Rome: The Mechanics of the Food Supply System." In *Ancient Rome: The Archaeology of the Eternal City*, edited by Jon Coulston and Hazel Dodge, 142–165. Monograph 54. Oxford University School of Archaeology, 2000.

Misson, Maximilien. *A New Voyage to Italy*. London, 1714.

——— . *Nouveau voyage d'Italie*. The Hague: Henri van Bulderen, 1702.

Montaigne, Michel de. *The Journal of Montaigne's Travels in Italy by Way of Switzerland and Germany in 1580 and 1581*. Translated and edited by W. G. Waters. Vol. 2. London: John Murray, 1903.

Montfaucon, Bernard de. *Diarium italicum*. Paris: Joannem Amesson, 1702.

Morelli, Roberta. "Gli uomini del Tevere: Fonti per la storia degli edili Romani tra 1450 e 1550." In *Le technicien dans la cité en Europe occidental, 1250—1650*, edited by Mathieu Arnoux et Pierre Monnet, 77–92. Rome: École Française de Rome, 2004.

Morgan, Lady Sydney Owenson. *Italy*. Vol. 2. London: Henry Colburn, 1824.

Mozley, Robert. *Letters from Rome on the Occasion of the Œcumenical Council, 1869–1870*. London: Longmans, Green, 1891.

Muratorio, Ludovico Antonio. *Antiquitates Italicae Medii Aevi*. Milan: Typographia Societatis Palatinae, 1740.

Myers, Henry A. *The Book of Emperors: A Translation of the Middle High German Kaiserchronik*. Morgantown: West Virginia University Press, 2013.

Namatianus, Rutilis. *De reditu suo*. Translated by J. Wright Duff and Arnold M. Duff. New York: Loeb, 1934.

Newman, Paul B. *Daily Life in the Middle Ages*. London: McFarland, 2001.

Newth, Michael A. H., ed. and trans. *Fierabras and Floripas: A French Epic Allegory*. New York: Italica, 2010.

Nicassio, Susan Vandiver. *Imperial City: Rome, Romans, and Napoleon, 1796–1815*. Welwyn Garden City, UK: Ravenhall Books, 2005.

Nixon, C. E. V., and Barbara Saylor Rodgers. *In Praise of Later Roman Emperors: The Panegyrici Latini*. Berkeley: University of California Press, 1994.

Orbaan, Johannes Albertus Franciscus. *La Roma di Sisto V negli avvisi*. Rome: Società Romana di Storia Patria, 1910.

———. *Sixtine Rome*. New York: Baker and Taylor, 1911.

Ossicini, Adriano. *Un'isola sul Tevere: Il Fascismo al di là del ponte*. Rome: Editori riuniti, 2005.

Pardoe, Rosemary, and Darroll Pardoe. *The Female Pope: The Mystery of Pope Joan; The First Complete Documentation of the Facts behind the Legend*. Wellingborough, UK: Crucible, 1988.

Pastor, Ludwig von. *History of the Popes from the Close of the Middle Ages*. London: Kegan Paul, Trench, Trübner, 1900.

Patterson, David O. "Adversos paganos: Disaster, Dragons, and Episcopal Authority in Gregory of Tours." *Comitatus: A Journal of Medieval and Renaissance Studies* 44 (2013).

Pesce, Ugo. *Come siamo entrati in Roma*. Milan: Fratelli Treves, 1895.

Petronius. *Satyricon*. Translated by Alfred R. Allinson. New York: Panurge, 1930.

Piccolomini, Aeneas Sylvius. *The Tale of the Two Lovers*. Translated by Flora Grierson. London: Constable, 1929.

Pick, Daniel. *Rome or Death*. London: Pimlico, 2006.

Piozzi, Hester Lynch. *Observations and Reflections Made in the Course of a Journey through France, Italy, and Germany*. Vol. 1. London: A. Strahan and T. Cadell, 1789.

Pius II. *The Commentaries of Pius II*. Translated by Florence Alden Gragg. Northampton, MA: Smith College Studies in History, 1937.

Platina, Bartolomeo. *Lives of the Popes*. Translated by W. Benham. Vol. 1. London: Griffith, Farran, Okeden & Welsh, 1888.

Pliny. *Letters*. Translated by Betty Radice. Cambridge, MA: Harvard University Press, 1969.

Pliny the Elder. *Natural History*. Edited and translated by H. Rackham. 10 vols. Cambridge, MA: Harvard University Press, 1938–1962.

Portelli, Alessandro. *The Order Has Been Carried Out: History, Memory, and Meaning of a Nazi Massacre in Rome*. New York: Palgrave Macmillan, 2015.

Procopius. *Vandalic War*. Translated by H. B. Dewing. London: Heinemann, 1916.

Propertius. *Elegies*. Translated by G. P. Goold. Cambridge, MA: Harvard University Press, 1990.

Pulvers, Marvin. *Roman Fountains: 2000 Fountains in Rome; A Complete Collection*. Rome: L'Erma di Bretschneider, 2002.

Quinlan-McGrath, Mary. "Blosius Palladius, 'Suburbanum Augustini Chisii': Introduction, Latin Text, and English Translation." *Humanistica Lovaniensia: Journal of Neo-Latin Studies* 39 (1990).

Rabelais, François. *The Complete Works of François Rabelais*. Translated by Donald M. Frame. Berkeley: University of California Press, 1991.

Rendina, Claudia. *Guida insolita ai misteri, ai segretti, alle leggende e alle curiosità del Tevere*. Rome: Tradizioni Italiane Newton, 1999.

Rickman, Geoffrey. *The Corn Supply of Ancient Rome*. Oxford: Clarendon, 1980.

Ridley, Robert. *The Eagle and the Spade*. Cambridge: Cambridge University Press, 2009.

Ridley, Ronald T. *The Pope's Archaeologist: The Life and Times of Carlo Fea*. Rome: Quasar, 2000.

Rinne, Katherine W. "Water: The Currency of Cardinals in Late Renaissance Rome." In *La civiltà delle acque tra Medioevo e Rinascimento*, edited by A. Calzona and D. Lamberini, 367–387. Florence: Olshki, 2010.

Roger of Hoveden. In *Monumenta Germaniae historica*. SS.27. Edited by G. H. Pertz. Hannover: Impensis Bibliopolii Hahniani, 1885.

Ronna, A. *Le Tibre et les travaux du Tibre*. Paris: Chamerot et Renouard, 1898.

Rowland, Ingrid. *The Culture of the High Renaissance*. Cambridge: Cambridge University Press, 1998.

Ruiz, Juan. *The Book of Good Love of the Archpriest of Hita*. Translated by Elisha Kent Kane. Newark, DE: William Edwin Rudge, 1933.

Sallares, Robert. *Malaria and Rome: A History of Malaria in Ancient Italy*. New York: Oxford University Press, 2002.

Sannazaro, Jacopo. *Opera omnia latine scripta*. Venice: Aldus Manutius, 1535.

Sanudo, Marino. *I diarii di Marino Sanuto (MCCCCXCVI–MDXXXIII) dall' autografo Marciano ital. cl. VII codd. CDXIX–CDLXXVII*. Venice: F. Visentini, 1879–1903.

Saxoferrato, Bartolomeo de. *Tyberiadis: Tractatus de fluminibus*. Bonn: Ioannes Roscius, 1576.

Scobie, A. "Slums, Sanitation, and Mortality in the Roman World." *Klio* 68 (1986): 399–433.

Seneca. *On Taking One's Own Life—Moral Letter to Lucilius*. Translated by Richard Mott Gummere. London: Heinemann, 1961.

Setton, Kenneth. *The Papacy and the Levant, 1240–1571*. Philadelphia: American Philosophical Society, 1983.

Sidonius Apollinaris. *Sidonius: Poems and Letters*. Edited and translated by W. B. Anderson. Cambridge, MA: Harvard University Press, 1936–1965.

Sigismondo dei Conti da Foligno. *Le storie de' suoi tempi dal 1475 al 1510*. Rome: G. Barbera, 1883.

Smith, Norman A. F. "The Roman Dams of Subiaco." *Technology and Culture* 11, no. 1 (January 1970).

Smith, Strother A. *The Tiber and Its Tributaries: Their Natural History and Classical Associations*. London: Longmans, Green, 1877.

Smollett, Tobias. *The Works of Tobias Smollett*. London: Bickers, 1872.

Southey, Robert. *See* Espriella, Don Manuel Alvarez.

Sprenger, Johan Theodor. *Roma nova*. Frankfurt: Sebastisan Rohneri, 1660.

Sprenger, Kai-Michael. "The Tiara in the Tiber: An Essay on the damnatio in memoria

of Clement III (1084–1100) and Rome's River as a Place of Oblivion and Memory."
Reti Medievali Rivista 13, no. 1 (April 2012).

Stendhal [Marie-Henri Beyle]. *Promenades dans Rome*. Paris: Delaunay, 1829.

Story, William Wetmore. *Castle St. Angelo and the Evil Eye*. London: Chapman and Hall, 1877.

Strabo. *Geography of Strabo*. Translated by H. C. Hamilton and W. Falconer. London: George Bell & Sons, 1903.

Straparola da Caravaggio, Giovanfrancesco. *Le piacevoli notti*. Venice: Francesco Lorenzini da Turino, 1560.

Suetonius. *Live of the Emperors*. Translated by J. C. Rolfe. Cambridge, MA: Harvard University Press, 1913.

Symmachus. *Relationes*. Translated by R. H. Barrow. Oxford: Clarendon, 1973.

Tacitus. *Annales*. Translated by J. Jackson. Cambridge, MA: Harvard University Press, 1931.

Tafur, Pero. *Travels and Adventures, 1435–1439*. Translated by Malcolm Letts. New York: Harper & Bros., 1926.

Taylor, Lily Ross. *The Cults of Ostia*. Bryn Mawr, PA: Bryn Mawr College, 1912.

Thurston, Herbert. *The Holy Year of the Jubilee: An Account of the History and Ceremonial of the Roman Jubilee*. St. Louis: B. Herder, 1900.

Tosti, Luigi. *History of Pope Boniface VIII and His Times*. Translated by Eugene J. Donnelly. New York: Christian Press Association, 1911.

Totti, Pompilio. *Ritratto di Roma*. Rome: Il Mascardi, 1638.

Trollope, Frances Milton. *A Visit to Italy*. Vol. 2. London: R. Bentley, 1842.

Ungaretti, Giuseppe. *A Major Selection of the Poetry of Giuseppe Ungaretti*. Translated by Diego Bastianutti. Toronto: Exile Editions, 1997.

Vacco, Flaminio. *Memorie di varie antichità trovate in diversi luoghi della città di Roma*. Rome: Stamperia de Romanis, 1820.

Varner, Eric R. *Mutilation and Transformation: Damnatio Memoriae and Roman Imperial Portraiture*. Leiden: Brill, 2004.

Vasari, Giorgio. *Le vite de' più eccellenti pittori, scultori ed architettori*. Edited by Gaetano Milanesi and Cornelius von Fabriczy. Florence: G. C. Sansoni, 1881.

Villani, Giovanni. *Cronica*. Edited by G. Porta. Parma: Fondazione Pietro Bembo, 1991.

Virgil. *Aeneid*. Translated by Rolfe Humphries. New York: Scribners, 1951.

Volterra, da. *See* Gherardi, Jacopo.

Whitehead, William. *An Ode to the Tiber*. London: R. and J. Dodsley, 1757.

Wickham, Chris. *Medieval Rome: Stability and Crisis of a City, 900–1150*. Oxford: Oxford University Press, 2015.

Williams, Robert, trans. *Selections from the Hengwrt Mss*. London: T. Richards, 1876.

Wright, John. *Life of Cola di Rienzo*. Translated by John Wright. Ontario: Pontifical Institute of Mediaeval Studies, 1975.

Wylie, James Aitken. *Pilgrimage from the Alps to the Tiber; or the Influence of Romanism on Trade, Justice, and Knowledge*. Edinburgh: Sheapherd and Elliot, 1855.

Zanazzo, Giggi. *Novelle, favole, e leggende romanesche*. Turin: Società Tipografico-Editrice Nazionale, 1907.

———. *Usi, costumi e pregiudizi del popolo di Roma*. Turin: Società Tipografico-Editrice Nazionale, 1908.

Zimmerman, T. P. *Paolo Giovio: The Historian and the Crisis of Sixteenth-Century Italy*. Princeton, NJ: Princeton University Press, 1996.